Present and Future of E-Learning Technologies

Present and Future of E-Learning Technologies

Guest Editors
**Antonio Sarasa Cabezuelo
Covadonga Rodrigo San Juan**

Basel • Beijing • Wuhan • Barcelona • Belgrade • Novi Sad • Cluj • Manchester

Guest Editors

Antonio Sarasa Cabezuelo
Department of Computer
systems and Computing
Complutense University
of Madrid
Madrid
Spain

Covadonga Rodrigo San Juan
Department of Computer
Languages and Systems
National Distance
Education University
Madrid
Spain

Editorial Office
MDPI AG
Grosspeteranlage 5
4052 Basel, Switzerland

This is a reprint of the Special Issue, published open access by the journal *Computers* (ISSN 2073-431X), freely accessible at: https://www.mdpi.com/journal/computers/special_issues/eLearning_Tech.

For citation purposes, cite each article independently as indicated on the article page online and as indicated below:

Lastname, A.A.; Lastname, B.B. Article Title. *Journal Name* **Year**, *Volume Number*, Page Range.

ISBN 978-3-7258-4016-8 (Hbk)
ISBN 978-3-7258-4015-1 (PDF)
https://doi.org/10.3390/books978-3-7258-4015-1

© 2025 by the authors. Articles in this book are Open Access and distributed under the Creative Commons Attribution (CC BY) license. The book as a whole is distributed by MDPI under the terms and conditions of the Creative Commons Attribution-NonCommercial-NoDerivs (CC BY-NC-ND) license (https://creativecommons.org/licenses/by-nc-nd/4.0/).

Contents

About the Editors vii

Preface ix

Marcos Chacón-Castro, Jorge Buele, Ana Dulcelina López-Rueda and Janio Jadán-Guerrero
Pólya's Methodology for Strengthening Problem-Solving Skills in Differential Equations: A Case Study in Colombia
Reprinted from: *Computers* 2023, 12, 239, https://doi.org/10.3390/computers12110239 1

William Villegas-Ch and Joselin García-Ortiz
Enhancing Learning Personalization in Educational Environments through Ontology-Based Knowledge Representation
Reprinted from: *Computers* 2023, 12, 199, https://doi.org/10.3390/computers12100199 22

William Villegas-Ch., Joselin García-Ortiz, Isabel Urbina-Camacho and Aracely Mera-Navarrete
Proposal for a System for the Identification of the Concentration of Students Who Attend Online Educational Models
Reprinted from: *Computers* 2023, 12, 74, https://doi.org/10.3390/computers12040074 41

Husam M. Alawadh, Amerah Alabrah, Talha Meraj and Hafiz Tayyab Rauf
English Language Learning via YouTube: An NLP-Based Analysis of Users' Comments
Reprinted from: *Computers* 2023, 12, 24, https://doi.org/10.3390/computers12020024 58

Joaquim Escola, Natália Lopes, Paula Catarino and Ana Paula Aires
Portuguese Teachers' Conceptions of the Use of Microsoft 365 during the COVID-19 Pandemic
Reprinted from: *Computers* 2022, 11, 185, https://doi.org/10.3390/computers11120185 76

Shanmugam Sivagurunathan and Sudhaman Parthasarathy
A Framework for a Seamless Transformation to Online Education
Reprinted from: *Computers* 2022, 11, 183, https://doi.org/10.3390/computers11120183 97

Lamis Al-Qora'n, Omar Al Sheik Salem and Neil Gordon
Heuristic Evaluation of Microsoft Teams as an Online Teaching Platform: An Educators' Perspective
Reprinted from: *Computers* 2022, 11, 175, https://doi.org/10.3390/computers11120175 108

Pierpaolo Limone, Sandra Pati, Giusi Antonia Toto, Raffaele Di Fuccio, Antonietta Baiano and Giuseppe Lopriore
Literature Review on MOOCs on Sensory (Olfactory) Learning
Reprinted from: *Computers* 2022, 11, 32, https://doi.org/10.3390/computers11030032 121

Sehrish Abrejo, Hameedullah Kazi, Mutee U. Rahman, Ahsanullah Baloch and Amber Baig
Learning from Peer Mistakes: Collaborative UML-Based ITS with Peer Feedback Evaluation
Reprinted from: *Computers* 2022, 11, 30, https://doi.org/10.3390/computers11030030 140

Christos Troussas, Akrivi Krouska and Cleo Sgouropoulou
Enriching Mobile Learning Software with Interactive Activities and Motivational Feedback for Advancing Users' High-Level Cognitive Skills
Reprinted from: *Computers* 2022, 11, 18, https://doi.org/10.3390/computers11020018 158

Akrivi Krouska, Christos Troussas and Cleo Sgouropoulou
A Cognitive Diagnostic Module Based on the Repair Theory for a Personalized User Experience in E-Learning Software
Reprinted from: *Computers* **2021**, *10*, 140, https://doi.org/10.3390/computers10110140 . . . . . . **170**

Giusi Antonia Toto and Pierpaolo Limone
Motivation, Stress and Impact of Online Teaching on Italian Teachers during COVID-19
Reprinted from: *Computers* **2021**, *10*, 75, https://doi.org/10.3390/computers10060075 . . . . . . **182**

Hugo Montiel and Marcela Georgina Gomez-Zermeño
Educational Challenges for Computational Thinking in K–12 Education: A Systematic Literature Review of "Scratch" as an Innovative Programming Tool
Reprinted from: *Computers* **2021**, *10*, 69, https://doi.org/10.3390/computers10060069 . . . . . . **194**

Nam-gyeong Gim
Development of Life Skills Program for Primary School Students: Focus on Entry Programming
Reprinted from: *Computers* **2021**, *10*, 56, https://doi.org/10.3390/computers10050056 . . . . . . **209**

Antonio Sarasa-Cabezuelo and Covadonga Rodrigo
Development of an Educational Application for Software Engineering Learning
Reprinted from: *Computers* **2021**, *10*, 106, https://doi.org/10.3390/computers10090106 . . . . . . **226**

About the Editors

Antonio Sarasa Cabezuelo

Antonio Sarasa Cabezuelo is an Associate Professor in the Department of Computer systems and Computing at the Complutense University of Madrid. His research career has been shaped by a strong interdisciplinary focus, integrating computer science with digital humanities, educational technology, and accessibility. His main scientific interests include semantic web technologies, linked data, digital preservation, inclusive learning environments, and the application of artificial intelligence to improve access to information and education.

Over the past two decades, he has contributed to and led numerous research and development projects at national and European levels. These projects have addressed challenges in areas such as the digitization and open dissemination of cultural heritage, the design of accessible educational platforms, and the development of ontologies and metadata schemas to enhance interoperability in digital archives. His work frequently bridges the gap between technological innovation and social impact, with a focus on inclusivity and accessibility.

He is currently involved in projects that explore the use of semantic technologies and artificial intelligence to support adaptive and accessible digital learning systems, as well as initiatives for the integration of cultural data sources using linked open data. His academic output includes a substantial number of scientific publications, technical reports, and participation in expert committees related to digital transformation in education and cultural institutions.

His research contributions have been recognized with two national research evaluation awards ("sexenios") granted by the Spanish Ministry of Science and Innovation, acknowledging the quality and impact of his scientific output.

Covadonga Rodrigo San Juan

Covadonga Rodrigo San Juan is a tenured faculty member in the Department of Computer Languages and Systems at the National Distance Education University (UNED) and currently serves as First Deputy Director for Knowledge Transfer, Research, and Innovation at the School of Computer Engineering (ETSI Informática). Her research interests lie in digital education, inclusive learning technologies, learning analytics, and the ethical dimensions of AI in education. She co-directs the research group DiNeLLL (Digital Innovation for Inclusive Life Long Learning) and coordinates the Ethics in Informatics working group within Informatics Europe.

She has led and collaborated on national and international initiatives focused on digital inclusion, quality assurance in e-learning, and institutional strategies for technology-enhanced learning. Her work includes participation as an auditor in the E-XCELLENCE and OpenupED quality frameworks, as well as contributions to standardization efforts such as UNE 71362 and UNE 66181. She previously held executive roles as Vice-Rector for Technology at UNED and directed the University-Enterprise Chair on Digital Inclusion in collaboration with Fundación Vodafone España. Her current projects explore the intersection of educational innovation, AI, and ethics in digital learning ecosystems.

Preface

The past few decades have witnessed a profound transformation in the domain of education, driven by the proliferation of e-learning technologies. What began as an alternative or supplementary mode of instruction has matured into a critical pillar of contemporary educational and professional training systems. This evolution has been characterized by increasing openness, accessibility, and ubiquity, facilitating learning experiences that transcend traditional spatial and temporal constraints.

The advancement of e-learning has necessitated the development and refinement of a broad spectrum of technological tools and frameworks—ranging from learning management systems and educational content generation tools to digital repositories and interoperability standards. More recently, a new technological paradigm has emerged, shaped by artificial intelligence, big data analytics, cloud computing, and the Internet of Things. These technologies hold the potential to significantly enrich and personalize e-learning environments, enabling adaptive and learner-centered educational experiences.

Concomitantly, new research trajectories have surfaced, including learning analytics, gamification, virtual assistants, and the integration of sensor technologies for real-time assessment and feedback. These developments raise critical questions regarding the future trajectory of e-learning and the extent to which these emerging technologies will be seamlessly integrated with existing software architectures and pedagogical methodologies.

This volume, Present and Future of E-Learning Technologies, seeks to engage with these questions by presenting scholarly contributions that explore the intersection of learning design and technological innovation. The chapters herein aim to provide both theoretical insights and practical frameworks for understanding how current and future technologies can support the creation of more inclusive, effective, and personalized learning environments.

Antonio Sarasa Cabezuelo and Covadonga Rodrigo San Juan
Guest Editors

Article

Pólya's Methodology for Strengthening Problem-Solving Skills in Differential Equations: A Case Study in Colombia

Marcos Chacón-Castro [1], Jorge Buele [2], Ana Dulcelina López-Rueda [3] and Janio Jadán-Guerrero [1,*]

1. Centro de Investigación en Mecatrónica y Sistemas Interactivos—MIST, Universidad Indoamérica, Quito 170103, Ecuador; mchacon10@indoamerica.edu.ec
2. SISAu Research Group, Facultad de Ingeniería, Industria y Producción, Universidad Indoamérica, Ambato 180103, Ecuador; jorgebuele@indoamerica.edu.ec
3. Grupo de Investigación Gincap, Universidad Autónoma de Bucaramanga, Bucaramanga 680006, Colombia; adulceli@unab.edu.co
* Correspondence: janiojadan@uti.edu.ec; Tel.: +593-996-339-372

Abstract: The formation of students is integral to education. Strengthening critical thinking and reasoning are essential for the professionals that today's world needs. For this reason, the authors of this article applied Pólya's methodology, an initiative based on observing students' difficulties when facing mathematical problems. The present study is part of the qualitative and quantitative research paradigm and the action research methodology. In this study, the inquiry process was inductive, the sample is non-probabilistic, and the data interpretation strategy is descriptive. As a case study, six students were enrolled onto a differential equations course at the Universidad Autónoma de Bucaramanga. A didactic process was designed using information and communication technologies (ICTs) in five sequences that address first-order differential equation applications. As a result of the pedagogical intervention, problem-solving skills were strengthened. All this was based on asking the right questions, repeated reading, identifying and defining variables, mathematization, communication, and decomposing the problem into subproblems. This research study seeks to set a precedent in the Latin American region that will be the basis for future studies.

Keywords: didactic strategy; differential equations; ICT; problem solving; Pólya method

Citation: Chacón-Castro, M.; Buele, J.; López-Rueda, A.D.; Jadán-Guerrero, J. Pólya's Methodology for Strengthening Problem-Solving Skills in Differential Equations: A Case Study in Colombia. *Computers* **2023**, *12*, 239. https://doi.org/10.3390/computers12110239

Academic Editors: Antonio Sarasa Cabezuelo and Covadonga Rodrigo San Juan

Received: 30 September 2023
Revised: 5 November 2023
Accepted: 7 November 2023
Published: 18 November 2023

Copyright: © 2023 by the authors. Licensee MDPI, Basel, Switzerland. This article is an open access article distributed under the terms and conditions of the Creative Commons Attribution (CC BY) license (https://creativecommons.org/licenses/by/4.0/).

1. Introduction

Mathematics comprehension is a fundamental pillar in the education of young people in modern society, as indicated by the Organization for Economic Cooperation and Development (OECD) [1]. Mathematics is not just an academic subject but an essential tool to address a wide range of challenges in everyday life, as well as in professional, scientific, and natural contexts [2–4]. According to the results of the PISA tests in 2018, which assess critical reading, science, and mathematics, Colombia ranks 58th out of 79 countries. This is a concern, given the poor results and the impact on the level of competence in mathematics required for entry into education. In Colombia, the Ministry of National Education (MEN) states that students nationwide need to strengthen their ability to justify, assert, and express criteria in situations involving quantitative information or mathematical objects based on mathematical considerations or conceptualizations [5].

The Colombian Association of Engineering Schools (ACOFI) administered a test to engineering students from affiliated public and private universities. The purpose was to assess the set of fundamental knowledge that should be incorporated through courses related to basic sciences (Mathematics, Statistics, Physics, Chemistry, and Biology). According to the results [6], ACOFI states that 55% of the evaluated students need to improve their ability to interpret, represent, and synthesize presented problems. This is evidenced by their limited capacity to recognize the necessary mathematical model for a specific situation, even if it is of low complexity [7,8]. Due to this issue, this article will focus on designing a strategy that allows students to manipulate mathematical objects, activate their mental capacity, exercise their creativity, and enhance the development of thinking processes [9]. In this line of thought, it is essential to bridge theory and practice, connecting students to real-world problems to foster conceptual understanding, because a significant portion of classroom time has traditionally been focused on repetitive exercises, limiting opportunities for practical applications that give meaning to what is learned [10–12]. To address this, students need competency in problem solving that relates to their daily experiences [13].

In response to these challenges, this study was conducted within the context of a mathematics course during the fourth semester of an engineering course at the Universidad Autónoma de Bucaramanga (UNAB). The primary research question that guided this study was: "How can problem solving competency in students taking a Differential Equations course at UNAB be enhanced through the application of mathematics didactics?" The answer to this question was sought through the implementation of a didactic strategy designed to foster contextualized and innovative learning practices. Problem solving stands as a fundamental pillar within mathematics education. From an epistemological perspective, it involves the application of mathematical logic to analyze statements and mathematical objects, ultimately leading to the formulation of estimates and hypotheses [14]. This skill is considered indispensable, serving as the foundation for the exploration of techniques and the development of self-study skills.

In 1945, George Pólya introduced "How to Solve It" [15], a groundbreaking work that outlines a structured approach to teaching and learning mathematics centered on the problem solving process. Pólya's method comprises four essential phases: understanding the problem, devising a plan, executing the plan, and critically evaluating the results. These phases provide a systematic and effective framework for approaching mathematical problems, emphasizing deep comprehension, careful planning, meticulous execution, and critical reviewing as foundational principles. The choice of methodology plays a pivotal role in achieving effective results in education and in sustaining student engagement and motivation throughout courses. The use of active methodologies is particularly effective in improving the teaching–learning process and reshaping any negative perceptions some students may hold about mathematics. By constructing mathematical concepts through problem solving, students can establish meaningful connections between the subject matter and their daily lives, fostering a deep understanding as opposed to mere rote memorization [16].

The classification of mathematical problems plays a pivotal role in education and research. This classification serves as a crucial tool for understanding the diversity of the mathematical challenges that arise. Consequently, it becomes an essential element for systematically and efficiently addressing problems. In this regard, Figure 1, developed by Foong [17], represents a classification of mathematical problems that holds significant relevance in comprehending the nature and diversity of the mathematical challenges faced by students and mathematicians. This classification eases the identification of problems and one's approach to them, contributing to the reinforcement of learning and advances in mathematical research.

According to Piñeiro et al. [18], there exists a classification of mathematical problems: (i) Closed structure problems—these are well-formulated problems in which the answer can be found within the problem statement itself. This type of closed structure is further divided into routine and non-routine problems. In routine problems, one studies the mathematics of a specific topic to solve this type of problem. In non-routine problems, the subject matter is not inherently specific due to several assumptions that need to be considered. (ii) Open structure problems—these problems are poorly formulated, resulting in a lack of clarity. This category encompasses real applied problems, mathematical investigations, and short open-ended problems. In real applied problems, the focus is on reality, and a mathematical solution is sought. In mathematical investigation problems, students engage in various exploratory and testing activities to find the solution. Short open-ended problems offer different possible solutions.

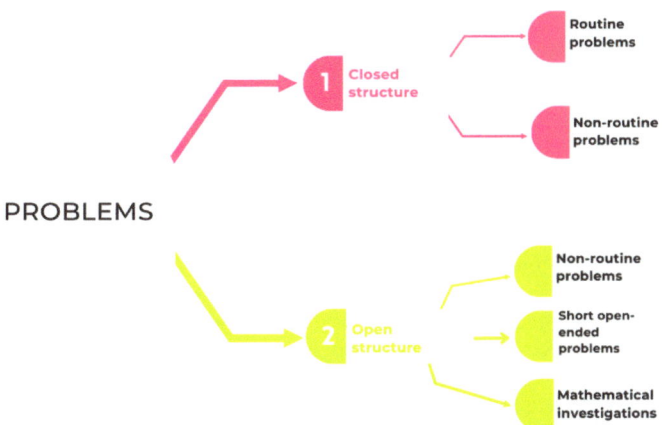

Figure 1. Mathematical problem classification.

To date, the teaching of differential equations (DEs) courses has predominantly emphasized the presentation of analytical procedures for tackling abstract mathematical problems. However, this overreliance on analytical methods, rather than incorporating numerical and qualitative approaches, has resulted in only partial learning outcomes for students. This presents a challenge, as according to both national and international standards, the memorization of analytical procedures no longer suffices for the comprehensive education of future professionals [19]. Today's students need to develop competencies that extend beyond the mere acquisition of mathematical problem-solving knowledge; they must also be able to apply these skills in real and specific professional contexts.

In this context, Pólya's proposal has had a significant influence on problem-solving instruction, yet it is also criticized for its rigidly defined stages. Some authors argue that problem solving is a more intricate process than simply applying predefined phases. As Schoenfeld [20] suggests, "problem-solving entails the use of heuristics and the management of the solver's cognitive resources", indicating that effective problem solving relies not only on applying specific phases but also on cognitive strategies and metacognitive control. Additionally, Santos Trigo [21] states, "problem-solving is an interactive process, where phases are not always linear; they can overlap or alternate". Furthermore, it underscores that "factors such as the solver's beliefs, attitudes, and emotions play a significant role". From a more contextual perspective, Campistrous and Rizo [22] argue that "problem-solving is a cyclical process, with constant evaluation between phases, rather than a simple sequential application". They also emphasize "the importance of considering the context and meaning of the problem for the solver" [23].

We deemed it essential to address the Pólya approach, which has proven valuable for problem-solving training but has also faced criticism [24]. While this method is often deemed suitable for routine problems, it may not be as effective when dealing with non-routine, real-world, or ill-defined mathematical challenges. Therefore, considering the incorporation of the Pólya methodology, we must explore ways to adapt it to address broader and more diverse mathematical challenges [25].

Furthermore, information and communication technologies (ICTs), though not a definitive solution to educational challenges in mathematics, have significantly transformed the teaching landscape. These technologies offer various ways to represent mathematical problems, allowing students to develop problem-solving strategies and a deeper understanding of the mathematical concepts they are studying [26]. Notably, ICTs, particularly simulators and applications, have gained increasing importance in mathematical education. Computational simulators can represent processes or phenomena, whether natural or artificial, through computational models. Users can interact with these simulators, adjusting model parameters to gain a better understanding of the system under study.

The combination of the Pólya approach with modern technology has empowered students to actively and collaboratively engage in solving complex mathematical problems, particularly in the context of differential equations. The use of simulators and applications, in conjunction with appropriate instruction, not only motivates and involves students but also provides them with a deeper and more practical understanding of a subject that might otherwise seem overwhelming. These technological tools enable students to explore and experiment, thereby strengthening their cognitive and mental processes in mathematical problem solving [27].

2. Materials and Methods

The research work conducted for the creation of this paper was qualitative. It involved directly engaging with students in their contextualized academic environment. The inductive method was employed. An analysis of the findings in each intervention facilitated the observation of the progression from the specific to the general. This paper is a descriptive study. Each action and process were interpreted from both individual and group perspectives [28]. The study followed the dynamics of action research, a methodology of inquiry and reflection conducted through collaboratively developed cycles involving teachers and students [29,30]. The pedagogical intervention was structured into didactic sequences, aiming for meaningful learning. The structuring of mathematical thinking to enhance problem-solving competence, specifically in the application of first-order differential equations, is conceptually rooted in Pólya's method. The application of its phases facilitated the exploration and comprehension of the method through critical and reflective progress within each sequence [15]. This type of proposed task serves as a potential tool for fostering logical reasoning. It utilizes data and information to formulate, summarize, strategize, and comprehend mathematical concepts.

Classes are generally taught in a traditional manner, without the incorporation of technological tools such as computers, simulators, or applications. Class dynamics do not involve group work; instead, students complete quizzes and assignments individually. Thus, during classes, the teacher adopts a traditional approach, and students remain in their seats, participating in the class passively. Our research was carried out using the research activity method and didactic sequencing. The information gathered allowed us to analyze the combination of Pólya's methods and technologies to develop applications for solving differential equations. This proposed combination is a potential tool for developing logical reasoning using data and information to formulate, summarize, strategize, and understand mathematical concepts.

To facilitate the development of this study, an initial test was formulated and validated by two experts in the fields of mathematics education and pedagogy. The primary objective of this test was to assess students' prior knowledge concerning problem solving in differential calculus and integral calculus. The outcomes of this assessment enabled the formulation of five sets of dynamic activities: radioactive decay, Newton's Law of Cooling, mixing problems, orthogonal trajectories, and Newton's second law. These sequences were meticulously crafted to promote active participation and enhance student engagement throughout their learning journey. They are presented as follows:

- Radioactive decay: This sequence commences by introducing the concept of radioactive decay, which is fundamental in solving differential equations. During this phase, students explore energy-related equations that depict this phenomenon. The sequence culminates with practical exercises that challenge students to solve differential equations pertaining to radioactive decay, thereby solidifying their comprehension of this phenomenon.
- Newton's Law of Cooling: The behavior in heat transfer is essential in modeling temperature as a function of time. Therefore, this sequence allows students to relate the law with differential equations by solving heat transfer problems in different systems. In this way, exercises are proposed to apply the cooling law in situations contextualized to the level of the course.

- Mixing problems: Within the realm of mixing problems, different concepts involving the variation of quantities of substances are employed to modify variables. In this subject, changes in quantities of substances as a function of time are applied, enabling an understanding of dynamic systems in real situations. As a result, participants engage in solving mixture-related problems pertinent to engineering and chemistry.
- Orthogonal trajectories: Orthogonal trajectories allow for an understanding of the relationship between solutions of differential equations and their behavioral interactions, facilitating an analysis within vector fields and dynamical systems. Thus, the development of orthogonal trajectories within vector fields and analysis in dynamical systems is proposed within this phase.
- Newton's second law: Within the Law of Force and Acceleration, the relationship between the force applied to an object and its resultant acceleration is discovered. As part of this phase, applications of the concepts related to the law are proposed under situations of motion, particle dynamics, and rigid bodies. Finally, the sequences conclude with exercises applied to complex systems, reflecting the academic challenges in the field.

2.1. Participants

The research period was from August to November during an academic cycle, and the study population consisted of 18 fourth-semester students of the Biomedical Engineering program at UNAB. The sample was a non-probabilistic sample of six students enrolled onto the Differential Equations course.

2.2. Techniques and Instruments

For this section, a mixed empirical approach that involved employing observation techniques, interviews, questionnaires, and educational interventions to gather information was used [30]. First and foremost, a diagnostic test was administered to identify prior knowledge, establish connections with new knowledge, and assess the strengths and weaknesses in students' problem solving processes. A field diary was maintained to record the most relevant events that significantly contributed to the research. The observations and the analytical methodology developed allowed for inferences to be made about students' behavior in each phase of Pólya's method. Furthermore, video recordings were utilized to obtain detailed observations of each educational intervention workshop construction session. These recordings assisted in identifying the researcher's behavior, interactions between the researcher and the participants, and the role of the students in the course and their performance in approaching problem solutions following Pólya's Problem phases [28]. Lastly, didactic sequences were employed as a source of pedagogical intervention, enabling the identification of students' actions, the researcher's role, and interactions between the researcher and the students. Throughout these interventions, applications such as GeoGebra, Matlab, and Wolfram Alpha, among others, were incorporated.

2.3. Procedure

Each of the suggested didactic sequences was planned according to Pólya's theory in such a way that it led to its conceptual and procedural empowerment. Action research methods were proposed by Kemmis and McTaggart [29], and they conceptualize research as a circular spiral process with four stages: observation, planning, action, and reflection. Figure 2 shows the procedure followed in this study (derived from this theoretical approach), where long-term reflection embodies the construction of knowledge and enriches practice.

Figure 2. Stages of action research according to Kemmis and McTaggart [29].

2.3.1. Planning: Diagnostic or Preparatory

The first action research cycle is enacted when the problem becomes evident [31]. From there, the approach focuses on questions, concerns, and objectives that indicate the progress of the work. This phase begins with identifying the problem to be investigated [29].

2.3.2. Action

In this stage, we applied didactic strategies through a series of steps focusing on using the Pólya model proposed above. During this phase, we collected information through observations and recorded the most relevant facts for the present research paper.

2.3.3. Observation: Redesign and Verification

During this phase, activities that were part of a didactic strategy designed to enhance problem-solving skills were analyzed, and data were collected through other tools, as reported by [31].

2.3.4. Reflection

This is the cycle's final stage in which the information is organized for presentation and evaluation according to categories of analysis relevant to the problem posed and the proposed purpose. Conclusions are drawn from the results, and the triangulation exercise is carried out for validation.

2.4. Methodology

Thanks to the design of didactic sequences and evaluation instruments, students were evaluated before and after the training. Once the diagnostic test was applied, the development of the problem-solving strategy was carried out using Pólya's method and ICT tools.

Each of the five didactic sequences focused on making the application of mathematics visible in solving problems requiring a first-order differential equation (FDE) approach. In this case, based on the categories/subcategories—problem solving (problem posing, mathematical processes, problem analysis, problem relationship, and review), perception (level of satisfaction, model recognition, benefits, retrospective view), implementation of the didactic strategy (understanding, mastery of the methodology, analysis)—elaborated through the theoretical elements of content, algebraic thinking, operations and algorithms, visualization and graphical representation, and problem solving, notes on each category were taken synchronously in a Google Drive (Word) document to facilitate interactions among students and the use of the method of Pólya, who defined a series of steps that lead to guiding questions for problem solving.

2.4.1. Understanding the Problem

Based on the numerous studies on the theory of the Pólya method, it is clear that this stage is necessary to make manipulating objects in mathematics more understandable to students. For this, students should ask and answer questions such as the following: Are you familiar with the problem? Is this a student problem? What data can solve the problem? Is the information complete, or is there a redundancy of data? What variables or unknowns should be configured to solve the problem? Do you need a drawing or diagram to solve your problem? What is your doubt? What is the theoretical operation or rules that allow you to ask the question? What units does it present, or does it not have dimensions?

2.4.2. Conceiving the Plan

This stage attempts to find similar or analogous problems. In this stage, we used questions to identify simple problems for use as a starting point for more complex problems, such as the following: We must solve the minor problem in question, but have you solved a similar problem? Can you restate the problem in your own words? Are all the data or conditions used correctly? Are all the basic concepts, theorems, or theoretical problem-solving elements emphasized? After you organize and structure the problem solution into a series of steps, do you have a single model? What is your plan or strategy for solving the problem? How else could you solve this problem?

2.4.3. Executing the Plan

During the development of this phase, mathematical operations are performed step by step to verify the stated results. Thus, the crucial questions in this phase are as follows: What has been obtained in these processes? Are there answers to the questions?

2.4.4. Retrospective View

This stage allows students to examine each step taken in each previous stage and to cross-check the questions, data, and information presented by the problem situation. This step is necessary to check or verify the results obtained, provide a way to generalize the problem, and answer the following questions: Does the result match the sentence? Do you have a problem? Is the solution correct? Is it possible to validate the solution? Is the data used part of the information problem? Can the problem be generalized, and can the results or processes be used to solve similar problems, and if so, how?

3. Results

This study was carried out for the module on applications of first-order ODEs; it was executed throughout the academic semester using five didactic sequences that include the following topics: radioactive disintegration, Newton's Law of Cooling, mixing problems, orthogonal trajectories, and Newton's second law. The results obtained regarding each of the proposed activities are discussed below.

3.1. Educational Interventions
3.1.1. Diagnostic Test

The tests show the need to implement methods that allow students to solve problems and relate theory to practice using concepts and procedures. We obtained the correspondence between the questions and the answers. In the answers, there needed to be more clarity when reading the contextualized question. In these cases, the situation had to be modeled from a function. In this regard, Arias-Rueda et al. [32] point out that machine learning represents the process that students prefer to use to solve problems and that most students substitute numbers in formulas and results, choosing to limit counting because it does not mean anything to them. For example, in one of the diagnostic tests, the students were expected to easily calculate the rate at which the volume increased concerning the radius of a spherical globe. Answers to this question are shown in Figure 3 below.

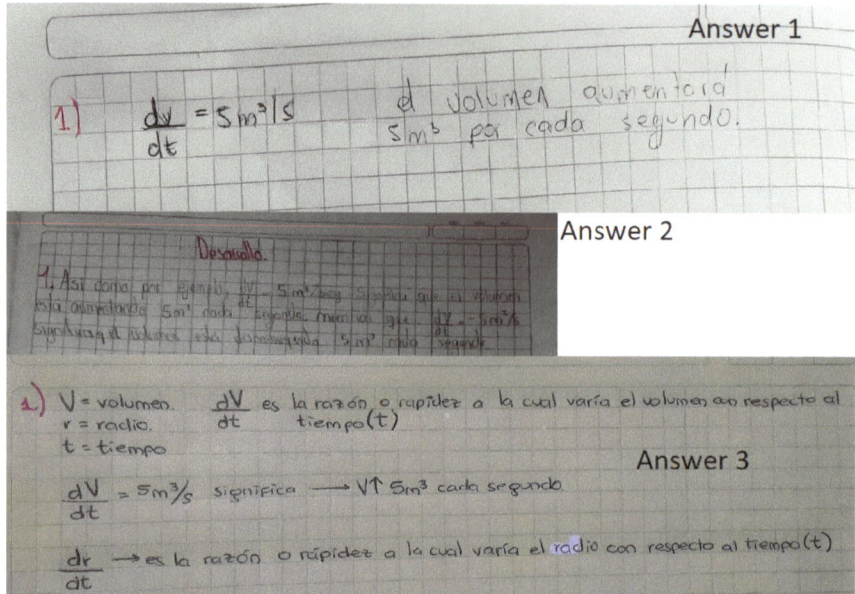

Figure 3. Diagnostic test results of three students to question 1. **Note:** The translation of answer 1 says, "the volume will increase by 5 m³ for each second". The translation of answer 2 says, "So for example, dv/dt = 5 m³/s means that the volume is increasing 5 m³ every second, while dv/dt = −5 m³/s means that the volume is decreasing 5 m³ every second".

The student writes the formula for the volume change rate shown in the problem statement. In addition to taking III the same ratio, he uses the words increase and decrease to see if they are negative instead of positive. Student E31 shows relevant variables, which represent changes in the volume–radius ratio. We observed that the participants had an intuitive idea of the rate of change. However, the students could not determine the volume function of the sphere and failed to establish the necessary relationship from the derivative of the variables concerning time. All three students left a blank and responded that they did not remember the topic when asked about their condition. Here are some basic actions to solve this problem.

3.1.2. Didactic Strategy

Once we completed the diagnostic test, we began implementing the five didactic strategies, starting with explaining Pólya's method as a strategy for solving mathematical problems, the results are shown below.

3.1.3. Radioactive Disintegration

In the didactic sequence, radioactive disintegration, and following the respective phases, it is evident that the students needed to comprehensively read the problem statement. The expression of the data, the unknowns, and the initial conditions show that they still need to gain the competence to develop and execute a plan that leads to the solution to the situation posed. Figure 4 describes this stage.

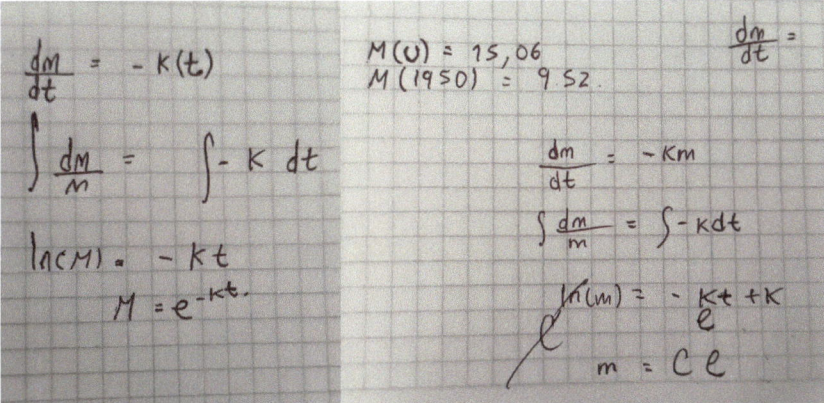

Figure 4. Mathematical model approach.

Group 1 showed that students could not establish an algebraic relationship between the data and the initial conditions of the problem. Group 2, on the other hand, did not use initial conditions to find the parameters "c" and "k". Due to the data required for specific ODE solutions, both groups left the problem's solution unfinished. Finally, no student successfully compared the results during the retrospective period.

3.1.4. Newton's Law of Cooling

We observed that the students gradually appropriated the methodology, identifying the variables (temperature and time); they used their excel skills to represent the situation. However, as expected, they did not analyze the graphical representation of the time–temperature relationship. There was no correspondence between the data presented, as shown in Figure 5.

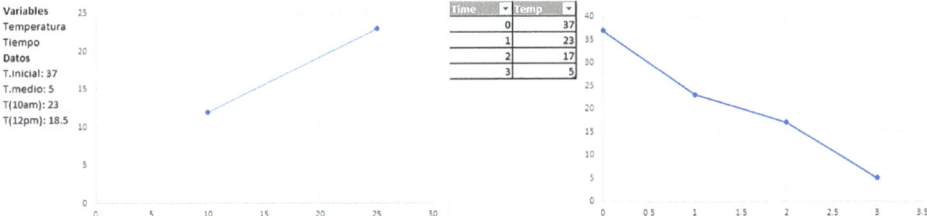

Figure 5. Graphical representation of the interpretation of the exercise. **Note:** Figure translation: "Variables: Temperature vs. Time, Data: Initial temperature: 37, Average time: 5, Temperature at 10 am: 23, Temperature at 12 pm: 18.5".

When observing group work, students read the problem in detail to find relevant variables and data and show progress using their prior knowledge. However, they did not use their graphs to reflect on the magnitudes of the problem and did not relate the data to the given situation (Figure 6). In the next phase of plan development and execution, students identified the cooling models and Newton's laws and applied their knowledge of integrals to find the mathematical model corresponding to the differential equation closely related to the problem statement.

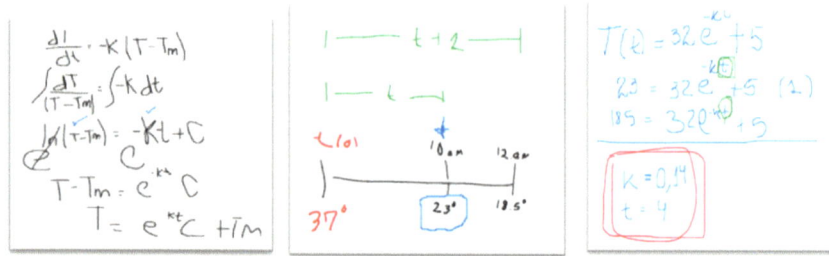

Figure 6. Elaboration of the plan: Newton's Law of Cooling.

In the process, the students presented errors in identifying the initial conditions and the approach to the problem situation, as described in Figure 7. This situation required the intervention of the research teacher; we posed theoretical questions and gave effective feedback to facilitate the student's progress and learning. In this phase, we observed an evolutionary advance in the use of the methodology in the students; despite not achieving the respective solution, they reached the retrospective phase using applications such as Symbolab, Wolfram Alpha, and GeoGebra to verify what had been performed and achieved in the previous steps.

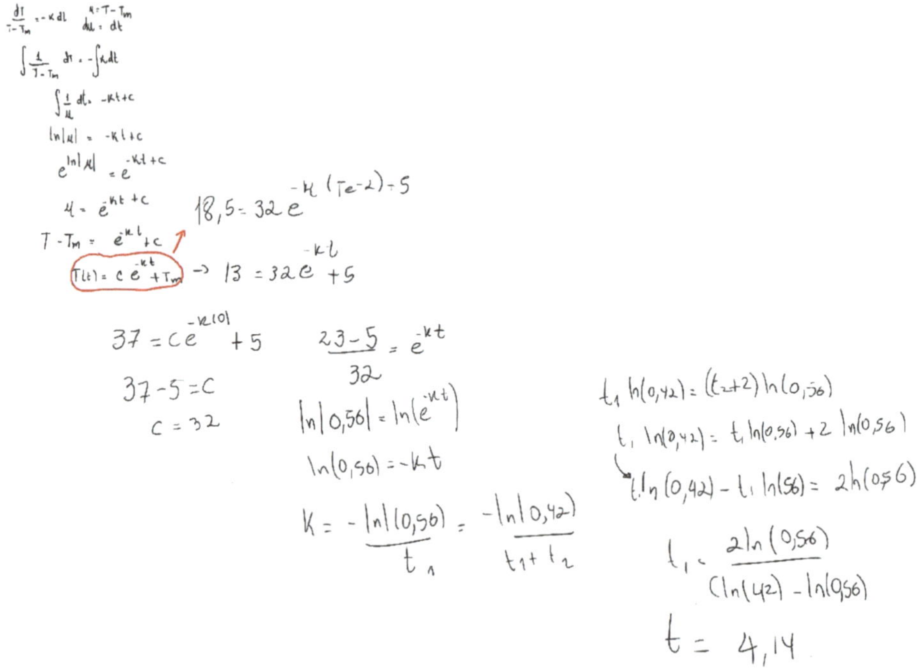

Figure 7. Plan execution and problem review.

3.1.5. Mixing Problem

This workshop exhibited a simulation where the liquid in the tank mixes with the contents and changes color. Therefore, differential equation models are built intuitively through rate of change and chain rules. The resolution is shown in Figure 8.

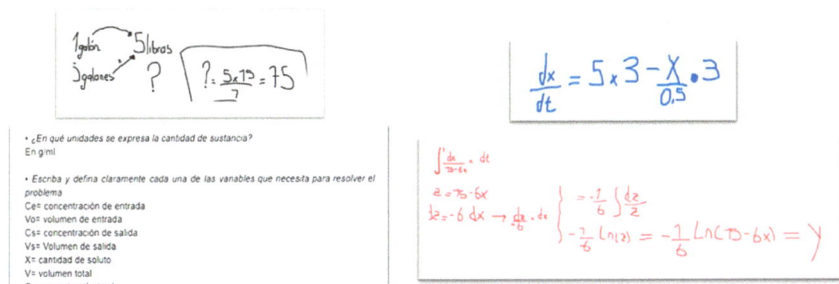

Figure 8. Relationship between the simulation and the guiding questions. **Note:** Translation of each response. Answer 1: 1 gallon, 5 gallons, 5 pounds. Answer 3: "What units is the amount of substance expressed in? In g/mL. Write and clearly define each of the variables needed to solve the problem. Ce = Inlet concentration. Vo = Inlet volume. Cs = Outlet concentration. Vs = Outlet volume. X = Amount of solute. V = Total volume. C = Total concentration".

In the execution of this didactic sequence and from the dynamizing action of the learning process that has been achieved with the two previous experiences, the students showed significant progress in using the methodology. In addition, with the implementation of the proposed guiding questions, they broke down the problem with repeated reading, identified the variables and data, answered the guiding questions, and analyzed the problem. An example of the progress described is shown in Figure 9.

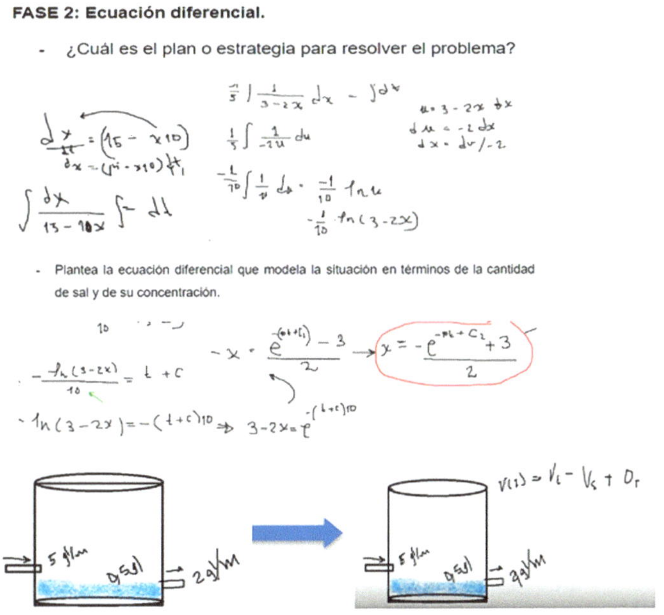

Figure 9. Volume variation modeling method. **Note:** Figure translation: "Phase 2. Differential Equation", "What is the plan or strategy to solve the problem?", "Formulate the differential equation that models the situation in terms of the quantity of salt and its concentration".

The students were able to create an outline of the problem situation, working as a team and in continuous dialogue to analyze the planned situation. This dialogue was led by the teacher–researcher, posing questions that allowed the students to understand and argue the solution to the question posed. Finally, in the retrospective view, the students, when checking the answer, discovered that they had made a mistake in one of the data points, which allowed them to rethink the mathematical process (Figure 10).

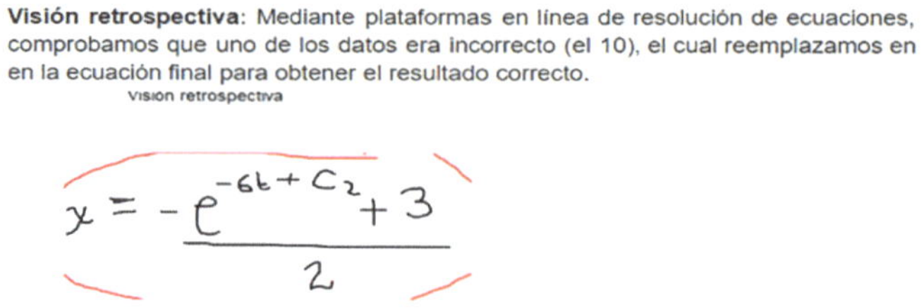

Visión retrospectiva: Mediante plataformas en línea de resolución de ecuaciones, comprobamos que uno de los datos era incorrecto (el 10), el cual reemplazamos en en la ecuación final para obtener el resultado correcto.
Visión retrospectiva

$$x = -\frac{e^{-6t+C_2}+3}{2}$$

Figure 10. Problem solution used to compare with the Symbolab calculator result.

During the execution of this didactic sequence, we employed the GeoGebra tool to conduct blending exercises. This tool offered an active and dynamic alternative that sustained the students' interest and attention in the learning process. Through the GeoGebra simulation, we presented a scenario in which the tank's liquid mixed with its contents, resulting in a color change that piqued the students' curiosity, as depicted in Figure 11.

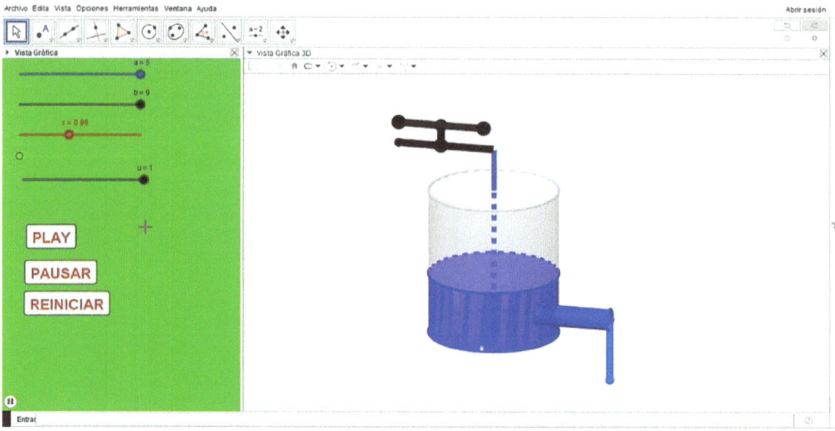

Figure 11. Activity carried out using the GeoGebra tool.

In this context, differential equation models were intuitively developed by examining rates of change and chain rules. Students actively engaged in problem decomposition, identified relevant variables and data, responded to guiding questions, and engaged in problem analysis. This approach fostered collaboration and an ongoing dialogue among the students, who worked together to analyze the planned situation.

The teacher–researcher played a crucial role in leading the dialogue and posing questions that prompted students to understand and articulate their solutions. In a reflective process, students, while verifying their response, identified an error in one of the data points, providing them with the opportunity to reconsider the mathematical process and correct their approach. The use of GeoGebra as an active and dynamic tool, coupled with the didactic sequence and guiding questions, enabled students to advance their competence in addressing mathematical problems and enhance their understanding of the concepts involved in the blending problem.

3.1.6. Orthogonal Trajectories

In this workshop, the process of strengthening knowledge and applying the mathematical problem solving method according to Pólya's theory continued. The aim was to find the family of orthogonal curves belonging to a given family of curves via the application of first-order ordinary differential equations. The pedagogical activity prompted the use of a graphical environment to visualize the orthogonality, all through drawing a pair of tangent lines to the orthogonal curves, respectively, at a given point. For this, a simulation created in GeoGebra was used. Figure 12 shows the result of the process that involved repeated reading, using graphical representations in GeoGebra, and following up on guiding questions. It is important to mention that Geogebra and Winplot were employed for these activities to visualize the slope fields and the orthogonal families of curves, respectively.

Fase 1. Comprensión del problema

- ¿Qué relación existe entre la recta y los círculos?

Rta. La relación que existe entre la recta y los círculos, es que las rectas son perpendiculares a ellos.

- Si un círculo tiene centro (h,k) y radio r. ¿Cuál es la ecuación cartesiana de dicho círculo?

Rta: $(x-h)^2 + (y-k)^2 = r^2$

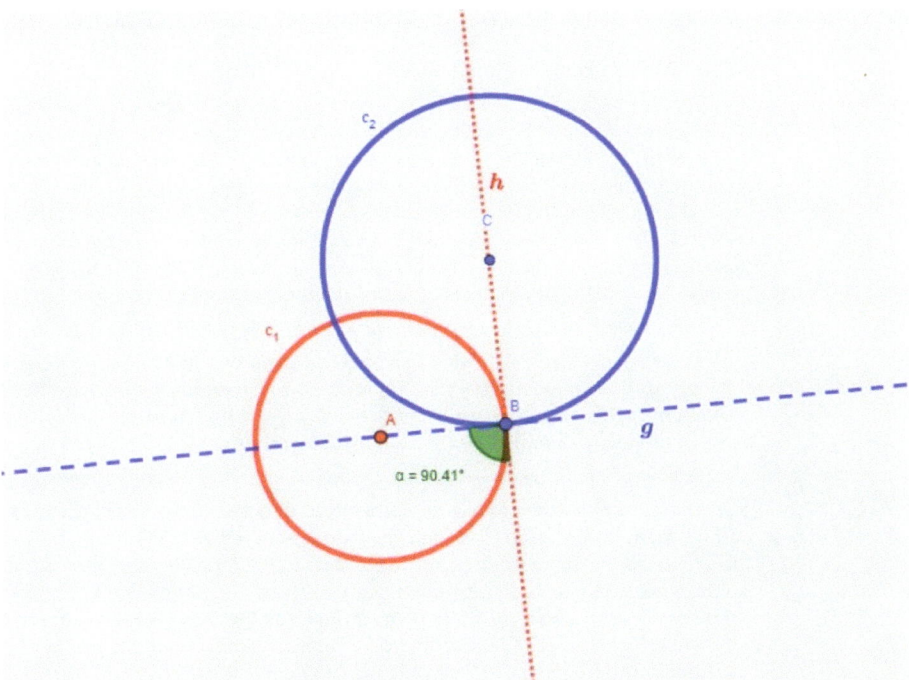

Figure 12. Relationship between the simulation and the guiding questions. **Note:** Figure translation. Phase 1. "Understanding the problem", "What relationship exists between the line and the circles?", "Answer: The relationship that exists between the line and the circles is that the lines are perpendicular to them", "If a circle has a center (h, k) and a radius r, what is the Cartesian equation of that circle?".

The student's progress in using and formulating guiding questions is fundamental to concretize the learning of the methodology and the application of the ODEs. The use of the GeoGebra application allowed the students to contrast the graphical representation with the algebraic one and to make their assessments of the questions posed. In summary, the analysis of the product made by the group that integrated the reading questions given as a fundamental element of the development of new questions to define data and variables clearly and previous link knowledge showed a significant improvement in the students' learning. This activity allowed for them to reflect on what happens when teachers use simulated guided questions to establish dialogues and face situations in a fun way; it is interesting to develop strategies that lead to the realization of a planned position.

3.1.7. Newton's Second Law

After the accompanying process, the students became aware of the methodological support that George Pólya's theory represents as a didactic strategy for solving problems. Here, it is worth noting that the students of the differential equations course improved significantly in their ability to solve problems, particularly those related to first-order ordinary differential equations. This is because the process led to the development of aspects of identifying variables or data and connecting existing knowledge in their cognitive structure with the new contents to calculate and analyze the effect of algebraic processes and consider how to solve situations in mathematics. In addition, with the help of previously formulated questions, the role of the teacher as a facilitator of the proposed problem is vital. The teacher becomes a spectator and active participant in the dialogue of the students (organizers) and builds meaningful learning. The dynamic classroom exercise encourages students to understand, reason, discuss, establish relationships, work in groups, reflect on and validate the results obtained, and facilitate critical thinking and research.

3.2. Analysis of Educational Intervention

For this study, interviews with a group of six university students were performed to carry out an analysis of the educational interventions. The aim was to qualitatively evaluate the impact of the pedagogical strategies implemented to enhance the problem-solving competence of the students. This analysis of educational interventions was centered around comprehending how the student responded to the pedagogical strategies designed to bolster their problem-solving skills. Throughout the interviews, the individual's perceptions, experiences, and challenges in the learning process were probed. Below are the most precise and recurring responses collected during these interviews.

Before participating in this research, had you used Pólya's methodology in problem solving?

The students generally stated that they had not seen this problem solving methodology throughout their education. Only one student commented that he had met a secondary education teacher who had used similar steps. He did not know of the Pólya methodology but had used some methodologies with many similarities.

Briefly explain the phases recommended by Pólya for effective problem solving.

The participating students explained that they should focus on reading the problem and understood the need to review the data (i.e., what are the unknowns or variables of the problem). In this way, they relate the data to elaborate a plan (how are they going to do it?) and take into account the strategy, execute the plan, solve it, and verify that the solution is correct. One of the students emphasized that it is necessary to read the problem very carefully and identify the required variables and how to organize it before developing the equation that can be used to solve the problem. The last step is to receive feedback on whether the result answers the question and whether the methods used were effective.

This process made one of the students recall the methodology of his high school physics teacher. The stages of this methodology were very similar to that of Pólya's, but this student emphasized that it was not practiced in other subjects, obstructing its consolidation within the learning process.

What mistakes did you make before working with Pólya's method?

Each student stated they needed to understand the problem, elaborate a plan, and review the solution (i.e., concentrating only on execution). It was identified that high-speed reading and not having a broad vision of the problem makes it difficult to solve it correctly. One student explained that he needed to learn how to differentiate between the variables that are necessary and those that are not. Using variables that do not contribute to the resolution is a distractor that could confuse the student. Another strategy used was to perform a process and start again with another option when not finding a solution. This strategy involves investing a lot of time and guarantees good results. In general, each student was able to significantly strengthen their ability to relate numerical data to their respective variables and identify the appropriate model needed to solve the problem. It was also validated as a tool used by the teacher to change the conventional process, motivating them.

Regarding student E11, he stated, "Before using this method, I was accustomed to following a step-by-step process for each exercise, like following a sequence rather than asking myself which variables are relevant and which are not. I used all the given variables, but I couldn't differentiate which ones weren't useful. So, this method helped me to address these kinds of doubts".

What new skills did you achieve using the Pólya methodology in your academic semester?

The students commented that it allowed them to approach each of the phases—understanding the problem, conceiving and executing the plan, and the retrospective review—in a more orderly and structured way. Now that they are familiar with it, they highly recommend using this methodology in other scenarios.

What recommendations do you propose for the solution of mathematical situations?

The practice of a more critical analysis allows us to identify what we have and how to orient it to the results. One of the students recommends using animations, drawings, and graphics in the classroom to learn visually; the teacher must implement this in their daily work. In physics, understanding the concept under study allows for a more straightforward resolution of exercises since physical phenomena need, in the first instance, a general knowledge of their conception for later treatment.

How was your academic performance in the differential equations course when participating in the pedagogical strategy proposed in this research?

In general, the students stated that they were delighted with the process used to strengthen their problem-solving skills, since their academic performance in the differential equations course was superior to that of previous semesters in the mathematics courses.

A knowledge assessment was conducted concurrently with the intervention, and its results are presented in Table 1. The diagnostic assessment results indicate a mean of 0.57, with a standard deviation of 0.18, out of a possible 5 points. This reflects a very low level of performance in solving first-degree differential equation problems. Following the implementation of the five sequences, the scores experienced a substantial increase; starting from the fourth sequence, the scores are higher than 4 out of 5. In the post-test, the mean score was 4.57 (with a standard deviation of 0.2), demonstrating a noticeable improvement. To analyze these data, the nonparametric Wilcoxon test was employed; with a p-value of 0.024, the existence of a statistically significant increase was confirmed. The results demonstrate an enhancement in problem-solving capabilities, with improved performance evident from the initial sequences. Nevertheless, the outcomes for the remaining sequences displayed a more modest improvement, indicating the effectiveness of this methodology for such exercises. However, there is still unexplored data that warrant analysis. The utilization of alternative methodologies could offer a deeper understanding of these phenomena, which should be corroborated through future experiments.

Table 1. Results of the application of the didactic sequences.

Participants	Test 1		Intervention					Test 2
	Pretest	Sequence 1	Sequence 2	Sequence 3	Sequence 4	Sequence 5		Post-Test
1	0.5	0.8	3.8	3.8	4.2	4.5		4.5
2	0.7	0.8	3.8	3.8	4.6	4.8		4.8
3	0.3	0.8	3.3	3.3	4	4.3		4.3
4	0.5	0.8	3.3	3.3	4.2	4.5		4.5
5	0.8	1.7	3.8	3.8	4.6	4.8		4.8
6	0.6	1.7	3.8	3.8	4.2	4.5		4.5
Average	0.57	1.1	3.63	3.63	4.3	4.57		4.57

4. Discussion

The practices learned in secondary education are carried over to higher education, which shows that the methodologies used will affect students in the future. The bibliography indicates that some proposals use this method in primary education [15,26] and high school [33,34]. There is a need-to-know new alternative to improve learning processes. The implemented sequence allowed for the strengthening of problem-solving competencies. The phases of Pólya's method prioritize repeated reading, the identification and definition of variables, graphic productions, materialization, dialogue between students and teachers, and decomposition into subproblems. This process began with a diagnostic evaluation to assess the subjects' prior knowledge of differential and integral calculus. The results showed a reduced understanding of linear functions and derivative concepts. In addition to this were problems of factoring and differential equations that obstruct the development of differential equations. These results highlight the need to strengthen problem-solving skills. The difficulty in interpreting mathematical problems should be contemplated as part of a comprehensive academic policy.

As the process progressed, students improved their levels of understanding. In terms of mathematization, prior knowledge is essential for establishing relationships and devising planning. Despite this, some differential equations were challenging and required specific algorithms. Collaboration among students and a more significant connection with the teacher–researcher are also encouraged [35]. This allows for the generation of questions and provision of correct feedback through pertinent discussion spaces. Group activities allow for better argumentation, relationships, reflection, and teamwork. The didactic sequences allow for rigorous work that strengthens the students' critical and investigative thinking. In addition, the incorporation of field diaries, videos, transcripts, and interviews serve to enhance this methodology [36].

The systematization of this method is an essential tool in the engineering field since it improves the organization of procedures. This strengthens the relationship between previous and developing knowledge. Mnemonic skills are also involved in remembering the necessary algorithms to follow the path to resolution. This can be enhanced using technological tools such as GeoGebra, MATLAB, Symbolab, and Wolfram Alpha, among others.

The results of this study are satisfactory from an academic point of view; however, the interviews allowed us to identify other considerations that are only sometimes considered. Students commented that the benefits are based on solving everyday life problems modeled using a differential equation in a more analytical, argumentative way and asking key questions that are not usually considered. They consider that they can recall similar problems to know what should happen, relate it to the current problem, and use mathematical theory to obtain the correct solution. It is also important to note that there was active and constant participation on the part of the students, strengthening their capacity to analyze daily life problems.

According to "*Reconstructing School Mathematics*" by Stephen Brown [34], the teaching of mathematics should be approached from broader perspectives, where students are educated as critical thinkers and well-rounded individuals, as he suggests, by solving problems in a more analytical and argumentative manner. Brown proposes that mathematics can be approached through metaphors or analogies that allow us to understand the world and ourselves simultaneously. Thus, the humanistic approach proposed by Brown, in which students are not only trained in technical skills but are also educated comprehensively as reflective, ethical individuals prepared for life's challenges, was of great interest and utility when preparing and carrying out this research study. Therefore, within this study, his approach was used under the question "What if not?" not only after solving a problem but even before attempting to solve it, where teaching is carried out with the expectation that errors, generated questions, and resulting doubts will enable the student to change the way they view any aspect of knowledge or experience. In this way, Brown suggests that by providing a problem and its solution to the student, they should be asked questions such as the following: "Why might this solution have been difficult to reach even though it is quite easy to follow?" "Have you found other mathematical ideas that could be described that way?" "Are there similar phenomena in your life (non-mathematical)?" In this way, students will become more engaged in problem solving.

In the context of Pólya's methodology for mathematical problem solving, Stephen Brown's proposal offers an alternative approach that promotes critical thinking and reflection, with an emphasis on the relationship between the problem and its context. Both authors agree on the importance of questioning both the problem itself and its relevance in the surrounding environment. This encourages students to explore various approaches and methods to solve the problem, even considering those that may lead to incorrect answers. This freedom in exploration aligns with Brown's approach, which recognizes errors, questions, and doubts as essential elements for learning and developing the student's perspective. Furthermore, metacognitive reflection is promoted, urging students to analyze not only the final solution but the entire problem solving process, encouraging them to identify the strengths and weaknesses of their approach and to establish connections between what they have learned during the process and its application in everyday situations. Therefore, the integration of Brown's methodology into Pólya's approach enriches mathematical problem solving by providing a broader and more reflective perspective.

During the diagnostic or preparatory planning phase, a diagnostic test, didactic sequences, and a review of technological tools were designed. The instruments used were validated by the researchers in the company of two experts to review the reliability of the theoretical references addressed, including the appropriate adjustments. During the action phase (design or implementation), the active participation of the students was evident, promoting their autonomous development, which was facilitated by the teacher. The development of group activities favors work through brainstorming, debates, and creativity in problem solving. In the observation phase (redesign and verification), the significant advances in the process of problem solving demonstrated by the students were considered. The last step of reflection, the presentation of results, emphasizes the improved academic performance of the participants. They combined theory with practice during the development of first-order ordinary differential equations. However, these questions were not enough since the teacher's guidance was essential. The methodological support discussed in the present research study paves the way for improving the teaching practice and incorporating digital tools that facilitate the teaching process. The promotion of spaces for strengthening pre-knowledge and the incorporation of new knowledge increases the confidence of students, who will then apply what they have learned in real-life situations [11,37].

As mentioned by the authors of [38], teaching mathematics has become a challenge for teachers in recent years. Not only does one's teaching approach need to be attractive to students, but it needs to factor in learnings that can also be applied in real life. The student's anxiety while studying the different branches of mathematics is an emotional response that can be considered typical, but it is not expected [39]. This may be a product of outdated teaching processes that do not allow the student to visualize the applications of mathematics and become passionate about learning them. This should be a wake-up call to teachers around the world, but especially in Colombia, where it has been observed that there are low levels of performance in regional evaluations. This type of tool builds new concepts that can enhance the problem-solving skills of future professionals; it is an aspect that goes beyond a knowledge test.

While George Pólya's model pioneered problem solving in education with well-defined phases, it has faced substantial criticism. Critics argue that it exhibits limitations due to its sequential and rigid nature, failing to encapsulate the true complexity and multidimensionality of the problem solving process. Theoretically, it has been acknowledged that effective mathematical problem solving involves intricate cognitive processes such as heuristic strategies and metacognitive skills on the resolver's part. Additionally, emphasis is placed on the interactive and recursive nature of the involved actions, which do not rigidly adhere to a predefined sequence but fluidly overlap and alternate. It is worth mentioning that not only prior knowledge influences problem-solving ability; attitudinal, motivational, and emotional factors also play significant roles in how students approach problem solving, and the importance of context in particular, as well as the meaning and significance that the problem holds for the resolver, given its impact on the process, should also be considered.

Therefore, it is crucial for students to approach a problem without prior knowledge of the solution process, provoking a conscious and intentional cognitive search for the solution. Consequently, not every exercise or task qualifies as a genuine problem unless it elicits this cognitive search activity from the student. In other words, problem solving is a multifaceted process that encompasses multiple factors. Thus, it is necessary to move beyond mechanistic views based solely on predefined steps and instead consider the cognitive processes and genuine searching involved in a problem's resolution, coupled with the contextual and subjective dimensions that mediate their approach. A multidimensional understanding offers a more comprehensive view of this fundamental mathematical competence.

Techniques must be applied to allow future generations to face an increasingly demanding world that requires rapid adaptation [40,41]. The results presented in this study align with those of other publications in the literature, showing how a methodology from the last century can be adapted to contexts worldwide. Despite this, there is still limited information on how students can apply this knowledge in the real world, which shows that there is still much to study in this field. Following what is stated in [42], it can be discerned that the planning students achieve can be transferred to non-mathematical contexts. Problem solving constitutes one of the essential skills in professional life. This type of tool, which does not include linear processes, should be simplified to be generalized according to the student's needs and situation. All of this will improve their critical thinking, as reflected via an increase in their efficiency and, consequently, in their productivity [43].

Modeling and representations play a crucial role in problem solving and deepening mathematical comprehension. Mathematical models, abstract constructions used to represent real-world situations and mathematical concepts, offer students a more profound and practical understanding. These models are pivotal in structured and logical problem solving, and as noted by Appelbaum [42], the mathematical modeling process may give rise to "ignorances". These gaps in knowledge or understanding should be seen as learning opportunities, motivating students to overcome them in their problem solving journey. Therefore, Appelbaum argues that the role of mathematical modeling in problem solving is of the utmost importance. Through models, students have the ability to address and resolve issues in a structured and evidence-based manner. These models provide a solid framework for reasoning and making informed decisions, essential aspects in contexts related to engineering applied to real situations, where the effectiveness of solutions is critical. By adopting this practice, students develop skills in asking questions, exploring novel perspectives, and challenging prior assumptions, which not only contributes to a deeper understanding of mathematics but also encourages creativity and critical thinking.

Regarding the limitations of this study, although Pólya's method is a support tool in problem solving, it does not have the greater innovation and appropriation of mathematical processes. Pólya's method and its implications for the teaching of differential equations and, in general, in higher education has presented few advances in the incorporation of technological tools. This is reflected in the few changes in the curriculum and by the fact that the methods of problem solving have not been significantly updated. This represents an obstacle from an epistemological and ontological point of view in the teaching–learning process of students. Mastering mathematical problem solving is a fundamental requirement for the development of learning from a historical–cultural perspective, and previous research has identified that the deficiencies begin in the teacher training model. These deficiencies are observed both in the deployment of this skill during the learning processes of teachers and undergraduate students, as well as in the pedagogical practices of these professionals in the school environment [44].

However, these criticisms should not be perceived as insurmountable obstacles but as valuable opportunities to improve and adjust the approach, especially when we take advantage of the technological tools provided by ICT [45]. Therefore, teachers should undergo an initial assessment to gauge their prior knowledge of mathematics, pedagogy, and technology. Once weaknesses have been identified, training programs focused on strengthening the teacher's most obvious areas of weakness could be implemented. Then, a joint intervention with teachers and students could be carried out to obtain better learning outcomes [46]. Students in the era of artificial intelligence deserve renewed plans, activities, and evaluations to improve the class environment through the use of new emerging technologies [47]. In this vein, we urge that mathematical problem solving should also benefit from other models such as TPACK and the use of gamification, given that it incorporates content knowledge, pedagogical knowledge, and technological knowledge [48]. In addition, future research could consider implementing mixed-method approaches that provide greater clarity and rigor in the measurement of outcomes. This would allow for a more accurate assessment of the impact of the applied pedagogical strategies in terms of improving students' academic performance and their effectiveness in improving problem-solving skills.

Furthermore, it is recommended to conduct a more comprehensive analysis of the strategies employed in each phase of the process, considering possible adjustments and supplements that could further improve results. The incorporation of additional strategies at different stages of the methodology might contribute to enriching the students' learning experience and increasing the transferability of their skills to non-mathematical contexts. This approach aligns with the metacognitive challenge posed to students, offering a more holistic view of their learning and problem-solving abilities.

Author Contributions: Conceptualization, M.C.-C., J.J.-G. and A.D.L.-R.; methodology, M.C.-C., J.B. and A.D.L.-R.; software, M.C.-C.; validation, M.C.-C. and J.J.-G.; formal analysis, M.C.-C. and J.B.; investigation, M.C.-C. and A.D.L.-R.; resources, M.C.-C. and J.J.-G.; data curation, M.C.-C., A.D.L.-R. and J.B; writing—original draft preparation, M.C.-C., J.J.-G. and A.D.L.-R.; writing—review and editing, J.B.; visualization, M.C.-C., J.J.-G. and A.D.L.-R.; supervision, J.B.; project administration, M.C.-C., J.B., J.J.-G. and A.D.L.-R.; funding acquisition, J.J.-G. All authors have read and agreed to the published version of the manuscript.

Funding: This research was funded by Universidad Indoamérica through the 305.254.2022 project, titled "Tecnología Educativa para discapacidad-TEDI".

Data Availability Statement: Data are contained within the article.

Acknowledgments: To Universidad Indoamérica and Universidad Autónoma de Bucaramanga for providing the resources necessary for developing this research study.

Conflicts of Interest: The authors declare no conflict of interest.

References

1. PISA Para el Desarrollo. *Programa Para la Evaluación Internacional de Alumnos*; OECD: Paris, France, 2017.
2. Chai, C.S. Teacher Professional Development for Science, Technology, Engineering and Mathematics (STEM) Education: A Review from the Perspectives of Technological Pedagogical Content (TPACK). *Asia-Pac. Educ. Res.* **2019**, *28*, 5–13. [CrossRef]

3. Engelbrecht, J.; Llinares, S.; Borba, M.C. Transformation of the Mathematics Classroom with the Internet. *ZDM-Math. Educ.* **2020**, *52*, 825–841. [CrossRef] [PubMed]
4. Pepin, B.; Xu, B.; Trouche, L.; Wang, C. Developing a Deeper Understanding of Mathematics Teaching Expertise: An Examination of Three Chinese Mathematics Teachers' Resource Systems as Windows into Their Work and Expertise. *Educ. Stud. Math.* **2017**, *94*, 257–274. [CrossRef]
5. Ochoa, J.A.; Vahos, H.M. Modelación En Educación Matemática: Una Mirada Desde Los Lineamientos y Estándares Curriculares Colombianos. *Rev. Virtual Univ. Catól. Norte* **2009**, *27*, 1–21.
6. Asociación Colombiana de Facultades de Ingeniería (ACOFI). *Resultados Generales Examen de Ciencias Básicas EXIM 2021*; ACOFI: Bogotá, Colombia, 2020.
7. Cai, J.; Hwang, S. Learning to Teach through Mathematical Problem Posing: Theoretical Considerations, Methodology, and Directions for Future Research. *Int. J. Educ. Res.* **2020**, *102*, 101391. [CrossRef]
8. Yuanita, P.; Zulnaidi, H.; Zakaria, E. The Effectiveness of Realistic Mathematics Education Approach: The Role of Mathematical Representation as Mediator between Mathematical Belief and Problem Solving. *PLoS ONE* **2018**, *13*, e0204847. [CrossRef] [PubMed]
9. Verschaffel, L.; Schukajlow, S.; Star, J.; Van Dooren, W. Word Problems in Mathematics Education: A Survey. *ZDM-Math. Educ.* **2020**, *52*, 1–16. [CrossRef]
10. García Retana, J.Á. La Problemática de La Enseñanza y El Aprendizaje Del Cálculo Para Ingeniería the Problem of Teaching and Learning Calculus in Engineering. *Rev. Educ.* **2013**, *37*, 2215–2644.
11. Valoyes-Chávez, L. On the Making of a New Mathematics Teacher: Professional Development, Subjectivation, and Resistance to Change. *Educ. Stud. Math.* **2019**, *100*, 177–191. [CrossRef]
12. Sultanova, L.; Hordiienko, V.; Romanova, G.; Tsytsiura, K. Development of Soft Skills of Teachers of Physics and Mathematics. *J. Phys. Conf. Ser.* **2021**, *1840*, 012038. [CrossRef]
13. Li, Y.; Schoenfeld, A.H. Problematizing Teaching and Learning Mathematics as "given" in STEM Education. *Int. J. STEM Educ.* **2019**, *6*, 44. [CrossRef]
14. Gagne, R.M. *The Conditions of Learning*; Holt, Rinehart and Winsto: New York, NY, USA, 1977.
15. Polya, G. *How to Solve It*; Princeton University Press: Princeton, NJ, USA, 1965.
16. Al-Mutawah, M.A.; Thomas, R.; Eid, A.; Mahmoud, E.Y.; Fateel, M.J. Conceptual Understanding, Procedural Knowledge and Problem-Solving Skills in Mathematics: High School Graduates Work Analysis and Standpoints. *Int. J. Educ. Pract.* **2019**, *7*, 258–273. [CrossRef]
17. Foong, P.Y. The Role of Problems to Enhance Pedagogical Practices in the Singapore Mathematics Classroom. *Math. Educ.* **2002**, *6*, 15–31.
18. Piñeiro, J.L.; Pinto, E.; Díaz-Levicoy, D. Qué Es La Resolución de Problemas? *Boletín REDIPE* **2015**, *4*, 6–14.
19. Lee, C.I. An Appropriate Prompts System Based on the Polya Method for Mathematical Problem-Solving. *Eurasia J. Math. Sci. Technol. Educ.* **2017**, *13*, 893–910. [CrossRef]
20. Schoenfeld, A.H. Making Sense of "out Loud" Problem-Solving Protocols. *Artic. J. Math. Behav.* **1985**, *4*, 171–191.
21. Santos Trigo, L.M. Revista Mexicana de Investigación Educativa. *Rev. Mex. Investig. Educ.* **1997**, *2*, 11–30.
22. Campistrous, L.; Rizo, C. *Aprende a Resolver Problemas Aritméticos*; Editorial Pueblo y. Educación: La Habana, Cuba, 1996.
23. Perez, L.E.H. Abordaje Teórico de La Resolución de Problemas Matemáticos Desde Los Postulados de Polya. *Sinop. Educ. Rev. Venez. Investig.* **2020**, *20*, 318–326.
24. Voskoglou, M.G. Problem-Solving from Polya to Nowadays: A Review and Future Perspectives. *Prog. Educ.* **2011**, *22*, 65–82.
25. Simpol, N.S.H.; Shahrill, M.; Li, H.C.; Prahmana, R.C.I. Implementing Thinking Aloud Pair and Pólya Problem Solving Strategies in Fractions. *J. Phys. Conf. Ser.* **2018**, *943*, 012013. [CrossRef]
26. Nurkaeti, N. Polya'S Strategy: An Analysis of Mathematical Problem Solving Difficulty in 5th Grade Elementary School. *EduHumaniora/J. Pendidik. Dasar Kampus Cibiru* **2018**, *10*, 140. [CrossRef]
27. González-pérez, L.I.; Ramírez-montoya, M.S. Components of Education 4.0 in 21st Century Skills Frameworks: Systematic Review. *Sustainability* **2022**, *14*, 1493. [CrossRef]
28. Hernández, R.; Fernández, C.; Baptista, P. *Metodología de La Investigación*; McGrawHill: Mexico City, Mexico, 2014.
29. Kemmis, S.; McTaggart, R.; Nixon, R. *The Action Research Planner: Doing Critical Participatory Action Research*; Springer Science and Business Media LLC: Dordrecht, The Netherlands, 2014; pp. 1–200. [CrossRef]
30. Latorre, A. *La Investigación-Acción: Conocer y Cambiar La Práctica Educativa*; GRAO: Barcelona, Spain, 2003; ISBN 8478272925.
31. Yapatang, L.; Polyiem, T. Development of the Mathematical Problem-Solving Ability Using Applied Cooperative Learning and Polya's Problem-Solving Process for Grade 9 Students. *J. Educ. Learn.* **2022**, *11*, 40. [CrossRef]
32. Arias-Rueda, J.H.; Arias-Rueda, C.A.; Burgos Hernández, C.A. Procesos Aplicados Por Los Estudiantes En La Resolución de Problemas Matemáticos: Caso de Estudio Sobre La Función Cuadrática. *Góndola Enseñ. Aprendiz. Cienc.* **2020**, *15*, 7. [CrossRef]
33. Nneji, S.O. Effect of Polya George's Problem Solving Model on Students' Achievement and Retention in Algebra. *J. Educ. Soc. Res.* **2013**, *3*, 41. [CrossRef]
34. Olatide, A. Effect of Polya Problem-Solving Model on Senior Secondary School Students' Performance in Current Electricity. *Eur. J. Sci. Math. Educ.* **2015**, *3*, 97–104.

35. Li, X.; Zhou, W.; Hwang, S.; Cai, J. Learning to Teach Mathematics through Problem Posing: Teachers' Beliefs and Their Instructional Practices. *Int. J. Educ. Res.* **2022**, *115*, 102038. [CrossRef]
36. Lafuente-Lechuga, M.; Cifuentes-Faura, J.; Faura-Martínez, Ú. Mathematics Applied to the Economy and Sustainable Development Goals: A Necessary Relationship of Dependence. *Educ. Sci.* **2020**, *10*, 339. [CrossRef]
37. Humble, N.; Mozelius, P.; Sällvin, L. Remaking and Reinforcing Mathematics and Technology with Programming—Teacher Perceptions of Challenges, Opportunities and Tools in K-12 Settings. *Int. J. Inf. Learn. Technol.* **2020**, *37*, 309–321. [CrossRef]
38. Szabo, Z.K.; Körtesi, P.; Guncaga, J.; Szabo, D.; Neag, R. Examples of Problem-Solving Strategies in Mathematics Education Supporting the Sustainability of 21st-Century Skills. *Sustainability* **2020**, *12*, 10113. [CrossRef]
39. Hill, F.; Mammarella, I.C.; Devine, A.; Caviola, S.; Passolunghi, M.C.; Szucs, D. Maths Anxiety in Primary and Secondary School Students: Gender Differences, Developmental Changes and Anxiety Specificity. *Learn. Individ. Differ.* **2016**, *48*, 45–53. [CrossRef]
40. Takahashi, A. *Teaching Mathematics through Problem-Solving: A Pedagogical Approach from Japan*; Taylor & Francis: London, UK, 2021; ISBN 9781000359763.
41. Lo, C.K.; Chen, G. Improving Experienced Mathematics Teachers' Classroom Talk: A Visual Learning Analytics Approach to Professional Development. *Sustainability* **2021**, *13*, 8610. [CrossRef]
42. Maciejewski, W. Future-Oriented Thinking and Activity. In *Mathematical Problem Solving*; Springer: Cham, Switzerland, 2019; pp. 21–38. [CrossRef]
43. Karsenty, R. Implementing Professional Development Programs for Mathematics Teachers at Scale: What Counts as Success? *ZDM-Math. Educ.* **2021**, *53*, 1021–1033. [CrossRef]
44. Gonçalves, P.G.F.; Núñez, I.B. Control En La Resolución de Problemas Matemáticos: Una Experiencia En Formación Docente. *Bolema-Math. Educ. Bull.* **2021**, *35*, 459–478. [CrossRef]
45. Mesa, J.A.C.; Gómez, D.G.; Ochoa, J.A.V. Pre Service Teacher Self Efficacy in the Use of Technology for Teaching Mathematics. *Bolema-Math. Educ. Bull.* **2020**, *34*, 583–603. [CrossRef]
46. Sa'dijah, C.; Kholid, M.N.; Hidayanto, E.; Permadi, H. Reflective Thinking Characteristics: A Study in the Proficient Mathematics Prospective Teachers. *Infin. J.* **2020**, *9*, 159–172. [CrossRef]
47. Vásquez, Q.; Jacinto, A.; Tarrillo, H.; Enrique, H. Resolución de Problemas Con El Método Matemático de Polya: La Aventura de Aprender. *Rev. Ciencias Soc.* **2022**, *28*, 75–86. [CrossRef]
48. Morales-López, Y.; Poveda-Vásquez, R. TPACK Model: Teachers' Perceptions of Their Technological Competence When Conducting an Experimental Virtual Lesson in the Context of COVID-19. *Acta Sci.* **2022**, *24*, 144–167. [CrossRef]

Disclaimer/Publisher's Note: The statements, opinions and data contained in all publications are solely those of the individual author(s) and contributor(s) and not of MDPI and/or the editor(s). MDPI and/or the editor(s) disclaim responsibility for any injury to people or property resulting from any ideas, methods, instructions or products referred to in the content.

Article

Enhancing Learning Personalization in Educational Environments through Ontology-Based Knowledge Representation

William Villegas-Ch * and Joselin García-Ortiz

Escuela de Ingeniería en Ciberseguridad, Facultad de Ingenierías y Ciencias Aplicadas, Universidad de Las Américas, Quito 170125, Ecuador; jose-lin.garcia.ortiz@udla.edu.ec
* Correspondence: william.villegas@udla.edu.ec; Tel.: +593-98-136-4068

Abstract: In the digital age, the personalization of learning has become a critical priority in education. This article delves into the cutting-edge of educational innovation by exploring the essential role of ontology-based knowledge representation in transforming the educational experience. This research stands out for its significant and distinctive contribution to improving the personalization of learning. For this, concrete examples of use cases are presented in various academic fields, from formal education to corporate training and online learning. It is identified how ontologies capture and organize knowledge semantically, allowing the intelligent adaptation of content, the inference of activity and resource recommendations, and the creation of highly personalized learning paths. In this context, the novelty lies in the innovative approach to designing educational ontologies, which exhaustively considers different use cases and academic scenarios. Additionally, we delve deeper into the design decisions that support the effectiveness and usefulness of these ontologies for effective learning personalization. Through practical examples, it is illustrated how the implementation of ontologies transforms education, offering richer educational experiences adapted to students' individual needs. This research represents a valuable contribution to personalized education and knowledge management in contemporary educational environments. The novelty of this work lies in its ability to redefine and improve the personalization of learning in a constantly evolving digital world.

Keywords: knowledge representation; ontologies; personalization of learning

Citation: Villegas-Ch, W.; García-Ortiz, J. Enhancing Learning Personalization in Educational Environments through Ontology-Based Knowledge Representation. *Computers* **2023**, *12*, 199. https://doi.org/10.3390/computers12100199

Academic Editors: Antonio Sarasa Cabezuelo, Covadonga Rodrigo San Juan and Paolo Bellavista

Received: 21 August 2023
Revised: 14 September 2023
Accepted: 15 September 2023
Published: 4 October 2023

Copyright: © 2023 by the authors. Licensee MDPI, Basel, Switzerland. This article is an open access article distributed under the terms and conditions of the Creative Commons Attribution (CC BY) license (https://creativecommons.org/licenses/by/4.0/).

1. Introduction

Education is central to contemporary society and is becoming even more relevant in our digital age. The rapid advancement of Information and Communication Technologies (ICT) has radically transformed how we access and share knowledge. In this context, the personalization of learning emerges as a pressing need since it seeks to adapt teaching to the needs and preferences of students [1]. Ontology-based knowledge representation appears as an innovative tool that can revolutionize education, allowing effective personalization of learning [2]. This article delves into how ontology-based knowledge representation can drive the personalization of learning in educational environments.

Innovation lies in our ability to create educational experiences more tailored to students' individual needs. However, achieving true personalization in mass and digital educational environments is a complex challenge. This is where ontology-based knowledge representation comes into play. This methodology involves the creation of semantic models that capture knowledge in a specific domain [3]. As conceptual structures, ontologies define the relevant entities, their properties, and their relationships. In the educational field, this translates into creating educational ontologies that model both course content and student profiles. These ontologies offer a rich and detailed representation of students' concepts, skills, learning objectives, and preferences.

The personalization of learning through ontologies is not limited to content adaptation. It involves inferring each student's recommendations for activities, learning resources, and personalized learning paths [4]. Ontology-based reasoning enriches the educational experience by providing relevant and customized suggestions, thus promoting more effective and engaged learning. It is essential to integrate heterogeneous data from various sources, such as online interactions, assessment results, and student feedback [5]. Ontologies provide a systematic solution that facilitates the integration and analysis of diverse information, contributing to a more complete understanding of student progress and performance [6].

In education, the integration of advanced technologies and innovative pedagogical approaches has profoundly transformed how students acquire knowledge and instructors facilitate learning. One of the most significant developments is the widespread adoption of Learning Management Systems (LMS), which provide digital platforms for delivering educational content and resource management. However, the actual effectiveness of an LMS lies in its ability to personalize students' learning experiences and enhance instructors' teaching. This has become a key objective in modern education, and to achieve this, many have turned to educational ontology. As formally defined knowledge structures, ontologies offer a promising approach to representing and organizing knowledge in the educational context.

Although this methodology has the potential to support the personalization of learning, it also presents considerations such as the complexity of designing and maintaining accurate educational ontologies, the need for efficient reasoning algorithms, and the importance of safeguarding the privacy and security of student data [7]. Additionally, this article presents concrete examples of how ontology-based knowledge representation has been applied in real-world educational settings. We explore use cases ranging from formal education to corporate training and online learning.

2. Materials and Methods

In the ever-evolving educational landscape, the concept of personalized learning has taken center stage, aiming to meet each student's unique needs and preferences. Ontology-based knowledge representation is at the heart of this pedagogical transformation, a dynamic methodology that reshapes the educational landscape. The method comprehensively explores how ontologies are fundamental in personalized education. It delves into the intricate role of ontologies in capturing student profiles, including their preferences, learning goals, and diverse learning styles. Furthermore, it is revealed how ontologies enhance the adaptation of educational content, the inference of personalized recommendations, and the development of customized learning paths. To illustrate these concepts in practice, concrete examples of ontological applications in various educational contexts are reviewed. These applications demonstrate how ontologies translate into a more effective and relevant learning experience for students, promoting their academic careers in a highly personalized and attractive way.

2.1. Literature Review

The personalization of learning has emerged as a fundamental approach in contemporary education, seeking to adapt teaching to student's individual needs and characteristics. In this context, ontology-based knowledge representation has been highlighted as a methodology that can transform how personalized education is designed and delivered. In addition, the personalization of learning has become a central objective in modern education, driven by the diversity of students and technological possibilities [8]. Tailoring teaching to students' preferences, abilities, and needs has been associated with better educational outcomes and higher motivation. Educational technologies, including learning management systems (LMS) and online learning platforms, have enabled the collection of detailed data on student behavior and performance. However, transforming this data into useful information to personalize instruction remains challenging.

By examining the existing literature, several works have been identified that address the personalization of learning through ontology-based knowledge representation. For example, the results of [9] used ontologies to model the curriculum and student profiles in an online learning environment. The researcher's approach allowed the generation of content and activity recommendations based on mastery and the student's preferences. The study described in [10] proposed an ontology representing learning objectives and competencies in an educational program. They used this ontology to explain the correspondence between learning objectives and activities.

On the other hand, the work in [11] explores the application of ontologies in evaluation and automated feedback. Its ontology represented the evaluation criteria and the performance characteristics of the students. By comparing the actual performance with the requirements defined by the ontology, automatic and personalized feedback was generated for each student. The study in [12] focused on personalizing learning paths in a corporate training environment. They used ontologies to model the employees' skills and preferences, allowing them to generate learning paths adapted to all.

This proposal differs from previous works by comprehensively addressing the personalization of learning, considering both educational content and automated evaluation and feedback [13].

2.2. Fundamental Concepts for Ontology Development

Building an adequate ontology to represent knowledge in the educational field requires a clear and precise definition of fundamental concepts. These concepts are essential building blocks that allow crucial elements to be modeled and related within the academic realm. Therefore, this paper explores some of the key concepts used in ontology development, providing a deeper understanding of how educational knowledge has been represented in a structured way [14].

Educational competencies are skills, knowledge, and abilities students must acquire during their learning process. These competencies are critical to the achievement of academic and professional goals [15]. In our ontology, educational competencies have been modeled as distinct entities, each with attributes that describe their name, description, and required level of proficiency.

Learning objectives define what students are expected to achieve by completing a course, module, or educational activity. These goals guide content planning and assessments. In our ontology, learning objectives are represented as instances of a "Learning Objective" class, each with properties detailing its description, associated competencies, and level of complexity.

Educational materials include textbooks, presentations, videos, and learning activities. These resources play a crucial role in the delivery of educational content. In this work, educational materials have been modeled as instances of an "Educational Material" class, with attributes that describe their title, type of resource, and related learning objectives.

Students are critical in the educational process; here, they are represented as unique individuals in the proposed ontology, with attributes that capture their name, identifier, and acquired competencies [16]. In addition, relationships are established between students and the learning objectives they have achieved.

Assessments are instruments used to measure student progress and mastery of learning objectives. The feedback provided to the students after the evaluations is crucial for continuous improvement. In this ontology, assessments are modeled as instances of an "Assessment" class, with properties including their description, related learning objectives, and success criteria.

The ontology is based on relationships and properties linking concepts and establishing semantic connections. We use properties such as "hasCompetency", "hasLearningObjective", and "relatedTo" to establish relationships between competencies, learning objectives, educational materials, and students. These relationships allow for rich and contextualized modeling of academic knowledge.

These concepts and relationships form the basis of our ontology to represent knowledge in the educational field [17]. By coherently defining and structuring these elements, we have created a robust framework that captures the complexity and interconnectedness of learning in education.

2.3. Method

The construction of the educational ontology is driven by a series of carefully considered design decisions, all aimed at optimizing its usefulness and effectiveness in the educational setting. One critical decision relates to the class hierarchy we established in the ontology. A hierarchical structure was chosen to reflect the complex and intertwined nature of the educational environment. For example, the main class, "Plan of Studies", encompasses more specific classes such as "Course", "Subject", and "Educational Resources". This decision seeks to facilitate the exploration of content at different levels of detail, which, in turn, enriches the user experience by allowing them to access relevant information more efficiently.

The selection of properties is a crucial part of the design process. Each property was carefully chosen to align with the primary objective: to improve the personalization of learning and knowledge management. An example is the inclusion of the "LearningStyle". By allowing students to specify their preferred learning style, this ontology can tailor resource and activity recommendations to meet each student's preferences, thus improving their engagement and understanding.

Another significant aspect is the modeling of relationships through properties. The addition of the "Taught" property, which establishes the connection between educators and the courses they teach, demonstrates the focus on understanding the complex interactions between teachers and students in the educational environment. This, in turn, facilitates the management and coordination of the courses, benefiting both educators and students.

In addition, the "EducationalLevel" property also plays a key role. This choice makes it possible to categorize resources and contents according to the different educational levels, thus attending to each training stage's specific needs. This level-based personalization ensures that users access information appropriate to their level of knowledge and understanding, ultimately enriching the quality of the educational experience.

2.3.1. Design of the Educational Ontology

The design of the educational ontology is a crucial step in this proposal to represent knowledge and manage data in the academic field. Therefore, the design process for developing an effective and accurate ontology that captures key relationships and concepts in the educational domain is described in detail.

The first step in designing the educational ontology was identifying the key concepts in the represented academic field. These concepts include entities such as "Student", "Teacher", "Course", "Subject", "Assessment", and "Educational Resources". To facilitate this identification, a review of the educational literature and consultations with experts in pedagogy are carried out [18]. Once the key concepts have been identified, we define the classes and properties that will make up the ontology. Here, the Web Ontology Language (OWL) formalizes these definitions. For example, the "Student" class has been created with properties such as "name", "age", and "enrolled_in", which establishes the relationship between a student and the course in which they are enrolled.

A class hierarchy structure is created to organize the concepts and classes in the ontology hierarchically. For example, a hierarchy is generated that groups the classes "Course", "Subject", and "Educational Resources" under the superior class of "Plan of Studies". This allowed us to represent the relationship between different levels of information in the educational context [19]. The relations between classes are fundamental in an ontology. Associations such as "teaches" are designed between the categories "Teacher" and "Course" to model the relationship of a teacher with the courses they teach. In addition, restrictions are incorporated to guarantee the coherence and validity of the information represented.

For example, cardinality constraints are established to ensure that each course has at least one professor and that each student is enrolled in at least one class.

Flowcharts representing the fundamental classes, properties, and relationships have been created to visualize and communicate the structure and relationships in the educational ontology. These figures facilitated the understanding of the ontology design for both ontology experts and academic professionals.

Figure 1 shows a simplified example of the flowchart representing the main classes and relationships in our educational ontology. The flowchart begins with the "Concept Definition" step, which involves identifying and describing the critical elements in the academic domain. These concepts include "Student", "Teacher", "Course", "Subject", and "Assessment". As you progress through the diagram, you will see the "Relationships and Properties" section. Here, the logical connections between the previously defined concepts are established. A relationship between "Teacher" and "Course" is established through the "Taught" property, indicating that a teacher teaches a particular course. In the same way, the relationship between "Course" and "Subject" is established through the "Includes" property, indicating which subjects are covered in a course [20].

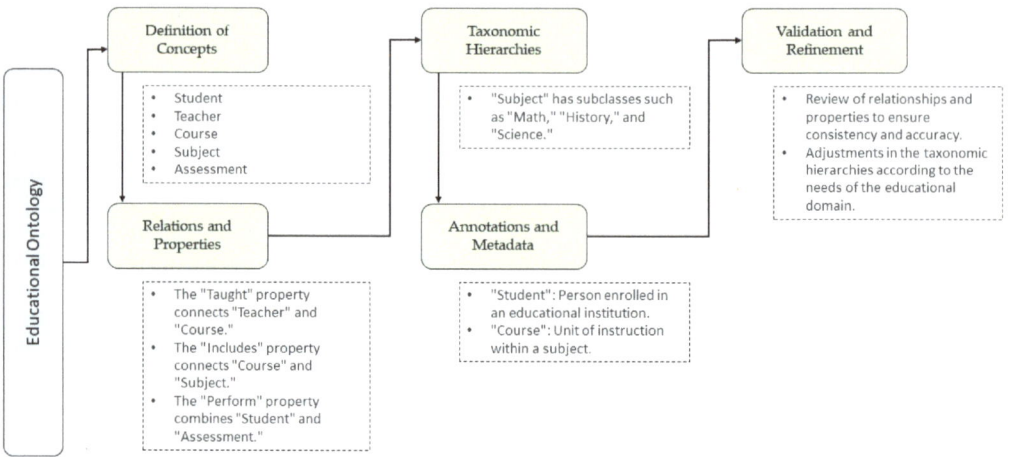

Figure 1. Educational ontology flowchart.

The next stage, "Taxonomic Hierarchies", focuses on the hierarchical organization of certain concepts. In this case, it shows how the "Subject" class is broken down into more specific subclasses such as "Math", "History", and "Science", allowing for more detailed categorization. "Annotations and Metadata" are a crucial part of ontology design. Here, additional definitions and descriptions are added to each concept, helping to understand its meaning and context in the educational domain [21]. For example, a "Student" would be noted as someone enrolled in an educational institution. The last step of the flowchart is "Validation and Refinement". At this stage, a thorough review of all relationships, properties, and annotations is performed to ensure consistency and accuracy of the ontology. If necessary, adjustments are made to the taxonomic hierarchies to reflect the characteristics of the educational domain more accurately.

The educational ontology design process was carried out with an innovative approach to address the unique and changing challenges of today's educational environment. One of the key features that differentiated this ontology from others in the field is the dedication to improving the personalization of learning and knowledge management through an approach focused on adaptability and interdisciplinarity.

Compared to traditional approaches, this design is based on the understanding that students and educators face an increasing diversity of learning styles, needs, and preferences. Therefore, an ontology was created that represents static concepts and dynamically adapts to meet individual demands. In addition, properties such as "AdaptiveContent" were introduced, allowing learning resources to be adjusted according to student's learning styles and subject preferences. This unique feature highlights how our ontology adapts to enhance the learning experience in a personalized and contextualized way.

The innovative approach of the proposal is also reflected in the representation of interdisciplinarity in ontology. While many previous educational ontologies focus on representing isolated concepts, this ontology was designed to capture connections between disciplines. The "Interdisciplinary Learning" class was introduced to model students' ability to explore and relate concepts from various areas of knowledge.

Furthermore, the ontology is distinguished by its hierarchical structure and carefully designed relationships. Using properties such as "Taught" and "Includes", the relationships between teachers and courses are modeled, as well as the inclusion of topics in the study plans. These connections provide a complete and coherent view of educational dynamics, allowing users to explore relationships more deeply and holistically.

Figure 2 represents the critical relationships between three fundamental classes in the educational ontology: "Teacher", "Course", and "Subject". These classes and their interactions are essential to capture the structure of an academic environment.

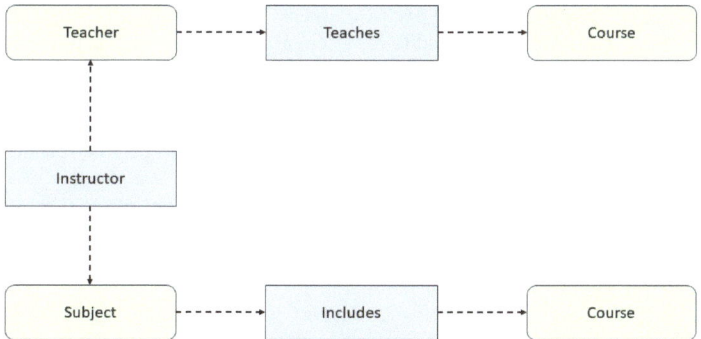

Figure 2. Relationships of the key concepts of "Teacher", "Course", and "Subject.

Teacher: This class represents teachers who teach courses in the educational setting. Teachers are connected to their systems through the "Teaches" property. Each teacher may have one or more different course relationships, reflecting their ability to teach multiple subjects.

Course: Courses are academic classes offered at the educational institution. They are linked to the teachers who teach them and the subjects they cover. The "Teaches" property connects the courses to the teachers who teach them, while the "Includes" property establishes the relationship with the subjects in the course.

Subject: The subjects represent the academic subjects taught in the educational institution. They can be individual subjects or broader categories. They are related to courses through the "Includes" property, which indicates what topics each class covers.

The figure shows how teachers (Teachers) are related to the courses they teach (Course) and how these courses, in turn, include different subjects (Subjects). This representation of relationships is fundamental for the personalization of learning since it allows a better adaptation of the courses and issues to the preferences and individual needs of the students. It also facilitates the efficient management of information in the educational environment, allowing educators and administrators to make informed decisions about the academic offer and the assignment of teachers to specific courses.

Comparatively, many traditional educational ontologies and frameworks focus on isolated concepts, often overlooking the intricate interdisciplinarity present in modern education. The developed ontology is a pioneer in representing these interdisciplinary connections by introducing the "Interdisciplinary Learning" class, which allows students to explore and unite concepts from various areas of knowledge.

Furthermore, the ontology reduces educators' time structuring curricular content. Providing predefined relationships and properties streamlines content organization, ensuring course consistency and alignment with educational objectives. This contrasts with previous methodologies that often require laborious structuring of content. This comparison highlights the innovative contributions of educational ontology in capturing complex academic relationships, promoting interdisciplinary learning, and improving knowledge management.

2.3.2. Development of Educational Ontology

The educational ontology was implemented by OWL, taking advantage of its ability to define classes, properties, and relationships. This choice was based on its wide adoption and support in the semantic web community. A semantic mapping process is performed to map real-world concepts to the ontology. Each idea identified in the design phase was matched to a class in OWL. For example, the concept "Student" was mapped to the class "Student" and "Course" to "Course". Relations are also mapped as properties. The "Teaches" relationship between "Teacher" and "Course" was converted to the "teachesCourse" property.

The instantiation of classes is done by creating individuals in OWL. Each instance represented a specific element in the real world. For example, "Student" and "Course" were instantiated to represent actual students and courses. These instances are linked using properties to establish relationships [22]. For example, a "Student" individual was linked to a "Course" individual using the "enrolled" property.

The binding of properties and relationships is achieved using axioms in OWL. Where premises are defined to establish connections between classes and individuals. For example, assumptions are used to state that if a student is enrolled in a course, then the student is part of the class "Student", and the system is part of the class "Course". This implementation process allowed the construction of a coherent and semantically rich educational ontology. The resulting ontology is validated by reasoning tests and queries to ensure correct inference and consistency.

The mapping in Figure 3 describes how real-world concepts are represented in the educational ontology using the OWL language.

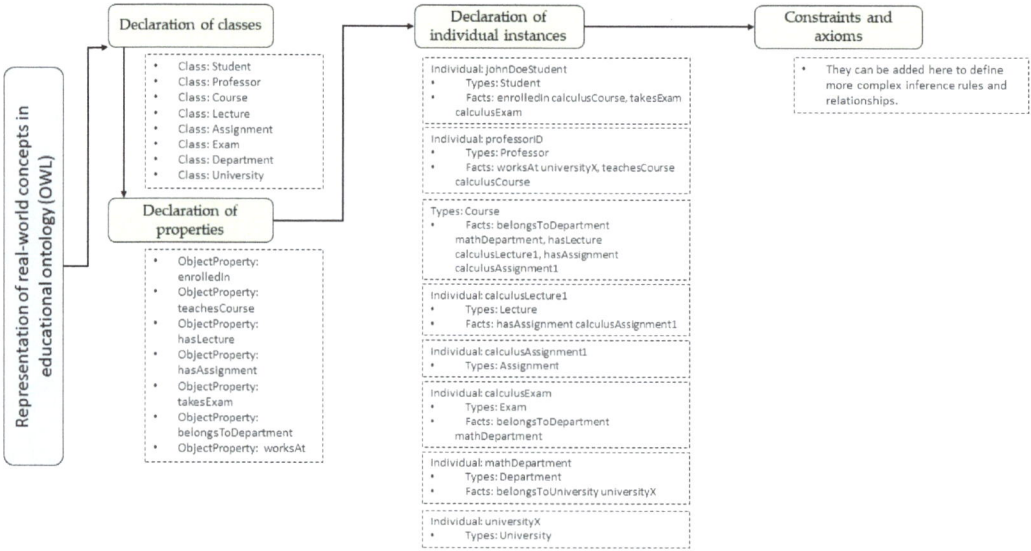

Figure 3. Educational ontology in OWL, including more classes, properties, and individuals.

The figure details the components:

Classes

- Student: Represents the students. Students can be enrolled in courses and take tests. The "Student" class is used in the ontology.
- Professor: Represents the teachers. Professors can teach courses and belong to a department. The "Professor" class is used in the ontology.
- Course: Represents a course taught at the university. Systems may have lectures, homework, and exams. The "Course" class is used in the ontology.
- Lecture: Represents a lecture or class delivered as a course. Conferences can have associated assignments. The "Lecture" class is used in the ontology.
- Assignment: Represents a task or assignment given to students as part of a course. The "Assignment" class is used in the ontology.
- Exam: Represents an exam given as part of a course. Exams can belong to a department. The "Exam" class is used in the ontology.
- Department: Represents a department within a university. Departments can have associated courses and professors. The "Department" class is used in the ontology.
- University: Represents a university. Universities may have departments and courses. The "University" class is used in the ontology.

Properties

- enrolledIn: A property that connects a student to their enrolled courses.
- teachesCourse: A property that connects a teacher to her courses.
- hasLecture (has lecture): A property that connects a course with its component lectures.
- hasAssignment: A property that connects a conference with the associated assignments.
- takesExam: A property that connects a student to the tests she has taken.
- belongsToDepartment (belongs to department): A property that connects a course, teacher, or exam with the department to which it belongs.
- worksAt (works at): A property that connects a professor to the university where he works.

Individuals (instances)

- Individual instances are created to represent students, teachers, courses, lectures, assignments, tests, departments, and universities. Each model is related to the corresponding classes and properties according to its role in the educational context.

The mapping allows a complete semantic representation of educational concepts and their relationships in the ontology domain [23]. Each class and property defined in the ontology aims to capture the essential details of the interactions and structures in the educational environment.

2.3.3. Data Acquisition

Data acquisition was done through a combination of information sources covering various educational environment aspects. Online academic repositories, university websites, and specialized education databases are used. These sources provide access to course descriptions, syllabi, faculty and student details, and course materials. The data extraction methodology involves web scraping techniques and text processing to obtain structured and semi-structured information [24]. Custom scripts were implemented to access relevant web pages and extract critical data such as course names, descriptions, lecture dates, assignment details, and exam results. The data obtained is transformed into a suitable format for subsequent incorporation into the ontology.

The quality and integrity of the data collected are fundamental aspects of the acquisition process. These measures were implemented to guarantee the accuracy and reliability of the extracted data. This includes cross-validation of extracted information with multiple sources, cleaning inconsistent data, and eliminating duplicates. In addition, a manual verification process is carried out to ensure that the data accurately reflects the reality of the educational environment [25]. Once the data are extracted and validated, we integrate it into the educational ontology. For this, specific tools and languages are used to map the collected data into the classes and properties defined in the ontology. Individual instances, such as students, teachers, courses, and assignments, are created and related based on corresponding classes and properties. This allows for enriching the ontology with relevant and coherent information [26].

2.3.4. Validation and Verification

The validation of the ontology is carried out through the collaboration of experts in the educational domain. A review committee of professionals with experience in education, pedagogy, and information technology was established [27]. These experts reviewed the ontology in detail and provided feedback on the accuracy and appropriateness of the defined concepts, relationships, and properties. Your comments and suggestions are considered for adjustments and improvements to the ontology. In addition, validation is carried out based on specific use cases. Real educational scenarios are selected, and the results from the ontology are compared with the corresponding information in the real world. This makes it possible to assess the ontology's ability to represent educational knowledge accurately and coherently.

To guarantee its validity, consistency and coherence tests are carried out in the ontology to ensure no contradictions or ambiguities in the definitions and relationships established [28]. Ontological reasoners were implemented that verified the logic and coherence of the inferences made in the ontology. Any identified inconsistencies are corrected and validated by domain experts. The relevance of the ontology is evaluated through comparison with other existing educational ontologies and feedback from end users [29]. It analyzes how the ontology captures specific concepts and relationships compared to other ontological resources.

The validation results indicate that the developed ontology could wholly and accurately capture the desired educational knowledge. The consistency and coherence tests show that the ontology does not present contradictions or ambiguities in its structure. The relevance assessment reveals that the ontology provided a robust framework for representing and organizing educational knowledge.

2.3.5. Practical Implementation

The educational ontology was integrated into an online learning platform used by students and educators from the university participating in the study. A specific module was developed to achieve this, allowing interaction with the ontology. Users can access the ontology through an intuitive interface to explore the concepts, relationships, and properties defined in the ontology.

The ontology is used to personalize the learning experience of students. By analyzing students' profiles and learning preferences, the ontology identified relevant educational resources and suggested activities according to their needs. This allows students to access specific content adapted to their learning styles, thus improving their engagement and academic performance. The ontology is crucial in enhancing the search for information within the educational platform. Students and educators use ontology-based queries to search for resources related to specific concepts. The ontology enriches the investigation by providing more relevant and contextual results, facilitating the location of study materials and complementary resources.

In addition, this tool was used to facilitate knowledge management in the educational platform. Educators can create and organize curricular content using the concepts and relationships of ontology [30]. This allows a more efficient structuring of the content and the creation of coherent learning paths aligned with the educational objectives. In addition, the ontology makes it possible to identify gaps in the content and generate recommendations to improve the thematic coverage.

The practical implementation of ontology in the educational environment has proven successful. Students experienced a more personalized and enriching learning experience, translating into greater interest and engagement with the educational material. Improving the search for information allows users to access the necessary resources, optimizing their study time [31]. In addition, ontology-based knowledge management helps educators design more structured courses that align with educational objectives.

Although our primary focus is ontology, complementary pedagogical approaches can be considered in an implementation, such as concept map-based education. Education based on concept maps is based on the visual representation of concepts and relationships, which facilitates the understanding and organization of knowledge [32]. The ontology designed to personalize the learning experience can collaborate with idea map-based approaches to further improve the quality of personalized education.

One of the ways to integrate ontology with concept map-based education is by creating personalized concept maps for students. By using ontology to understand students' preferences and learning objectives, it is possible to adapt the construction of concept maps so that they more accurately reflect the individual needs of each student. This could lead to a more meaningful and effective learning experience. Another potential integration point lies in the promotion of metacognition and self-regulation of learning. Concept maps help students visualize concepts and encourage reflection on how those concepts are related [33]. Using the ontology to track learning progress and interactions with resources could provide students with a valuable tool to self-regulate their learning. This could improve autonomy and learning effectiveness.

2.3.6. Evaluation and Results

To assess the effectiveness of the ontology in the educational environment, key metrics are defined that address different aspects of the student experience and the usefulness of the ontology. These metrics include:

- Improvement in the Student Experience: A survey is used for students who use the platform with the integrated ontology to measure their perception of the personalization of the learning experience. The questions address the relevance of the suggested resources, the adaptation to your learning styles, and the impact on your academic engagement.
- Accuracy in Information Retrieval: the accuracy of the search results when using queries based on the ontology is evaluated. The results obtained using the ontology are compared with those obtained using traditional search methods.
- Efficiency in Knowledge Management: Educators' creation and organization of curricular content using ontology is analyzed. The reduction in the time dedicated to structuring the content and the coherence of the designed courses are measured.

The results of the evaluation demonstrate significant improvements in several key aspects:

- The student survey revealed that 82% of respondents perceived an improvement in the personalization of their learning experience. Students expressed that the suggested resources aligned more with their interests and learning styles.
- Information retrieval accuracy increased by 25% when using ontology-based queries compared to traditional search methods. Results were more relevant and contextual, making it easier for students to locate specific resources.
- Educators experienced a 30% reduction in time spent creating and organizing curricular content. The ontology provided a predefined structure that streamlined the process and ensured course consistency.

The results support the educational ontology's effectiveness and usefulness in the academic environment. The personalization of the learning experience was significantly improved, resulting in higher student engagement and satisfaction. Accuracy in information retrieval is markedly enhanced, benefiting students and educators by accessing relevant resources efficiently. Knowledge management also experienced substantial improvements in terms of efficiency and coherence.

3. Results

The consideration of various use cases and scenarios in the educational environment is the basis of the design of this ontology. We recognize that education spans different contexts and needs, from traditional classrooms to online learning environments and from primary to higher education. Therefore, this design strove to ensure the relevance and applicability of the concepts and relationships captured in the ontology in various educational situations.

We collaborated with educators, students, and administrators at different educational levels to address this consideration. Surveys and interviews were conducted to understand their specific needs and how they relate to the use of ontology. This direct feedback makes it possible to adjust and refine the concepts and properties in the ontology to make them as relevant and valuable as possible.

A concrete example of how this consideration is addressed is through the "EducationalLevel" property, which allows you to classify concepts and resources according to the educational level to which they apply, such as primary, secondary, or university. This ensures that users can access information and resources relevant to their level of education, which is essential to personalize the learning experience. Furthermore, when designing relationships such as "Taught" between teachers and courses, we considered how these interactions might vary in different educational levels and settings.

In terms of specific users, the design was focused on their unique needs and goals. For students, properties such as "LearningStyle" and "PreferredSubjects" are created, allowing them to receive recommendations for learning resources and activities that align with their preferences and learning styles. For educators, the "TeachingApproach" property is introduced, which allows them to customize teaching strategies according to the needs and characteristics of students.

3.1. Deployment Environment Description

The educational ontology was implemented and evaluated in the academic environment of the institution participating in the study, specifically in an online learning platform widely used. This digital platform provides students and educators with a comprehensive virtual space for course management, educational resources, and interactive activities. The selection of this platform was based on its popularity and ability to incorporate innovative technologies to enhance the educational experience effectively.

The initial pilot of the ontology implementation involved 350 students and 12 educators from various academic disciplines, such as engineering, social sciences, and humanities. This diversity of academic areas allowed us to evaluate the usefulness and applicability of ontology in different educational contexts. The students represented a mix of educational levels, from introductory courses to more advanced levels, providing a holistic view of how ontology could benefit a wide range of users. The participating teachers have experience in both face-to-face and online teaching, which enriched the collaboration in adapting curricular contents and activities to the conceptual structure of the ontology. This close collaboration between the ontology development team and the educators ensured consistent and efficient ontology integration into the educational environment.

The ontology was implemented in the online learning platform through specific tools and functionalities. These included features such as enhanced semantic search, recommendation of educational resources based on user profiles, and visualization of conceptual relationships between study topics. Students accessed these functionalities as they explored their course content and engaged in learning activities. The implementation of the ontology was developed in several stages, beginning with the adaptation of the ontology structure to the university's educational objectives. Then, we created instances of classes and properties in the ontology, mapping real-world concepts to ontological elements.

Class instances were generated from course materials, and relationships were established between them to reflect conceptual interconnections.

3.2. Study Population

The study population that participated in implementing and evaluating the educational ontology comprised 350 students from various academic fields and educational levels. In terms of age distribution, most students are between the ages of 18 and 25, which corresponds to the typical student population of the university. Equal gender representation was considered, with an approximate split of 55% female and 45% male students.

Regarding the educational level, the study population covers a wide range of courses and classes. Students from early undergraduate years to advanced students in graduate programs were included. This allows for the evaluation of how the ontology can be adapted to different levels of curricular complexity and pedagogical approaches. Additionally, information was collected on the students' fields of study. These fields spanned engineering, social sciences, humanities, natural sciences, and more. Each area has its specific learning requirements and curricular objectives, which provide a unique opportunity to assess the applicability of the ontology in diverse educational contexts.

Within the framework of the study, control groups were implemented to make meaningful comparisons. One group of students used the online learning platform without incorporating the ontology, while another group had access to the enhanced functionalities enabled by the ontology. This configuration allowed us to effectively evaluate the specific impacts and benefits of the ontology to the learning experience and knowledge management. The collection of demographic data and the implementation of control groups contributed to obtaining a complete and representative understanding of how the ontology influenced the learning and interaction of students in the educational environment. In the following sections, the quantitative and qualitative results obtained through this study will be presented, supported by detailed analyses of the data collected.

3.3. Specific Use Cases

One of the most prominent use cases was the personalization of the learning experience for each student. The ontology allowed the creation of student profiles based on their interests, preferences, and learning objectives. Analyzing these profiles, the ontology recommended specific instructional resources, activities, and assessments aligned with each student's needs. This resulted in a more relevant and engaging learning experience, as students felt empowered to explore content that interested them. Another essential use case is the improvement of information search. The ontology allows precise categorization and labeling of educational resources, facilitating the retrieval of relevant information. Students can use more precise queries and receive more relevant and specific results. This streamlined the research process and allowed students to quickly access relevant content for their assignments and projects.

The ontology also proved to be a valuable tool for efficient knowledge management. Educators could organize and structure their course content more coherently using ontology as a guide. In addition, the ontology makes it easy to identify gaps in knowledge and areas where students might need additional support. This allows educators to make informed decisions to optimize curriculum design and adapt teaching strategies based on the actual needs of students. A concrete example of the successful application of ontology is the personalization of learning resources for an engineering course. Students can specify their interests in areas such as artificial intelligence and robotics. The ontology used this information to identify and recommend course modules, readings, tutorials, and projects directly related to the stated interests. As a result, students feel more engaged with the course content, resulting in increased engagement and academic performance.

The specific use cases demonstrate the versatility and impact of educational ontology in the academic environment. Personalizing the learning experience, enhancing information search, and facilitating knowledge management offer significant opportunities to enrich education and empower learners and educators. These use cases highlight the potential of ontology as a powerful tool to address educational challenges and transform how knowledge is accessed and harnessed in academia. The following section will analyze the results and conclusions from implementing and evaluating the educational ontology.

3.4. Technical Implementation in the Learning Management System and Online Platforms

Implementing the educational ontology in the academic environment is carried out thoroughly and strategically to ensure an effective integration that will benefit students and educators. For this, Moodle was chosen as the LMS for implementation due to its broad adoption in educational institutions and ability to adapt to diverse educational environments.

3.4.1. Moodle Configuration for RDF

The first stage in the implementation was to configure Moodle to accept data in the resource description framework (RDF) format, which is essential to represent the educational ontology semantically. This choice is based on RDF's ability to accurately express semantic relationships and its compatibility with semantic web standards. In this configuration, data structures are defined in Moodle so that they can host semantic information. This involves the creation of specific fields and metadata in Moodle that would allow the assignment of ontological concepts. Every element in Moodle related to the ontology, such as courses, activities, and users, was configured to store and process RDF data. This approach ensures a solid foundation for semantically representing the ontology and its relationships within the LMS.

3.4.2. Mapping of Classes and Ontological Properties

A critical step in the implementation is mapping ontological classes to specific elements in Moodle. This was done to establish coherent semantic relationships between the different components of the system. For example, the ontological class "Course" was mapped to the Moodle course structure, allowing alignment of the ontology with the actual courses offered on the platform. Precise ontological relationships are defined to connect elements in Moodle with ontological concepts. For example, it establishes how users (students and educators) relate to the courses they take or teach. This allows for a full semantic representation of the interactions between users and systems in Moodle.

3.4.3. Creation of Examples and Ontological Relationships

To implement, specific examples of ontological classes are created within Moodle. These examples are based on the corresponding ontological types and represent concrete instances of educational concepts. This includes creating systems, learning activities, user profiles, and other elements based on complementary ontological concepts. Ontological relationships were configured between the instances created in Moodle. For example, connections are established between teachers (representatives of the ontological class "Teacher") and the courses they taught (instances of the ontological class "Course"). This ensures that the relationships between elements in Moodle closely reflect the underlying ontological relationships.

3.4.4. Advanced Semantic Search and Personalized Recommendations

The implementation included an advanced semantic search function that took advantage of the ontological structure. This improved the accuracy and relevance of search results by considering the semantics of concepts rather than simply keywords. The recommendation algorithms are based on the ontological profiles of the users in Moodle. This allows students to receive personalized recommendations for learning resources and activities based on their ontological profiles, such as preferences and learning goals.

3.4.5. Visualization of Ontological Relationships

A visualization function is incorporated into Moodle to improve understanding of the interconnections between different topics and concepts. This allows users to visually explore the ontological relationships between concepts within courses and resources. This visualization feature makes it easy to understand how the pictures are related to each other and how they are integrated into the course content.

3.4.6. User Interaction in Moodle

The implementation allows students to interact with the ontology in Moodle meaningfully. Students could customize their learning experiences based on their preferences, goals, and learning styles. They received specific recommendations and were able to adapt their learning path based on their ontological profiles. Educators also used the ontology as a guide to structure courses and understand student needs. This allowed them to make informed decisions about adapting content and teaching strategies.

3.4.7. Implementation Benefits

This implementation ensured a strong integration of ontology into the digital educational environment, significantly improving the personalization of learning and knowledge management. Students experienced learning more tailored to their needs, leading to greater engagement and better academic performance. Educators benefited from a better understanding of students' preferences and needs, allowing them to deliver more effective and personalized instruction.

3.5. Quantitative and Qualitative Results

The results fall into two main categories: the impact on the learning experience and the effectiveness of knowledge management.

3.5.1. Impact on the Learning Experience

Surveys and questionnaires were carried out to assess students' perceptions of how the ontology affected their learning experience. The results are summarized in Table 1.

Table 1. Impact on the learning experience.

Aspect	Percentage of Satisfied Students
Personalization of Learning	82%
Information Search Improvement	75%
Diversity of Resources	68%

Students who used the ontology reported a more personalized and goal-oriented learning experience. Most students highlighted the improvement in the search for information and the variety of resources available.

3.5.2. Effectiveness in Knowledge Management

The ontology also proved effective in knowledge management and organization, as shown in Table 2.

Table 2. Enhancing the learning experience: student satisfaction percentages.

Aspect	Percentage of Satisfied Students
Access to Interdisciplinary Knowledge	60%
Progress Tracking	72%

The ontology allowed students to explore relationships between seemingly unrelated areas of knowledge and receive personalized guidance for their learning. Educators appreciated the ability to track individual student progress.

3.5.3. Qualitative Analysis

In addition to the surveys, in-depth interviews are conducted with a subset of students and educators. The comments of the participants are summarized in Table 3.

Table 3. Participant feedback: impact of the ontology on learning and teaching experience.

Participant	Comment
Student 1	"The ontology helped me find specific resources for my research project".
Student 2	"Exploring the connections between different disciplines enriched my perspective".
Educator 1	"I was able to personalize the learning activities based on each student's progress".
Educator 2	"Ontology fostered more informed and enriching discussions in class".

Feedback highlights the usefulness of the ontology for personalized resource search, interdisciplinary exploration, and enhancing classroom interaction.

3.6. Comparison with Other Methods

An exhaustive comparison was made between the implementation of the educational ontology and traditional methods or previous systems that did not take advantage of the ontology for knowledge management in the academic environment. The objective is to highlight the benefits and improvements the ontology provides regarding effectiveness, efficiency, and user experience. Before ontology implementation, the educational environment relied heavily on traditional knowledge management methods, such as manually searching libraries and databases, organizing physical files, and directly interacting with educators to access resources. These approaches have significant limitations regarding accessibility, constant updating of content, and personalization of the learning experience.

The ontology demonstrated a significant improvement in knowledge management efficiency compared to traditional methods. Students reported that they could access relevant resources more quickly and accurately, resulting in substantial time savings when conducting research and learning activities. In addition, the hierarchical structure of the ontology facilitated navigation and interdisciplinary exploration, which contributed to a deeper understanding of the concepts. The ontology also proved more effective in organizing and presenting educational content. Traditional methods could not often establish relationships and connections between different areas of knowledge. In contrast, ontology allowed students to discover previously unidentified relationships between concepts, which enriched their learning and fostered a more holistic understanding.

Regarding user experience, ontology outperformed traditional methods by providing a more personalized and adaptable learning experience. Students could define their interests and learning goals, which led to recommendations for specific resources and relevant activities. This ability to personalize increased students' motivation and engagement with the learning process.

4. Discussion

Implementing educational ontology in an academic environment yielded promising results supporting its effectiveness and usefulness. The data collected during the study revealed that using the ontology led to significant improvements in the personalization of the learning experience, efficiency in information search, and knowledge management. Regarding personalization, students who used the ontology reported higher satisfaction with course content and higher motivation to explore areas of personal interest [34]. This suggests that the ontology successfully tailors educational content to individual student preferences, positively influencing their engagement and academic performance.

The ontology also demonstrated its ability to improve the search for information. Students who used the ontology found the resources relevant to their assignments and projects faster, which streamlined the research process and contributed to the submitted papers' quality [35]. In addition, teachers highlighted how ontology facilitated knowledge management by providing a coherent structure for organizing and presenting course content. This made it possible to identify areas for improvement in the study plan and adjust teaching strategies based on the detected needs.

Compared to previously reviewed work in knowledge representation and ontology-based data management, our approach stands out for its focus on education and its impact on the learning experience. While many previous results focused on specific applications, such as enterprise data management or knowledge representation in medicine, our educational ontology spans a broader spectrum of academic disciplines and aims to improve education.

In terms of effectiveness and efficiency, our results show similarities with previous works that applied ontologies to personalize the user experience and improve information retrieval. For example, the work [36] used an ontology to recommend personalized educational resources to university students. While our approaches are similar, our educational ontology addresses a broader range of use cases, including knowledge management and improving the learning experience [37].

The successful implementation of educational ontology suggests several practical and theoretical educational implications. From a practical perspective, our ontology offers an innovative solution to address common academic challenges, such as lack of customization and difficulty in knowledge management [38]. The ability to tailor educational content to individual student needs and preferences can significantly contribute to student retention and academic achievement.

In addition, the educational ontology can serve as the basis for future research and development in technology-assisted education [39]. For example, integrating artificial intelligence technologies and data analysis can further enhance the personalization of the learning experience and improve educational decision-making. Furthermore, the ontology could be extended to address specific challenges, such as formative assessment and content adaptation for students with special needs. In theoretical terms, our research contributes to the growing understanding of how ontologies can transform education and improve the student experience. By highlighting the importance of accurate and structured knowledge representation in education, our educational ontology highlights the need for interdisciplinary approaches that combine information technology with pedagogy and educational psychology.

The essence of the design of this educational ontology lies in its ability to enrich the personalization of learning, allowing a more precise adaptation of educational resources to the individual needs and preferences of students. One of the crucial aspects in this regard is the "LearningStyle". By capturing each student's preferred learning style, our ontology can recommend resources and activities that align with their cognitive preferences, thus optimizing their engagement and understanding in the learning process. For example, suppose a student demonstrates a visual learning style. The ontology might suggest resources with more prominent optical components, such as graphics and videos, to maximize their retention and comprehension.

The "EducationalLevel" property also plays a crucial role in personalizing learning. By categorizing resources and activities according to the educational level of the students, the ontology ensures that users access content appropriate for their level of knowledge. For example, a beginner-level student might receive recommended activities to reinforce fundamental concepts, while a more advanced student might receive suggestions for exploring more complex and challenging topics. This adaptation based on educational level optimizes the relevance and relevance of the materials presented, enhancing the academic experience.

In addition, the "Interest" property further amplifies the personalization of learning. By capturing students' individual interests, the ontology can identify areas of greatest attraction and motivation for each one. For example, if a student is interested in marine biology, the ontology could recommend resources and projects related to this field, fostering greater immersion and engagement in learning.

Through these design features, this ontology significantly impacts the personalization of learning. Understanding and addressing students' cognitive preferences, educational levels, and areas of interest, ontology becomes a powerful tool for delivering an enriching and individualized learning experience. The precise adaptation of the resources and activities improves the comprehension and retention of the contents and fosters a tremendous enthusiasm and commitment to the educational process. Ultimately, ontology design creates a more satisfying and practical learning experience for each student.

5. Conclusions

The implementation and evaluation of the educational ontology in an academic environment has given us a revealing vision of its transformative potential in contemporary education. Through this study, we have provided a comprehensive and practical approach to address critical educational challenges, such as personalizing the learning experience, improving information search, and knowledge management. Our results support the idea that ontologies can play a fundamental role in improving the efficiency and effectiveness of educational processes, establishing a new horizon for education based on semantic technologies.

One of the most notable conclusions of this study is the ability of educational ontology to personalize students' learning experiences. Tailoring educational content to individual student preferences and needs has significantly impacted their engagement and academic performance. Our ontology has proven to be an effective tool for delivering a more student-centered education, which could contribute to higher student retention and more substantial educational outcomes.

In addition, educational ontology has proven to be a valuable tool to improve the efficiency of information search and knowledge management. The ability to organize and present educational content in a structured and coherent manner has made it easier for students and educators alike to find and access the resources needed for their academic pursuits. This translates into greater productivity in research and more informed educational decision-making.

By comparing our results with previous work in knowledge representation and ontology-based data management, we can highlight the breadth and versatility of our educational ontology. While many previous works focused on specific applications, such as business management or healthcare, our ontology covers various disciplines and use cases in the educational context. This further reinforces the idea that ontologies can be powerful and adaptable tools in multiple domains.

However, we recognize limitations and areas for improvement in our study. While the results are promising, it is essential to note that the implementation and evaluation were carried out in a specific setting and with a population of individual learners and educators. The scalability and generalization of our ontology to different educational contexts may require additional adjustments and adaptations. In addition, integrating emerging technologies, such as artificial intelligence and data analytics, could offer other opportunities further to improve the personalization and efficiency of ontology-based education.

Looking to the future, it is essential to recognize the need to continue advancing this line of research. Additional future work that expands and strengthens our educational ontology would be valuable. These works could include adapting the ontology to different educational contexts, exploring new emerging technologies such as artificial intelligence and data analytics, and collaborating with various educational institutions to further evaluate its effectiveness in multiple settings. Furthermore, it is essential to explore how our ontology can contribute to the continued evolution of education in the digital age. These additional research efforts will contribute to the development of a continuously improving educational ontology and its application in modern education.

Author Contributions: Conceptualization, W.V.-C.; methodology, W.V.-C.; software, J.G.-O.; validation, J.G.-O.; formal analysis, W.V.-C.; investigation, J.G.-O.; data curation, W.V.-C. and J.G.-O.; writing—original draft preparation, J.G.-O.; writing—review and editing, J.G.-O.; visualization, W.V.-C.; supervision, W.V.-C. All authors have read and agreed to the published version of the manuscript.

Funding: This research received no external funding.

Data Availability Statement: Not applicable.

Conflicts of Interest: The authors declare no conflict of interest.

References

1. Capuano, N.; Mangione, G.R.; Pierri, A.; Salerno, S. Personalization and Contextualization of Learning Experiences Based on Semantics. *Int. J. Emerg. Technol. Learn.* **2014**, *9*, 5. [CrossRef]
2. Mylonas, P. A Fuzzy Contextual Approach towards Intelligent Educational Content Adaptation. In Proceedings of the SMAP07—Second International Workshop on Semantic Media Adaptation and Personalization, Uxbridge, UK, 17–18 December 2007.
3. Romero, L.; Gutierrez, M.; Caliusco, M.L. Conceptual Modeling of Learning Paths Based on Portfolios: Strategies for Selecting Educational Resources. In Proceedings of the Iberian Conference on Information Systems and Technologies (CISTI), Caceres, Spain, 13–16 June 2018.
4. Dağ, F.; Erkan, K. A Personalized Learning System Based on Semantic Web Technologies. In *Intelligent Tutoring Systems in E-Learning Environments: Design, Implementation and Evaluation*; Stankov, S., Glavinic, V., Rosic, M., Eds.; IGI Global: Hershey, PA, USA, 2010.
5. Silva-Lopez, R.B.; Sanchez-Arias, V.G.; Mendez-Gurrola, I.I. Ontological Model to Represent the Student's Learning Profile. In Proceedings of the 6th International Conference of Education, Research and Innovation (ICERI 2013), Seville, Spain, 18–20 November 2013.
6. Rtili, M.K.; Khaldi, M.; Dahmani, A. Modeling Approach to Learner Based Ontologies for the Recommendation of Resources in an Interactive Learning Environments. *J. Emerg. Technol. Web Intell.* **2014**, *6*, 340–347.
7. Băjenaru, L.; Smeureanu, I. Learning Style in Ontology-Based E-Learning System. In Proceedings of the International Conference on Informatics in Economy, Cluj-Napoca, Romania, 2–3 June 2018; Volume 273.
8. Machado, J.B.; Martins, G.L.; Isotani, S.; Barbosa, E.F. An Ontology-Based User Model for Personalization of Educational Content. In Proceedings of the International Conference on Software Engineering and Knowledge Engineering (SEKE), Boston, MA, USA, 27–29 June 2013.
9. Zhu, Y.; Zhang, W.; He, Y.; Wen, J.; Li, M. Design and Implementation of Curriculum Knowledge Ontology-Driven SPOC Flipped Classroom Teaching Model. *Kuram Uygulamada Egit. Bilim.* **2018**, *18*, 1351–1374. [CrossRef]
10. Costa, L.A.; Pereira Sanches, L.M.; Rocha Amorim, R.J.; Salvador, L.D.N.; dos Santos Souza, M.V. Monitoring Academic Performance Based on Learning Analytics and Ontology: A Systematic Review. *Inform. Educ.* **2020**, *19*, 361–397. [CrossRef]
11. Sami, B.; Yasin, H.; Mohammad Yasin, M. Automated Score Evaluation of Unstructured Text Using Ontology. *Int. J. Comput. Appl.* **2012**, *39*, 19–22. [CrossRef]
12. Engel, A.; Coll, C. Hybrid Teaching and Learning Environments to Promote Personalized Learning. *RIED-Rev. Iberoam. Educ. A Distanc.* **2022**, *25*, 225–242. [CrossRef]
13. Carbonaro, A. Concept Integration to Develop Next Generation of Technology-Enhanced Learning Systems. In *Project and Design Literacy as Cornerstones of Smart Education, Proceedings of the Smart Innovation, Systems and Technologies, 27 September 2019*; Rehm, M., Saldien, J., Manca, S., Eds.; Springer: Singapore, 2020; Volume 158, pp. 121–129.
14. Blanco-Fernández, Y.; Pazos-Arias, J.J.; Gil-Solla, A.; Ramos-Cabrer, M.; López-Nores, M.; García-Duque, J.; Fernández-Vilas, A.; Díaz-Redondo, R.P.; Bermejo-Muñoz, J. A Flexible Semantic Inference Methodology to Reason about User Preferences in Knowledge-Based Recommender Systems. *Knowl. Based Syst.* **2008**, *21*, 305–320. [CrossRef]
15. Labib, A.E.; Canos, J.H.; Penades, M.C. Integrating Product Line and Learning Style Approaches to Enforce Reusability and Personalization of Learning Objects. In Proceedings of the IEEE 17th International Conference on Advanced Learning Technologies (ICALT), Timisoara, Romania, 3–7 July 2017.
16. Terzieva, V.; Ivanova, T.; Todorova, K. Personalized Learning in an Intelligent Educational System. In *Novel & Intelligent Digital Systems: Proceedings of the 2nd International Conference (NiDS 2022)*; Krouska, A., Troussas, C., Caro, J., Eds.; Springer: Berlin/Heidelberg, Germany, 2023.
17. Yessad, A.; Faron-Zucker, C.; Laskri, M.T. Ontology-Based Personalization of Hypermedia Courses. *Int. Rev. Comput. Softw.* **2008**, *3*, 1–28.
18. Wang, H.C.; Huang, T.H. Personalized E-Learning Environment for Bioinformatics. *Interact. Learn. Environ.* **2013**, *21*, 18–38. [CrossRef]
19. Pham, Q.D.; Adina, M.F. Adaptation to Learners' Learning Styles in a Multi-Agent E-Learning System. *Internet Learn.* **2013**, *2*, 11–20. [CrossRef]

20. Siino, M.; La Cascia, M.; Tinnirello, I. WhoSNext: Recommending Twitter Users to Follow Using a Spreading Activation Network Based Approach. In Proceedings of the IEEE International Conference on Data Mining Workshops (ICDMW), Sorrento, Italy, 17–20 November 2020.
21. Guan, Y.; Wei, Q.; Chen, G. Deep Learning Based Personalized Recommendation with Multi-View Information Integration. *Decis. Support Syst.* **2019**, *118*, 58–69. [CrossRef]
22. Behera, R.K.; Gunasekaran, A.; Gupta, S.; Kamboj, S.; Bala, P.K. Personalized Digital Marketing Recommender Engine. *J. Retail. Consum. Serv.* **2020**, *53*, 101799. [CrossRef]
23. Castro, F.; Alonso, M.A. Learning Objects and Ontologies to Perform Educational Data Mining. In Proceedings of the 2011 International Conference on Frontiers in Education: Computer Science and Computer Engineering (FECS'11), Las Vegas, NE, USA, 18–21 July 2011.
24. Iatrellis, O.; Kameas, A.; Fitsilis, P. An Ontological Approach for Semantic Modeling of Learning Pathways. In Proceedings of the 2017 IEEE 26th International Conference on Enabling Technologies: Infrastructure for Collaborative Enterprises (WETICE), Poznan, Poland, 21–23 June 2017.
25. Iatrellis, O.; Kameas, A.; Fitsilis, P. Educ8: Self-Evolving and Personalized Learning Pathways Utilizing Semantics. In Proceedings of the 2018 IEEE International Conference on Evolving and Adaptive Intelligent Systems (EAIS), Rhodes, Greece, 25–27 May 2018.
26. Sharma, S.; Shakya, H.K.; Marriboyina, V. A Location Based Novel Recommender Framework of User Interest through Data Categorization. *Mater. Today Proc.* **2021**, *47*, 7155–7161. [CrossRef]
27. Iatrellis, O.; Kameas, A.; Fitsilis, P. Personalized Learning Pathways Using Semantic Web Rules. In Proceedings of the 21st Pan-Hellenic Conference on Informatics, Larissa, Greece, 28–30 September 2017.
28. Adorni, G.; Battigelli, S.; Brondo, D.; Capuano, N.; Coccoli, M.; Miranda, S.; Orciuoli, F.; Stanganelli, L.; Sugliano, A.M.; Vivanet, G. CADDIE and IWT: Two Different Ontology-Based Approaches to Anytime, Anywhere and Anybody Learning. *J. E-Learn. Knowl. Soc.* **2010**, *6*, 53–66.
29. Kovatcheva, E.; Nikolov, R. An Adaptive Feedback Approach for E-Learning Systems. *IEEE Multidiscip. Eng. Educ. Mag.* **2009**, *4*, 1–3.
30. Kerkiri, T.; Manitsaris, A.; Mavridis, I. How E-Learning Systems May Benefit from Ontologies and Recommendation Methods to Efficiently Personalise Resources. *Int. J. Knowl. Learn.* **2009**, *5*, 347–370. [CrossRef]
31. Amine Alimam, M.; Seghiouer, H. Personalized E-Learning Environment Based on Ontology to Improve Students' School Levels. *Int. J. Comput. Appl.* **2013**, *84*, 1–12. [CrossRef]
32. Sharif Ullah, A.M.M. W-12 Manufacturing Engineering Courses and Web-Based Education. *JSEE Annu. Conf. Int. Sess. Proc.* **2013**, *2013*, 72–77. [CrossRef]
33. Ullah, A.S. What Is Knowledge in Industry 4.0? *Eng. Rep.* **2020**, *2*, e12217. [CrossRef]
34. Hsu, T.Y.; Ke, H.R.; Yang, W.P. Knowledge-Based Mobile Learning Framework for Museums. *Electron. Libr.* **2006**, *24*, 635–648. [CrossRef]
35. Ivanova, T.; Terzieva, V.; Ivanova, M. Intelligent Technologies in E-Learning: Personalization and Interoperability. In Proceedings of the 22nd International Conference on Computer Systems and Technologies, New York, NY, USA, 18–19 June 2021.
36. Taurus, J.; Niu, Z.; Khadidja, B. E-Learning Recommender System Based on Collaborative Filtering and Ontology. *Int. J. Comput. Inf. Eng.* **2017**, *11*, 256–261.
37. Bajenaru, L.; Smeureanu, I. An Ontology Based Approach for Modeling E-Learning in Healthcare Human Resource Management. *Econ. Comput. Econ. Cybern. Stud. Res.* **2015**, *49*, 18–34.
38. Ruiz-Iniesta, A.; Jiménez-Díaz, G.; Gómez-Albarrán, M. A Semantically Enriched Context-Aware OER Recommendation Strategy and Its Application to a Computer Science OER Repository. *IEEE Trans. Educ.* **2014**, *57*, 255–260. [CrossRef]
39. Raud, Z.; Vodovozov, V. Ontology-Based Design of the Learner's Knowledge Domain in Electrical Engineering. *Electr. Control Commun. Eng.* **2019**, *15*, 47–53. [CrossRef]

Disclaimer/Publisher's Note: The statements, opinions and data contained in all publications are solely those of the individual author(s) and contributor(s) and not of MDPI and/or the editor(s). MDPI and/or the editor(s) disclaim responsibility for any injury to people or property resulting from any ideas, methods, instructions or products referred to in the content.

Article

Proposal for a System for the Identification of the Concentration of Students Who Attend Online Educational Models

William Villegas-Ch. [1,*], Joselin García-Ortiz [1], Isabel Urbina-Camacho [2] and Aracely Mera-Navarrete [3]

[1] Escuela de Ingeniería en Tecnologías de la Información, FICA, Universidad de Las Américas, Quito 170125, Ecuador
[2] Facultad de Filosofía, Letras y Ciencias de la Educación, Universidad Central del Ecuador, Quito 170129, Ecuador
[3] Departamento de Sistemas, Universidad Internacional del Ecuador, Quito 170411, Ecuador
* Correspondence: william.villegas@udla.edu.ec; Tel.: +593-98-136-4068

Abstract: Currently, e-learning has revolutionized the way students learn by offering access to quality education in a model that does not depend on a specific space and time. However, due to the e-learning method where no tutor can directly control the group of students, they can be distracted for various reasons, which greatly affects their learning capacity. Several scientific works try to improve the quality of online education, but a holistic approach is necessary to address this problem. Identifying students' attention spans is important in understanding how students process and retain information. Attention is a critical cognitive process that affects a student's ability to learn. Therefore, it is important to use a variety of techniques and tools to assess student attention, such as standardized tests, behavioral observation, and assessment of academic achievement. This work proposes a system that uses devices such as cameras to monitor the attention level of students in real time during online classes. The results are used with feedback as a heuristic value to analyze the performance of the students, as well as the teaching standards of the teachers.

Keywords: artificial intelligence; computer vision; blink rate

1. Introduction

E-learning is a teaching modality that uses information and communication technologies (ICT) to facilitate learning through the Internet [1,2]. In e-learning, students can access educational materials online, interact with content at their own pace, and communicate with teachers and other students through online tools such as discussion forums, chat rooms, and video conferencing [3]. E-learning can take many different forms, from online courses complete with videos and assessments, to short, self-administered learning modules. It can also be used in combination with other teaching methods, such as face-to-face classes or tutorials [4]. E-learning has proven to be an effective tool for distance learning and online training, allowing students to access educational resources from anywhere and at any time, making them more accessible and convenient.

Even though e-learning has many advantages, it also presents some challenges and problems. For example, within e-learning, some sessions are carried out asynchronously, which means that students may feel isolated by not having the social interaction they have in a traditional classroom [5]. This can affect the motivation and commitment of students. In addition, this requires a structured plan that generates motivation and discipline in the student to remain committed to the learning process. Some students may have difficulty staying motivated and focused on online content. Additionally, there are technical problems such as Internet connection, software, or hardware problems that can affect access to educational resources and, therefore, the learning process. In some cases, students may find it difficult to receive immediate feedback from their teachers and peers, which can hinder the learning process and the improvement of their skills [6].

Works like [7] mention that there are different methods and tools to measure student concentration in e-learning. For example, quizzes are common tools used to measure student concentration and engagement in e-learning [8]. These may include questions that measure student attention, level of engagement, and interest in the content. In addition, some systems use gaze tracking software to monitor student eye movement as they interact with online course content [9]. These systems provide information on student attention and concentration at different times of the course. Other systems using biometric sensors can measure a student's physiological activity, such as heart rate, brain activity, and sweating, to determine the student's level of concentration and engagement. There are also methods included in learning management platforms (LMS) that integrate online interaction analysis tools, which present online interaction data, such as the frequency and type of interactions in discussion forums or online chats, can provide information about the level of participation and commitment of the students in the course.

In this work, a blink counting system is proposed to determine the level of concentration, relating the resulting statistics with similar works that determine the average blink rate of a person from 8 to 21 blinks per minute [10]. However, when a person is deeply focused on a specific visual task, the blink rate is significantly reduced to an average of 4.5 blinks per minute [11,12]. The blink rate increases to more than 32.5 blinks per minute when the individual's concentration level is low. In addition, this system integrates the development of an algorithm for the classification of emotions through the identification of gestures that the student generates during an academic activity. The study [13] explores how the emotional state of students varies during the learning process and how emotional feedback can improve learning experiences. In addition, there are emotional factors such as happiness, boredom, surprise, and neutrality that denote a positive, constructive learning experience, while emotions such as sadness, fear, anger, and disgust represent a negative experience [14,15].

The design of systems that use artificial intelligence (AI) to identify the level of concentration of e-learning students has garnered great interest and motivation on the part of researchers in the educational sector. First, one of the main goals of online education is to make sure that students are fully engaged and focused during the learning process. Inattention or distraction can negatively affect student performance and ultimately affect their ability to learn and retain information. Therefore, the use of AI systems to measure student attention can help ensure that students are fully engaged in the learning process. Second, the development of systems that use AI to measure the concentration level of students through blink counts and emotion identifications helps to improve the quality of online education [16]. The information collected by these systems helps educators identify when students are distracted or having difficulty concentrating. Armed with this information, tutors can tailor their teaching approach and provide additional resources to help students stay focused and engaged during the learning process.

Third, the use of AI systems to measure student attention also helps improve the efficiency of online learning. By providing alerts when students are distracted or inactive, AI systems help students refocus and become more productive in their study time. This allows students to complete their work more efficiently and improve their ability to retain information. Finally, the motivation to develop systems that use AI to measure student attention is related to competitiveness in the online education market. With the growing popularity of this educational model, institutions are constantly looking for ways to improve the quality and efficiency of the learning process to remain competitive in the market.

2. Materials and Methods

The method consists of two components to define the concentration level of students in e-learning. In the first stage, a blink-counting algorithm is developed and used to measure the frequency and duration of eye blinks [17]. Systems with this capability use sensors to detect flicker and then record the information in a database. Blink frequency measurement is useful for measuring a person's attention and concentration in different situations, including e-learning. Studies have shown that blink frequency can decrease when a person is highly focused on a task [11,18]. Blink counting systems use different detection techniques, such as cameras, electro-oculography sensors, and motion sensors. These systems are portable and non-invasive, making them easy to use in a variety of situations. The results obtained with a blink counting system should be evaluated in conjunction with other measures, such as questionnaires, analysis of online interactions, identification of emotions, etc., to obtain a more complete understanding of the level of concentration and attention of the students [12].

In the second component, an algorithm is designed to identify student emotions in an e-learning environment. An algorithm for emotion classification uses different techniques, such as the detection of facial expressions, the measurement of electrical activity in the brain, and the detection of physiological changes such as heart rate and respiration [19]. These systems use algorithms and machine learning models to identify and classify a person's emotions into different categories, such as happiness, sadness, fear, anger, and surprise. In the context of e-learning, emotion rating systems can be useful for measuring students' emotional responses to different course elements, such as learning materials and interactions with other students and teachers [20]. This information is used to personalize online content and interactions and enhance the learning experience for students.

In this work, the use of the images of the students and the objective of this study were revealed. Therefore, informed consent was obtained from the people participating in this study. The design of the student concentration level identification system with the use of AI involves several technical details; among these details considered, signal processing and the data collected by sensors or cameras are processed by signal processing techniques to extract relevant characteristics that can indicate the level of concentration of the student. Machine learning: machine learning techniques are used to train models that can classify the concentration level of the student based on the extracted features. The integration of software and hardware is for the system to work effectively. Performance evaluation and improvement: the system must be continuously evaluated to measure its accuracy, and improvements must be made when necessary. Privacy and security: appropriate measures must be taken to ensure that data are secure, and that student privacy is respected. The implementation in real-time: the system must be able to process the data and classify the concentration level of the student in real time so that it can be used in an educational environment.

2.1. Review of Related Works

This paper proposes the use of AI algorithms to identify the level of concentration in university students; the use of AI techniques has the potential to be useful to improve education and academic performance. However, in works such as [11,12], it is mentioned that it is important to consider that any AI application must be carefully designed and developed to guarantee that it is accurate, fair, safe, and ethical. Furthermore, according to [21], there must be transparency as to how student data are collected and used so that users can trust the tool and feel comfortable using it.

Online education or e-learning has gained popularity in recent years due to its accessibility, flexibility, and convenience for students. However, one of the most important concerns for educators is how to ensure students are fully focused and engaged during online learning. One solution that has been explored is the use of AI systems to monitor and measure the concentration level of students. Currently, several research papers have addressed the issue of the use of AI systems to identify the level of concentration of students in e-learning. An example of this is the study carried out by [22], where they developed an AI model to measure students' attention using their device's webcam. The model was based on tracking the student's gaze and head movement to determine their level of concentration. The study yielded positive results, showing that the model was able to accurately identify the level of attention of the students.

Another interesting study was conducted by [23], where a machine learning-based AI system was used to analyze mouse cursor behavior and student keystrokes. The system was able to detect when students were distracted or inactive and provide alerts to help keep their attention during learning. In addition, the work of [24] focused on the use of physiological sensors to measure the attention level of students. Electroencephalography (EEG) sensors were used to measure the students' brain activity, and skin conductance sensors measured their emotional responses. The study demonstrated that physiological data can be used to assess students' attention and emotions during online learning.

Among the problems identified in e-learning, several studies emphasize the identification of the concentration level of students in this modality of study. In the results and conclusions of these works, it is determined that the levels of concentration are affected by various factors such as the design of the course, the technology used, and the level of student participation, among others. However, other related work suggests that students' concentration in e-learning can be affected by factors such as the amount of social interaction, the level of difficulty of the content, the amount of material to be covered, and the quality of feedback. For example, a study published in the journal *Computers & Education* [25] found that the amount of social interaction, such as online communication with classmates and teachers, can improve students' concentration and performance in e-learning. Another study published in the *Journal of Educational Psychology* [26] suggests that the complexity and level of difficulty of content can affect students' concentration. Additionally, other studies have found that information overload can affect student concentration in e-learning. Therefore, it is recommended that online courses be designed with an adequate amount of information, organized into manageable modules, and allow frequent feedback to maintain students' attention and motivation.

Works like [27] mention that there are different methods and tools to measure student concentration in e-learning. For example, quizzes are common tools used to measure student concentration and engagement in e-learning. These may include questions that measure student attention, level of engagement, and interest in the content. In addition, some systems use gaze tracking software to monitor student eye movement as they interact with online course content [28]. These systems provide information on student attention and concentration at different times of the course. Other systems using biometric sensors can measure a student's physiological activity, such as heart rate, brain activity, and sweating, to determine the student's level of concentration and engagement. There are also methods included in LMS that integrate online interaction analysis tools, which present online interaction data, such as the frequency and type of interactions in discussion forums or online chats, and can provide information about the level of participation and commitment of the students in the course.

While these studies show promising results, it is important to note that the use of AI systems to measure students' attention levels has also raised ethical concerns. Some argue that the constant monitoring of students can violate their privacy and create an environment of mistrust. Therefore, AI systems must be implemented with transparency, and the rights of students must be respected.

2.2. Identification of the Environment and the Population

This work is carried out with the participation of students from a university in Ecuador. The sample size is given by all the students enrolled in the 2020 promotion at the Faculty of Administrative Sciences. In this cohort, there are a total of 229 students. The volume of students is not high; therefore, the entire cohort is considered. By including the entire population, a more precise result is sought, and this research is applied to matters that are directly related to the use of ICT. Therefore, the data included are those obtained in the subject of office automation II. In this matter, the use of computing devices is a priority for the development of different activities. In the structure of the subject, synchronous and autonomous activities have been defined, in which the student must comply with the use of the algorithms that measure the student's concentration.

The synchronous activities are guided by the tutor; for the development, it is essential to use personal computer equipment such as computers, cameras, tablets, etc. The activities are varied, from reading articles to developing practical exercises. Autonomous activities, such as synchronous ones, depending on the use of a computer, include readings, research, the development of mental maps, exercises, etc. The course where the system is implemented is made up of three sessions per week, 60 min each, one of which is synchronous.

2.3. Method

This study makes use of two parameters to calculate the attention level of the e-learning student. The ability to concentrate is calculated using blink rate and facial expression, and this process is continuously updated over 5 s. Instead of a sequential run, all the models needed to calculate the concentration level are run in parallel once the online class starts. This is obtained by using multi-threading in all functions, which plays an important role in reducing the time consumption of each model as well as the whole system [29]. Every 5 s, the model will generate the attention span score and provide real-time feedback to students in the form of live graphs that are plotted for each parameter, as well as the calculated attention span score [30,31]. The general architecture of the proposed system is shown in Figure 1; it is composed of several stages that focus on image processing, classification, and categorization.

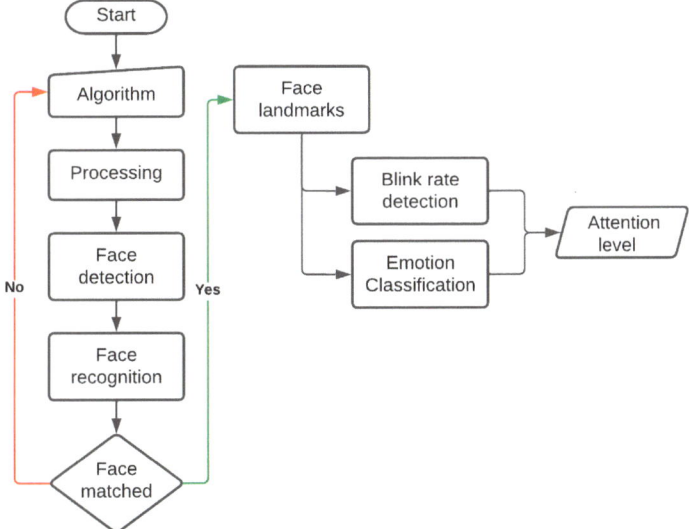

Figure 1. Proposed architecture for a concentration level identification system in an e-learning educational model.

2.4. Design and Development of the Blink Count Algorithm

The blinking of the human eye is the object of study by psychologists, psychiatrists, ophthalmologists, neurophysiologists, etc., due to the numerous applications attributed to it. Blinking can be used as a criterion for the diagnosis of certain medical conditions of a patient or to determine the level of concentration of a person before an activity is carried out with the use of computing devices. There are a lot of variations when it comes to blinking, and several studies mention that, depending on the task that is performed and the conditions that are performed, the influence on blinking will be different. Thus, when a person performs tasks with a high degree of concentration, the number of blinks is reduced. A fundamental part of the design of an image processing algorithm is that it can detect if there is a specific object in an area [32]. In Figure 2, the phases for the count of blinks are presented. In these, the proposed algorithm with the objective of counting blinks is represented; its initial process must establish if there is a face within an image. Once a face has been identified, the algorithm must identify and detect the desired area, in this case, the person's eyes, for a subsequent count of blinks during a defined period.

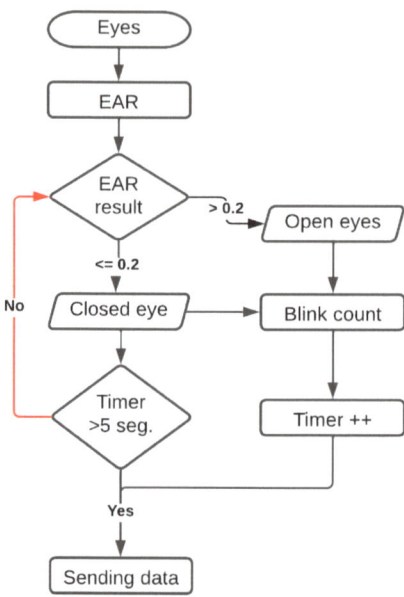

Figure 2. Architecture for blink rate detection.

There are several computer vision techniques and libraries that automatically detect flickers in a video sequence or streaming. These techniques are based on an estimate of movement in the region of the eye; the face and eyes are detected by a Viola–Jones-type detector [33]. When applied, movement in the eye area is estimated from the optical flow by sparse tracking or by applying the intensity difference from frame to frame and adaptive thresholding. This process allows for identifying if the eyes are covered by the eyelids or not.

For blink detection, the regions containing the pairs of eyes are cut out, and each eye is divided into two halves. With this, the eye aspect ratio (EAR) is calculated using Euclidean distances, which are observed in Figure 3 for each frame according to Equation (1), and identify if the eyes are open or closed [34]. A countdown timer has also been incorporated into the algorithm design. This is activated once a blink is detected and keeps track of the number of seconds the eyes are closed. The purpose of this event is to conclude that the user enters a sleepy state (loss of attention) by detecting that the eyes are closed for more than two seconds. For the calculation of the frequency of blinks, the number of blinks is taken continuously at an interval of 5 s to determine the average blink rate of the user. The EAR threshold value is set to 0.2 based on the experiments performed.

$$\text{EAR} = \frac{\|p2 - p6\| + \|p3 - p5\|}{2\|p1 - p4\|} \tag{1}$$

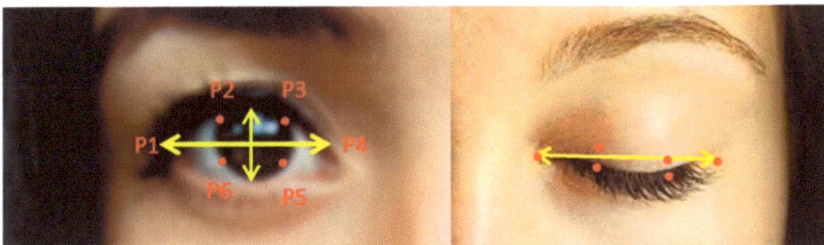

Figure 3. Eye measurements for eyelid movement identification.

In the equation, $p1, p2, pn$, etc., are the reference point locations. Since the blinking is performed by both eyes synchronously, the EAR is averaged to determine whether there is complete blinking.

The algorithm proposed for the design of the blink counter is developed in Python. In this, several libraries are applied, among which MediaPipe Face Mesh stands out, from which 468 referential points distributed on the person's face are obtained when it is detected [35,36]. Of all the reference points, 12 points are taken to detect the eyes, six for the left eye and six for the right eye, as shown in Figure 3.

In classification, generally, a low EAR value does not mean that a person is blinking. A low EAR value can occur when a subject intentionally closes their eyes for a long time or makes a facial expression, yawns, etc., or the EAR captures a brief random fluctuation of the reference points. In these cases, it is possible to use a classifier that takes as input a time window greater than one frame. Figure 4 shows an example of an EAR signal in the video sequence, in which the student is wearing a mask and glasses. However, the algorithm easily detects the student's eyes through the reference points and counts a blink, as shown by the fluctuation generated in the graph.

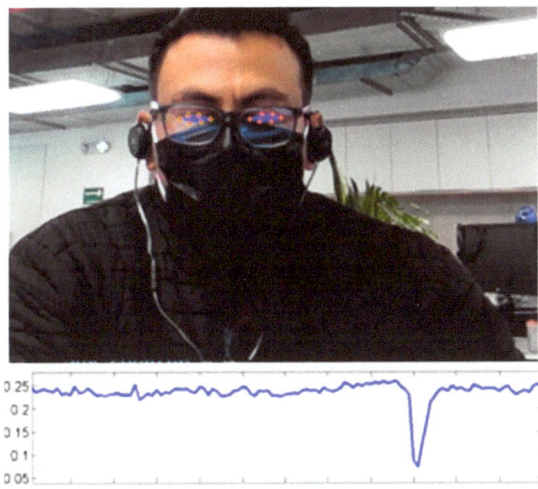

Figure 4. Identification of the frequency of blinks in a video in real-time.

The algorithm uses the mediapipe, OpenCV, Numpy, and Matploylib libraries; these libraries oversee face detection and blink counting. For the use of these libraries, several functions are created where the detection of eye coordinates is declared using the reference points detected on the face [37,38]. The drawing_output function allows coloring the eye area and displaying the results, as can be seen in the previous figure. The eye_aspect_ratio function calculates the three distances shown in Figure 5. The eye aspect ratio is involved in the calculation and returns the result of the EAR equation.

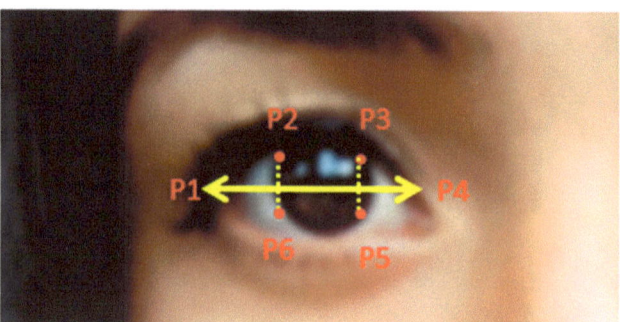

Figure 5. Application of the eye aspect ratio function that determines the EAR calculation to identify the eye distances.

2.5. Design and Development of the Algorithm for the Recognition of Emotions

For the development of the algorithm, three fundamental bases are considered that guarantee the operation of the identification of the emotions of the students through the gestures that their faces generate in a didactic environment, as represented in Figure 6. The bases considered are bases of image data, affective computing, and emotion recognition systems with artificial intelligence.

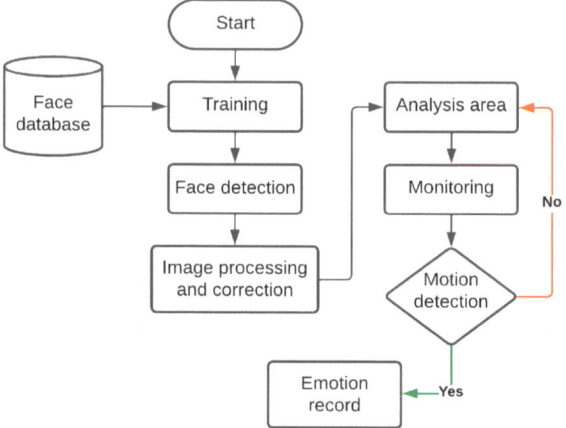

Figure 6. Flowchart of the architecture for the detection of emotions by means of computer vision.

2.5.1. Image Database and Algorithm Training

The image base in the design of the gesture and emotion recognition algorithm refers to a collection of data used to train the recognition model. For this, the algorithm uses deep learning techniques, such as convolutional neural networks (CNN), to train the gesture recognition model. As the model learns to recognize patterns in images, it can identify gestures in new images that it has not seen before. The accuracy of the model will largely depend on the quality and diversity of the image base used to train it [39,40]. In Python, different libraries and tools are used to create and manipulate image bases in a gesture recognition algorithm. For the development of the algorithm, a practical comparison of libraries such as OpenCV, TensorFlow, and Keras was carried out. Of these libraries,

TensorFlow was the one used in the algorithm, since it presented better characteristics about the available hardware requirements.

Affective computing arises from the need to provide computer equipment with a certain capacity to interact with people. This task is carried out using artificial vision techniques and machine learning algorithms; the objective of human–machine interaction is for the system to be capable of producing an effective response in people [20]. According to [21,22], affective computing is subdivided into four research areas, as follows:

- The analysis and characterization of affective states that identify through natural interactions the relationships between effect and cognitive processes in learning;
- Automatic recognition of affective states by analyzing facial expressions and extracting features from linguistic expressions, posture, gaze tracking, and heart rate, among others;
- The adequacy of the systems to respond to a particular affective state of the users;
- The design of avatars that show appropriate affective states for better interaction with the user.

As for emotions, these are classified into two groups, primary or basic and secondary or alternative. In [41], six basic emotions were identified, anger, disgust, fear, happiness, sadness, and surprise, and the gestures that appear on the face, as shown in Figure 7. Secondary or alternative emotions are complex emotions that appear after primary emotions and depend on the situation and context of the person. For example, a person who is afraid (primary emotion) can turn it into anger or rage (secondary emotion) and provoke an aggressive reaction.

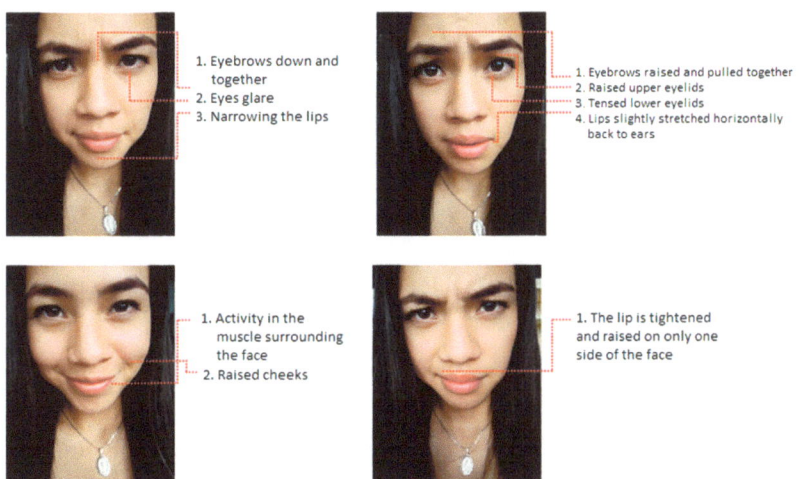

Figure 7. Examples of recognizable gestures on people's faces that demonstrate an emotion.

Facial expression analysis is applied in different areas of interest, such as education, video games, and telecommunications, to name a few. In addition, it is one of the most used in human–machine interactions. Facial expression recognition is an intelligent system that identifies a person's face and, from it, obtains certain characteristics that it analyzes and processes to know the affective state of the person [42].

2.5.2. Face Detection, Gesture Identification, and Emotion Classification

Face recognition depends on four steps shown in Figure 8; the first step is to detect faces in an image, applying the oriented gradient histogram algorithm. In the second step, the facial landmark estimation algorithm is used, which identifies 68 landmarks on each face. In the third step, 128 measurements are created for each face through deep learning, which corresponds to the unique characteristics of the faces; finally, with the unique characteristics of each face, the person is identified.

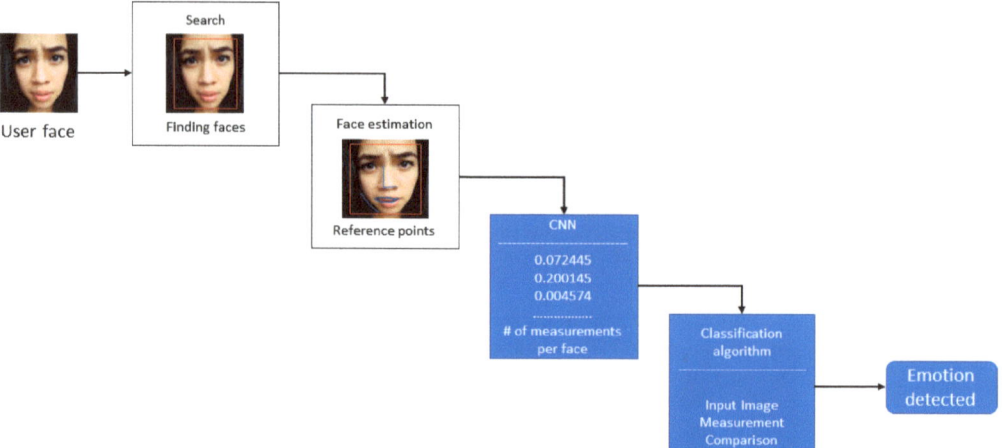

Figure 8. Detection phases applied in a convolutional neural network.

Figure 9 shows the stages that the system performs to correctly identify the emotion. The initial stage validates that the image received by the recognizer contains a face; if the algorithm does not find it, it discards the image. Next, a gray filter is applied to remove the different color channels to later detect some important parts of the face, such as the nose, eyes, eyebrows, and mouth. In the next stage, facial points are marked on the detected parts, and an initial reference point is placed in the center of the nose to identify various facial points on the face parts. Geometric calculations of the distance between the initial reference point and each facial point detected on the face are then performed. The result of the calculations is a matrix of facial features that are processed by the support vector algorithm with their emotion label so that it can learn to classify facial expressions. Finally, the trained neural network is sent more facial feature vectors to test whether the algorithm has learned to classify gestures and recognize emotions.

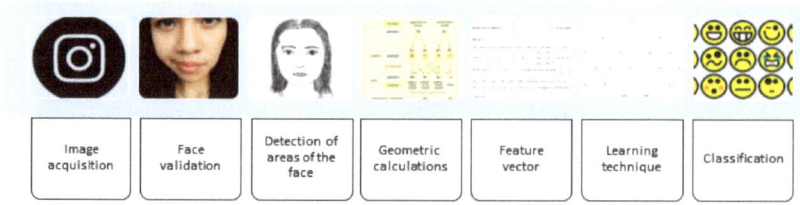

Figure 9. Architecture for gesture detection and emotion identification.

3. Results

According to the results obtained, the values obtained from the parameters measured by the developed algorithms are presented. These parameters correspond to the blink rate detection and emotion classification; these values are normalized to calculate the attention score according to Equation (2). Figure 10 shows the live graphs of the EAR with the student's expected attention level updated in real time. The figure shows the variation of the parameters measured with the designed algorithms. Figure 10a detects the blinking frequency; Figure 10b shows the classification of the emotion, and Figure 10c presents the level of care. Facial recognition data are not presented because they do not contribute to determining the level of attention of the student; this parameter is specific to the system to offer personalized treatment to students.

$$Att = \frac{\sum score(i)}{n} * 100 \qquad (2)$$

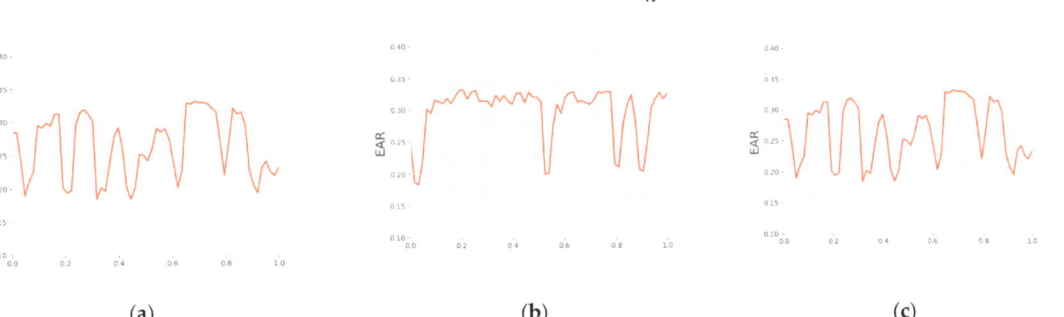

Figure 10. This figure shows the graphs of the parameters measured with the algorithms designed: (**a**) detection of the blink frequency; (**b**) classification of emotion; (**c**) level of care.

To determine the performance of the system, a data set of 45 students corresponding to the 2020 cohort was analyzed. Even though the entire cohort is under analysis, two parallels were established as a sample that takes the subject of office automation 2. The groups evaluated are composed of 27 women and 18 men. For the evaluation, students were asked to attend online tutorials on specific topics of the subject. The tutorials lasted 45 min, divided into three sections of 15 min (900 s) each. During these sessions, students must turn on their web cameras and enable the blink frequency counting and emotion identification applications. The measurements are made online, and the data are stored in the cloud, where they are consumed by experts to determine the level of concentration per session. The mechanics of the tutorials has been determined considering three activities: one is the tutor's explanation of a subject, and the second section is given by the development of a reading-type activity, especially scientific articles. In the third section, the development of a practical activity related to the theme developed is proposed. The sections within the session do not have a specific order, so the student does not generate a plan and affect the measurement.

Table 1 presents the results obtained from the evaluation; at this stage, the aim is to identify the number of students who are concentrated, distracted, and sleepy during the development of the activities of a session. According to the results obtained during the activity developed by the tutor (a class on a specific subject), 27 students are within the range of concentrating. This calculation is obtained according to the blink frequency count; that is, the blink rate is between four and five per minute. Within this same activity, 13 students were distracted; the calculation corresponds to their blink rate being greater than eight per minute. In this group, it was found that five students were in a sleepy state; for this identification, the algorithm identifies the time that the eyelids are closed. If this time is greater than two seconds, it is established that the student entered a state of sleepiness.

Table 1. Identification of the level of concentration of students by counting the frequency of blinks.

	Tutoring	Reading	Practical Exercise
Concentrated	27	19	37
Distracted	13	18	6
Sleepy	5	8	2

In the second activity, a reading of an article on a specific theme of the subject was established. This activity lasted 15 min; at the end of this period, it was found that

19 students were concentrated during reading, 18 had distraction stages, and 8 people presented drowsiness. These results indicate that this type of activity is usually not very effective during an online tutorial. In the third section of the tutorial, students are proposed to develop a practical activity; the results reflect a high concentration in most of the students, amounting to 37 with 82% concentration identified in the group. Of the group, only six students presented a distracted attitude toward the activity, and two of them were in a state of drowsiness.

Table 2 presents the results of the emotion classification algorithm. The Support Vector Machine (SVM) algorithm is used to classify students' emotions into seven different classes: anger, disgust, fear, happiness, sadness, surprise, and neutral. Each emotion is given a score based on its effect on the user's level of attention. The designed algorithm considers four classes of emotions: concentration, boredom, surprise, and neutral, these states being those identified within the classroom. However, it is necessary to consider that these emotions are based on those supported by SVM and the six universal emotions of people [43]. According to the results of the tutoring activity, 13 concentrated people were identified, 7 were bored, 15 were surprised, and 10 had neutral emotions. Regarding the results obtained for the blink rate, it can be mentioned that the emotion of surprise and neutrality can be classified as emotions that have a certain relationship with distraction and drowsiness. For example, a student during the activity can demonstrate her interest in the topic by showing joy or with a neutral gesture. Similarly, a bored person can generate gestures that the algorithm detects as neutral emotions. This relationship is similar in the following activities; even in the development of the practical exercise, the relationship between the algorithms is more noticeable.

Table 2. Identification of the concentration level of students with the use of an emotion detection algorithm.

Emotion	Tutoring	Reading	Practical Exercise
Concentration	13	11	35
Boredom	7	13	3
Surprise	15	10	2
Neutral	10	11	5

The acceptable limits of quality metrics vary depending on the specific application. Quality metrics are tools that allow you to assess the accuracy of models and predictions and are used to compare different models or to determine if a model is accurate enough for your application. Common quality metrics include root mean square error (RMSE), mean absolute error (MAE), coefficient of determination (R2), and mean absolute percentage error (MAPE). These metrics are presented in Table 3, with the values corresponding to the performance of the system. By relating the results obtained from each algorithm and the EAR, it is possible to evaluate the general performance of the system. The table shows the performance metrics of the system.

Table 3. Values obtained from the system pressure versus the limits established in the system tests.

Metric	RMSE	MAE	R2	MAPE
Value	11.351	10.924	0.803	15%
Boundaries	15.000	13.000	1 (100%)	20%

According to the results obtained, it has been identified that the operation of the system is on the real state of the students during the educational environment developed. The general precision of the system was developed for the identification of the level of concentration, taking the average of the precisions of each module. Compiling the OpenCV DNN module with Deepface support improved performance and significantly reduced the inference time in the algorithms, as shown in Table 4. We achieved an overall accuracy of 96.16%.

Table 4. Metrics obtained from the application of the concentration level identification system in an e-learning model.

Module	Accuracy	Inference Time
Blink rate detection	92.54%	0.0293 ms
Emotion classification	89.11%	0.024 ms
Facial recognition	95.21%	0.061 ms
Overall system	92.16%	0.1143 ms

4. Discussion

According to the results obtained, it was identified that the system, when using the AI libraries to recognize the level of concentration of the students, must process a large volume of data to guarantee its effectiveness. For this, the training and test data set that contains information on the characteristics of emotions and the times that a person blinks when they generate a state of concentration requires a wide variety of images in different states, as well as different environments and settings. With a data set that allows the model to be adjusted and its performance to be evaluated, an adequate result that can be used in education is guaranteed. For this, unlike other works, several quality metrics have been used in a set of tests before the system goes to a production stage. The results of the quality metrics obtained in the set of tests are presented below:

- RMSE: 11.351
- MAE: 10.924
- R2: 0.803
- MAPE: 15%

Now, to determine the acceptable limits of these quality metrics, it is necessary to consider the context of the problem and the accuracy expectations of the model. For example, in testing, the model is expected to have acceptable accuracy if it can predict a student's concentration level with an average error of +/−15.000. In this case, the RMSE value of 11.351 is less than the precision expectation, so the model could be considered acceptable in terms of precision. However, the MAE value of 10.924 indicates that the model has a systematic bias in its predictions, and adjustments may be necessary to improve its accuracy. The R2 value of 0.803 indicates that the model explains 80% of the variability in concentration levels demonstrated by a student, which would be considered acceptable in many cases. On the other hand, the MAPE value of 15% indicates that the model has an average percentage error of 15% in the predictions, which may or may not be acceptable, depending on the context and expectations of the problem.

It is important to consider that concentration in learning is a subjective experience, where there is great individual variability in what is considered "concentration". Therefore, any AI algorithm used for concentration level identification should be designed to account for this individual variability and should not rely solely on technology to assess student performance [44]. Other works mention that there are potential advantages of using AI tools in e-learning that allow personalization of learning; this can help to maximize the learning of each student and ensure that the material is adjusted to their individual needs. It is proposed to improve immediate feedback by allowing errors to be identified and corrected immediately. This can help students improve their understanding and retain information better, saving time and costs by automating many tasks where time and costs can be saved for teachers and educational institutions.

The work carried out uses computer vision techniques with AI techniques to perform a blink count to measure a person's concentration [39,40]. This is based on similar studies where it has been identified that when a person is focused, they blink less than when they are distracted or bored. Therefore, if it is possible to measure a person's number of blinks per minute, their level of concentration can be inferred. One advantage of blink counting with the developed algorithm is that it is a simple and non-invasive way to measure a person's concentration, but it has limitations and should not be considered a precise and universal measure of concentration [10]. To overcome this limitation, another algorithm that classifies students' emotions during certain activities is used to evaluate multiple factors to obtain a complete picture of a person's concentration.

The identification of emotions using an AI algorithm is a useful tool to measure the concentration level of students in an e-learning model [42,45]. Excitement and concentration are closely related, and a person who is excited or interested in a subject is more likely to be focused on it. Therefore, if a student's emotion can be measured, the level of concentration can be inferred from it [42,43]. AI algorithms need large amounts of data to learn to accurately identify emotions; therefore, Python libraries are used that are previously trained. With this, the system improves its accuracy percentages and guarantees the results obtained [44].

Compared to related works, the system developed using Python with AI libraries has several advantages. First, Python is a popular programming language in the AI community due to its ability to handle large data sets and its wide selection of AI libraries. AI libraries, such as TensorFlow, Keras, and Scikit-Learn, provide powerful tools for data processing and predictive modeling, allowing you to build complex and accurate models. Secondly, the developed system allows greater automation in the data analysis process, which reduces the time and costs necessary to perform this type of analysis. Third, the proposed system is highly customizable and adaptable to the specific needs of the educational institution or the online learning program. Machine learning algorithms can be trained to recognize specific patterns of student behavior and adapt to different student needs. In addition, the developed system can be integrated with other online learning management systems by using Python and its libraries, which allows a more integrated and complete analysis of student behavior [33].

However, there are also some limitations identified in the development of the proposed system; these are focused on the use of Python with AI libraries for the identification of the concentration level of e-learning students. First, the use of sensors or cameras to capture student data may raise privacy and security concerns. Additionally, the accuracy of AI models can be affected by factors such as the quality of the input data, feature selection, and the choice of the machine learning algorithm [46]. Finally, the developed system has several advantages compared to related works on the identification of the concentration level of e-learning students. The use of AI libraries allows for greater automation, customization, and adaptability to the specific needs of students and educational institutions. However, it is important to keep in mind the limitations in terms of privacy and data security, as well as the accuracy of the AI models.

5. Conclusions

Blink counting can be a useful technique for determining a student's concentration level, as there is a correlation between attention and blink pattern. When a student is more focused, they generally blink less frequently, and their blinks are longer. However, the blink count only provides a rough estimate of the concentration level and is not a precise measurement. The blink pattern can be affected by factors such as eye strain, ambient lighting, the position of the student's head, and individual blink habits. Additionally, blink counting can be difficult to perform in practical situations, such as in an e-learning environment where the student may be in different positions or moving around. Therefore, it is necessary to consider a methodological update in the way knowledge is provided. In the proposed environment, three activities have been established that can be considered a guideline to follow in the pedagogical development of a class.

On the other hand, the use of techniques for the identification of emotions using AI algorithms is useful to determine the level of concentration of a student in an e-learning environment. Emotions are closely related to attention and motivation and can indicate whether a student is interested in the learning material or is distracted or bored. However, it is important to note that emotion identification is an active field of research, and there are still challenges in accurately detecting emotions in different contexts and cultures.

Additionally, emotion identification can be affected by the quality of the data set and the accuracy of the AI algorithm used. Therefore, although emotion identification can be a useful technique to determine a student's concentration level in an e-learning environment, it should be used in combination with other monitoring and evaluation techniques to obtain a more accurate and complete picture of student performance.

This work makes use of AI as an integral part of education, considering that these tools are currently gaining ground in the educational sector. Additionally, the integration of AI into e-learning has the potential to significantly improve the quality of learning by providing students with a more personalized and adaptive learning experience. For example, AI algorithms can analyze the learning behavior of students, such as their progress in the course, their strengths and weaknesses, and their interaction patterns with course content. With this information, e-learning systems can offer students content recommendations and personalized learning activities that are tailored to their individual needs. In addition, technical limitations and the need for proper system design must be considered to ensure that AI is used effectively and efficiently in e-learning.

The designed concentration level identification system has demonstrated effectiveness in its usability and efficiency. Therefore, several recommendations can be made that may be useful in the use of the system or for institutions that design a similar system. Among the most important ones, an important recommendation is to ensure that any information collected by the system is used solely to improve the learning experience of students and is not shared with third parties without their consent. It is important to validate the system through rigorous testing, to ensure that the system works accurately and reliably before deploying it in a production environment. It is important to validate the system to ensure that the results are accurate and reliable. In the same way, it is important to provide feedback to students; the results of the system must be shared to provide feedback to students and help them improve their level of concentration and performance. Feedback can include advice on how to improve your concentration and suggestions on how to adjust your learning environment to increase your focus. Considering the context of learning, it must be taken into account that the level of concentration of students can be affected by external factors, such as the learning environment or the level of stress. Therefore, it is necessary to consider the learning context when interpreting the results of the system. Finally, it is a priority to evaluate the impact of the system, considering the performance and learning experience of the students.

Author Contributions: Conceptualization, W.V.-C. and A.M.-N.; methodology, W.V.-C.; software, J.G.-O.; validation, I.U.-C.; formal analysis, W.V.-C.; investigation, J.G.-O.; data curation, W.V.-C. and I.U.-C.; writing—original draft preparation, A.M.-N.; writing—review and editing, J.G.-O.; visualization, J.G.-O.; supervision, A.M.-N. All authors have read and agreed to the published version of the manuscript.

Funding: This research received no external funding.

Conflicts of Interest: The authors declare no conflict of interest.

References

1. Fuchs, K. The Difference Between Emergency Remote Teaching and E-Learning. *Front. Educ.* **2022**, *7*, 921332. [CrossRef]
2. Hariyanto, D. The Design of Adaptive Learning System Based on the Collaboration of M-Learning and e-Learning Platform. *J. Adv. Comput. Netw.* **2014**, *2*, 311–314. [CrossRef]
3. Chen, C.; Lee, H.; Chen, Y. Personalized E-Learning System Using Item Response Theory. *Comput. Educ.* **2005**, *44*, 237–255. [CrossRef]
4. Villegas-Ch, W.; Luján-Mora, S. Systematic Review of Evidence on Data Mining Applied to LMS Platforms for Improving E-Learning. In Proceedings of the International Technology, Education and Development Conference, Valencia, Spain, 6–8 March 2017; Chova, L.G., Martinez, A.L., Torres, I., Eds.; EDULEARN: Palma de Mallorca, Spain, 2017; pp. 6537–6545.
5. Rodriguez-Ascaso, A.; Boticario, J.G.; Finat, C.; Petrie, H. Setting Accessibility Preferences about Learning Objects within Adaptive Elearning Systems: User Experience and Organizational Aspects. *Expert Syst.* **2017**, *34*, e12187. [CrossRef]

6. Zamzuri, Z.F.; Manaf, M.; Ahmad, A.; Yunus, Y. Computer Security Threats Towards the E-Learning. In Proceedings of the In International Conference on Software Engineering and Computer Systems, Kuantan, Pahang, Malaysia, 27–29 June 2011; Springer: Berlin/Heidelberg, Germany, 2011; pp. 335–345.
7. Lin, H.-M.; Wu, J.-Y.; Liang, J.-C.; Lee, Y.-H.; Huang, P.; Kwok, O.-M.; Tsai, C.-C. A Review of Using Multilevel Modeling in E-Learning Research. *Comput. Educ.* **2023**, *198*, 104762. [CrossRef]
8. Lindgren, R.; Morphew, J.W.; Kang, J.; Planey, J.; Mestre, J.P. Learning and Transfer Effects of Embodied Simulations Targeting Crosscutting Concepts in Science. *J. Educ. Psychol.* **2022**, *114*, 462–481. [CrossRef]
9. Ali, M.; Hussein, A.; Al-Chalabi, H.K.M. Pedagogical Agents in an Adaptive E-Learning System. *SAR J.-Sci. Res.* **2020**, *3*, 24–30. [CrossRef]
10. Boumiza, S.; Souilem, D.; Bekiarski, A. Workflow Approach to Design Automatic Tutor in E-Learning Environment. In Proceedings of the International Conference on Control, Decision and Information Technologies, Saint Julian's, Malta, 6–8 April 2016; IEEE: Saint Julian's, Malta, 2016; pp. 263–268.
11. Lee, J.; Song, H.D.; Hong, A.J. Exploring Factors, and Indicators for Measuring Students' Sustainable Engagement in e-Learning. *Sustainablity* **2019**, *11*, 985. [CrossRef]
12. Heishman, R.; Duric, Z. Using Image Flow to Detect Eye Blinks in Color Videos. In Proceedings of the Proceedings-IEEE Workshop on Applications of Computer Vision, Austin, TX, USA, 21–22 February 2007; IEEE: Austin, TX, USA, 2007.
13. Sofia Jennifer, J.; Sree Sharmila, T. Edge Based Eye-Blink Detection for Computer Vision Syndrome. In Proceedings of the International Conference on Computer, Communication, and Signal Processing: Special Focus on IoT, Chennai, India, 10–11 January 2017; IEEE: Chennai, India, 2017.
14. Clavijo, G.L.R.; Patino, J.O.; Leon, D.M. Detection of Visual Fatigue by Analyzing the Blink Rate. In Proceedings of the 2015 20th Symposium on Signal Processing, Images and Computer Vision, STSIVA 2015-Conference Proceedings, Bogota, Colombia, 2–4 September 2015; IEEE: Bogota, Colombia, 2015.
15. Zeng, H.; Shu, X.; Wang, Y.; Wang, Y.; Zhang, L.; Pong, T.C.; Qu, H. EmotionCues: Emotion-Oriented Visual Summarization of Classroom Videos. *IEEE Trans. Vis. Comput. Graph.* **2021**, *27*, 3168–3181. [CrossRef] [PubMed]
16. Kim, Y.; Soyata, T.; Behnagh, R.F. Towards Emotionally Aware AI Smart Classroom: Current Issues and Directions for Engineering and Education. *IEEE Access* **2018**, *6*, 5308–5331. [CrossRef]
17. Tzacheva, A.; Ranganathan, J.; Mylavarapu, S.Y. Actionable Pattern Discovery for Tweet Emotions. *Adv. Intell. Syst. Comput.* **2020**, *965*, 46–57. [CrossRef]
18. Vijayalaxmi; Sudhakara Rao, P.; Sreehari, S. Neural Network Approach for Eye Detection. *arXiv* **2012**, arXiv:1205.5097.
19. Onners, J.; Alam, M.; Cichy, B.; Wymbs, N.; Lukos, J. U-EEG: A Deep Learning Autoencoder for the Detection of Ocular Artifact in EEG Signal. In Proceedings of the 2021 IEEE Signal Processing in Medicine and Biology Symposium, SPMB 2021-Proceedings, Philadelphia, PA, USA, 4 December 2021; IEEE: Philadelphia, PA, USA, 2021.
20. Scherer, K.R.; Coutinho, E. How Music Creates Emotion: A Multifactorial Process Approach. *Emot. Power Music* **2013**, *1*, 121–145.
21. Greene, G. Guidelines for Assessing and Minimizing Risks of Emotion Recognition Applications. In Proceedings of the 2021 9th International Conference on Affective Computing and Intelligent Interaction (ACII), Nara, Japan, 28 September–1 October 2021; IEEE: Nara, Japan, 2021.
22. Madureira, J.; Pereira, C.; Paciência, I.; Teixeira, J.P.; de Oliveira Fernandes, E. Identification and Levels of Airborne Fungi in Portuguese Primary Schools. *J. Toxicol. Environ. Health-Part A Curr. Issues* **2014**, *77*, 816–826. [CrossRef]
23. Kobai, R.; Murakami, H. Effects of Interactions between Facial Expressions and Self-Focused Attention on Emotion. *PLoS ONE* **2021**, *16*, e0261666. [CrossRef]
24. Alzbier, A.M.T.; Cheng, H. Real Time Tracking RGB Color Based Kinect. *Mod. Appl. Sci.* **2017**, *11*, 98. [CrossRef]
25. Lai, H.Y.; Ke, H.Y.; Hsu, Y.C. Real-Time Hand Gesture Recognition System and Application. *Sens. Mater.* **2018**, *30*, 869. [CrossRef]
26. Ismael, K.D.; Irina, S. Face Recognition Using Viola-Jones Depending on Python. *Indones. J. Electr. Eng. Comput. Sci.* **2020**, *20*, 1513–1521. [CrossRef]
27. Huang, J.; Shang, Y.; Chen, H. Improved Viola-Jones Face Detection Algorithm Based on HoloLens. *EURASIP J. Imag. Video Process* **2019**, *41*. [CrossRef]
28. Liu, F.; Kromer, P. Early Age Education on Artificial Intelligence: Methods and Tools. In *Advances in Intelligent Systems and Computing*; Springer: Cham, Switzerland, 2020; Volume 1156 AISC.
29. Sciarrone, A.; Bisio, I.; Garibotto, C.; Lavagetto, F.; Hamedani, M.; Prada, V.; Schenone, A.; Boero, F.; Gambari, G.; Cereia, M.; et al. Early Detection of External Neurological Symptoms through a Wearable Smart-Glasses Prototype. *J. Commun. Softw. Syst.* **2021**, *17*, 160–168. [CrossRef]
30. Uranishi, Y. OpenCV: Open Source Computer Vision Library. *Kyokai Joho Imeji Zasshi/J. Inst. Image Inf. Telev. Eng.* **2018**, *72*, 736–739. [CrossRef]
31. Emami, S.; Suciu, V.P. Facial Recognition Using OpenCV. *J. Mob. Embed. Distrib. Syst.* **2012**, *4*, 1.
32. Naveenkumar, M.; Ayyasamy, V. OpenCV for Computer Vision Applications. In Proceedings of the National Conference on Big Data and Cloud Computing (NCBDC'15), Trichy, India, 20 March 2016.
33. Sigut, J.; Castro, M.; Arnay, R.; Sigut, M. OpenCV Basics: A Mobile Application to Support the Teaching of Computer Vision Concepts. *IEEE Trans. Educ.* **2020**, *63*, 328–335. [CrossRef]

34. Zhu, Z.; Cheng, Y. Application of Attitude Tracking Algorithm for Face Recognition Based on OpenCV in the Intelligent Door Lock. *Comput. Commun.* **2020**, *154*, 390–397. [CrossRef]
35. Kumar, Y.; Mahajan, M. Machine Learning Based Speech Emotions Recognition System. *Int. J. Sci. Technol. Res.* **2019**, *8*, 722–729.
36. Drowsiness Detection Using Eye-Blink Frequency and Yawn Count for Driver Alert. *Int. J. Innov. Technol. Explor. Eng.* **2019**, *9*, 314–317. [CrossRef]
37. Rosique, F.; Losilla, F.; Navarro, P.J. Using Artificial Vision for Measuring the Range of Motion. *IEEE Lat. Am. Trans.* **2021**, *19*, 1129–1136. [CrossRef]
38. Serrano-Ramírez, T.; Lozano-Rincón, N.D.C.; Mandujano-Nava, A.; Sámano-Flores, Y.J. Artificial Vision System for Object Classification in Real Time Using Raspberry Pi and a Web Camera. *Rev. Tecnol. Inf. Y Comun.* **2021**, *5*, 20–25. [CrossRef]
39. Ouyang, F.; Jiao, P. Artificial Intelligence in Education: The Three Paradigms. *Comput. Educ. Artif. Intell.* **2021**, *2*, 100020. [CrossRef]
40. Xue, Y.; Wang, Y. Artificial Intelligence for Education and Teaching. *Wirel. Commun. Mob. Comput.* **2022**, *2022*, 1–10. [CrossRef]
41. Tonguç, G.; Ozaydın Ozkara, B. Automatic Recognition of Student Emotions from Facial Expressions during a Lecture. *Comput. Educ.* **2020**, *148*, 103797. [CrossRef]
42. Nct Emotion Recognition Training for Young People. 2015. Available online: https://clinicaltrials.gov/show/NCT02550379 (accessed on 16 February 2023).
43. Hossain, M.S.; Muhammad, G. An Emotion Recognition System for Mobile Applications. *IEEE Access* **2017**, *5*, 2281–2287. [CrossRef]
44. Wani, T.M.; Gunawan, T.S.; Qadri, S.A.A.; Kartiwi, M.; Ambikairajah, E. A Comprehensive Review of Speech Emotion Recognition Systems. *IEEE Access* **2021**, *9*, 47795–47814. [CrossRef]
45. Mohammad, S. NRC Emotion Lexicon. *Saif Mohammad*. 2015. Available online: https://saifmohammad.com/WebPages/NRC-Emotion-Lexicon.htm (accessed on 16 February 2023).
46. Scraping of Social Media Data Using Python-3 and Performing Data Analytics Using Microsoft Power Bi. *Int. J. Eng. Sci. Res. Technol.* **2020**, *9*. [CrossRef]

Disclaimer/Publisher's Note: The statements, opinions and data contained in all publications are solely those of the individual author(s) and contributor(s) and not of MDPI and/or the editor(s). MDPI and/or the editor(s) disclaim responsibility for any injury to people or property resulting from any ideas, methods, instructions or products referred to in the content.

Article

English Language Learning via YouTube: An NLP-Based Analysis of Users' Comments

Husam M. Alawadh [1], Amerah Alabrah [2], Talha Meraj [3,*] and Hafiz Tayyab Rauf [4]

[1] Department of English Language and Translation, College of Languages and Translation, King Saud University, Riyadh 11451, Saudi Arabia
[2] Department of Information Systems, College of Computer and Information Sciences, King Saud University, Riyadh 11451, Saudi Arabia
[3] Department of Computer Science, COMSATS University Islamabad—Wah Campus, Wah Cantt 47040, Pakistan
[4] Independent Researcher, Bradford BD8 0HS, UK
* Correspondence: talhameraj32@gmail.com

Abstract: Online teaching and learning has been beneficial in facilitating learning of English as a foreign language (EFL). In online EFL learning, YouTube is one of the most utilized information and communication technology (ICT) tools because of its inherent features that make it a unique environment for learners and educators. Many interesting aspects of YouTube-based learning can be beneficial in supplementing conventional classroom methods, and, therefore, such aspects must be identified. Previous scholarly work aimed at improving YouTube learning environment was predominantly conducted manually by gathering learners' impressions through interviews and questionnaires to analyze the differences between YouTube- and classroom-based EFL learning. However, such methods are tedious and time-consuming and can lead to results that are of less generalizable implications. User comments on YouTube channels are useful in identifying such aspects, as they present a wealth of information related to the quality of the content provided, challenges the targeted audience faces, and areas of potential improvement. Therefore, in our current study, YouTube API is used to collect the comments of three randomly selected and popular YouTube channels. Following a data cleaning process, people's sentiments about EFL learning were first identified via a TextBlob method. Second, the automated latent semantic analysis (LSA) method of topic finding was used to collect global and open-ended topics of discussion on YouTube-based EFL learning. Users' sentiments on the most popular topics of discussion are discussed in this paper. Further, based on the results, hypothetical findings on YouTube EFL learning are provided as recommendation for future content, including more variety of the content covered, introduction of the meanings and punctuation following words, the design of the course such that it addresses a multinational audience of any age, and targeted teaching of each variety of English, such as British and American. We also make suggestions for learners of English who wish to utilize online and offline learning, which include finding the course of interest first based on one's needs which can be discussed with a tutor or any English teacher to optimize the learning experience, participating in fearless educator–learner interaction and engagement, and asking other EFL learners for their previous experiences with learning online in order for the learner to maximize benefit.

Keywords: English learning; online education; sentiment analysis; topic modeling; YouTube learning

Citation: Alawadh, H.M.; Alabrah, A.; Meraj, T.; Rauf, H.T. English Language Learning via YouTube: An NLP-Based Analysis of Users' Comments. *Computers* 2023, 12, 24. https://doi.org/10.3390/computers12020024

Academic Editors: Antonio Sarasa Cabezuelo and Covadonga Rodrigo San Juan

Received: 4 November 2022
Revised: 20 December 2022
Accepted: 22 December 2022
Published: 19 January 2023
Corrected: 17 February 2025

Copyright: © 2023 by the authors. Licensee MDPI, Basel, Switzerland. This article is an open access article distributed under the terms and conditions of the Creative Commons Attribution (CC BY) license (https://creativecommons.org/licenses/by/4.0/).

1. Introduction

English is considered to be the international language of communication and is termed English as a foreign language (EFL) for its learners. Therefore, proficiency in speaking and listening to English has become necessary in communicating about and understanding worldwide matters [1]. Moreover, there is a growing need for EFL learners' proficiency levels to be reliably assessed for a variety of reasons ranging from enrolling in higher education to migrating to an English speaking country for professional reasons. This is determined by certain international organizations [2] which categorize EFL learners into different groups based on their English proficiency levels. The age of technology has resulted in technology becoming popular in each aspect of current modern life, with teaching and learning being in the forefront of this transition. Many people are studying various topics using Internet sources such as YouTube videos, webpages, etc., [3].

Similarly, many people are currently learning English from YouTube videos. Moreover, traveling and enrolling in educational institutes require good command of English, and with the advances of and availability of different ICTs, this process has now become more flexible [3]. As a result of using ICT, learning has become more flexible, creative, and enriched in quality [4]. Learning in any domain using ICT results in benefits in various areas; according to a report published by the National Institute of Multimedia Education in Japan, ICT-technology-based learning is more effective compared with traditional study in classrooms. Further, it is reported that ICT-based learners have higher presentation skills, creativity, and understanding [5] of topics.

The use of electronic devices allows the provision of more visually appealing illustrations of topics via audio and video description, graphical representation, animated description, etc. Although these ICT technologies are also being utilized in classroom-based studies to increase student interactivity, remote access to YouTube-like platforms makes learning more accessible for anyone [6]. Smart choices for a more flexible learning environment are being abundantly adopted, including in the form of mobile learning, social interaction, personal grooming and growth, global networking and engagements, etc. [7–9]. Personal growth is one of the soft critical skills that any individual needs for development and involves autonomous learning of an individual at their own pace and environment to cater to those specific needs they desire.

Further, linking and structuring elements of any specific topic is also more beneficial to the learner to gain broader and stronger conceptualization [10]. Interactivity and socialization are other vital factors in learning environments. Individuals interacting with others in academic life helps others to learn from them and explore more ideas [11]. Inclusiveness is another factor in learning environments, and it highlights the barriers that cause issues when teaching students. In this way, the students, regardless of social, national and religious status, can receive equal opportunities in their studies [12].

All these above mentioned qualities of a learning environment are available on a single ICT platform, YouTube, for learning and teaching the English language. Further, a greater variety of authentic teachers [13] from different native languages are available, providing a more specialized experience for EFL learners. Pun et al. [14] state that the content delivered on online multimedia is more functional and has more up-to-date data than textbooks. Further, learning English from YouTube can lead to more up-to-date learning compared with regular institutional studies. At present, many professors in universities and colleges have started their own YouTube channels in which they upload their lectures as a complete course, which helps many students in revising the lectures with flexibility with reference to time, and absent students can also benefit from this through remote learning.

However, many recent studies on YouTube-based English language learning have focused on conducting interviews and questionnaires of EFL learners that seek English from YouTube videos. This highlights the significance of YouTube-based learning and raises specific research questions. The use of manual interpretation of YouTube-based EFL learning can be misguided and biased, as discussed in reports on previous studies of YouTube-based English learning. Therefore, analysis of the real-time collected comments, likes, and responses to those comments by other users can give practical information regarding YouTube-based English language learning. Further, examination of the YouTube comments provided by citizens of different nations can provide greater insight into YouTube-based English language learning. Our current study solves the following challenges regarding YouTube-based EFL learning:

- An automated solution was established to collect multinational data about YouTube-based EFL learning and analyze the most discussed topics and the sentiments of learners regarding these topics.
- How and why does English learning from YouTube videos influence students compared with conventional EFL learning? Is YouTube helping or misleading online consumers?
- What are the challenges and difficulties of learning from internet sources?
- Suggestions and hypotheses were derived based on LSA-based topic modeling of user feedback in the form of YouTube video comments.

To answer these questions, in our study, the data of comments and other information from several popular YouTube channels were collected. These include the benefits of learning from YouTube videos and the gaps that some viewers lack. The remaining sections of this work are Section 2: Related Work; Section 3: Material and Methods; Section 4: Findings and Discussions; Section 5: Hypothetical Findings and Suggestions; and Section 6: Conclusion, which includes future suggestions.

2. Related Work

Many of the studies that investigated YouTube-based English language learning highlight the benefits of learning from YouTube. They mostly relied on manual collection of datasets via conducting interviews and the use of questionnaires. This targeted specific users, while it also did not involve real-time comments or data. However, we highlight a few studies which were experimental in nature here.

A study conducted by a Taiwanese university reported certain facts about YouTube-based English learning and included 20 students in the hypothetical experimentation, and answers to certain predefined questions were obtained from these students. The three major areas of concern were highlighted in terms of three questions asked by the interviewers and classified into multiple options based on the EFL learners. Essentially, classroom- and YouTube-based EFL learning were differentiated. Further, the study explored whether learning is self-regulatory or not using the responses of EFL learners. The study was based on SRL models and focused on six goals. The inter-rater agreements were calculated based on EFL responses and the SRL models, and the responses were correspondingly classified. Lastly, the differences and similarities between EFL and regular classroom learners were highlighted [15]. In another example, YouTube-based language learning research was used as the basis for a conceptual study that marked the advancements and limitations of YouTube-video-based language learning environments. It reported that classroom-based language learning could be more effective if YouTube-based assistance is added to guide the students. Further, due to the availability of authentic content, the learners can be more involved in the selection of the instructor in the YouTube videos [16]. The study was conducted in a school where English was studied as a subject, and for data collection, 14 randomly selected students were enrolled. The students had both online and offline experiences, and the conducted study based its conclusions on student reviews.

In another study, three main questions were analyzed based on the responses of students to certain questions on (1) the differences in offline and online studies for EFL learners, (2) user interaction regarding study using ICT tools or YouTube as a learning environment, interaction, and engagement to multimedia, and (3) the learner's personal experience of learning and speaking English using ICT tools. For the quantitative exploration of the results, the Pearson correlation test and regression analysis were used. The time range of YouTube channel videos was analyzed, wherein the exposure between these watching times was analyzed. For qualitative analysis, the improvement in writing skills and the affordance of YouTube videos were reported by asking all learners simple questions. The study also concluded that negative aspects were related to personal growth and the accuracy in the fluency of learning and writing English [17].

Wahyuni et al. conducted a study on YouTube-based English language learning in an Indonesian setting, and a class of 40 students was observed. It was reported that the learning environment of any learning is highly significant. Therefore, the English language learning-based study was conducted by applying a qualitative approach in the experimental setup. Mainly English speaking was analyzed, where four steps were repeatedly applied to answer the questions asked in the questionnaire reported in that study. The statistical measures of mean, standard deviation, maximum, and minimum were applied to the questions and their answers. It was concluded, based on the statistical analysis, that YouTube provides a good environment for learning English speaking [18].

The author of another study claimed that there are two modes of learning: audio and video. The study recommends video illustration over audio for English speaking. The cognitive reasoning regarding the use of video and audio media is described in the methodology section, where the multiple styles of learning and effective reasons are further described. It was reported that when using video-based EFL learning, there is less cognitive load on the learners. It was further stated that YouTube is not only useful for entertainment but can also be beneficial for language learning [19].

Putri et al. [20] reported in their study that YouTube is a more flexible, entertaining, and fun environment to learn the English language. The study included experimental data based on 12 students. Qualitative analysis was performed by asking questions on different cultural, social, meta-cognitive, resource, effectiveness, and goal commitment aspects. The analysis was based on the different factors, concerned with their effect on how swiftly the English language can be learned.

Another study based on making and uploading English-speaking videos on YouTube was conducted based on 10 participants and qualitative analysis of their answers to questions was performed. The questionnaire in use comprised five questions with an 80% response rate, which showed that before making English-speaking assignment videos and uploading them on YouTube, extensive practice was conducted on correcting their English pronunciation. Therefore, to ensure correct English pronunciation, English speaking could be improved by uploading English-speaking videos. The different suggestions to improve English pronunciation made by all learners were also provided [21].

To analyze YouTube-based EFL learners, the authors of [22] stated, in their study, that this platform contributes to developing individual participation as well as critical thinking and social engagement. Authentic English teaching material is available on YouTube. Additionally, a few channels also provide supplementary materials for English language learning. Including all these aspects results in YouTube being an effective source of learning for EFL learners. Another study on YouTube-based EFL learning included 32 students [23]. The pros and cons of the learning environment were discussed by presenting students with open-ended questions. The report concluded that YouTube is a very familiar, cheap, and flexible platform for EFL learning. However, participants encountered difficulties that could be resolved by using different YouTube-video-watching features and by discussing problems with teachers and friends.

A study in an Indonesian university included students participating in EFL learning via YouTube [24]. This involved the use of the Web 2.0 program of the YouTube platform, which provides many other benefits over traditional EFL learning. This research uncovered the benefits of YouTube-based learning over classroom learning. Certain practices were also suggested for improving teaching in the future to ensure students felt more at ease in that environment.

There are many areas of EFL learning in which different people are weak and wish only to improve in that specific aspect. To investigate this, a study was conducted on YouTube-based EFL learning for improving pronunciation [25]. The benefits of using YouTube were revealed through such remarks as videos are free to watch, different speakers from different nations even with good British and American English could be found to improve pronunciation, in particular, and the possibility to watch videos anywhere and also on different devices. The recommendations given were to learn pronunciation while watching YouTube videos, where important points were also given before and after watching videos.

In another study, student reviews were collected using Google Forms, and based on the questionnaire answers, it was concluded that YouTube-based EFL learning occurs most specifically according to the content given in the course with the addition of attractive and flexible features [26].

The different recent studies on EFL learning discussed above highlight the use of YouTube in English language learning for improving writing, speaking, grammar, and pronunciation.

However, the data that such studies utilized were only manually collected, and qualitative and quantitative analysis was mostly performed on only certain and specific questions. The research questions in those studies were built upon personal impressions and analyzed with some statistical approaches. Therefore, to bridge a clear research gap related to identifying wider challenges of YouTube-based English language learning, an automated solution to collect real-time responses from channel comments is needed. Moreover, qualitative and quantitative discussion of EFL learner responses is also required. In this way, the problems and benefits can be highlighted. Further, inter-comparison of the different YouTube-based channels could allow pedagogical implications to be formulated and shared with content makers to facilitate more positive responses from their viewers.

3. Materials and Methods

In the current study, user comments on three popular YouTube English teaching channels were collected via an API provided by Google developer services. The data were cleaned after scraping from the API, and playlist-wise topic modeling was performed, where each channel playlist topic was compared to check the user response to the topic. The primary purpose of this was to increase the audience and enhance their interest by proposing suggestions for new and already existing and popular YouTube channels. The results obtained form the current study may also carry important implications which can pour into the improvement of traditional EFL classroom environment. All primary steps of the current study are shown in Figure 1.

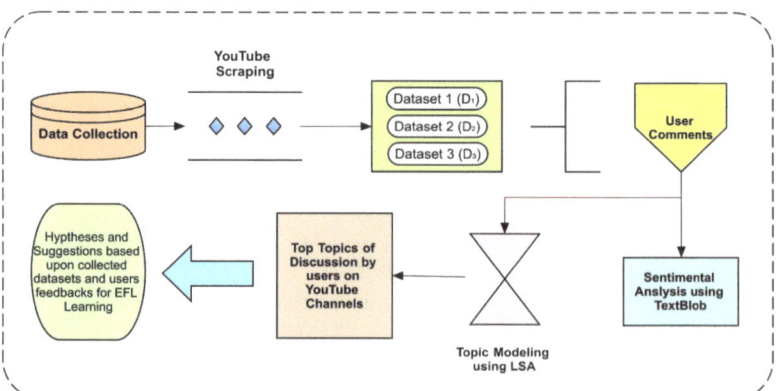

Figure 1. Flowchart containing all steps included in the current study to analyze YouTube-based EFL learning using computer-assisted methods.

Data acquired from YouTube were then subjected to cleaning. The user response on each topic of each channel is important. Therefore, at first, the sentiment of the user was checked using the TextBlob method of sentiment analysis, and, secondly, their topics of discussion in the comments box were discussed following topic modeling via the LSA method. The most popular topics and their associated used words were discussed, and suggestions were proposed by determining people's sentiments on these topics.

3.1. Data Collection and Cleaning

In previous studies, authors mostly selected interested students from different semesters and assigned them to watch videos and share narratives/notes describing their impressions. After that, interviews and questionnaires were conducted and completed to analyze the topics and behavior. The predefined questions asked mostly answer the following major and basic questions: Is YouTube a good source of learning for EFL learners or not? Similarly, are the sources on YouTube trustworthy and authentic or not?

However, in all previously used approaches, automated and real-time collection from a multinational audience was lacking. In this way, the known issues and benefits of using YouTube-based EFL learning would also be lacking. In our study, we manually selected the three of the most viewed channels on EFL learning on YouTube and scraped people's comments on them together with their likes and responses on each playlist. A YouTube developer account was created and the API key was used, and the collection of user responses according to channel and playlist was performed. The selected channel names are (1) Learn English with Englishclass101.com (D_1) [27]; (2) Learn English with Jessica (D_2) [28]; (3) Speak English with Vanessa (D_3) [29].

The textual data of comments on these channels contained stop words, URLs, and other redundant information that was removed using the regular expression library of Python. After collecting and cleaning data on all playlists, a topic wise analysis was performed. We highlight the main findings from this step below.

3.2. Dataset Topics

Different topics of discussion were found on the three different channels. The user response and interest in all topics were analyzed and included negative, positive, and neutral responses. First, the video topics are discussed here, and the findings related to these are discussed in Section 4. Table 1 describes the datasets and their discussed topics.

Table 1. Topics of videos in the three datasets used in this study.

Datasets	Topic ID	Topics of Discussion in Videos
D_1	D_1T_1	"Learn basic English vocabulary"
	D_1T_2	"English conversational phrases"
	D_1T_3	"Fun and easy"
	D_1T_4	"American English intermediate reading practice"
	D_1T_5	"American English advanced reading practice"
	D_1T_6	"British English advanced reading practice"
	D_1T_7	"English listening comprehension for absolute beginners"
	D_1T_8	"English listening comprehension for beginners"
	D_1T_9	"English listening comprehension for intermediate learners"
	D_1T_{10}	"English listening comprehension for advanced learners"
D_2	D_2T_1	"Practice English speaking conversations"
	D_2T_2	"Learn English speaking using daily life conversations"
D_3	D_3T_1	"How to learn English"
	D_3T_2	"American vs. British English"
	D_3T_3	"English listening lessons"
	D_3T_4	"English vocabulary"
	D_3T_5	"Business English"
	D_3T_6	"Travel English"
	D_3T_7	"English pronunciation"
	D_3T_8	"English grammar"
	D_3T_9	"Phrasal verbs"
	D_3T_{10}	"Live English lessons"
	D_3T_{11}	"Skype tests"
	D_3T_{12}	"Fearless discussion"
	D_3T_{13}	"Interviews in English"

We can see in Table 1 that there are several different topics discussed in the videos. The first dataset contains the topics of English vocabulary, conversational phrases, listening, and speaking at beginner and advanced levels in both British and American contexts. The second dataset involves creating animated videos containing anonymous objects. Most of the videos in this dataset contain the regular use of English regarding speaking.

The third dataset contains interesting topics compared with both of the above-discussed datasets. It contains the regular content for EFL learners as well as live interviews and the fearless discussions of its users/subscribers through Skype and other live interactions. It also contains different levels of the syllabus for EFL learners according to their usages, such as business and travel English. The user response on all these datasets and their topics is more interesting and is discussed in the following section of this manuscript.

3.3. User Sentiment in Dataset Topics via Sentiment Analysis

In previous studies, statistical analysis was performed on answers to predefined questions in questionnaires asking about YouTube videos. The analysis concerned user sentiment and suggestions to watch YouTube videos for EFL learning. Similarly, there was an automated collection of user sentiment based on open-ended comments, sentiment analysis of all comments on different topics in the videos was performed for each dataset, and the sentiments on each topic are shown in Section 4. TextBlob was used to perform sentiment analysis.

3.4. User-Response-Based Topic Modeling via Latent Semantic Analysis (LSA)

In previous studies, most of the questions and topics were user-defined and collected and provided by authors. In our study, we examined user comments on different YouTube channels in which there were different topics of discussion. To analyze the topics of discussion in comments, topic modeling based on LSA [30] was performed.

The cleaned textual data were first provided to the LDA model [31], and the most frequently occurring unique topics from each playlist of each channel were analyzed. The mathematical representation of applied steps on documents or input data are shown in Equations (1)–(3).

$$d_n(i) = p_n(i) \qquad (1)$$

In Equation (1), D_n represents the three datasets, where n varies from 1 to 3, and i represents a certain comment or text document that is passed from the preprocessing step to clean the document from stop words, URLs, etc. The cleaned data are stored in D_n. These cleaned data are then used to create the count vector document matrix. The mathematical representation is shown in Equation (2).

$$d_c = d_n[count] \qquad (2)$$

D_c represents the document count against the cleaned data matrix (D_n). The count is the term count in each document or text comment in this case study. To obtain multi-matrix decomposition as acquired by the LSA model, the singular value decomposition (SVD) method is used, where topics on each channel's comments data are manually specified here. SVD is a matrix term that is used to reduce the matrix dimensionality [32]. The mathematical representation is shown in Equation (3).

$$T_m = SVD(m, D_c) \qquad (3)$$

In Equation (3), two input parameters are specified while making the SVD matrix that will generate the unique topics of discussion. Topics are represented by T_m, where m is the number of topics, and the output is calculated by using specific topics (m) and the cleaned count vectorizer of each document. After obtaining user topics of discussion via each dataset, sentiment analysis is performed to determine user sentiment as being either positive, negative, or neutral.

4. Findings and Discussion

There are two types of topics that need to be discussed in this section about the EFL learning topics and the user responses to them. First, let us explore the collected datasets and the sentiments of people about them.

4.1. Sentiment Analysis of Collected Datasets

There are three datasets collected where the basis of the collection was their different playlist topics. To identify people's sentiments on each topic of channels, the three basic sentiments of people were collected based on the polarity of their comments. The sentiments for each topic are shown in Table 2.

Table 2. User sentiments on topics of three YouTube channels about EFL learning.

Topics of Discussion in Videos	Sentiments (%)		
	Positive	Negative	Neutral
D_1T_1	75	5	20
D_1T_2	75	15	10
D_1T_3	72.7	9.1	18.2
D_1T_4	27.3	9.1	63.6
D_1T_5	58.3	0	41.7
D_1T_6	75	10	15
D_2T_1	75	5	20
D_2T_2	80	0	20
D_3T_1	92.5	2.5	5.0
D_3T_2	92.5	2.5	5.0
D_3T_3	96.7	0	3.3
D_3T_4	92.5	2.5	5.0
D_3T_5	95.0	2.5	2.5
D_3T_6	85.0	2.5	12.5
D_3T_7	93.8	2.5	3.8
D_3T_8	94.0	1.0	5.0
D_3T_9	95.0	0	5
D_3T_{10}	100	0	0
D_3T_{11}	90	0	10
D_3T_{12}	100	0	0
D_3T_{13}	77.5	10	12.5

There are many topics, and the different sentiments regarding these can be seen in Table 2. Regarding our first dataset topics and their sentiments, we can see that there are six unique topics for which the user sentiment analysis was performed. The sentiments regarding basic vocabulary remain less negative compared with those on the discussion of conversational phrases.

Fun and ease, which is the third topic of sentiment analysis in the table, is also associated with 9% negative sentiment, and this could be due to the critical thinking about this topic of discussion. The fourth topic is associated with far less positive sentiment and is American English intermediate, and the next topic D_1T_5 is more negative and is advanced-level American English reading practice.

The British English reading-based comments received more positive feedback compared with American readings, as can be seen in D_1T_6. This could be attributed to higher quality exposure of and practice in the British variety of English compared with the American context, though this needs to be formally established in a future study utilizing validation and triangulation techniques.

Regarding the second dataset, which specifically utilized animated videos to teach spoken English, the self-made objects were made and used to practice spoken English. Both playlists were associated with positive sentiments and some (5%) negative sentiments. Therefore, it can be said that increasing excitement by employing non-traditional and innovative techniques such as making animated videos for object-based English practice and learning can lead to positive impressions amongst the target audience.

4.2. LSA-Based Topic Modeling of User Comments

Topic modeling based on user comments was performed, where the most popular topics are also identified with the use of the most significant words in them. The count-vector-based feature vector is provided to the SVD matrix maker and the LSA model is then applied.

4.2.1. Dataset 1 (D_1) Topics Discussed by Users

The topics of user comments from each playlist of datasets were collected, and those for dataset D_1 are shown in Table 3.

Table 3. User topics of discussion in YouTube videos in D_1.

Topic IDs	Topics Discussed by Users
$D_1 T_1$	"English lesson like learn thanks speaking teacher thank lot good" "Words described entire learn language kashmir just jammu imagine good"
$D_1 T_2$	"Like engineering faculty lesson helpfuli petroleum continue awesome student studying useful" "Maximum respect appreciate coz daily improving madam really aliciai saudi great alisha" "Thank language improving saudi arabia learn english helpfuli great going faculty" "Videos going marathon yamaximum department anyone hi helpfuli"
$D_1 T_3$	"Important jobs sends bookstores branch brands details rights restaurants"
	"Live pay afford bills guys bangladesh" "Cost transportation afghanistan mount education semester lot living city like home"
$D_1 T_4$ and $D_1 T_5$	"english help wash mim dificil fokor hi hmmm improv want" "alisha 00am practice im enjoy like btw boring beautiful simples" "Thanks video nice"
$D_1 T_6$	"World known billgates channel hello 2nd position portuguese nice love" "Good uploading content thanks achi baat billgates bot british caption channel" "english sure british world achi baat billgates bot caption channel" "portuguese caption world english achi baat billgates bot british channel" "Speak nice world english achi baat billgates bot british caption" "Thank love world english achi baat billgates bot british caption"

The table of topics in the dataset (D_1) shows the major discussed topics based on videos of each topic. The first topic ($D_1 T_1$) shows the type of topics that are more likely to be associated with positive sentiments and even show that the user Jammu Kashmir belongs to and is inspired by the English teaching of this channel.

Secondly, we can see in $D_1 T_2$ that people from Saudi Arabia and Bangladesh follow this channel and strongly recommend the language learning style used here for conversational phrases videos. In the third topic of this channel, the user mentions that it is a fun and easy way to learn English. It includes user-interaction-based activity to comment in English for a given phrase. Therefore, the user comments are almost the same, talking about bills, electricity, education, etc., again and again.

Only three topics of discussion are listed in the table where other similar topic related comments are discarded. The fourth and fifth topics, which are on American English learning, already showed slightly negative sentiments of people compared with British English on this channel. In the user comments, the user is saying that the video is boring but simple and has given suggestions for where improvement is needed.

The next topic on British English learning received positive comments, and it also came from a multinational audience learning British English from this channel that positively recommended taking British English lessons through this YouTube channel.

4.2.2. Dataset 2 (D_2) Topics Discussed by Users

The users of the second channel gave mostly positive responses on data, where their discussed topics are discussed in Table 4.

Table 4. Users topic of discussion on topics of YouTube videos on D_2.

Topic IDs	Topics Discussed by Users
D_2T_1	"Really English know video dear thank wish improved love maker" "Heart efforts thank wish god know improved happy great good" "Want does practice good love know improved heart happy great" "Video thanks good wish god know improved heart happy great" "Wish god thank know improved heart happy great good fluently" "Mam super god know improved heart happy great good fluently" "Waiting to wish god know improved heart happy great good" "Pronunciation great wish maker know improved heart happy good god" "Congratulations efforts good love know improved heart happy great god" "Nice wish maker knows improved heart happy great good god"
D_2T_2	"Absolutely time listen" "English Channel story"

In the second dataset, channel comments where animated videos were given received many positive comments and best wishes, whereas comments about the video maker and story maker being nice were given. Now, it can be noted that by making objects and animated videos, plays, and by making small stories in an innovative fashion, we can increase the efficacy of EFL teaching utilizing ICT. Again, this is an area of potential future research focusing on innovative content creation in ICT and how it can increase its utility and impact in the learning process. Certain areas of language learning such as expressions, pronunciation, and vocabulary can be easier to deliver using innovative content as compared to other areas such speaking.

4.2.3. Dataset 3 (D_3) Topics Discussed by Users

The third channel includes interesting topics, compared with the two other channels, that essentially use the same strategy to teach English, which also works in regular classrooms and courses for EFL learners. The users on this channel and its topics also showed a higher proportion of comments and sharing compared with the other two channels. To examine the differences and reasons for more interaction of users of this channel, the most discussed topics are shown in Table 5.

Table 5. Topics of discussion of users of YouTube videos on D_3.

Topic IDs	Topics Discussed by Users
D_3T_1	"Day english like learn vanessa" "English doing vanessa really way"
D_3T_2	"English just vanessa interesting time use really native video expressions" "Piano asked said practice plan shoot daughter scene ready discussion" "Lot helped videos thanks dear vanessa fluency write glad friends" "Vanessa lovely write love educational exactly excellent expressions fabulous mood" "Great lesson like shoot know family breeze bless understand thank"
D_3T_3	"Vanessa thanks videos accent learning make new excited English rock" "Just years bless speaking growing teach past confidence important following" "Know useful ex situations really easy demise make love certain" "Videos learned helpful routine did thank daily things new watch" "Podcast listen amazing app beautiful, best videos vanessa teacher hope" "Lesson lot life English thanks just learning wow amazing learned"

Table 5. *Cont.*

Topic IDs	Topics Discussed by Users
D_3T_4	"Learning years hard English hope simple day daily comment good" "Regard appreciate enjoyed watching warm Indonesia video pet vanessa really" "YouTube channel really subscriber helped new relaxing love watch australia" "Like listening positive speech thank useful lot clear videos watching" "Dislike video people thanks loved vanessa class wonderful important indonesia" "Vanessa lessons dear love thank youtube hard helped hope important" "Enjoyed fun talking session learning learn just intensive inspiration indonesia"
D_3T_5	"Thank great english vanessa don lessons hello expression lesson love"
D_3T_6	"Lesson marek looking subscriber nice realy regards rent response new" "Vanessa thanks going thank english glad teacher help learning kisses" "Want bother lessons grammar don excuse world hotel helpful hey"
D_3T_7	"Love videos 70 help thanks thank enjoy teacher teach good" "Summer ll headed think wish instead lesson place portugal great" "Vanessa thanks mood nice smiling instead help helps hi hope" "Clear muchlove sweet helps pronunciation improves english india vanessa hello"
D_3T_8	"Lesson great words job beautiful vanessa thanks english hi helpful" "Thank vanessa chinese varied advanced creating media mainland love lessons"
D_3T_9	"Learn english videos different symbols fluently smile difficult" "Learn accidentaly fun channel clear success speech dear" "Lesson ve youtube easy simple sooooooo did practical" "Lessons like enjoyed struggling teach love brought vanessa" "Make isn possible plans vacations vanessa years amazing like lessons"
D_3T_{10}	"Happiness wish following tips month people relationship great" "Lots of useful love lesson thanks expressions lot channel"
D_3T_{11}	"Understand movies teacher" "youtube videos speakers"
D_3T_{12}	"Really like natural shock reverse remembered face speaking culture country" "Understand like conversations problem try speak advanced 90 listening hours"
D_3T_{13}	"Good say experienced identified inmersion interacte knowledge deep" "Learnt lot good debate work different identified hello"

As previously discussed, there are certain unique topics of discussion that are distinguished and described by the LSA model. For example, the users of dataset (D_3) showed more interest compared with those of datasets 1 and 2, and there are many aspects that seem to engage the audience. At first, the very basic start of this channel poses the question "How to learn English?", a very basic question in itself to which there are many different answers, and even people of different ages and language backgrounds could all learn English. People's sentiments and comments all remained positive and they appreciated the way to start EFL learning.

Secondly, there is a global issue of whether to learn either British or American English. The differences are highlighted when people discuss this topic, and excellent differences are highlighted with acquired expressions to speak the English of both varieties. The third topic D_3T_3, to take English lessons again, engages many audiences, the teacher's accent and expressions are, again, much appreciated, and the lesson is also much appreciated by the audience and viewers.

Acquiring and retaining Vocabulary can be a challenge for many EFL learners. Users who visited the YouTube channels under investigation appear to agree with this. On this topic, D_3T_4, many people from different countries, such as from Australia, say that Indonesian people watching a video on this topic feel more relaxed and inspired after watching these videos. The next topics of the video are related to English on business and travel demonstrating a narrower focus on a less targeted EFL learning area especially in a free online resource.

However, business English with topic ID D_3T_5 showed all positive responses with, again, expressions-based acknowledgment. The English grammar topics and the phrasal verbs are much appreciated, and people immensely enjoyed these difficult topics. Some users found the channel to be unique and rare with interesting topics and expressions based on EFL learning. In D_3T_8, the people appreciated the advancement of this course of EFL learning and showed immense appreciation to this teacher. For this topic, it was also mentioned that a practical and easy way of learning was introduced, and teachers are increasingly struggling to teach lessons in an interesting way.

The people commenting on topic D_3T_9 also mention that they accidentally found an amazing and fluent English-speaking channel. The last topics are all practice- and interaction-based and lead to different, but fully positive, sentiments. The live sessions with students, users, and regular viewers are a unique and fruitful activity to teach English. The people themselves give positive remarks such as that they can never forget this fluent way of speaking English full of expressions and that they are more likely to understand it based on the positive expressions of the teacher.

4.3. User Difficulties Found in the Collected Datasets

In the collected datasets, although the sentiments mostly remained positive, there are a few concerns highlighted in all topic-based data from the scraping of datasets. The remarks of interest are represented as a word cloud in Figure 2, which summarizes the negative topics and remarks of dataset 1.

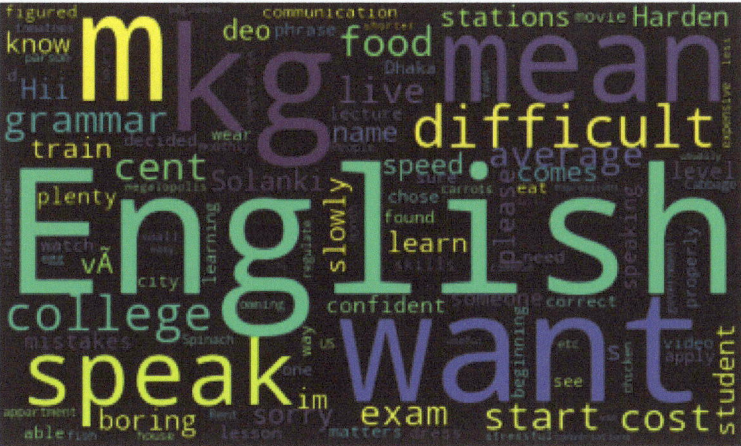

Figure 2. Word cloud of negative words in dataset 1 (D_1).

We can see from the word cloud that the topics of discussion are narrow in words such as that the user "wants" something; for example, "speak" loudly, "boring", "exams", "slowly", etc., are the top negative words used in dataset D_1 channel comments. The negative comments can be seen in detail in Table 6, which shows user negative remarks more deeply for the difficulty level.

Table 6. Top negative commented topics in dataset (D_1).

Serial Number	Topics
1	"im sorry this video is very boring"
2	"Why train stations i mean over and over again"
3	"Could you speak more slowly please It's very difficult to learn with that speed"
4	"exam is not easy exam is difficult"

Users' negative comments mainly revolved around a few areas which we discuss here. First, word repetition made videos according to users boring to watch. Speaking loudly is also a topic causing negativity in users' discussion, and speaking slowly is also another issue. In addition, exam difficulty, where applicable, is another source of negative sentiments that can be exhibited as a user's personal problem with the site.

To determine the difficult topics in dataset D_3, the top words of interest are also shown as a word cloud in Figure 3. The top words show, again, the positive remarks, and why a comment is marked as negative should be discussed. The negative topics are listed in Table 7.

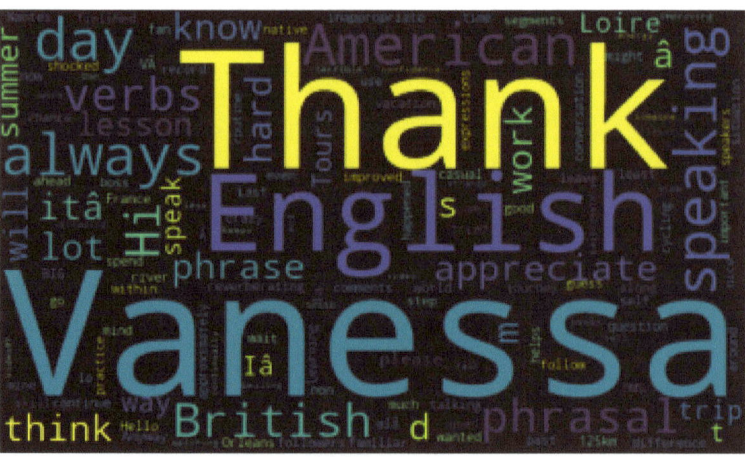

Figure 3. Word cloud of negative words in dataset 3 (D_3).

There is a mix of positive and negative words in negative marked comments in dataset 3. Words such as "thanks", "British", and "phrasal" need to be examined in more depth when looking at topics that are listed in Table 7.

Table 7. Top negative commented topics in dataset (D_3).

Serial Number	Topics
1	"Hi, this question has been reverberating in my mind for the past few days Is there any difference between American and British English phrasal verbs Does American use British phrasal verbs"
2	"Don't you think that is strange how they are always smiling"
3	"She speaks very fast Please someone needs tell him SLOW DOWN YOUR SPEED"

The topics with the highest keywords found in comments categorized as negative from TextBlob methods are shown in Figure 3, and the filtered topics are shown in Table 7. Most of the comments were expressing thanks to the content creator Vanessa, whereas the negative or questioning comments are showing that some users are asking whether British and American phrasal verbs are the same or different, and what the differences are. The other topic is the same as in dataset (D_3): "Slow down the speed of speaking where you speak very fast". The other topic is that the "user feels strange that teacher always keep smiling".

The topics of discussion with negative sentiment are quite the same and show that the user feels difficulty when they are learning. However, slowing the speed, which was found to be a common difficulty in users of different datasets, could be solved using the YouTube feature to slow down the video playback. The other remarks regarding always smiling is a single person's opinion, where most of the users that commented on dataset 3 videos highlighted the importance and happiness toward the expression of its teachers. Word repetition in video creation could be an irritating point while learning English. The created video does not need to be long, and if long, it should not be boring, ensuring that interesting facts and activities are added to avoid boredom.

4.4. Key Features of YouTube-Based EFL Learning

The most prominent key feature of YouTube-based EFL learning is its remote access and control. Restrictions such as those regarding time and speed are not relevant. YouTube also provides subtitles and options for speed increase and decrease when playing videos that could be more beneficial for listening and understanding video topics according to user interest. Punctuation and pronunciation problems can be addressed in either British or American Englishes, as both can be found on YouTube. The live streaming feature is now also of interest to engage students globally to ask questions and to give suggestions for acquiring a different set of skills within the EFL learning environment. We saw reviews from people that are mostly positive regarding online or YouTube-based EFL learning. This positivity relies on many key factors. The key points or features of YouTube-based EFL learning are video sharing among friends or classmates by teachers, which reduces the reproduction of the same lecture by the instructor. It also assists absent students to catch up on certain topics. The other feature could be its larger and more extraordinary syllabus or content compared with regular classroom-based textbook learning. Global viewership is another important feature which can be considered a strength of YouTube-based EFL learning. People from different nationalities watch these YouTube-based EFL learning channels and it would be interesting to gather more information of this global viewership (e.g. where the user posting the comment is actually from). The people that respond in comments are visually illustrated according to the country in Figure 4.

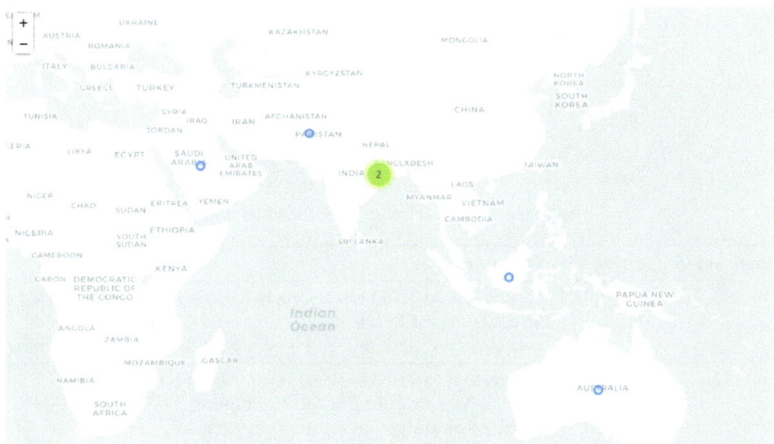

Figure 4. Users engaged in collected YouTube datasets from different regions of the world.

We can see that people from mostly the Asia Pacific region engaged in collected datasets viewership, whereas a few of them also belong to Saudi Arabia, Australia, and Indonesia. Few users are found in the United Kingdom, United States, and other European countries. Therefore, we could emphasize here that regions that people are mostly from may need more English learning, and those from other countries may also need EFL learning but not as much as people from Asia.

5. Hypothetical Findings and Suggestions

The topics of three different YouTube channels and discussions of their users were investigated in this study. Many new findings were uncovered, compared with previous studies, and the summarized hypothetical findings are discussed here and shown in Table 8. In H_1, classroom-based textbook learning has a traditional old syllabus, whereas it is found that YouTube channels include a larger syllabus and new content compared with textbooks. An issue for consideration, as stated in H_2, is determining how to learn English vocabulary and pronunciation, which is a basic topic discussed by one of the investigated YouTube channels. Therefore, it is found to be an important factor to be included in learning. It is also found that expression-based EFL learning is important as it includes the necessary accent, expression, etc., and is described in H_3. Fearless discussions between teachers and students are also an important factor in EFL learning that increases the confidence of learners and is shown in H_4. This will boost EFL learning. EFL learning varies according to people's interests, such as regarding British, American, and business English. Therefore, an acquired syllabus and content are needed in EFL learning, as mentioned in hypothesis H_5. A general and specific age-based understanding of EFL learning is required when designing an EFL course. H_6 shows this general requirement that needs to be added in courses.

In S_1, user-based suggestions are specifically given to learn English according to your interests. In S_2, trainer authentication needs to be cross-checked to determine whether the user is learning correctly or not. In S_3, each type of question asked in comments or live interaction should be answered to engage an increasingly larger audience. In S_4, ask the EFL learner what new things, improvements, and suggestions for things need to be added in future videos or courses. In S_5, one of the channels included animated videos and stories in which topic-wise discussion was added for listening and viewing by users. There are certain problems, challenges upon exploration, and discussion of datasets that are found listed in tabular format. There are two types of categories of findings from the YouTube channel datasets, and the user discussions on them were explored and used as a basis for deriving certain hypotheses and suggestions. From H1 to H5, how things are happening on different YouTube channels based on EFL learning is discussed.

The positive and dominant factors compared with regular classroom-based textual studies are discussed. These hypotheses play major roles in YouTube-based EFL learning compared with regular classroom EFL learning. However, a few suggestions made on user responses in comments were collected that could improve both classroom- and YouTube-based EFL learning.

Table 8. Hypothetical findings and suggestions (for better convergence) based upon dataset and user response upon watching YouTube videos.

Hypothetical Finding IDs	Hypothesis
H_1	Classroom-based EFL learning is confined to textbook-based old syllabus, whereas online YouTube-based EFL learning contains new, updated, and a variety of topics in EFL learning.
H_2	Suggestion to add a basic start topic in EFL learning such as how to learn English and how to learn vocabulary, conversation phrases, etc.
H_3	Real-time expressions while teaching English are much appreciated by users and are needed and play an important role in EFL learning.

Table 8. *Cont.*

Hypothetical Finding IDs	Hypothesis
H_4	For fearless discussion and student–teacher interaction, it is suggested that online YouTube-based EFL learning is added to regular practice in classrooms.
H_5	Each topic of EFL learning needs to be categorized and separately taught, such as British and American English, business and traveling English, etc.
H_6	Make and design courses in such a way that people of all ages can easily learn and understand English.
S_1	For online EFL learning, reach out to and search for a channel particular to your interest.
S_2	Authenticate the teacher/trainer from your classroom and instructor so that you do not learn incorrectly.
S_3	Respond to subscribed users to answer their silly and important questions to increase the audience and to ensure a better teaching style.
S_4	Ask users specifically what kind of EFL learning they want and what kinds of improvements could be made to their online courses.
S_5	Animated and object-based story creation can also be used to improve EFL learning, and live interaction is essential as it engages more users in topic-based discussion according to the findings of datasets.

6. Conclusions

The current study scraped the comment data of three different YouTube channels, using the YouTube developer-provided API service. The scraped data were collected and cleaned over a textual preprocessing phase and then assessed to determine user sentiments on topics discussed in them. Then, the user comments based on top and unique topics were collected to obtain user reviews of these. To obtain topics of user discussion, the LSA method was used, which works on the sentiments of a given document. In previous studies, manual inspection of YouTube-based EFL learning was conducted on limited datasets of mostly less than 100 people. Thus, they do not highlight the benefits and challenges of global users. However, this study used an automated method for data collection as well as to find topics in user comments. This resulted in making hypotheses regarding the importance and uniqueness of YouTube-based EFL learning. The benefits of this learning are also discussed, such as having a larger syllabus on YouTube as compared to textbook learning, expressions and punctuation following words, course design that covers a multinational audience and is suitable for learning by a student of any age, and allowing separate learning of each variety of English, such as British and American. Further, classroom-based EFL learning could also be improved by implementing the following suggestions: find the course of interest first based on one's needs which can be discussed with a tutor or any English teacher to optimize the learning experience, participate in fearless educator–learner interaction and engagement, and ask other EFL learners for their previous experiences with learning online in order for the learner to maximize benefit.

Author Contributions: Conceptualization, T.M. and H.M.A.; Methodology, T.M.; Software, T.M.; Validation, A.A. and H.T.R.; Formal analysis, H.M.A. and T.M.; Investigation, A.A.; Writing–review and editing, H.T.R. and H.M.A.; Supervision, H.M.A.; Project administration, H.M.A. All authors have read and agreed to the published version of the manuscript.

Funding: This research received no external funding.

Institutional Review Board Statement: Not applicable.

Informed Consent Statement: Not applicable.

Data Availability Statement: All data has been present in main text which is collected via YouTube platform and publically available to collect using available APIs.

Acknowledgments: This research was supported by the Researchers Supporting Project (RSPD2023R799), King Saud University, Riyadh, Saudi Arabia.

Conflicts of Interest: The author declare no conflict of interest.

References

1. Getie, A.S. Factors affecting the attitudes of students towards learning English as a foreign language. *Cogent Educ.* **2020**, *7*, 1738184. [CrossRef]
2. Macaro, E.; Jiménez Muñoz, A.; Lasagabaster, D. The importance of certification of English medium instruction teachers in higher education in Spain. *Porta Linguarum* **2019**, *32*, 103–118. [CrossRef]
3. Tahat, K.M.; Al-Sarayrah, W.; Salloum, S.A.; Habes, M.; Ali, S. The influence of YouTube videos on the learning experience of disabled people during the COVID-19 outbreak. In *Advances in Data Science and Intelligent Data Communication Technologies for COVID-19*; Springer: Berlin/Heidelberg, Germany, 2022; pp. 239–252.
4. European Commission (EC). *Making a European Area of Lifelong Learning a Reality*; European Commission: Brussels, Belgium, 2001.
5. Aoki, K. The use of ICT and e-learning in higher education in Japan. *Int. J. Educ. Pedagog. Sci.* **2010**, *4*, 986–990.
6. Reinders, H.; Benson, P. Research agenda: Language learning beyond the classroom. *Lang. Teach.* **2017**, *50*, 561–578. [CrossRef]
7. Buchem, I.; Pérez-Sanagustín, M. Personal learning environments in smart cities: Current approaches and future scenarios. In Proceedings of the PLE Conference 2013, Berlin, Germany, 10–12 July 2013; pp. 136–154.
8. Mikulecký, P. Smart environments for smart learning. In Proceedings of the DIVAI 2012 9th International Scientific Conference on Distance Learning in Applied Informatics, Sturovo, Slovakia, 2–4 May 2012; pp. 213–222.
9. Libbrecht, P.; Müller, W.; Rebholz, S. Smart learner support through semi-automatic feedback. In *Smart Learning Environments*; Springer: Berlin/Heidelberg, Germany, 2015; pp. 129–157.
10. Vaughan, T. *Multimedia: Making It Work*; McGraw-Hill, Inc.: New York, NY, USA, 2006.
11. Al-Mukhaini, E.M.; Al-Qayoudhi, W.S.; Al-Badi, A.H. Adoption of social networking in education: A study of the use of social networks by higher education students in Oman. *J. Int. Educ. Res.* **2014**, *10*, 143–154. [CrossRef]
12. Rice, D. Appendix 1: Use of ICTs for Inclusive Education. 2020. Available online: http://inova.snv.jussieu.fr/evenements/colloques/colloques/article.php?c=70&l=en&a=361 (accessed on 15 May 2022).
13. Grzeszczyk, K.B. Using multimedia in the English language classroom. *World Sci. News* **2016**, *43*, 104–157.
14. Pun, M. The use of multimedia technology in English language teaching: A global perspective. *Crossing Bord. Int. J. Interdiscip. Stud.* **2013**, *1*, 29–38. [CrossRef]
15. Wang, H.c.; Chen, C.W.y. Learning English from YouTubers: English L2 learners' self-regulated language learning on YouTube. *Innov. Lang. Learn. Teach.* **2020**, *14*, 333–346. [CrossRef]
16. Dizon, G. YouTube for Second Language Learning: What Does the Research Tell Us? *Aust. J. Appl. Linguist.* **2022**, *5*, 19–26.
17. Alobaid, A. Smart multimedia learning of ICT: Role and impact on language learners' writing fluency—YouTube online English learning resources as an example. *Smart Learn. Environ.* **2020**, *7*, 1–30. [CrossRef]
18. Wahyuni, A.; Utami, A.R.; Education, E. the Use of Youtube Video in Encouraging Speaking Skill. *Pustakailmu. Id* **2021**, *7*, 1–9.
19. Nasution, A.K.R. YouTube as a media in English language teaching (ELT) context: Teaching procedure text. *Utamax J. Ultim. Res. Trends Educ.* **2019**, *1*, 29–33. [CrossRef]
20. Putri, F.H. Youtube for self-regulated language learning: An EFL perspective. *Engl. Educ. J. Tadris Bhs. Ingg.* **2019**, *12*, 42–57.
21. Rahayu, S.P.; Putri, W.S. Uploading speaking assignment to YouTube channel as an effort in increasing student's pronunciation skill. *EnJourMe (Engl. J. Merdeka) Cult. Lang. Teach. Engl.* **2018**, *3*, 35–45. [CrossRef]
22. Aprianto, D. To what extent does youtube contents-based language learning promote An English proficiency? *J. Engl. Lang. Teach. Lit.* **2020**, *3*, 108–126. [CrossRef]
23. Khoiroh, S.A. Using YouTube for speaking in online learning: EFL students' perception and difficulties. *Res. Engl. Lang. Teach. Indones* **2021**, *9*, 202–211.
24. Novawan, A.; Alvarez-Tosalem, S.M.; Ismailia, T.; Wicaksono, J.A.; Setiarini, R.B. Students' Experiences of Online English Language Learning by Using YouTube. In Proceedings of the The First International Conference on Social Science, Humanity, and Public Health (ICOSHIP 2020), Online, 7–8 November 2020; Atlantis Press: Dordrecht, The Netherlands, 2021; pp. 220–226.
25. Al-Jarf, R. YouTube videos as a resource for self-regulated pronunciation practice in EFL distance learning environments. *J. Engl. Lang. Teach. Appl. Linguist.* **2022**, *4*, 44–52. [CrossRef]
26. Simanjuntak, U.S.; Silalahi, D.E.; Sihombing, P.S.; Purba, L. Students'perceptions of using youtube as English online learning media during COVID-19 pandemic. *J. Lang. Lang. Teach.* **2021**, *9*, 150–159. [CrossRef]
27. Learn English with EnglishClass101.com—youtube.com. Available online: https://www.youtube.com/c/EnglishClass101 (accessed on 3 November 2022).

28. Learn English with Jessica—youtube.com. Available online: https://www.youtube.com/c/LearnEnglishwithJessica (accessed on 3 November 2022).
29. Speak English with Vanessa—youtube.com. Available online: https://www.youtube.com/c/TeacherVanessa (accessed on 3 November 2022).
30. Landauer, T.K. LSA as a theory of meaning. In *Handbook of Latent Semantic Analysis*; Psychology Press: London, UK, 2007; pp. 15–46.
31. Martinez, A.M.; Kak, A.C. Pca versus lda. *IEEE Trans. Pattern Anal. Mach. Intell.* **2001**, *23*, 228–233. [CrossRef]
32. Wall, M.E.; Rechtsteiner, A.; Rocha, L.M. Singular value decomposition and principal component analysis. In *A Practical Approach to Microarray Data Analysis*; Springer: Berlin/Heidelberg, Germany, 2003; pp. 91–109.

Disclaimer/Publisher's Note: The statements, opinions and data contained in all publications are solely those of the individual author(s) and contributor(s) and not of MDPI and/or the editor(s). MDPI and/or the editor(s) disclaim responsibility for any injury to people or property resulting from any ideas, methods, instructions or products referred to in the content.

Article

Portuguese Teachers' Conceptions of the Use of Microsoft 365 during the COVID-19 Pandemic

Joaquim Escola [1,2], Natália Lopes [1], Paula Catarino [3,4] and Ana Paula Aires [3,4,*]

[1] Department of Education and Psychology, University of Trás-os-Montes e Alto Douro, 5000-801 Vila Real, Portugal
[2] IF—Institute of Philosophy, University of Porto, 4150-564 Porto, Portugal
[3] Department of Mathematics, University of Trás-os-Montes e Alto Douro, 5000-801 Vila Real, Portugal
[4] CIDTFF—Research Centre on Didactics and Technology in the Education of Trainers, 3810-193 Aveiro, Portugal
* Correspondence: aaires@utad.pt

Citation: Escola, J.; Lopes, N.; Catarino, P.; Aires, A.P. Portuguese Teachers' Conceptions of the Use of Microsoft 365 during the COVID-19 Pandemic. *Computers* **2022**, *11*, 185. https://doi.org/10.3390/computers11120185

Academic Editors: Antonio Sarasa Cabezuelo and Covadonga Rodrigo San Juan

Received: 4 November 2022
Accepted: 9 December 2022
Published: 14 December 2022

Publisher's Note: MDPI stays neutral with regard to jurisdictional claims in published maps and institutional affiliations.

Copyright: © 2022 by the authors. Licensee MDPI, Basel, Switzerland. This article is an open access article distributed under the terms and conditions of the Creative Commons Attribution (CC BY) license (https://creativecommons.org/licenses/by/4.0/).

Abstract: In 2020, education found itself involved in a whirlwind of metamorphosis, of transformations that required responses to the emergencies dictated by the pandemic. In Portugal, many schools opted for Microsoft 365 as the platform of choice for providing adequate resources for teaching and learning processes, while also ensuring remote teaching in an integrated and inclusive way. In this context, we carried out an investigation with the objectives of knowing the opinion of teachers about the use of Microsoft 365 in their classes and identify their degree of satisfaction with its use. The methodology adopted had a descriptive and exploratory nature, following a mixed paradigm. A total of 101 primary and secondary school teachers from schools in Northern Portugal participated in the study. A questionnaire and an interview were used as data collection instruments. The results showed that the most respondents revealed a high level of satisfaction with the use of Microsoft 365, and that its use was accompanied by the employment of active methodologies. Moreover, despite the lack of initial or ongoing training of teachers in the use of this technology and the students' lack of digital competence, Microsoft 365 proved to be an adequate response to the confinement and ensured students' learning in a safe environment.

Keywords: Microsoft 365; digital platforms; distance learning; active methodologies; good practices

1. Introduction

In the same way that work contexts have shifted—seeing an increase in teleworking and the use of devices to support remote working—in the last two years, distance learning has proven to be a practical, cheaper, and pedagogically viable option for students and teachers from all corners of the world. The pandemic situation experienced demanded profound changes in education. All citizens felt a deep need to adjust behavior, practices and, in the educational universe, we were invited to reinvent ourselves. Teachers felt the imperative need to change their practices and adapt their way of teaching. In this sense, to promote the development of teachers' digital skills, necessary for the effective use of digital technologies, and to respond to the demands of an increasingly digital society, the Directorate General for Education (DGE) developed the Digital Teacher Training Plan, which is still in progress. In this framework of digital transformation of schools, digital platforms gradually achieve a more evident centrality. In fact, it is no longer possible to delay the curricular integration of technologies into teaching practices, to stop exploring them as allies in the demanding task of increasing students' motivation, arousing in them the desire to search for and build knowledge. Thus, the teacher will have the difficult mission of adapting methodologies that lead an effective learning, promoting the use of active methodologies, and the curricular integration of digital technologies. For this to happen, the teacher will have to maintain availability to receive and train themselves to learn and continue the path of constant updating. However, the principal objective of teacher training for educational use cannot be limited to the instrumental domain of technological resources. It is imperative to identify needs, to understand the potential of each device, and to develop skills for their use even before their application for educational purposes [1]. Every day, teachers have many teaching platforms at their disposal and use them to better organize students' learning activities, fostering a classroom climate more conducive to knowledge construction and teacher collaboration [2,3]. Digital educational learning platforms are programs that bring together an extensive group of tools that facilitate the activities of teachers and students and are intended to support distance learning [4]. They allow organizing communication processes, interaction between teachers and students, transmitting content, providing activities, or even assessing students' learning. At the same time, by using synchronous and asynchronous communication tools, the platforms facilitate the constitution of virtual learning communities, exploring themes of common interest, carrying out joint activities [5].

Microsoft 365, along with other platforms, gained extraordinary importance and attention from education systems—especially with the pandemic that invaded the world. As a result of the difficulties caused by COVID-19, Microsoft 365 became one of the most chosen supports by Portuguese schools, as it continued to provide tools agile and powerful enough to promote learning, collaboration, and communication. At the same time, it continued to provide a safe and trusted environment for teachers and students to work. However, we must ask: are teachers happy with the uptake of this platform? What kind of use is being made of Microsoft 365 by teachers? Which methodologies are most used with Microsoft 365 by teachers? Our study will seek to answer these questions.

Certainly, technology will continue to gain the recognition of all and will prevail in teaching and teachers will continue the arduous task of integrating it, overcoming the more rigid dimensions of the traditional school. More technology, more practical teaching and assessment methods, and more autonomous and creative students are some of the trends that schools can hardly escape.

2. Microsoft 365 and Education in Times of Pandemic

The presence of Digital Information and Communication Technologies in citizens' daily lives has contributed to their more systematic and critical integration by teachers in educational institutions. In this sense, it is agreed that the use of digital technologies of information and communication can play a relevant role in educational processes, providing new supports and diversified strategies for teaching and learning content established in curricula [6–8]. In the last two years, because of the difficulties of the pandemic context, learning platforms have gained an extraordinary visibility and constitute an essential—even unquestionable—means in the promotion of teaching and learning. The fact that they are hosted on the web makes it easier for teachers and students to access content or software, regardless of space and time, reinforcing their ubiquitous nature. It thus seems unquestionable that the inclusion of platforms in education has become an irrefutable fact. Moreover, the adoption of a learning platform lends greater dynamism to teaching by making it possible to combine different formats in the same space. Currently, the platforms provide a considerable number of resources and tools that can include video, animations, access and participation in forums, chat, tests, assessments, and that enrich the students' experience [5]. It is important to note that these are not only used in the school context, within what is established as the academic period, but also as a central place for complementary learning outside of this context and school time [9]. Learning platforms, especially in the framework of formal education, present more and more possibilities for pedagogical exploration that cannot be ignored, with emphasis on communication, collaboration, inclusion, and innovation processes. Microsoft 365 imposes itself today as a space for pedagogical innovation, where collaborative and inclusive learning takes place. Aware of the pedagogical potential that this platform has, and drawing upon the lessons of the last two years, it has become increasingly urgent that teachers have specific training to explore the possibilities at its disposal, always inviting students to participate actively in building their learning. The fact that they were born, grew up, and continue to be involved in a digital environment—increasingly global and technological—reinforces a growing confidence in these devices as being suitable for learning. To that extent, they challenge teachers—with each new activity proposal—to investigate its potentialities, to explore the possibilities of students' involvement, interaction, and participation in learning that they provide [10]. This facility with which students deal with technological devices does not correspond—as Cabero-Almenara [11] (p. 3), and Cabero-Almenara and Valencia-Ortiz [12] (p. 224) argue—to the effective existence of digital competencies on their part. In fact, in these authors' studies the students revealed difficulties in adapting to the virtual teaching context, which shows that students lack digital literacy. Wang et al. [13], against the widespread idea that there is some idea of the difference in digital skills between teachers and students, argue that there is no evidence that teachers have less digital competence than students.

Microsoft 365 covers a huge variety of applications, features, and possibilities, so it was and is a powerful ally in distance learning that imposes itself as an extraordinary solution for a learning experience in hybrid contexts, accessible through mobile communications, cell phone, tablet, or computer [14]. Over the past few years, the possibilities of distance learning have been an increasingly present reality in the education system of all countries in the world due to the possibilities of digital platforms, made visible by teachers' practices. These involve different types of tools which guarantee the most suitable conditions for distance learning to take place [4]. Building virtual learning environments supported by Digital Information and Communication Technologies is one of the priority functions of the platforms, in which teachers can carefully manage the contents to be taught, organize communication processes, and carry out tutorial monitoring of students [15]. Exploring the various aspects that the platforms offer, we find that they can be used to transmit content and propose activities, monitor student work, solve doubts by providing appropriate feedback, create spaces for interactive communication, and promote the assessment of student progress. Furthermore, it should not be forgotten that they are also useful for creating discussion and workspaces for research groups or even for implementing virtual communities and wider learning networks that are so relevant at all levels of education [16,17]. The use of the platform reinforced the need for the use of active methodologies to support learning activities and teaching strategies that would better respond to the integration of digital technologies in teachers' practice. The flipped classroom [18], project pedagogy [19], project-based learning, gamification [20–22], and STEAM [23–25], are—among other active methodologies—the ones that received most attention from the teachers we interviewed about the use of Microsoft 365. Thus, we wanted to know the opinion of teachers from some northern Portuguese schools on the use of this platform in their teaching practice. The digital skills they show, the changes in practices resulting from the use of Microsoft 365, the transformation of their conception of teaching, the modification of methodological options and the more systematic use of active methodologies were some of the dimensions that the survey by questionnaire and the survey by interview aimed to explain.

This paper aims to analyze the ways in which Microsoft 365 has been used during the last two years with regard to pedagogical dimensions and the organization of teaching and learning processes.

3. Methods

3.1. Methodological Options

In order to analyze the way of Microsoft 365 has been used during the last two years, with regard to pedagogical dimensions and the organization of teaching and learning processes, we conducted one study with Portuguese teachers. The methodology selected to carry out the study is based on a mixed paradigm [26–28], combining both quantitative and qualitative dimensions. They are used and articulated data collection instruments adjusted to the selected paradigm and methodology, as is the case of the survey by questionnaire and the survey by interview.

In this context, we formulated the following research objectives:

1. To understand how the schools in the northern interior of Portugal that chose Microsoft 365 made use of it;
2. To appreciate the level of teacher satisfaction with the use of Microsoft 365;
3. To understand teachers' perceptions about the advantages or disadvantages of using the platform to organize the teaching and learning processes;
4. To understand teachers' perceptions about the advantages and disadvantages of using the platform to improve results and practice;
5. To analyze if the use of Microsoft 365 has been accompanied by the use of active methodologies;
6. To analyze if the use of Microsoft 365 has facilitated the teachers' actions;
7. To identify the type of training needs experienced by schools and teachers in using Microsoft 365 over the past two years.

3.2. Participants

As for the research context, we chose schools in the northern interior of Portugal. In total, 101 teachers from all study cycles of the Portuguese education system participated in this study, 69 of whom were female and 32 males. Regarding the age of the participants in the study, we have: 34.7% of the teachers between 41 and 50 years of age; 17.8% from 31 to 40 years of age; and 26.7% in the 51 to 60 age bracket. At the extremes, we note that only 3% are under 30 years of age and 17.8% are over 60. If we consider between the age of 41 and retirement age (67 years) we find that almost 80% of the teachers who participated in the study are in this range.

The Portuguese education system consists of four study cycles:

- Basic education: first cycle, from first to fourth year (ages 6 to 10); second cycle, from fifth to sixth year (ages 11 to 12); third cycle, from seventh to ninth year (ages 13 to 15).
- Secondary education consists of three years: 10th, 11th, and 12th years (ages 16 to 18).

It should be noted that 63.3% of the participants in the research belong to the female gender and, in terms of age, most of them are over 40 years old. Teachers who participated in the research were from all study cycles of the Portuguese education system—13.9% from the first cycle of basic education, 23.8% from the second cycle of basic education, 35.6% from the third cycle of basic education, and 26.7% from secondary education.

Regarding teachers' professional situation, the data reveal a relatively high degree of stability, since 80.8% have an indefinitely labor contract with the state. Nineteen participants (18.8%) have a fixed-term contract with the state, and only one participant is in pedagogic internship.

A large majority of teachers (91.1%) are linked to teaching in public education, and only 8.9% work in the private sector.

Regarding their academic qualifications, 49.5% of teachers report having a degree. In addition, 36 teachers (36%) also hold a Master's degree, and 7 teachers (6.9%) also hold a Ph.D.

3.3. Procedures and Instruments

In the research design, we established three essential moments in the development of the process. In the first moment, a questionnaire was given to teachers in schools in the northern interior of Portugal. In the second moment, the questionnaires were analyzed in order to identify teachers, distributed among the various study cycles of the Portuguese education system, who showed a better knowledge of the Microsoft 365 platform and who had good practices with this platform. From the analysis of the questionnaire, we identified eight teachers (here identified as E1, E2, E3, ... , E8), two for each study cycle, purposely concealing their identity.

In the third moment, a survey by interview was carried out with the chosen teachers.

Regarding the questionnaire, it was structured in two parts. The first part includes 10 closed-ended questions, called "Characterization of teachers and their school environment" and these questions aimed to collect information on aspects and dimensions that allow characterizing teachers—such as age, education, professional situation, and their school environment. The second part consisted of 15 questions which aimed to understand how teachers make use of the Microsoft 365 platform and, at the same time, to judge their level of satisfaction.

The questionnaire was specially designed for this study, having been subject to a validation process by two national and two international experts in the scientific field of Education Sciences, belonging to higher education institutions to understand the relevance of its content and the suitability of the established items. In the process of validating the questionnaire, we followed the guidelines of researchers Almeida and Freire [29], who recommend submitting the questionnaires to experts to check if the data collection instrument was properly designed; if the questions were carefully formulated so as to collect the desired information; if the information is available to be collected; if information is missing; and finally, if there is a lack of questions that may be essential to the achievement of the research objectives.

Within any research, the issues of credibility and validity—although they have different meanings—go hand in hand. In fact, the data collection instrument used in this research considered a series of requirements that fundamentally determine whether it is adequate and whether it serves to measure what is intended. For the data coming from the application of a data collection instrument to be interpreted, the data collection instrument must, according to Ribeiro and Ribeiro [30], have reliability and validity because they determine the quality of any measuring instrument. To correctly assess the accuracy of the applied questionnaire, we chose to use statistical analysis to obtain a coefficient of internal consistency also called Cronbach's alpha since the 'ideal' is almost impractical, given the time restrictions of our research. In our opinion, it makes sense to assess internal consistency by calculating Cronbach's Alpha when it comes to a set of items on the same Likert scale. Therefore, using the items in the question where they were asked to indicate their level of satisfaction with each of the components, the results show a good internal consistency of the questionnaire, with the alpha value equal to 0.869. According to Pestana and Gageiro [31] the alpha value that guarantees a good internal consistency of a questionnaire should be between 0.8 and 0.9. Thus, the alpha value found allows us to conclude that our questionnaire has a good internal consistency.

The survey by interview, applied to eight teachers that resulted from the analysis of the questionnaire, was organized into eight dimensions: (a) identification elements, (b) Microsoft 365 use context, (c) resource domain, (d) objectives for use, (e) description of the practice, (f) difficulties experienced, (g) results, and (h) future perspectives. For the analysis of the interview data, the content analysis [32] was used and the following categories were established a priori: academic training, professional experience, continuous training in the use of digital devices, digital skills, contexts of use of Microsoft 365, technical competences of use, purposes in the use of the Microsoft 365, good practices, difficulties/obstacles in the use of Microsoft 365, learning outcomes, and prognosis.

Table 1 presents the organization of the content analysis where in addition to the dimensions and categories, the respective indicators are listed.

For data analysis, we used Microsoft Excel 2010 software, which allowed us to process and prepare charts and tables, since it is an adequate tool for research and does not require complex statistical models which are not included in this study. We also used descriptive statistics to consider not only the frequencies, but also the percentages reached in each answer. For the analysis of the interviews, we used content analysis [32] employing the qualitative analysis software, Nvivo (Creator: QSR International, Version number: 13 (free version)).

Table 1. Dimensions, categories, and indicators for analysis.

Dimensions	Categories	Indicators
Identification elements	Academic training	Bachelor's degree Graduation Master's PhD
	Professional experience	Internship; time of service
	Continuous training in the use of digital devices	Did training on Microsoft 365 Did ICT training No training
Microsoft 365 use context	Digital skills	Basic user; Advanced user; Develops innovative resources.
	Contexts of use of Microsoft 365	Use: - less than 1 year ago - one year ago - two years ago - over 3 years ago Uses synchronous times Uses asynchronous times Uses with other platforms Use on computer Use on mobile phone
Resource domain	Technical competences of use	Know all the Microsoft 365 applications Knows some Microsoft 365 applications Uses all Microsoft 365 applications Use some Microsoft 365 applications
Objectives for use	Purposes in the use of the Microsoft 365	Organize teaching and learning materials Provide learning materials to students Assessing students Contacting students Contacting parents
Description of the practice	Good practices	Using Microsoft 365 synchronously and asynchronously Using Microsoft 365 together with other platforms Use of Microsoft 365 to develop teaching resources
Difficulties experienced	Difficulties/obstacles in the use of Microsoft 365	Difficulty in installation Difficulty in using some applications Difficulty sharing documents Difficulty in synchronous sessions Difficulty in asynchronous sessions. No difficulties
Results	Learning outcomes	Facilitates learning outcomes Improves learning outcomes Difficulties in achieving learning outcomes
Future perspectives	Prognosis	Continue to use Microsoft 365 Continue to use Microsoft 365 and increase your usage

4. Discussion and Results

The results of this research are collected, considering the results obtained in the survey by questionnaire and the survey by interview.

4.1. Survey by Questionnaire

Regarding the degree of satisfaction of teachers regarding the use of the Microsoft 365 platform, the results reveal that—regarding the level of competence in the use of Microsoft 365 education—most of the responding teachers (75.3%) consider that their level is not beginner, but medium (63.4%) or advanced (11.9%), and that they have not undergone adequate training for the use of this platform. The issue of training, specifically in relation to the lack of specific training for the use of distance learning platforms, is in concordance with the national results presented in other studies [2,3,33,34]. The teachers who received training in this area did so mainly during the period of confinement in which distance learning was used. 30% had training before the confinement, 66.7% during the period of confinement, and only 3.3% after this period. In fact, the results show that in the context of the pandemic, the teachers had not had specific training for a teaching context such as this, i.e., they had no training to respond to such a challenging circumstance for the entire school community. In such an adverse and emergency context, there is a clear need to create the conditions and structures that can respond to an adequate teacher training program. In line with Moreira and Schlemmer [35], we argue that the demands of the "new normal" show the imperative need to adjust to a complex reality where the multicultural, multidisciplinary, and multidimensional character is evident.

From the analysis of the participants' answers, we can see that when teachers needed help using the Microsoft 365 platform, 32.7% turned to someone in the school support structure, 30.7% looked for information on YouTube, 27.7% stated that they had the support of a colleague, and only 8.9% revealed that they had resorted to the help of the ICT coordinator of their school group. These results are in consonance with the study by Marôco [3], where 74% of the teachers stated that they had not appealed to the support of formal, institutional networks (ICT Coordinator of the School), and 90% of the respondents stated that they had not requested any help from specialized technical services or even consultants external to the school. In the same line, Escola [33] noted that the fact that teachers had not received initial or continuing training on distance learning platforms had not stopped them from continuing their teaching activities even when they were confined. Teachers kept in contact with students by using informal groups, social networks, colleagues, friends, or even family members. This context also helped the dialogue and collaboration between teachers [33].

From the point of view of the time when the teachers started using the Microsoft 365 platform, it can be seen from Figure 1 that most of the teachers participating in this study (42 respondents) only started using Microsoft 365 at the beginning of the confinement period imposed by COVID-19.

From the analysis of the data in Figure 2, the Microsoft 365 applications that teachers use the most are Teams, "synchronous interaction tool" [14], Word, Forms, Outlook, and PowerPoint. Skype is the tool that reaped the least use from the teachers who participated in the study.

The question about the advantages of using Microsoft 365 in education provided a set of data presented in Table 2 and worth reflecting on. Note that each participant could choose more than one option. For 26.3% of the teachers, the use of Microsoft 365 allows for proper management of classes and individual students, through the Notepad, a tool that allows for scheduling of activities, notes, communications with students or parents, among others. 21.2% of the teachers consider that the platform simplifies the organization of teaching and learning materials, and a very close percentage of teachers (19.2%) argue that it facilitates communication with students and promotes greater contact with them. 16.2% think that it allows additional learning material to be made available to students. Security issues attracted the attention of 15.1% of the teachers, who are convinced that the platform provides greater security for both teachers and students, since only registered teachers and students can access class content. A very small percentage of teachers (2%) consider that Microsoft 365 offers a suitable environment for conducting online tests or quizzes.

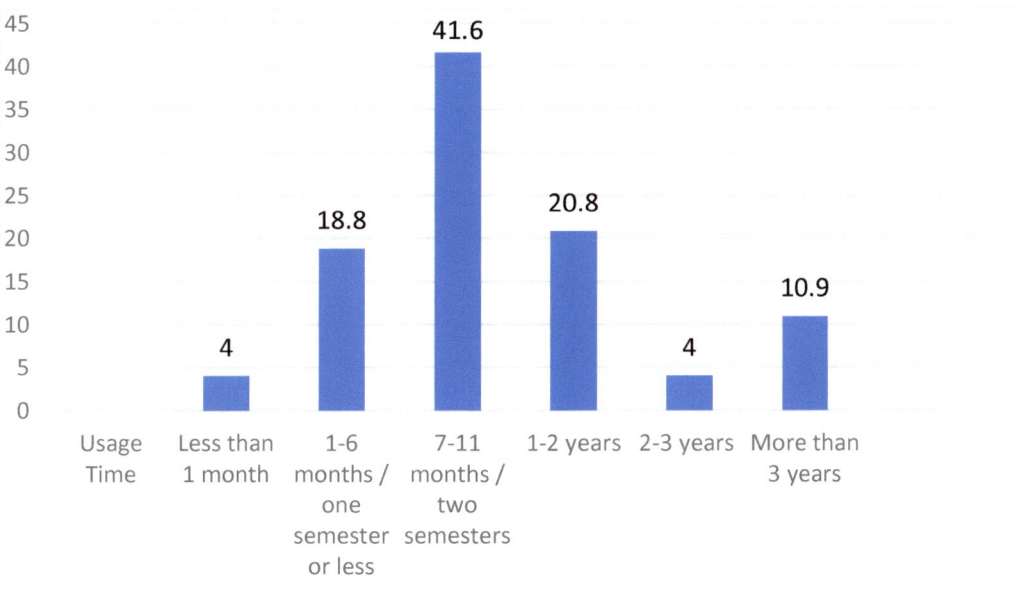

Figure 1. Microsoft 365 usage time.

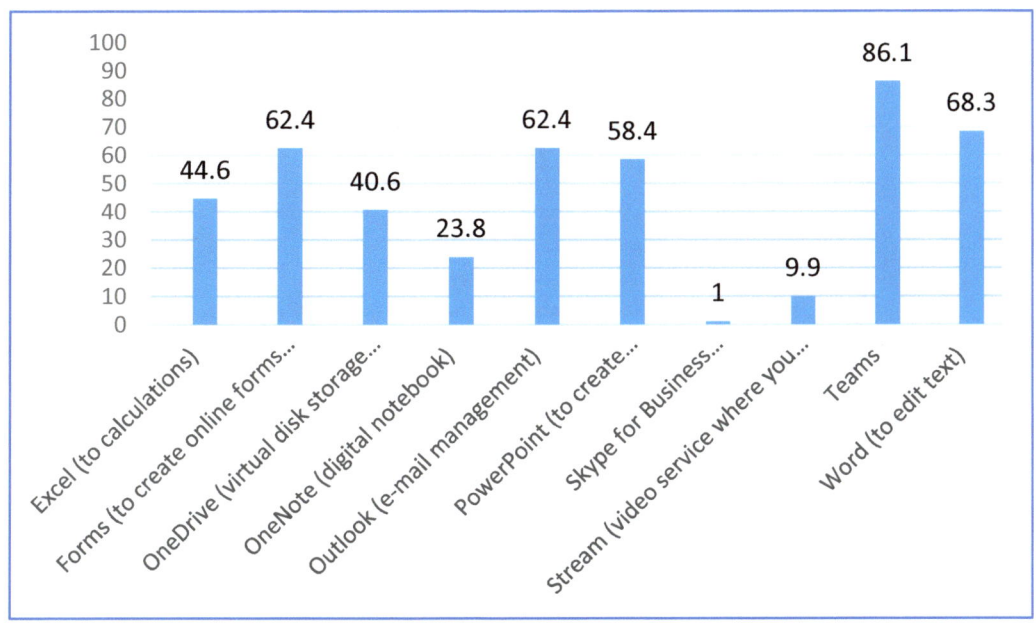

Figure 2. Microsoft 365 applications to carry out teaching activities.

Table 2. Most significant pedagogical advantage of using Microsoft 365 Education.

Most Significant Advantage of Using Microsoft 365 Education	Fr.	%
Gives security to students and teachers (only registered teachers and students have access to class contents)	15	15.1
Provides a suitable environment for conducting online tests or questionnaires	2	2
Provides an adequate management of classes and individual students (Notepad) (ex.: scheduling of activities, notes, communications to students or guardians, ...)	26	26.3
It facilitates greater contact with students	19	19.2
Organizes teaching and learning materials	21	21.2
Allows additional learning material to be made available to students	16	16.2
TOTAL	99(*)	100

(*) Total number of responses from 101 participants of this study.

A very relevant fact is that, with the end of the confinement and the return to face-to-face teaching, even if maintaining security measures and physical distance, digital platforms continued to be used, although at a lower level. It is important not to forget that, according to the results of Marôco's study [3], 35% of the teachers surveyed declared that they had never used a distance learning platform, (Moodle, Classroom, MSTeams, or any other) [34]. This study reinforces precisely this perception of ours (Cf. Table 3), since more than half of the responding teachers—equivalent to 45.6%—continued to use Microsoft 365 to support or complement face-to-face teaching (supplementary material is made available online for teaching or study); 27.2% use it for classes in mixed format, hybrid teaching (in some cases there are teaching units that are organized online); and 20.8% used it to contact parents. Only 6.4% use it to support and clarify students' doubts and to contact students and other teachers. Once more, we recall that each participant could choose more than one option.

Table 3. Use Microsoft 365 when teaching face-to-face.

Now that We Are in Face-to-Face Teaching, Use Microsoft 365:	Fr.	%
Just to contact the guardians	26	20.8
For mixed-format classes (some program units are taken online)	34	27.2
To complement face-to-face teaching (additional material is posted online)	57	45.6
Other	8	6.4
TOTAL	125(*)	100

(*) Total number of responses from 101 participants of this study.

The results obtained are in line with the results of some national research. Ribeirinha and Silva [2] consider that teaching in the future will tend to be hybrid, where we will be able to observe distance learning tools being integrated into teachers' teaching practices; in the research of Marôco [3] it is clear the intention to continue to use it in the future in a mixed regime. The interviews conducted with some of the teachers who responded to this questionnaire survey, already in the year 2022, confirm the continuity in the use of the Microsoft 365 platform.

It should be noted that teachers who responded to the questionnaire survey stated they use other platforms in addition to Microsoft 365. In fact, the data in Table 4 show that 14.2% of teachers also used Google Classroom, 19.1% used Leya's Aula Digital, 28.4% used Porto Editora's Virtual School, and 38.3% of teachers used Zoom/Colibri. This latter platform is very popular with Portuguese teachers. As we have mentioned before, each participant could choose more than one option.

Table 4. Other platforms used.

Other Platform(s) You Have Already Used, as A Student/Trainee or as a Teacher/Trainer	Fr.	%
Leya's Digital Class	39	19.1
Google Classroom	29	14.2
Porto Editora Virtual School	58	28.4
Zoom/Colibri	78	38.3
TOTAL	204(*)	100

(*) Total number of responses from 101 participants of this study.

As time goes by and despite the return to face-to-face teaching, the idea that the use of platforms will remain [2,31,32] is being consolidated. Regarding the question about the progression in the use of Microsoft 365 since the time it was implemented, it is perhaps important underlining very relevant data: only 1% of respondents reported making a lesser use of Microsoft 365 and, 66.3% of respondents state that they increasingly use this platform. Only 32.7% claim to make a similar use to the one they did in the initial period of the pandemic (Figure 3).

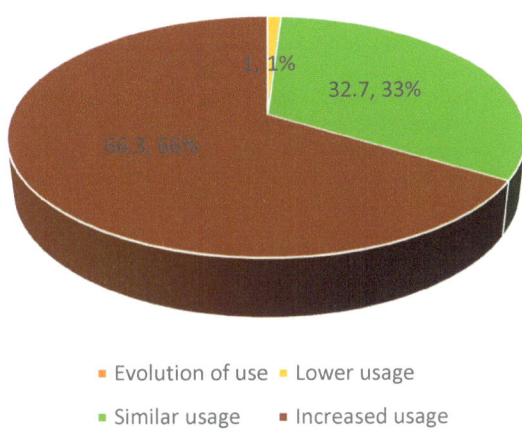

Figure 3. Evolution of the use of the Microsoft 365 platform since its implementation.

These results corroborate those of the study by Ribeirinha and Silva [2] who argue that, due to the needs imposed by the pandemic, we would see a reinforcement of the use of distance learning resources. The position of Cabero-Almenara [11], although referring to the Spanish educational context, considers that the pandemic led to profound transformations in the educational system, making it possible to observe the passage from a model centered on the transmission of information, with the emphasis on the face-to-face dimension, to a model strongly centered and mediated by technologies.

Concerning the possibilities offered by the Microsoft 365 platform, we can say that the satisfaction level of participants is very high. In fact, more than three four of the teachers (78.2%) are satisfied with what they can do with the platform. Teachers are of the opinion that the platform provides schools, teachers, and students with the resources they need to continue learning in a remote learning context, as shown in Figure 4. Only 3% are very dissatisfied.

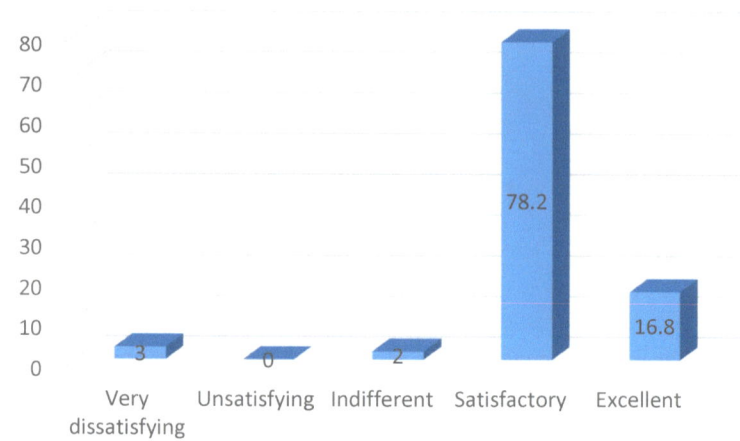

Figure 4. Overall satisfaction with the activities you can do with Microsoft 365.

To understand more clearly the degree of teachers' satisfaction about the dimensions: Intuitiveness and way of organizing materials on the platform; quickness/speed of learning the interface and way of navigating; assessment tools (tests, questionnaires, ...); help/Guidance Tools; collaborative features (sharing files and other resources; agenda, calendar, ...); communication features with other teachers from the same educational community; communication features with students; access to the educational contents of the course (materials format, e.g., flash, html, pdf); integration with mobile communication devices (e.g., tablet, mobile phone); integration with other collaborative applications (e.g., online whiteboards, forums, ...), we present Tables 5–8. To evaluate the degree of teachers' satisfaction regarding the different dimensions of Microsoft 365, a five-level Likert scale was used with the correspondence: 1—very dissatisfying; 2—unsatisfying; 3—indifferent; 4—satisfactory; and 5—excellent.

Table 5. Teachers' satisfaction regarding the intuitiveness and ways of organizing materials and quickness/speed of learning the interface and the way of navigating.

	Fr.	%	Fr.	%
	Intuitiveness and Way of Organizing Materials on the Platform		Quickness/Speed of Learning the Interface and Way of Navigating	
Very dissatisfying	2	2	0	0
Unsatisfying	2	2	3	3
Indifferent	8	7.9	7	6.9
Satisfactory	79	78.2	80	79.2
Excellent	10	9.9	11	10.9
TOTAL	101	100	101	100
Mean		3.92		3.98
Standard deviation		0.66		0.55

Table 6. Teacher satisfaction with assessment and help/guidance tools.

	Fr.	%	Fr.	%
	Assessment Tools (Tests, Questionnaires, ...)		Help/Guidance Tools	
Very dissatisfying	1	1.0	1	1
Unsatisfying	8	7.9	3	3
Indifferent	10	9.9	12	11.9
Satisfactory	66	65.3	76	75.2
Excellent	16	15.8	9	8.9
TOTAL	101	100	101	100
Mean	4.21		3.88	
Standard deviation	0.62		0.64	

Table 7. Teacher satisfaction regarding collaborative features, communication with other teachers, and students.

	Fr.	%	Fr.	%	Fr.	%
	Collaborative Features (Sharing Files and Other Resources; Agenda, Calendar, ...)		Communication Features with other Teachers from the Same Educational Community		Communication Features with Students	
Very dissatisfying	1	1	1	1	0	0
Unsatisfying	1	1	0	0	1	1
Indifferent	2	2	4	4	1	1
Satisfactory	69	68.3	67	66.3	67	66.3
Excellent	28	27.7	29	28.7	32	31.7
TOTAL	101	100	101	100	101	100
Mean	4.21		4.22		4.29	
Standard deviation	0.62		0.61		0.54	

Table 8. Teachers' satisfaction in accessing the contents of the subjects, integration with mobile communication devices and collaborative applications.

	Fr.	%	Fr.	%	Fr.	%
	Access to the Educational Contents of the Course (Materials Format, e.g., Flash, html, pdf)		Integration with Mobile Communication Devices (e.g., Tablet, Mobile Phone)		Integration with Other Collaborative Applications (e.g., Online Whiteboards, Forums, ...)	
Very dissatisfying	1	1	0	0	2	1.98
Unsatisfying	2	2	3	3	2	1.98
Indifferent	18	17.8	19	18.8	25	24.75
Satisfactory	71	70.3	61	60.4	62	61.39
Excellent	9	8.9	18	17.8	10	9.9
TOTAL	101	100	101	100	101	100
Mean	3.84		3.93		3.75	
Standard deviation	0.64		0.7		0.74	

Almost 10% of respondents considered Microsoft 365 an excellent platform with respect to the intuitiveness and organization of the materials on the platform, and 78.2% were satisfied with the platform in this dimension. Only 4.0% are unsatisfied or very unsatisfied. Regarding the speed/celerity of learning of the interface and form of navigation, four out of five teachers (79.2%) mentioned that they are satisfied and only 3% state that they are dissatisfied. About two-thirds of the respondents (65.3%) are satisfied with the assessment tools as well as the help and guidance tools (Table 6). However, if we look at the results where the question "What was the biggest educational advantage of Microsoft 365" was answered, a residual percentage considered that this platform provides a suitable environment for conducting online tests or quizzes. The study of Marôco [3] also indicated the difficulties revealed by teachers in the use of distance learning platforms for assessment tasks: 14% of the respondents reported experiencing difficulties in using software/digital applications to carry out the assessment.

The data in Table 7 illustrates a very positive perception of Microsoft 365's features in the collaborative, communication, and communication dimensions, both between teachers and between teachers and students. "Satisfactory" and "excellent" together aggregate 95% of the respondents, which shows the teachers' very positive representation of these features.

Regarding the question about teacher satisfaction regarding the educational content of the subject, only 3% of teachers say they are dissatisfied; for 17.8% they reveal that it is indifferent, and the majority confirms that they are satisfied as shown in Table 8. About the integration of mobile communication devices, whether tablet or mobile phone, most teachers (78.2%) say they are satisfied. With identical values (71.29%) of teachers considered the integration of Microsoft 365 with other collaborative applications (e.g., online whiteboards, forums, among others) as "satisfactory" or "excellent".

The data on teachers' level of satisfaction—given the results from the answers to the previous questions—helps explain that 60.4% of teachers said they would probably recommend Microsoft 365 to a friend and 35.6% would do so without doubt or hesitation. Only 4.0% are unlikely to recommend the Microsoft 365 platform to a friend.

4.2. Survey by Interview

The interview results are presented following the eight dimensions considered: (a) identification elements, (b) Microsoft 365 use context, (c) resources domain, (d) objectives for use, (e) description of practice, (f) difficulties experienced, (g) results, and (h) future prospects.

All translations of the interviewees' answers were made by the authors.

(a)   Identification Elements

Regarding Professional experience, we found a considerable variation for each of the subjects. The minimum length of service is three years, and the maximum is 32 years of service. Regarding contractual situation and professional stability, only one of the interviewees has a fixed-term contract with the state. Most interviewees have an indefinite labor contract with the state. From the point of view of the analysis of the results, this data is very relevant since through it we can see that the situation of these professionals confers considerable professional stability to the interviewed teachers.

Concerning Academic training, four of the interviewees hold a bachelor's degree, and the remaining ones hold a master's degree. One of the respondents has a Ph.D. and another is still studying for a Ph.D.

(b)   Microsoft 365 Use Context

All interviewees confirm their ability and competence to install Microsoft 365 on both computer and mobile devices, making use of it to support their teaching practice. What is at issue here is the technical competence to work with the hardware. The ability to perform software installation falls under this category.

Regarding the media for using the platform, all respondents mention that they use Microsoft 365 from various devices, giving as an example the school computer, laptop, tablet, or mobile phone.

E3 highlights the importance of using Microsoft 365 from mobile devices, highlighting the dimensions of interactivity and ubiquity. The comfort of use regardless of space and support facilitates ubiquitous learning. The mastery of devices allows for the development of digital skills that are facilitators of students' learning. In this regard, teacher E3 says:

"Yes. I installed it because it is easy and practical. It is practical because sometimes we must attend a department meeting and we still go on a trip, and we can attend the meeting. When the student has a question and puts it in the chat, I can answer it even though I am not at home and so solve the problem quickly to the student." (E3)

Concerning the full use of the Microsoft 365 features, all interview respondents confirm a very extensive use of them. The answers clearly fall within the domain of teachers' digital competences. The teachers' perception of the usability of the Microsoft 365 features is explored. Referring to the full use of the features E3 states:

"I use the ones I think are useful for my work as a teacher." (E3)

To the question regarding the production of innovative resources based on Microsoft 365 tools/applications all interviewees replied in the affirmative.

E3 answers:

"Yes, without a doubt. I launch assignments to be developed by students in Word, I create Quizzes in Forms, I organize and process data in Excel and PowerPoint. . . . " (E3)

Regarding training in the use of Microsoft 365, none of the interviewees revealed having received specific training in its use.

In this respect, E3 says:

"No, because I didn't have the opportunity. I would like to because I would like to improve my performance." (E3)

However, the reasons given to justify this absence relate to the fact that there was no opportunity before the actual need arose, from the closure of schools in March 2020 and the requirement to maintain the teaching activity in distance learning. It is very revealing to recall that Portuguese teachers were invited to use distance learning platforms as soon as the period of confinement began. Remote emergency teaching required the use of the platform by teachers and students; however, no training had been provided. The need for remote emergency teaching imposed the use, regardless of whether there had been training in the use of the platform.

In all interviewees, there is a clear recognition of the importance of training in the use of Microsoft 365. While on the one hand they recognize the relevance of training in teaching practice, on the other they draw attention to specific aspects that need to be addressed in the training domain. The respondents identified some tools that, in their opinion, needed improvement, be it OneNote, Excel, or network management software, among others.

Some interviewees' responses addressed the importance of training in the use of Microsoft 365:

"I think it is always important to have training, because we always learn and the sharing of experiences that usually occurs is very important. In the case of 365 I think it is essential to improve the mastery of OneNote which is a tool with a lot of potential and which many still don't use and can be a good alternative to the daily notebook." (E2)

"If you do not have previous relevant experience, you should carry out general training in productivity tools such as Excel and file management on the network." (E4)

"Yes. I think it is very important because we need to use it more and more with the students and we need to master its use to use it." (E1)

(c) Resource Domain

Regarding the mastery of the resource all respondents confirmed having Microsoft 365 installed on their school computer, personal computer, tablet, or their own mobile phone.

Considering its functionalities, all respondents consider that they know all the functionalities.

Regarding preferences for any of the tools, we found some variability in the answers:

"In the day to day, I use many tools: Word, Excel, Outlook, Forms, SharePoint, Teams, OneDrive, among others." (E1)

"OneDrive because I can put all the documents and access them anywhere. SharePoint is a document sharing tool where we can always add something which is good for those who work in collaboration and in group . . . Teams, word, excel . . . ." (E8)

(d) Objectives for Use

As for the objectives for the use of Microsoft 365, the purposes centered on the bureaucratic activities that teachers develop linked to the students are indicated.

Some answers:

"To give synchronous lessons through Teams e.g., to share information with students, to propose activity to students, to receive assignments, to assess students through quizzes e.g., to communicate with students and parents. . . . " (E3)

"Streamline/simplify daily tasks and promote greater communication and interaction with students and work colleagues." (E4)

With regard to the tools that respondents use most with their students, Teems was identified:

"Sharing materials, tutorial guidance of students, to communicate with them and parents/careers." (E1)

Other responses:

"Teams, Word, Excel, Outlook, Forms." (E3)

"Teams for communicating with students and answering questions; Microsoft OneNote—for filing information, carrying out work, monitoring and giving feedback; Forms for formative assessment." (E2)

"Microsoft OneNote—To archive information, carry out work, monitor and give feedback." (E4)

When analyzing the interviews, using the qualitative analysis software NVivo, regarding the dimension "objectives for use" of Microsoft 365 and its functionalities we obtained the following results which can be seen in Figure 5.

Figure 5. Objectives for use of Microsoft 365 and its functionalities.

From the analysis of Figure 5, the emphasis on communication, sharing and cooperation provided by the use of Microsoft 365 is quite evident.

(e) Description of the Practice

Regarding their practice as Microsoft 365 users, the interviewees stated that the platform fulfilled the following functions: as a basic user to produce simple documents for daily and mandatory use; as an advanced user to produce, store, and share information documents and resources; receive documents and information; receive and change information or resources for sharing; receive and change information or resources for personal use; develop innovative and different pedagogical resources for students all interviewees stated that they positively fulfilled these dimensions.

Concerning the dimension of specific moments when Microsoft 365 is used, the interviewees did not consider that a specific moment could be established for the use of Microsoft 365. In some cases, the interviewees referred that it is used at the beginning of the lesson, it is used for the organization of contents at different moments of the lesson or even to perform assessment moments. The situations of isolation and the consequent need to communicate with isolated students also dictated different moments for the use of Microsoft 365.

E1 said:

"No. I use it when I consider it important and essential. Of course, when I have sick students at home, so I necessarily use 365 for synchronous and asynchronous lessons." (E3)

All interviewees considered that since they started using Microsoft 365 their practice has become easier, there has been a simplification. E3 and E4 stated in this regard:

"Undoubtedly more streamlined. I have everything more organized." (E3)

"The work is more simplified but requires some preparation time that is easily recovered in the monitoring and feedback processes." (E4)

Regarding the methodologies used, there is a consensus among the interviewees about the need to use active methodologies with Microsoft 365. They all state that they use active methodologies in their practice. As stated by E2, E3, and E4:

"No doubt active methodologies." (E2)

"Active methodologies because my students are protagonists. The teaching process does not happen without their intervention and participation. Students don't just sit and listen, taking notes. They debate, criticize, do. They help build knowledge together with the teacher and with their colleagues. Hybrid teaching methodologies are conceptions that make use of the technological possibilities of current times. Among them is the flipped classroom, which as the name says, reverses the whole traditional classroom logic. In it, learning begins at home rather than at school. The student does his own research on the internet and online materials about previously passed themes, and arrives in class with knowledge in his baggage, which is then debated with teachers and colleagues. This method allows for the optimization of class time, which is then used to deepen the knowledge on the subject and answer questions. After class, the student can still do more learning with multimedia resources that can be made available by the teacher." (E3)

"Active methodologies, namely project-based learning, Design Thinking, and STEAM methodology. To create a stimulating and motivating environment that allows working on several skills simultaneously." (E4)

Concerning the question "Considers your practice with Microsoft 365 to be good practice", all the teachers interviewed maintained that they had good practice, although it was naturally subject to improvement processes (E5, E7, and E8). We can see the options that legitimize teachers' assessment from the descriptions:

"A good practice is one that leads the student to achieve essential learning, and as my practice has led them down that path then it is a good practice. So, I use it to get them to look for information, to get them curious and that to me is good practice." (E1)

"It's a good pedagogical practice because I provide information and materials for the student to work on at the time, he/she thinks is best. In addition, as I can clear up doubts by chat, video conference or call, the student feels more accompanied." (E2)

"Microsoft 365 allows me to perform active and flipped classroom methodologies, so I think it's a good practice." (E3)

"It is a good pedagogical practice because it allows planning and designing a strategy to reach an end. In a dynamic/interactive way the student autonomously, or accompanied, travels the defined path to achieve an objective/competence." (E4)

(f) Difficulties Experienced

Regarding the difficulties they experienced and the options to overcome them were similar. On the one hand, they warned about the difficulties of using Microsoft 365 due to lack of training and the support strategies that centered on seeking help not so much in the schools' support structures, but mainly seeking help from colleagues or even YouTube tutorials. We transcribe the statements of E1:

"Watching videos on YouTube or asking colleagues." (E1)

This practice is confirmed by Marôco's study [3]. Although institutions have provided support structures for teachers, focusing on the ICT coordinator for this function, most teachers sought help in informal groups on social networks, with colleagues from the institution or outside the institution, in YouTube tutorials.

E2 mentions the lack of digital literacy of parents and students, to be able to consistently support the teachers' effort to ensure teaching activities in distance learning context. Faced with difficulty, interviewee E2 explains what the strategy was chosen to overcome the lack of literacy: "I seek to increase the digital literacy of students and parents with short webinars." (E2)

Within the framework of the difficulties pointed out, the obvious lack of conditions for distance activities also merited negative comment, with the lack of quality of the network being a constant. The issues of digital divide became more evident during the pandemic period. The scarcity of equipment, the lack of Internet access, the lack of network quality in educational institutions, or low network quality in inland areas are effective dimensions of the digital divide. E3's statements attest to these difficulties when he says:

"Sometimes it is the internet network failure." (E3)

And E4:

"Security policies instituted by the institution that condition the sharing and easy transport of documents. And access difficulties in case of deficient internet networks. To overcome the difficulties, the options are to resort to local storage units and use offline applications." (E4)

About the difficulties experienced by participants while using Microsoft 365, the content analysis provided by NVivo generated the following responses (Figure 6).

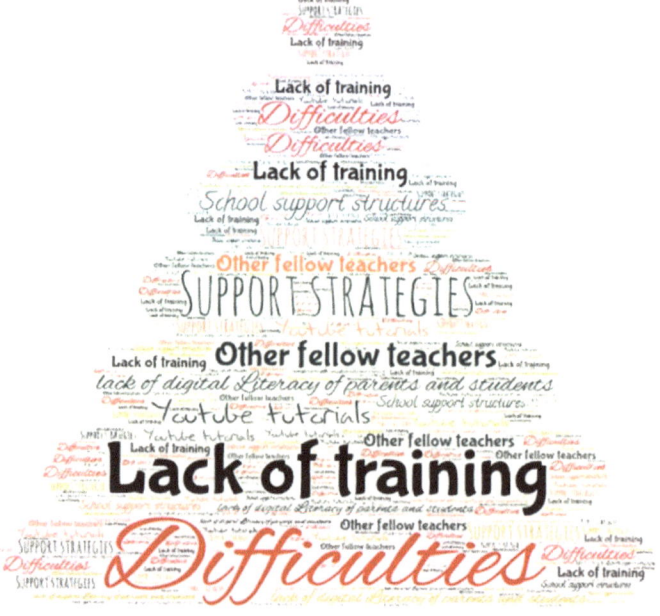

Figure 6. Difficulties experienced in using Microsoft 365.

(g) Results

When asked about the results obtained, the interviewees argued that students achieve better results and in less time with the use of this tool. Interviewee E2 is less categorical or at least retains some caution on the issue of obtaining better results in less time, although he leans towards this perception:

"I haven't used 365 for that long to say for sure if I need more or less time, but it seems to me that less time, as it is a platform with a lot of potential and very intuitive." (E2)

Regarding the changes in learning resulting from a more systematic use of Microsoft 365 with students, these seem evident. Increased autonomy (E1, E2), possibility to participate in online working groups, where the teacher guides, shares information, monitors and provides feedback (E1, E7, E8).

About changes in teachers' work, E1 said: "sharing of strategies and resources is highlighted." (E1)

The interviewees considered that the use of Microsoft 365 did not change the concept of teacher (E1, E2, E3, E4, E5, E6, E7, E8), but in the case of E1, it ensured a deepening of the concept of teacher. The traditional vision of the educational action was largely overcome by teachers when they assumed the centrality of the student in the learning processes, when they privileged learning over teaching, when they bet on the student as the builder of his/her own learning, using digital media as mediators in the communication processes. As teachers who stood out for their practice in the use of digital media, the answers confirm the deepening of the concept of teaching and teacher (E1).

E6 states that the use of Microsoft 365 "has not changed my belief of what it is to be a teacher, but it has improved it" (E6); and that the increased use of the platform "made me use more digital resources to teach the lessons, allowing me to organize the lessons in a less traditional way" (E6).

Regarding the level of usefulness of Microsoft 365, on a scale where 1 was not at all useful and 5 was very relevant, the answers were mostly between 4 and 5, with the majority at 5. Only E1 scored 4.

(h) Future Perspectives

In relation to the questions focusing on future perspectives on the continuity of a practice where the use of Microsoft 365 is integrated, all interviewees were unanimous in stating their intention to continue using this platform. At the same time, they expressed the expectation that some changes would be introduced—in a word, improvements allowing "facilitating and saving work" for the teacher and "allowing for pedagogical differentiation" (E1).

Within the framework of future perspectives, we also highlight the issue of digital literacy. The pandemic issue brought to the agenda the issue of literacy not only of teachers, but also of students.

E3 answers "I hope students will be more active and improve their digital literacy" (E3).

Regarding the ideal practice for using Microsoft 365 the interviewees highlighted some dimensions such as promoting students' autonomy, developing communication skills among peers and between students and teachers, facilitating students' learning. We transcribe some of the positions of the interviewees:

Some answers:

"One that promotes more autonomy, improves communication between students and teachers and teachers and students, facilitates the teacher's work and enhances students' learning." (E2).

"It would be one that allows all teachers and students to make learning." (E3).

"The development of greater autonomy and transversal skills." (E4).

5. Conclusions

In the last two years, teachers have resorted, as never before, to the aid of technological devices to promote the organization of the didactic processes in remote and hybrid learning contexts. This situation has highlighted the constraints and obstacles of the main actors in the teaching process and in the education system, in a very clear way in public education. However, learning platforms are today an unavoidable need to meet the challenges of 21st century education. To continue supporting teachers and students in creating a more integrative learning environment and raise the quality standards of Education, Microsoft 365 presented and explored new features for teachers, educators, and students that are important to understand if they were being useful in teaching and learning processes. It was in this sense that it was decided to proceed with the study previously presented [14].

We will now present some conclusions that emerged from the results obtained, taking into account the research objectives we formulated for this study.

Considering Objective 1: "To understand how the schools in the northern interior of Portugal that chose Microsoft 365 made use of it", the results obtained confirm that in the schools that have participated in the study, teachers have made very extensive use of Microsoft 365. All available tools were used; however, Teams, Forms, Outlook, Word, and Power Point were the most used.

Considering Objective 2: "To appreciate the level of teacher satisfaction with the use of Microsoft 365", we noticed that the respondents revealed a very high level of satisfaction, since 95% of the participants consider themselves satisfied or with an excellent level of satisfaction. It is also important to add that 60.4% of teachers stated that they would probably recommend Microsoft 365 to a friend and 35.6% stated that they would do so without any doubt or hesitation.

Considering Objective 3: "To understand teachers' perceptions about the advantages or disadvantages of using the platform to organize the teaching and learning processes", the survey and interview responses were very positive. With regard to the functionalities of Microsoft 365, two-thirds of the respondents are satisfied and more than a quarter consider the functionalities for cooperative communication, communication with colleagues, or even communication with students as excellent.

Considering Objective 4: "To understand teachers' perceptions about the advantages and disadvantages of using the platform to improve results and practice", all respondents argued that the use of the platform has improved student academics outcomes and express a positive perception about the change in practices.

Considering Objective 5: "To analyze if the use of Microsoft 365 has been accompanied by the use of active methodologies", we have seen that all the interviewees confirmed the need to adjust the methodologies in the teaching and learning processes, especially in hybrid teaching contexts. They also refer to the need to use active methodologies, identifying the flipped classroom, project-based learning, design thinking, and STEAM.

Considering Objective 6: "To analyze if the use of Microsoft 365 has facilitated the teachers' actions", all interviewees were unanimous in noting that Microsoft 365 facilitated the teachers' action in the pandemic period and stated that they intended to continue using it even in the face-to-face mode. This intention confirms the recognition that Microsoft 365 continues to provide conditions facilitating the teacher's actions.

Considering Objective 7: "To identify the type of training needs experienced by schools and teachers in using Microsoft 365 over the past two years", the results obtained in the survey and interviews are in accordance with the national studies cited [2,3], and confirm that teachers had not had specific training in the use of Microsoft 365 before the pandemic and felt they needed it for teaching. In the interviews we carried out, we noted that all interviewees considered it very relevant to obtain specific training in order for teachers to be able to do a more adequate teaching of the challenges involved in the use of Microsoft 365.

It is understood that the conclusions of the research presented should be interpreted with some caution. In fact, the type of research design presented, and the size of the sample imply some restrictions for the generalization of the results. In terms of future research, it is our intention to obtain a larger sample and carry them out in a wider geographical area. Thus, considering that many Portuguese schools have chosen Microsoft 365, our objective is to continue the research by getting answers from the majority of schools in Portugal that use Microsoft 365.

Considering the previously discussed, we are convinced of the importance of the results achieved by the study, in the sense that they show how the platform has been used, its integration in the teaching and learning processes, in the communication strategies, in the continuous teacher training, in the digital transition plan, and in the changes in teaching practices and methodologies.

Some relevant implications emerged from the study: Teacher training should include a distance learning curricular unit, with special attention to Microsoft 365. In this curricular unit, the construction of learning objects should be addressed. In didactic curricular units, active methodologies more adequate to distance education should be addressed. The offer of continuous teacher training should include assessment themes in distance learning platforms.

Author Contributions: Conceptualization, J.E. and P.C.; Methodology, A.P.A., J.E. and P.C.; Software, N.L. and J.E.; Validation, J.E., N.L. and A.P.A.; Formal analysis, J.E., P.C. and A.P.A.; Investigation, J.E. and N.L.; Writing—original draft preparation, J.E., N.L., A.P.A. and P.C.; Writing—review and editing, J.E., P.C. and A.P.A.; Supervision, J.E. and P.C. All authors have read and agreed to the published version of the manuscript.

Funding: This work was financially supported by University of Trás-os-Montes e Alto Douro.

Data Availability Statement: All data were presented in main text.

Acknowledgments: This work was financially supported by National Funds through FCT—Fundacão para a Ciêcia e a Tecnologia, I.P., under the project UIDB/00194/2020. The authors would like to thank the University of Trás-os-Montes e Alto Douro for the financial support, as well as the reviewers for their comments, which have greatly contributed to the improvement of this manuscript.

Conflicts of Interest: The authors declare no conflict of interest. The funders had no role in the design of the study; in the collection, analyses, or interpretation of data; in the writing of the manuscript; or in the decision to publish the results.

References

1. Rodrigues, A. Ensino Remoto na Educação Superior: Desafios e conquistas em Tempos de pandemia. SBC Horizontes, 2020. Available online: http://horizontes.sbc.org.br/index.php/2020/06/17/ensino-remoto-na-educacao-superior/ (accessed on 12 October 2022).
2. Ribeirinha, T.; Silva, B. Cinco lições para a educação escolar depois da COVID. *Interfaces Científicas* **2020**, *10*, 194–210. [CrossRef]
3. Maroâco, J. Experiências de Ensino a Distaância em Tempos de pandemia. 2020. Available online: https://somossolucao.pt/2020/08/31/o-que-nos-dizem-os (accessed on 14 October 2022).
4. Prat, M. *Réussir Votre Projet e-Learning: Pédagogie, Méthodes et Outils de Conception, Déploiement, Évaluation*, 2nd ed.; Editions ENI: Herblain, France, 2012.
5. Lopes, N.; Gomes, A. O Boom das plataformas digitais nas práticas de ensino: Uma experiência do E@D no ensino superior. *Rev. Pract.* **2020**, *5*, 106–120. [CrossRef]
6. Kenski, V.M. Educação e Tecnologia: O novo ritmo das informações. *Práxis Educ.* **2012**, *7*, 285–290. [CrossRef]
7. Borba, M.C.; Silva, R.S.; Gadanidis, G. *Fases das Tecnologias Digitais em Educação Matemática: Sala de Aula e Internet em Movimento*, 2nd ed.; Autêntica Editora: São Paulo, Brazil, 2016.
8. Motta, M.S.; Kalinke, M.A. Uma proposta metodológica para a produção de objetos de aprendizagem na perspectiva da dimensão educacional. In *Objetos de Aprendizagem: Pesquisas e Possibilidades na Educação Matemática*, 1st ed.; Kalinke, M.A., Motta., M.S., Eds.; Life Editora: Campo Grande, Brazil, 2019; pp. 203–218.
9. Fiori, R.; Goi, M.E. O Ensino de Química na plataforma digital em tempos de Coronavírus. *Rev. Thema* **2020**, *18*, 218–242. [CrossRef]
10. Oliveira, N.R. A web 2.0 na formação docente. In Proceedings of the Trabalho Docente e Formação: Políticas, práticas e investigação: Pontes para a mudança, Porto, Portugal, 1–3 November 2013.
11. Cabero-Almenara, J. Learning from the time of the COVID-19. *Rev. Eletrónica Educ.* **2020**, *24*, 1–3. [CrossRef]
12. Cabero-Almenara, J.; Valencia, R. And COVID-19 transformed the educational system: Reflections and experiences to learn. *IJERI Int. J. Educ. Res. Innov.* **2021**, *15*, 218–228. [CrossRef]

13. Wang, S.K.; Hsu, H.; Campbell, T.; Coster, D.; Longhurst, M. An investigation of middle school science teachers and students' use of technology inside and outside of classrooms: Considering whether digital natives are more technology savvy than their teachers. *Educ. Technol. Res. Dev.* **2014**, *62*, 637–662. [CrossRef]
14. Aires, A.P.; Escola, J.; Lopes, N. Microsoft 365: A teaching and learning resource during the pandemic. In Proceedings of the 15th International Technology, Education and Development Conference, Virtual, Online, 8–9 March 2021. [CrossRef]
15. Charnet, C. La Plateforme D'Apprentissage: Un Artefact de Mediation? Université de Montpellier. 2009. Available online: http://citeseerx.ist.psu.edu/viewdoc/download;jsessionid=7F4ABD745B5A617767F40BDCD5155198?doi=10.1.1.174.1885&rep=rep1&type=pdf (accessed on 12 October 2022).
16. Raposo-Rivas, M.; Escola, J. Virtual Communities of and for learning. *J. Educ. Teach. Train. -JETT* **2016**, *7*, 7–10. Available online: https://jett.labosfor.com/index.php/jett/article/view/199 (accessed on 1 October 2022).
17. Raposo-Rivas, M.; Escola, J. Virtual Learning Communities: Review of a decade of Spanish-Portuguese scientific production. *J. Educ. Teach. Train. -JETT* **2016**, *7*, 11–24. Available online: https://jett.labosfor.com/index.php/jett/article/view/200/102 (accessed on 1 October 2022).
18. Bergmann, J.; Sams, A. *Flip Your Classroom: Reach Every Student in Every Class Every Day*, 1st ed.; International Society for Technology in Education (ISTE): Washington, DC, USA, 2012.
19. Kilpatrick, W.H. *Educação para uma Civilização em Mudança*, 1st ed.; Melhoramentos: São Paulo, Brazil, 1967.
20. Carvalho, A.A. Mobile-Learning: Rentabilizar os dispositivos móveis dos alunos para aprender. In *Aprender na Era Digital. Mobile-Learning*, 1st ed.; Carvalho, A.A., Ed.; De Facto Editores: Santo Tirso, Portugal, 2012; pp. 149–163.
21. Alves, L. Videojogos e Aprendizagem: Mapeando percursos. In *Aprender na Era Digital. Mobile-Learning*, 1st ed.; Carvalho, A.A., Ed.; De Facto Editores: Santo Tirso, Portugal, 2012; pp. 11–28.
22. Prensky, M. *Digital Game Basead Learning*, 1st ed.; MacGraw-Hill: New York, NY, USA, 2012.
23. Yakman, G. STEAM Education: An Overview of Creating a Model of Integrative Education. Ph.D. Thesis, Virgina Polytechnic and State University, Pulaski, VA, USA, 2008.
24. Riley, S.M. *STEAM Point: A guide to Integrating Science, Technology, Enginneering, the Arts, and Mathematics Throut thr Common Core*, 1st ed.; Createspace: Westminter, UK, 2012.
25. Bacich, L.; Holanda, L. *STEAM Em sala de Aula. A Aprendizagem Baseada em Projectos Integrando Conhecimentos na Educação Básica*, 1st ed.; Penso: Porto Alegre, Brazil, 2020.
26. Creswell, J.W. *Research Design: Qualitative, Quantitative, Mixed Methods Approache*, 3rd ed.; Sage Publications Inc.: Thousand Oaks, CA, USA, 2009.
27. Creswell, J.W.; Clarck, V. *Designing and Conducting Mixed Methods Research*; Sage Publications Inc.: Thousand Oaks, CA, USA, 2010.
28. Bryman, A. Integrating quantitative and qualitative research. how is it done? *Qual. Res.* **2006**, *6*, 97–113. [CrossRef]
29. Almeida, L.; Freire, T. *Metodologia de Investigação em Psicologia e Educação*, 5th ed.; Psiquilíbrios: Braga, Portugal, 2017.
30. Ribeiro, A.C.; Ribeiro, L.C. *Planificação e Avaliação do Ensino Aprendizagem*; Universidade Aberta: Lisboa, Portugal, 1990.
31. Pestana, M.H.; Gageiro, J.N. *Análise de Dados para Ciências Sociais. A Complementaridade do SPSS*; Edições Sílabo: Lisboa, Portugal, 2008.
32. Bardin, L. *Análise de Conteúdo*; Edições 70: Lisboa, Portugal, 1995.
33. Escola, J. Comunicação Educativa: Perspetivas e desafios com a COVID 19. *Educ. Real.* **2020**, *45*, e109345. [CrossRef]
34. Escola, J. Ensinar e Aprender: Desafios no Período de COVID em Portugal. *Rev. Educ. Ciências E Matemática* **2020**, *10*, 87–103. Available online: http://publicacoes.unigranrio.edu.br/index.php/recm/article/view/6592/3318 (accessed on 24 October 2022).
35. Moreira, J.A.; Schlemmer, E. Por um novo conceito e paradigma de Educção digital onlife. *Rev. UFG* **2020**, *20*, 63438. [CrossRef]

Article

A Framework for a Seamless Transformation to Online Education

Shanmugam Sivagurunathan [1,*] and Sudhaman Parthasarathy [2]

1 Department of Computer Science and Applications, Gandhigram Rural Institute (Deemed to be University), Gandhigram 624302, India
2 Thiagarajar College of Engineering, Madurai 625015, India
* Correspondence: svgrnth@gmail.com

Abstract: Online education is now widely used in schools and universities as a result of COVID-19. More than 1.6 billion children, or 80% of all school-aged children worldwide, have missed school as a result of the COVID-19 pandemic. The COVID-19 outbreak has been a significant concern for educational institutions since 2020 and has interfered with regular academic and evaluation practices. Organizational preparedness for online education must be assessed by institutions. To assist them, we present a case study carried out at an Indian educational institution that highlights the drawbacks and advantages of online education and that outlines a framework for its change. Additionally, we assessed the system and offered suggestions to improve the online instruction provided by institutions. We think that the proposed methodology will assist organizations in identifying challenges prior to launching online learning.

Keywords: online education; blended learning; e-learning; educational institutions; digital education

Citation: Sivagurunathan, S.; Parthasarathy, S. A Framework for a Seamless Transformation to Online Education. *Computers* **2022**, *11*, 183. https://doi.org/10.3390/computers11120183

Academic Editors: Antonio Sarasa Cabezuelo and Covadonga Rodrigo San Juan

Received: 16 November 2022
Accepted: 8 December 2022
Published: 12 December 2022

Publisher's Note: MDPI stays neutral with regard to jurisdictional claims in published maps and institutional affiliations.

Copyright: © 2022 by the authors. Licensee MDPI, Basel, Switzerland. This article is an open access article distributed under the terms and conditions of the Creative Commons Attribution (CC BY) license (https://creativecommons.org/licenses/by/4.0/).

1. Introduction

Teachers have always experimented with their craft in their efforts to be more effective. Through the adoption of new ideologies, strategies, techniques, resources, and technologies, teaching has advanced over the years to reach a larger audience. As technology changes, teachers must carefully use, evaluate, and adapt new tools to make the most of them and to determine how they work.

In higher education, online learning is well established [1]. The advantages of online education are well-known and include improved access, more flexible scheduling options, fewer space requirements, and lower delivery costs [2–4]. Additionally, there is a need for precise instructions and obligations, honest and open communication, the presence of both the students and the instructor, and prompt feedback [5–8]. When both students and teachers feel at ease, communities can begin to form [2,4,9].

The effects of the global COVID-19 pandemic have had a considerable impact on how higher education institutions currently provide their educational services. Students and educators from all study disciplines and levels were required to switch to online teaching, learning, and evaluation techniques immediately in order to be in accordance with national lockdown limitations. Work–life balance and welfare were severely impacted by this abrupt end to face-to-face learning, and many students and employees reported feeling particularly lonely and cut off from their friends and co-workers, who they had been interacting with regularly before the outbreak. Online learning can be defined as education carried out through the use of digital tools that are used to instruct others online.

All student groups, including mature students, commuters, disabled students, and those with mobility challenges, medical conditions, and care obligations, have experienced the benefits of online learning in terms of engagement, motivation, enjoyment, and satisfaction. It is well known that students prefer online instructors who are kind, sympathetic, approachable, upbeat, comfortable with technology, and who regularly give them opportunities to interact, collaborate, and form relationships with other students. This confirms that staff members still have a crucial role to play in facilitating student learning in online contexts.

Online learning has grown significantly over the past several years thanks to information and communication technology (ICT). Online learning has some advantages over more conventional offline education. By offering students personalized guidance and immediate feedback, online learning can, in the beginning, make the learning process more student-centered. Second, because online education is affordable, more people can more easily access high-quality education. Third, access to online education is simple. It provides more learning opportunities for people who reside in rural and distant areas where there may be few local educational resources. Given the benefits of online learning, techno-optimists think that its widespread use has the ability to raise educational standards and spread equality throughout the industry.

Due to the COVID-19 epidemic, online education has mostly replaced traditional education at all levels of learning, from elementary schools to colleges and universities. For close to 80% of the world's enrolled pupils, the COVID-19 pandemic has forced more than 1.6 billion students to stay home from school in 161 nations, causing them to miss out on normal class lectures and other academic activities [10]. The COVID-19 epidemic became a major problem for educational institutions starting in the beginning of 2020 and has severely limited their ability to carry out their regular academic and evaluation activities.

Digital tools and technologies are creatively used in online education for learning, assessment, and teaching. Online education is often referred to as TEL (technology-enhanced learning) or e-learning [11] and was enforced by the regulating bodies of educational institutions in every nation in order for students to stay sage while continuing their academic activities via online learning in the absence of a vaccination to reduce the rate of COVID-19 transmission. Educational institutions in nearly all of the world's nations have begun to transition their methods for holding lectures, assignments, seminars, and exams to online platforms. As a result, the system's resilience was placed under more stress, and both instructors and pupils had to learn how to use online platforms rapidly.

In spite of some faculty members and organizations having previously adopted online learning and being familiar with it, it was not until recently, as a result of the COVID-19 crisis, that a large number of people began using platforms for online learning and began to enjoy both the challenges and advantages that come with it. In fact, most institutions were compelled to change to an online learning environment overnight without any kind of planning, which may be why we are now hearing about "digital flops" [12–15].

To adopt online education successfully, educational institutions must evaluate their "organizational preparedness". Here, we use a case study carried out an Indian educational institution to highlight the advantages and drawbacks of online education, and we create a prospective framework for its transformation to aid institutions in their endeavors. As part of our review of the framework, we also conducted a preliminary assessment. Below, we provide our recommendations for institutions that are looking to offer students efficient and worthwhile online education. We think this approach will help educational institutions figure out their problems with online education before switching to online learning.

2. Review of Literature

Public life was severely constrained to slow the rate of COVID-19 infection in 2020. The majority of courses became digital, and all university facilities were unavailable to the general public. The term "emergency online learning" [16] refers to a moment in contemporary history in which the whole student population began to learn exclusively from home for a protracted period. Assuring the availability of all required courses inside study programs was the priority to keep the show going. However, now that we have completed over a year of emergency online learning, we can examine the many COVID-19 crisis-related activities as well as teaching strategies in more details from the perspectives of an online course for higher education professionals [17], of problem-based online learning, or by considering online learning methods that had been used before but that changed due to the real-world scenario (for example, statistics on the use of online learning in the past tense situations). Numerous educators and students were caught off guard when the transition from in-person to online learning happened virtually overnight.

It is reasonable to assume that teachers' knowledge, proficiency, and attitudes toward using digital technology to provide worthwhile learning experiences for their pupils will be influenced by a variety of other factors [18]. Numerous studies have shown that university teachers still mostly avoid utilizing digital techniques to provide online learning opportunities that are more than just digital slide presentations, and instructors usually lack the essential skills (e.g., [19,20]). In a similar vein, managing online education programs that are entirely online requires students to have the ability to self-regulate themselves and their learning strategies more than before.

When regular classroom meetings and teacher-directed direct external regulation are not organized, student learning is more dependent on metacognitive strategies and internal and external resource-related methods that help them to observe, organize, and regulate their learning methods in a goal-oriented manner [21,22]. Because online learning and digital skills go together so well, both teachers and students need fundamental technical skills to make the most of the opportunities that online learning offers.

The capacity to use digital techniques to find, manipulate, process, and produce data and information and the ability to communicate and collaborate with others online are all included in the category of digital skills [23]. The results of numerous large-scale examinations conducted internationally, on the other hand, suggest that the digital competence of secondary school teachers and pupils varies greatly [24,25].

It is logical to assume that as a result, the student body at higher education institutions will likewise be quite varied in terms of taking advantage of online learning and teaching. Indicators of the limitations within which online learning and teaching happens or does not occur may be found in the institutional, organizational, and administrative factors, with examples including infrastructure, digitalization policy, support systems, or equipment [20]. The research on this topic highlights both the range of contextual elements at play in the background and the variety of prospective ways in which online teaching and learning can be implemented.

3. Transformation to Online Education—Challenges and Advantages

Regarding their professional lives and work, faculty members across educational institutions are currently going through a transition period. The rapid shift to online forms of delivery to retain student engagement has resulted in drastically increased efforts for staff as they work to not only move instructional material and resources online but to also develop the necessary software navigation skills. Both instructors and students are affected differently. In some contexts, similar to many organizations, online and mixed delivery methods for courses are already well established; thus, increasing capacity along existing routes is now the responsibility. Due to the shift to the online environment, teachers in certain places are finding it very hard to adjust to what may be the "new normal" for a long time, especially in educational institutions.

During the past several years, a select number of educational establishments have begun to implement online education as part of their curricula. Worldwide, online education platforms such as Coursera and EdX have attracted a decent amount of acceptance. These programs have made it possible for educators to communicate with aspirational pupils located in different parts of the world. They have allowed educational organizations and individual instructors to not only conduct educational programs in a distance-learning format but have also allowed them to make a profit from doing so. For instance, the government of India created and promoted the online learning platform "National Programme on Technology Enhanced Learning (NPTEL)" in India, and in recent years, it has been determined to be quite popular among both professors and students. In India, the market for online education is predicted to increase by an eight-fold proportion over the next five years, reaching USD 1.96 billion in sales and 9.6 million subscribers by 2021, as per the research by KPMG.

Consulting teams and researchers advise that not all of these schools have or can mobilize the necessary campus resources to accommodate a 30 to 50% surge in students choosing on-campus education over the next 10–15 years. Enrolling students in online courses is both a logical solution and a need to expand capacity when neither the government nor private organizations are providing financial support for the construction of new structures or laboratories or for the establishment of new educational institutions. This is yet another strong argument for many nations to support and develop online educational opportunities. As a result, educational establishments are powerless to do anything besides seek out non-traditional teaching methods, such as online education, to assist their students in comprehending the pedagogical instructions provided by their faculties and in participating in evaluation activities.

One of the key issues that such alternative efforts bring with them is the capacity of the stakeholders (students and faculty) to adjust to the new learning system and to organize training to utilize online learning systems such as Coursera, Edx, or any custom-built learner-management system. Although there are some financial and campus infrastructure benefits to adapting to online education [26], such alternative initiatives also bring significant challenges for institutions with them. These key challenges include the availability of the requisite IT infrastructure. We decided to carry out a study using the right method, which will be explained in the next few paragraphs, to determine the problems that educational institutions have to deal with.

4. Research Methodology

The survey-based research methodology suggested by the research methodologist Yin [27] was used in this research. It involves two stages. The steps provided by Yin [27] are (i) to prepare a draft of the interview questions as suggested in King and Horrock [28]; (ii) to carry out a pilot interview with two or three interviewees to verify and validate the correctness and completeness of the questionnaire; (iii) to conduct the actual interview with the chosen interviewees using the final questionnaire; and (iv) to use interview findings as a basis to develop the proposed framework.

King and Horrock's [28] qualitative "focused semi-structured" interviewing techniques were employed for data collection. By "focused," we mean that the participants' understandings of online teaching and learning activities were the main emphasis of the interview and any interactions with them. The word "semi-structured" in this context means that the participants were asked to react to questions that had been prepared in advance but that the interviewer had the freedom to add a few more questions on the spot to obtain more detailed information from the interviewees.

It should be noted that 32 professors over the age of 30 years old were chosen from eight different educational institutions and interviewed in the first round. In the second phase, we conducted a case study at a particular institution. During March and April of 2021, the case study and the interview were conducted entirely online through several platforms, including Google Meet. Three of the eight universities from which the academics were selected found that they were already using online platforms in some capacity, while the other four had never used such internet services and were likely utilising then as a response to the limitations imposed by the circumstances of the COVID-19 outbreak. Based on what King and Horrock [28] have suggested, we carried out "focused semi-structured" qualitative interviews with the 32 academics. These academics were from eight universities, each of which contributed to 4 of the 32 professors overseeing the introduction of online learning at their institutions.

The academics were interviewed to determine the tactical, strategic, and operational facets of their institutions. All of the respondents were requested to provide further details regarding the preparations they took to adopt online education, their discussions with faculty colleagues and students that take place along the way, the planning tools they utilize, and other technical issues and challenges. The responses of the interviewees were documented and evaluated so that decision-making patterns could be deduced from the collected data. All of the people who were interviewed stated that they had not implemented any structured or in-depth planning and execution processes, nor had they prepared any documents to record their ongoing activities related to online education, including their performance or any problems that may have arisen. Nevertheless, some documentation needs to be improved in terms of its usability and efficacy. According to the results of our study, to save time, all of these educational institutions have recently started offering online versions of classes that were previously only available on campus. However, these online versions are not very well organized and only have a few guided exercises to help students prepare.

We concluded from the interviews that these eight institutions were struggling because of inadequate IT resources, a lack of awareness of online tools, and a lack of planned decisions to either buy new online education tools or to update current tools or pilot test some of the free online available resources available for e-learning before purchasing. Based on the analysis of the interviewees' responses, we have found that for a learning organization to start online education effectively and efficiently, it is necessary them to possess three characteristics (criteria for capability assessments): the necessary IT infrastructure, faculty and student adoption of online services, and software packages made for online learning. We suggest a "Capability Assessment Framework (CAF)" that takes such things into account and that is explained in the next paragraph.

5. CAF (Capability Assessment Framework) for Online Education Implementation

An institution will be able to evaluate both its existing capabilities and its potential to successfully implement online education with the assistance of CAF, as illustrated in Figure 1. This will help educational institutions to decide if online learning can be carried out effectively.

Attributes	The capability of the Institution		
	No change ('0')	Gradual change ('1')	Radical Change ('2')
IT Infrastructure	A1	B1	C1
People	A2	B2	C2
Product	A3	B3	C3

Figure 1. CAF Framework.

Each of the framework's attributes—IT infrastructure, products, and people—are assessed concerning three different capability measures: radical change, no change, and gradual change. The institution will receive a score of "0" if it is unable to make any modifications or improvements for the attribute "IT infrastructure," a score of "1" if it can make some minor adjustments, and a score of "2" if it can afford to make large modifications or remarkable progress within a short amount of time. In this way, the capacity is measured for the other attribute "people." An OEMT ("Online education management tool") is given a score of "1" if it can help people accept and cope with minor changes, a score of "2" if it can help people accept adjustments made by an OEMT at any time, and a score of "0" if the individuals in question cannot adapt to any changes.

The institution receives a score of "0" if it cannot manage to update its current product (OEMT), a score of "1" if it can be updated to meet current demands, and a score of "2" if it can afford to upgrade its current products or purchase new ones to satisfy the institution's current needs for its teachers and students. Ideal scoring for an institution would be "2" for each of these three factors, giving them a total score of "6," or C1-C2-C3. If the overall evaluation score in CAF is "0" (A1-A2-A3), then it is clear that educational institutions should either forgo offering online courses or think about only carrying out those that can be implemented with simpler resources.

The objective of the framework is to help the institution understand the strengths and the weaknesses with regard to the capability to get transformed to online education. As observed from the previous research studies, the significant parameters for this transformation are the Information Technology (IT) resources of the implementing institution, the IT team which will be involved in planning and executing this transformation and finally the IT product (i.e.,) the learning management system which is going to be used by the faculty and the students for online education. If all these parameters are taken into consideration by the implementing institution, then they would not face any hurdles during the post implementation.

The capability assessment decision framework is a collection of instruments and suggestions that provide direction and encourage the adoption of common standards for the conversion of institutions to online education. The CAF Framework, an instructional design model for creating and delivering online education that aims to alter behavior and improve performance, is based on a qualitative study carried out at an institution. It is also based on earlier research on online education, the principles of the blended learning model, and instructional design literature. It provides a methodical approach to needs analysis, designing, creating, and implementing online education through IT solutions, as well as assessing them in the context of people, IT products, and IT resources. The implementing institution is now given a streamlined, targeted approach by the framework, as well as feedback for ongoing progress.

6. Application of the Framework

To determine how practically applicable the suggested framework is, we carried out a case study at one of the eight universities. The case study research to analyze our proposed framework was conducted according to the strategy that was recommended by Yin [27]. The nature of our case study research can best be described as exploratory. The purpose of this project is two-fold: first, we wanted to demonstrate the usefulness of the framework by putting it to use in a real-world scenario so that we could communicate to the audience the kinds of outcomes that they might anticipate; second, we wanted to derive insights from the consequences of applying the framework. We arrived at the decision that the following procedures would be the best strategy to carry out the case study: the academics from the case study school would assist in data collection; second, we would make it easier for the case study participants to apply the framework by instructing them on how to assess their institutions' assessment ratings for each characteristic; and third, we would analyze and summarize findings and recommendations. We came to this conclusion after deliberating on the matter.

The institution known by the pseudonym "GIST" hosted the case study, which was conducted at the beginning of March 2021. "GIST" has been around for more than 30 years, and it now provides a total of 16 different post-graduate degree programs in addition to 12 undergraduate degree programs. Every year, approximately 1500 students graduate, and this number represents the national average. The university has a total faculty of 290 people and is equipped with fundamental information technology resources, along with additional conveniences. Over the course of conducting this case study, we spoke virtually with a team of seven academics who were tasked with assisting their faculty members and students while the institution under investigation implemented online education. They are highly experienced faculty members who have in-depth information regarding the development of teaching and learning procedures as well as of the evaluation system at their institution. They were acquainted with the aspects of the OEMT program that were used by their fellow staff members as well as with the methods in which their fellow staff members utilized online education platforms. During the current COVID-19 situation, which is still ongoing, we noticed that "GIST" was only beginning to become acquainted with the concept of online education.

Since February of 2020, the organization had been working with a freeware OEMT. The administration of this educational institution concluded that there was very little room for training to be provided to the institution's teachers and students; therefore, they decided to begin requiring them to utilize this instrument beginning in the last week of February 2020. To determine whether or not their institution was prepared to make a smooth transition to an online education platform, we asked those seven professors from the institution that served as our case study, GIST, to assign a point value to each of the CAF's features. Every professor was briefed on the significance of awarding a score for each attribute as well as the ramifications that this had. All seven academics were asked to meet in a single online venue, Google Meet, to debate the suggested framework known as CAF and to assign marks collectively and decisively for each of the following characteristics: the product, the IT infrastructure, and the people. The first writer was responsible for documenting all of the specifics of the conversations that took place with the academics while the case study was being conducted, including their results for "GIST." "GIST" only received a score of "2" (B1-A2-B3 in CAF) for its overall performance, with each attribute receiving a score of "1" (B1) for the infrastructure, "0" (A2) for the people, and "1" (B3) for the product. As we have already discussed, the best total score for online education should be "6" or as close to it as possible, with an example of appropriate scores being "4" (for example, C1-B2-B3) or "5" (for example, C1-C2-B3).

7. Lessons Learned

We were curious to see how the case study institution managed their online education practices with their professors and students since they only received a total score of "2" regarding the implementation of the framework. One of the professors who participated in this case study said that they were simply reactive and not proactive in anticipating the administrative or technological problems that the faculty and students would encounter, resulting in a mess that resulted in incomplete lectures, tardy faculty evaluations of assignments, lower student participation in discussion/clarification forums, and subpar preparation and delivery of digital content. In addition to poorly maintained IT assets and less user-friendly online learning tools, our case study institution even had trouble training its staff on how to utilize its newly launched online education management tool (OEMT). This shows how poorly educational institutions handle staff and student change management, which is crucial to the success of online learning.

The case study institution was ready to build up its IT resources, with examples of improvements including stronger internet connections and system upgrades or configurations. Since free products only offer a few functions, the case study institution was also interested in spending money to purchase a licensed version of their current online education software program. However, their biggest limitation was that, under their current approval and budget management methods, they would need additional time to make use of two features: the product and the IT resources. The case study participants acknowledged that implementing online education would be challenging and would not benefit faculty or students unless the institution's top management made a strategic action plan to prepare for it by allocating IT resources, assisting employees in adjusting to change, and recommending the use of an intuitive online platform.

8. Recommendations

Based on the application of our proposed Capability Assessment Framework (CAF) with the help of a case study guided by Yin [27] and by relying on the lessons learned from it, we now present our recommendations to institutions for a seamless transformation to online education.

Digital technology integration has great promise for creating opportunities for cognitively stimulating higher learning, not just in the face of present or upcoming crises (e.g., [29,30]). Because of the greater temporal and spatial/geographic flexibility, online learning systems also allow more varied students with various constraints (such as maternity, a distant place of residence, or part-time study) to benefit from a potentially excellent university education [31]. Without any face-to-face interaction, the digitization of education may not be as pervasive and all-encompassing as it was in traditional times, and change processes may be slower and less inevitable. In spite of these distinctions, there are many lessons to be learned by examining how teachers and students behave, interact, and think when faced with a challenging circumstance that pushes everyone outside of their comfort zones that necessitates a quick response. Based on the extensive and worldwide use of online teaching and learning in higher education, both the positive and negative characteristics are more obvious than ever before. Even though the factors we're discussing are the same whether we are in a crisis or not, quickly and rigorously implementing the derived measures is far more important in an emergency.

Here, we provide some suggestions to educational institutions to help them to smoothly move from in-person instruction to online instruction.

Choice of online product: It is not necessary to switch to new technology or new online platforms quickly without first thoroughly reviewing their features and other technical requirements for institutions that have already adapted to Google Classroom or Microsoft Systems, both of which are free for educational institutions. In reality, amid a crisis, such as the current on brought about by COVID-19, it is advisable to keep things simple and use the resources that an organization already has access to. Later on, organizations might investigate other online tools being offered.

Use the same online product: Whether it is a paid-for OEMT or a freeware OEMT, all faculty members are urged to use the same online software product. This will enable professors and learners to fully utilize the product's capabilities by immediately being able to share their own experiences with the product. Different software products used by different teachers will only make learning more difficult for students because each product will have a different user interface and operating system.

Leverage IT resources: Only when the institution is aware of the IT resources available to their professors and students can it advise them on the best methods to enhance it so that they can use online education services without any problems. Only then is uninterrupted teaching–learning via an online mode conceivable. For instance, internal computer maintenance cells may serve as their guide in defining the bare minimum hardware and software requirements that must be upheld for desktop or laptop computers at home.

Promote Blended Learning: During the interview, a few professors advised using a blended learning approach (also known as a "flipped class" model) [32] rather than an entirely online class-based course delivery. According to this concept, the faculty would share some or all of the audio/video lectures or online course materials with the students before engaging in any online interaction. Before online lectures, the students can download materials at their leisure and utilize them for fast reading/listening exercises. Depending on the institution's and the students' IT resources, the course faculty could decide whether to use this model or a full-fledged online platform for delivering courses.

Motivate and train people: Any business undergoing a digital transformation will only be successful if it invests in the staff members who will be responsible for putting the technology to use [32]. Regarding people (students/faculty), the most critical concerns for our case study institution were the lack of knowledge about online education on the part of some faculty and students, the lack of interest in such a mode of teaching on the part of others, and the difficulty, despite best efforts, experienced by the remaining group in using it effectively due to a lack of training and insufficient IT resources. To break out of this impasse, a team composed of a cross-section of faculty members should initially be assembled to adopt online education. After that, this team might receive training from a different corporation or from subject-matter experts from other organizations. They might then gradually train the students as well as the other academic staff members at their institution. Furthermore, by having their internal training team use the product, the institution will be able to fix a few technical issues or features. To effectively provide online lectures and implement cutting-edge evaluations using online platforms, the training staff and selected faculty members who are well-liked by their students should be given rewards. The institution may think about awarding them with incentives such as reward points or appreciation certificates.

Do not shrink IT investments too much: The organization should be ready to spend a small amount on IT to use the capabilities of their present product, if one already exists, or to buy a new one. These types of investments are essential since some online learning resources are only accessible on Android, while others may cost a little more than normal but may be compatible with a variety of operating systems, including Linux, Microsoft, and Android. Both mobile apps and web-based versions of these tools should be accessible.

9. Conclusions

In studies concentrating on the attitudes, abilities, and knowledge of instructors in higher education institutions, it also became clear how crucial it is to have personal experience to comprehend the effects of emergency online learning and teaching. This focus on resources is consistent with the Expectancy Value Theory [33], which holds that a person's motivation to engage in an activity is influenced by both their subjective task value in a particular domain and their expectations for success (i.e., competence-related beliefs). In the case of emergency online education, it may be hypothesized that both external and internal resources, particularly attitudes linked to competence, affect expectations for success. However, positive attitudes toward technology seem to boost student abilities to handle emergency online learning without regard to emotional–motivational student profiles, which is consistent with other research on the significance of ICT competencies and attitudes towards online learning [23]. In other words, with more positive ICT attitudes, emergency online learning can be seen as less risky.

If institutions are unwilling to invest in human capital, the benefits of online education cannot be fully realized, and institutions will have trouble properly utilizing their IT infrastructure and online learning platforms. If they do not invest, institutions risk lowering the sophistication of the employed electronic materials, frustrating both users and instructors. As recommended for most organizational changes [34], a comprehensive strategic method to change management is required for the implementation of online education. The potential of online education to reach as many students as possible all over the world can, if carried out well, increase revenue for educational institutions in addition to providing accessibility from anywhere and flexibility in delivery. The experience of learners using online education needs to be better understood through future research.

Author Contributions: Conceptualization, S.S.; methodology, S.P.; software, S.S; validation, S.P.; formal analysis, S.S.; investigation, S.P.; data curation, S.S.; writing—original draft preparation, S.S.; writing—review and editing, S.P.; visualization, S.S.; supervision, S.S.; project administration, S.P. All authors have read and agreed to the published version of the manuscript.

Funding: This research received no external funding.

Data Availability Statement: Data are contained within the article.

Conflicts of Interest: The authors declare no conflict of interest.

References

1. Allen, I.E.; Seaman, J. *Online Report Card: Tracking Online Education in the United States*; Babson Survey Research Group: Babson Park, MA, USA, 2016.
2. Bocchi, J.; Eastman, J.K.; Swift, C.O. Retaining the online learner: Profile of students in an online MBA program and implications for teaching them. *J. Educ. Bus.* **2004**, *79*, 245–253. [CrossRef]
3. Exter, M.E.; Korkmaz, N.; Harlin, N.M.; Bichelmeyer, B.A. Sense Of Community Within A Fully Online Program Perspectives of Graduate Students. *Q. Rev. Distance Educ.* **2009**, *10*, 177–194.
4. Rovai, A.P. Building classroom community at a distance: A case study. *Educ. Technol. Res. Dev.* **2001**, *49*, 33–48. [CrossRef]
5. Kang, H.; Gyorke, A.S. Rethinking distance learning activities: A comparison of transactional distance theory and activity theory. *Open Learn. J. Open Distance e-Learn.* **2008**, *23*, 203–214. [CrossRef]
6. Lee, Y.; Choi, J. A review of online course dropout research: Implications for practice and future research. *Educ. Technol. Res. Dev.* **2011**, *59*, 593–618. [CrossRef]
7. O'Shea, S.; Stone, C.; Delahunty, J. "I 'feel'like I am at university even though I am online." Exploring how students narrate their engagement with higher education institutions in an online learning environment. *Distance Educ.* **2015**, *36*, 41–58. [CrossRef]
8. Pigliapoco, E.; Bogliolo, A. The effects of psychological sense of community in online and face-to-face academic courses. *Int. J. Emerg. Technol. Learn.* **2008**, *3*, 60–69. [CrossRef]
9. Palloff, R.M.; Pratt, K. *Building Online Learning Communities: Effective Strategies for the Virtual Classroom*; John Wiley & Sons: New York, NY, USA, 2007.
10. Kumar, P.; Kumar, A.; Palvia, S.; Verma, S. Online business education research: Systematic analysis and a conceptual model. *Int. J. Manag. Educ.* **2019**, *17*, 26–35. [CrossRef]
11. Alcaraz, R.; Martínez-Rodrigo, A.; Zangróniz, R.; Rieta, J.J. Blending Inverted Lectures and Laboratory Experiments to Improve Learning in an Introductory Course in Digital Systems. *IEEE Trans. Educ.* **2019**, *63*, 144–154. [CrossRef]
12. Chi, M.T.; Adams, J.; Bogusch, E.B.; Bruchok, C.; Kang, S.; Lancaster, M.; Yaghmourian, D.L. Translating the ICAP theory of cognitive engagement into practice. *Cogn. Sci.* **2018**, *42*, 1777–1832. [CrossRef]
13. Englund, C.; Hofer, S.; Nistor, N. Designing for fake news literacy training: A problem-based undergraduate online-course. *Comput. Hum. Behav.* **2021**, *121*, 106796.
14. Leonardi, P. You're Going Digital—Now What? *Sloan Manag. Rev.* **2020**, *61*, 1–10.
15. Thomas, M. Digital Education: Opportunities, Challenges, and Responsibilities. In *Digital Education. Palgrave Macmillan's Digital Education and Learning*; Thomas, M., Ed.; Palgrave Macmillan: New York, NY, USA, 2011.
16. Murphy, M.P. COVID-19 and emergency eLearning: Consequences of the securitization of higher education for post-pandemic pedagogy. *Contemp. Secur. Policy* **2020**, *41*, 492–505. [CrossRef]
17. Miranda, P.; Isaias, P.; Costa, C.; Pifano, S. Validation of an e-Learning 3.0 Critical Success Factors Framework: A Qualitative Research. *J. Inf. Technol. Educ. Res.* **2017**, *16*, 339–363. [CrossRef] [PubMed]
18. Sathyan, A.R.; Funk, C.; Sam, A.S.; Radhakrishnan, A.; Ragavan, S.O.; Kandathil, J.V.; Vishnu, S. Digital competence of higher education learners in the context of COVID-19 triggered online learning. *Soc. Sci. Humanit. Open* **2022**, *6*, 100320.
19. Englund, C.; Olofsson, A.D.; Price, L. Teaching with technology in higher education: Understanding conceptual change and development in practice. *High. Educ. Res. Dev.* **2017**, *36*, 73–87. [CrossRef]
20. Schneckenberg, D. Understanding the real barriers to technology-enhanced innovation in higher education. *Educ. Res.* **2009**, *51*, 411–424. [CrossRef]
21. Broadbent, J. Comparing online and blended learner's self-regulated learning strategies and academic performance. *Internet High. Educ.* **2017**, *33*, 24–32. [CrossRef]
22. Fischer, C.; Fischer-Ontrup, C.; Schuster, C. Individuelle Förderung und selbstreguliertes Lernen. *Beding. Und Optionen Für Das Lehren Und Lern. Präsenz Und Auf Distanz* **2020**, *20226*, 136–152.
23. Carretero, S.; Vuorikari, R.; Punie, Y. *The Digital Competence Framework for Citizens with Eight Proficiency Levels and Examples of Use*; Publications Office of the European Union: Luxembourg, 2017.
24. Fraillon, J.; Ainley, J.; Schulz, W.; Duckworth, D.; Friedman, T. *IEA International Computer and Information Literacy Study 2018 Assessment Framework*; Springer Nature: Berlin, Germany, 2019; p. 74.
25. Hofer, S.I.; Holzberger, D.; Reiss, K. Evaluating school inspection effectiveness: A systematic research synthesis on 30 years of international research. *Stud. Educ. Eval.* **2020**, *65*, 100864. [CrossRef]
26. Mahlow, C.; Hediger, A. Digital Transformation in Higher Education–Buzzword or Opportunity? *ACM Elearn Mag.* **2019**, *2019*, 13. [CrossRef]
27. Yin, R.K. *Case Study Research*, 5th ed.; Sage: Thousand Oaks, CA, USA, 2013.
28. King, N.; Horrock, C. *Interviews in Qualitative Research*; Sage: New York, NY, USA, 2010.
29. Chi, M.; Wylie, R. The ICAP framework: Linking cognitive engagement to active learning outcomes. *Educ. Psychol.* **2014**, *49*, 219–243. [CrossRef]
30. Hillmayr, D.; Ziernwald, L.; Reinhold, F.; Hofer, S.I.; Reiss, K.M. The potential of digital tools to enhance mathematics and science learning in secondary schools: A context-specific meta-analysis. *Comput. Educ.* **2020**, *153*, 103897. [CrossRef]

31. Mahieu, R.; Wolming, S. Do Men Learn in Order to Earn? Motives for Lifelong Learners to Choose Web-based Courses and the Relationship with Age, Gender, Parenthood, and Rate of Studies. Proceeding of the 21st European Distance and e-Learning Network Annual Conference 2012 (EDEN 2012) EDEN Secretariat c/o Budapest University of Technology and Economics, Porto, Portugal, 6–9 June 2012; p. 51.
32. Frankiewicz, B.; Chamorro-Premuzic, T. Digital Transformation Is About Talent, Not Technology. *Harv. Bus. Rev.* **2020**, *6*, 1–8.
33. Eccles, J. Expectancies, Values and Academic Behaviors. In *Achievement and Achievement Motives*; Free Man: San Francisco, CA, USA, 1983.
34. Navarro, P. How economics faculty can survive (and perhaps thrive) in a brave new online world. *J. Econ. Perspect.* **2015**, *29*, 155–176. [CrossRef]

Article

Heuristic Evaluation of Microsoft Teams as an Online Teaching Platform: An Educators' Perspective

Lamis Al-Qora'n [1,*], Omar Al Sheik Salem [1] and Neil Gordon [2]

[1] Faculty of Information Technology, Department of Software Engineering, Philadelphia University, Amman 19392, Jordan
[2] School of Computer Science, University of Hull, Hull HU6 7RX, UK
* Correspondence: lalqoran@philadelphia.edu.jo

Abstract: The way that education is delivered changed significantly during the COVID-19 pandemic to be completely online in many countries for many institutions. Despite the fact that they are not online teaching platforms, virtual meeting platforms were utilized to deal with this transformation. One of the platforms Philadelphia University utilized for the unplanned shift to online teaching was Microsoft Teams. This paper examines how heuristic evaluation may be used to guide the evaluation of online meeting platforms for teaching and focuses on the use of heuristic evaluation to assess the level of usability of Microsoft Teams. The level of Zoom's usability is also evaluated using heuristic evaluation in order to compare it to that of Microsoft Teams and to assess Microsoft Teams' overall usability in comparison to other platforms being used for the same purpose. Microsoft Teams was identified as having a few issues that need to be addressed. Additionally, strengths, weaknesses, opportunities, and threats to Microsoft Teams' usability were assessed.

Keywords: Microsoft Teams; usability; usability evaluation; heuristic evaluation

Citation: Al-Qora'n, L.; Salem, O.A.S.; Gordon, N. Heuristic Evaluation of Microsoft Teams as an Online Teaching Platform: An Educators' Perspective. *Computers* **2022**, *11*, 175. https://doi.org/10.3390/computers11120175

Academic Editors: Antonio Sarasa Cabezuelo and Covadonga Rodrigo San Juan

Received: 7 November 2022
Accepted: 2 December 2022
Published: 4 December 2022

Publisher's Note: MDPI stays neutral with regard to jurisdictional claims in published maps and institutional affiliations.

Copyright: © 2022 by the authors. Licensee MDPI, Basel, Switzerland. This article is an open access article distributed under the terms and conditions of the Creative Commons Attribution (CC BY) license (https://creativecommons.org/licenses/by/4.0/).

1. Introduction

COVID-19, a new coronavirus disease, was identified as a 'pandemic' by the World Health Organization (WHO) on March 11, 2020, due to its quick global spread [1]. Following that, governments started to announce lockdowns, prompting educational institutions to suddenly take decisions on an unexpected and compulsory shift to online teaching. Academic institutions faced challenges as a result of this rapid academic revolution, as there was no prior preparation for both educators and learners, resulting in several challenges while practicing the online learning process. This complete transformation to online learning and online teaching requires a suitable evaluation that measures and reflects the quality of the entire learning and teaching experience [2]. An important aspect of this evaluation is evaluating the online meeting platforms considering how user-friendly these platforms are and how effective and efficient they are in achieving the specified goals for teaching.

Microsoft Teams was the primary platform used at Philadelphia University for the rapid shift to online teaching during COVID-19 and later. However, by all means, it was a big challenge to use this platform, not only within our university but also worldwide. This was due to the lack of knowledge in using these platforms for online teaching. As a teaching platform, it has been improving since then to match the needs of the users and to become easier to use. However, it has been reported by many lecturers that they are still facing lots of difficulties while using the platform.

Usability is a fundamental criterion for assessing e-learning technology and systems as it reflects the quality and prioritizes the users' actual needs [3]. Therefore, evaluating the usability of the used platform and investigating its contribution to the learning process is crucial. This paper evaluates the usability of Microsoft Teams as an online teaching platform. It also examines how other platforms such as Zoom, which are used for online teaching, meet the requirements of educators. Moreover, the paper identifies several shortcomings and challenges with Microsoft Teams as an online teaching platform in comparison to Zoom as a platform that is used for the same purpose. The paper does not consider more specialized Virtual Learning Environment (VLE) platforms, which tend to focus on supporting learners generally. The problem addressed here is on some of the most adopted platforms—notably Microsoft Teams and Zoom—that were used to supplement established VLEs to provide a synchronous learning environment.

2. Background

2.1. Usability and Usability Evaluation

Usability, as explained by the International Standards Organization [4], is the extent to which a product can be utilized by specific users to accomplish specific goals in a given application context with efficiency, effectiveness, and satisfaction [5]. Moreover, [6] defined usability as a metric that measures how efficiently, effectively, and successfully a specific user can use a product or design to achieve a specified objective in a given context. Therefore, usability is a quality metric that assesses how easy it is to use a user interface, and during the design phase, "usability" refers to techniques for enhancing the ease of use [7]. In this paper, usability is defined as a quality metric that assesses how easily, effectively, and efficiently a platform can achieve a user's goals.

Usability is important because it is one of the key factors in gaining users' satisfaction and confidence, which is essential to the survival of platforms such as MS Teams. If users were not satisfied with the existing platform, they would look for a reasonable alternative that delivers all of the features offered by the current platform.

Thus, from the previous definitions and as explained by [8], we perceived that in studying the usability of Microsoft Teams we have three important aspects to focus on as shown in Table 1: specified users (lecturers in our case), goal (delivering an online lecture in our case), and context (teaching in our case).

Table 1. Usability Aspects.

Usability Attribute	Application in Online Teaching
Specified users	Educators
Effectively meeting goal	Delivering online lecture
Context	Online Teaching in Higher Education institutions

Furthermore, studying the usability of Microsoft Teams should be directed to measure its effectiveness, efficiency, and the extent to which users are satisfied.

A review of the literature revealed that researchers can employ either usability testing (User Experience (UX) is another name for it) or Heuristic evaluation to examine and assess the usability of online learning platforms. Usability evaluation is the process of assessing a product or device's usability on several levels [9]. The process, that concentrates on observing users while interacting with a product when carrying out genuine and meaningful tasks, is called usability testing [8]. Usability tests and inspection methodologies may be performed to measure and evaluate the usability of a product that has already been designed into it [10]. Moreover, in usability tests, the focus is on the potential end users and their experience while using the product. In the case of e-learning systems, individual interviews, questionnaires, online surveys, heuristic evaluations, expert reviews, remote testing, and other approaches can be utilized for evaluating their usability [11].

A well-known technique for quick evaluation of the effectiveness of new technologies and interface problems is heuristic evaluation [3,12,13]. Daniela and Rusu [10] identified heuristic evaluation as one of these approaches, which is a type of inspection that finds usability issues using usability heuristics or principles. Moreover, remote usability testing is possible when the user is at a different location (either unmoderated or moderated) [11]. Additionally, [13,14] defined heuristic evaluation as a method for usability evaluation that is informed by heuristics analysis in which several specialists in the field are required to apply their specialized knowledge to speculate on an interface solution. The ten basic concepts of interaction, designed by Jakob Nielsen [15] that were updated in November 2020, are general rules of thumb rather than particular usability requirements or guidelines, thus, they are known as "heuristics". Therefore, using these ten heuristics while developing interfaces is regarded best practice. To determine whether a system adheres to usability standards, a system should be evaluated by three to five experts because using multiple evaluators has the potential to produce more accurate results.

Squires and Preece [16] originally proposed the use of heuristic evaluation to measure usability, quality, and potential for learning the applications with an educational focus. Albion and Benson et al. [17] also used Nielson's heuristics and added extra heuristics to them that are related to e-learning. Moreover, [18] applied the heuristics that were developed by [16] for pedagogic applications. Even though heuristic evaluation is frequently employed in online learning and other domains, not everyone follows Nielsen's suggested ten principles [9].

Thus, it can be seen that there are many methods for measuring usability in the literature, as without measurement, it is impossible to control usability requirements or to determine if a product has developed to meet its users' requirements [19].

This study evaluates the usability of Microsoft Teams as a platform for online teaching using heuristic evaluation. In other words, it evaluates how well Microsoft Teams fits the usability requirements of educators in higher education in order to deliver a lecture. Additionally, it aims to evaluate how Microsoft Teams is employed and how efficient and effective it is. Considering Nielsen's heuristics, the researchers built their technique.

2.2. Microsoft Teams

Microsoft Teams is a software that was developed by Microsoft in the Office 365 bundle. This communication platform offers file storing, chatting and video/voice conferencing, which has the potential to enable its users to perform group discussions as well as one-to-one meetings. Due to the pandemic, Microsoft Teams and some of its competitors such as Google Meet and Zoom gained much more interest and usage in the educational field.

The number of users of Microsoft Teams has increased significantly between 2019 and 2022. In 2019, the number of daily active users was 13 million [20], while in 2022 it reached more than 270 million monthly active users [21]. That increase was because of the improvement in the features that were provided by Microsoft Teams to its users as there are some features that help in enhancing the education process and virtual learning such as chatting, creating teams, conversations as groups, quizzes, assignments, and channels.

2.3. Evaluation of Microsoft Teams and Online Learning Platforms

The most popular technologies for lectures in higher education institutions recently have been Microsoft Teams and Zoom, and because these platforms were not created with education in mind at first, learning effectiveness was noticeably diminished [9]. Many studies such as [22,23] stated that during online lectures, both students and teachers reported numerous issues.

Throughout the COVID-19 pandemic and the sudden transfer to online learning, [24] conducted research in Jenin city to see how using technologies such as Microsoft Teams helped to enrich English education. The results of studying a sample of twenty-five (25) English language teachers showed that Microsoft Teams has features that enrich the interactive learning process by allowing users to share content and files, as well as screen sharing, which allows educators to present appropriate content while the class is online.

Sari and Nayir [25], on the other hand, looked at how teachers, administrators, and scholars felt about continuing online education. The data were analyzed by a working group of 65 teachers. The research revealed issues with students' Internet access, as well as a lack of infrastructure and classroom management as a result.

Moreover, [26] assessed and contrasted the online learning tools' usefulness using the System Usability Scale (SUS) questionnaire, which primarily focuses on efficiency, ease of use, and ease of learning. The findings of this research show that, compared to e-learning platforms and Microsoft Teams, Zoom performs better in terms of usability. Additionally, [27] combined the System Usability Scale (SUS), Human–Computer Interaction (HCI)-based technique, Technology Acceptance Model (TAM), and Information Systems (IS)-based approach to use them for the usability evaluation of Microsoft Teams. In their study, [27] assessed the efficiency of Microsoft Teams as an online learning platform in terms of how usable it is seen by students. However, educators (lecturers) are also on another side of this argument and knowing about their perspectives on the usability of online learning platforms is vital.

After reviewing the literature, we found that e-learning platforms' usability was the subject of many studies. These studies used many heuristics for evaluating the overall experience of online learning; however, they were frequently not focused on the teaching experience while delivering an online lecture. Accordingly, there is a scarcity of studies that consider evaluating the educators' experience while using online teaching platforms, especially the usability of Microsoft Teams as an online teaching platform. Thus, this paper utilizes Nielsen's heuristics for the evaluation of Microsoft Teams as an online teaching platform. In order to validate our results, Zoom is also evaluated as it is a platform that is in use for the same purpose. The results of the evaluation of the two platforms are compared to obtain an overall evaluation of Microsoft Teams.

3. Evaluation Procedure and Results

The study was initially approved by the Philadelphia University Research Ethics Committee (Faculty of Information Technology). For the purpose of evaluating Microsoft Teams, the authors used Nielsen's heuristics to evaluate both Microsoft Teams and Zoom, as indicated in Table 2. Zoom is assessed in order to compare Microsoft Teams with other platforms out there. Thus, a group of experts with proven expertise in e-learning and computer education research, as well as in teaching software engineering and computer science courses at the University level, evaluated the two platforms. Thus, the procedure served as an end-user evaluation to help in getting professional suggestions and recommendations for updating the platforms.

Any learning management system or any software that is in use as a learning management system should help in achieving key educational institutions' goals such as delivering and tracking courses, which can be subdivided into the following sub-goals: creating a course, managing a course and delivering a course. The sub-goal "Delivering a course" can be achieved by delivering online lectures, interacting with students, and tracking students' performance.

In order to deliver an online lecture, a lecturer is required to perform a variety of tasks. Thus, to determine the end tasks, the sub-goal of delivering a lecture is broken down into sub-goals and activities. The authors as experts developed a number of scenarios and embedded certain tasks to be carried out to evaluate the two platforms according to the same standards. Scenarios were prepared in a way that each scenario has a set of related tasks that are directed to achieve a sub-goal.

Then, scenarios that achieve the goal of "delivering an online lecture" are built, which enables us to reconsider the approach of delivering a traditional lecture. The scenarios required to deliver a virtual or online lecture are specified and created. The scenarios that are intended to achieve goals are used in order to achieve a consistent evaluation. The scenarios were given to the experts so they could complete the same tasks and assess them using the heuristics. Figure 1 below shows the process of specifying the tasks (actions) and functions that are required to achieve a goal.

Table 2. Nielsen's heuristics applied to evaluate Microsoft Teams on a scale of 1 to 5.

Heuristics	Experts' Evaluation (Microsoft Teams)	Experts' Evaluation (Zoom)
Ensures visibility of system status	4 4 2 3 Avg: 3.25	5 4 3 4 Avg: 4
Maximizes match between the system and the real world	5 4 3 4 Avg: 4	5 4 4 4 Avg: 4.25
Maximizes user control and freedom	4 3 4 3 Avg: 3.5	4 2 4 3 Avg: 3.25
Consistent and matches standards	4 4 4 4 Avg: 4	4 4 4 4 Avg: 4
Prevents Errors	4 4 2 3 Avg: 3.25	4 3 3 4 Avg: 3.5
Supports recognition rather than recall	3 2 3 2 Avg: 2.5	4 3 4 4 Avg: 3.75
Supports flexibility and efficiency	4 3 3 4 Avg: 3.5	3 3 3 4 Avg: 3.25
Uses aesthetic and minimalist design	4 4 4 4 Avg: 4	3 4 4 4 Avg: 3.75
Helps users recognize and recover from errors	4 3 4 3 Avg: 3.5	4 3 4 4 Avg: 3.75
Provides help and documentation	4 4 4 4 Avg: 4	4 4 2 4 Avg: 3.5

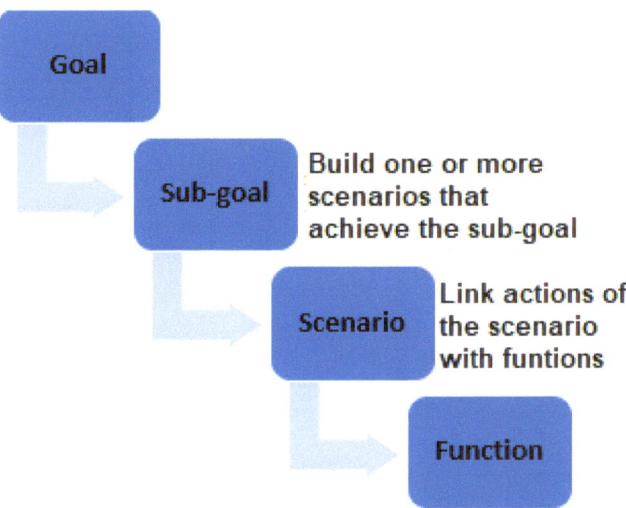

Figure 1. The process of specifying the tasks (actions) and functions that are required to achieve a goal.

The following is an example of one of the scenarios that achieves the goal: **deliver an online lecture**.

A 90-min online virtual lecture could be split up into different actions that are performed by the lecturer to start the lecture and to manage it. Moreover, there are a number of activities that have to be performed throughout the lecture and homework for the next lecture or that may even need to be submitted after one week.

To start an online lecture, the lecturer starts a meeting and makes sure that all his/her students are able to join before starting the online lecture. The lecturer then shares the material (such as lecture slides) and, if desired, begins to record the lecture. The lecturer may also need to share the whiteboard to demonstrate some concepts to the students. The lecturer will then give the students an assignment to complete as classwork, which must be turned in during the lecture. There is a chance that the lecturer will have to assign different tasks to various groups. The lecturer may also be required to engage with the class; for example, by encouraging a student, showing appreciation for what they said, or expressing surprise at something they observed. The lecturer may also need to record the lecture in addition to dividing the class into groups and interacting with each one separately. He or she should be able to finish the meeting after the lecture before leaving.

Then, the implementation phase started, where we began the evaluation procedure by having the experts perform tasks in each scenario and rating the platform according to the heuristics. Figure 2 demonstrates the phases of the evaluation procedure.

As shown in Table 2, in light of Nielsen's heuristics, four experts were asked to rate the platforms (Microsoft Teams and Zoom) on a scale of 1 to 5, with 1 being the worst and 5 being the best. Where the platform does not apply, they were asked to enter N/A. The average expert evaluation is then calculated and the results are shown in Table 2 and Figure 3. For more details on the mapping of each heuristic in Table 2 to the assessment carried out by the expert evaluator, see Table A1 in the Appendix A.

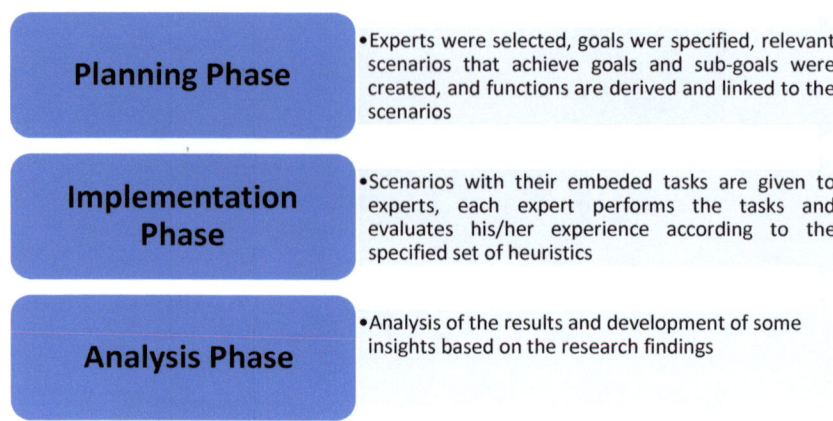

Figure 2. Evaluation Procedure.

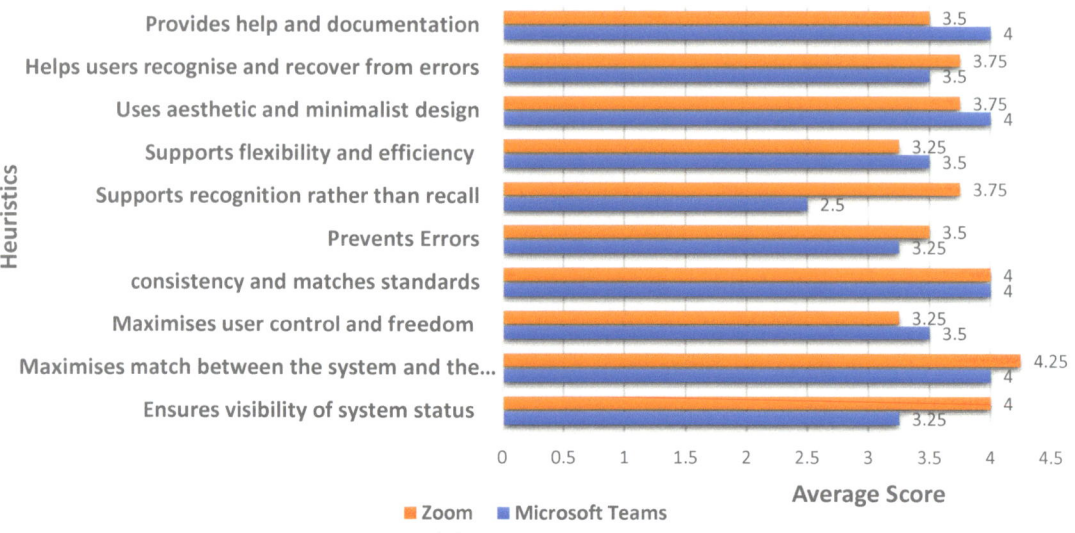

Figure 3. Comparison between Microsoft Teams and Zoom according to the evaluation procedure.

4. Discussion of Results

The focus was on the activities (functions) necessary for delivering an online lecture that should be available and obvious for lecturers to finish the lecture efficiently and satisfy educators. Some of the core activities were creating a Team or initiating a meeting, scheduling a meeting, and adding members to the meeting, enabling/disabling video and audio, sharing content, recording meeting, uploading content and chatting. According to Nielsen's heuristics, users should always be informed and provided with suitable feedback in a timely manner about what is going on. The average of experts' evaluation for this heuristic is 3.25 out of 5 for Microsoft Teams and 4 out of 5 for Zoom. Experts stated that Zoom provides the user with appropriate information regarding the current status such as: sharing the screen, activating the whiteboard or ongoing recording. Moreover, while idle, the status of the actions conducted on Zoom is clear, for example, Zoom shows the following message: ('The user does not have any upcoming meetings. To schedule a new meeting click Schedule a Meeting'). On the other hand, in Microsoft Teams, experts reported a few issues. For example, the status of the actions conducted on the platform is clear when interacting but while idle it is not clear. Additionally, when creating a team with the same name as an existing team, experts found that Microsoft Teams allows them to do so without alerting users that this is an existing team; currently, the user can search for the team's name first and if it does not exist, they can create it. According to Nielsen's heuristics, this is an action that the users should be informed about because it has consequences. Another example that is related to the same issue is that when the camera is open while the user's screen is shared, it does not tell the user that his camera is turned on. As mentioned before, the visibility of the system status is crucial, no action that has consequences may be made without telling the user, and feedback to a user should always be given straight away, in accordance with Nielsen's heuristics. When turning on the camera, providing the user with feedback such as a sound notification is recommended. In addition to that, when using Zoom for quizzes and polls, the host is informed of the results live, while in MS Teams, that is not the case.

The second heuristic states that the design should communicate with the user's language, employ concepts that the user is familiar with, and present the information in a way that is both natural and logical for the lecturer to find comfortable. It should also use terms, expressions, and concepts that are well-known to educators. When searching across Microsoft Teams and Zoom, all the used words and sentences are familiar to novice and expert users, and the conventions used on the interface are understandable and can be easily recognized by the user. The recently added and updated reactions such as: smileys, raising a hand, out/break, etc., eased the communication and simulated real-world interactions. As a result, Zoom exceeded Microsoft Teams in this regard, achieving an average of 4.25 out of 5 compared to Microsoft Teams' average of 4. For example, in this essence, MS Teams and Zoom could provide sign language interpretation features, which could be enabled by the user, so verbal and nonverbal communication are addressed on both platforms.

The third heuristic supposes that users can undo mistakes and stop unwanted actions through a clearly marked "emergency exit" available to them. On this, the experts rated Microsoft Teams with an average of 3.5 and Zoom with an average of 3.25. All experts suggested that several enhancements can still be achieved in this domain, such as modifying sent messages or undoing sending a file to a specific user or deleting a message sent to all. Therefore, Zoom and MS Teams would provide users with more than one option to be able to exit such as the cancelling, pausing or deletion of a team, member, meeting or many other items.

Regarding the consistency and matching standards heuristic, users should not have to guess whether actions, various phrases, or circumstances have the same meaning because the usual operating system standards are maintained. Similar to Zoom's average score of 4 out of 5, Microsoft Teams here receives an average score of 4. The home page of Microsoft Teams, for instance, offers two options for the same function: "invite people to join you" AND "search participants and share invitation", indicating a lack of consistency in this situation. Experts claim that there is a proper distinction between various actions in both platforms and no ambiguity in understanding the various phrasing. In this regard, Zoom and Microsoft Teams showed a reasonable level of consistency.

The error prevention heuristic assumes that good error messages are crucial for error prevention but better designs also deal with potential issues before they arise. Conditions that are prone to errors should be checked or eliminated and a confirmation option should be given before users agree to an action. Microsoft Teams achieved 3.25 in this regard while Zoom achieved 3.5. Experts specified that to some extent, Zoom has a good messaging system, such as: confirming exiting the meeting or confirming the acceptance of recording the meeting. However, further indications could be added such as: confirming sharing of a file with the participants. In addition, experts pointed out that in Microsoft Teams, some options with important frequently used functions were grouped next to each other in a way that could be confusing when using these objects. It was also found that the objects were placed in a way that is uncomfortable for the user; as an example of this, see Figure 4, which shows a screenshot of Microsoft Teams' objects. For instance, the leave button is next to the share button, thus it is quite easy to leave by mistake. Additionally, there is potential for the user to unintentionally click the camera button, which may result in the camera opening without telling the user that their camera was turned on, as criticized by the first heuristic "Ensures visibility of system status". On the other hand, in Zoom, it is less likely that the user would accidentally push the start video button without intending to do so.

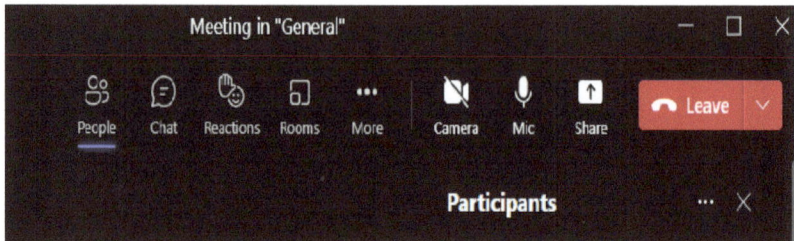

Figure 4. A Screenshot of Microsoft Teams Objects.

The heuristic known as "supports recognition rather than recall" precepts that by making elements, actions, and alternatives visible, the design should reduce the user's memory load. Moving from one user interface element to another should not need the user to recall or remember. Things such as menu items and field labels should be obviously visible or accessible. Zoom's average score is not particularly impressive here. A case that justifies this relatively low score is when looking at the case of switching from the normal session to the breakout sessions, all options could be retrieved and utilized; however, after exiting the system and it shutting down, (for instance, as a result of an internet outage), all previous settings (such as chat) were lost and could not be retrieved and recovered.

Microsoft Teams on the other hand receives a relatively low average score of 2.5, which is justified by the experts through many examples. For example, when looking at Microsoft Team's objects as in Figure 2, if the user presses the three dots, there are more than 15 options in the same dropdown menu to choose from including the meeting recording option, which may confuse the user. Returning to the "supports recognition rather than recall" heuristic, it can be observed that this is not fulfilled since Microsoft Teams' architecture does not eliminate memory overhead. In Zoom, as in Figure 5, the user is informed that there are alternatives for the video and they may select what they want, such as choosing a background or a video filter, due to the arrow to the top right of the video button. However, with Microsoft Teams, the user must point at the camera option in order to see the options, which are, according to lecturers, insufficient and do support the current heuristic.

Figure 5. A Screenshot of Zoom's Objects.

The seventh heuristic "Supports flexibility and efficiency", provides that to serve both inexperienced and experienced users, employing shortcuts may accelerate interaction for expert users while maintaining novice users' usability. Shortcuts also allow users to customize routine tasks. Microsoft Teams achieved an average score of 3.5 and Zoom achieved 3.25, which shows that there are some opportunities for both platforms to speed use.

According to the "Uses aesthetic and minimalist design" heuristic, interfaces should not contain unnecessary information that is infrequently used. Every extra piece of information that is added to an interface competes with the essential pieces and decreases their relative visibility. For this heuristic, Microsoft Teams and Zoom achieved an average score of 4 and 3.75, respectively, as both have little irrelevant information.

In terms of the "Helps users recognize and recover from errors" heuristic, which highlights the importance of error messages that are expressed in simple terms, clearly stating the issue, and offering a solution, Microsoft Teams achieved an average score of 3.5 and Zoom achieved 3.75.

The last heuristic is "Provides help and documentation" which states that in an ideal world, the system should be self-explanatory. However, it can be essential to provide documentation to ensure that users can complete their tasks. In this regard, Microsoft Teams receives an average of 4 and Zoom an average of 3.5.

Therefore, as shown in Figure 6, it is found that Microsoft Teams offers a number of strengths, including the simplicity of carrying out fundamental tasks necessary for delivering an online lecture. Furthermore, because there is help available, even tasks that are not obvious are simple to complete.

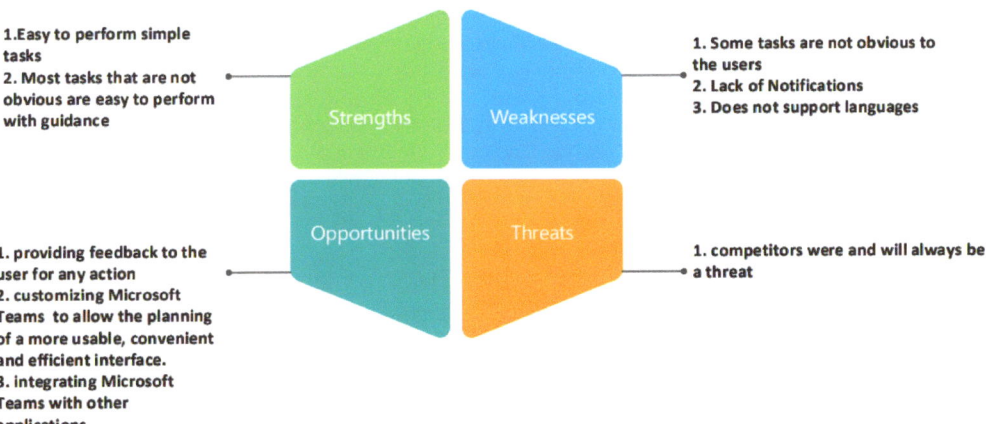

Figure 6. SWOT Analysis.

Additionally, there are many opportunities that should be taken to improve Microsoft Teams. For example, there is the opportunity to customize Microsoft Teams and modify its objects to allow the planning of a more usable, convenient and efficient interface. Moreover, it is important that Microsoft Teams provides feedback to the user for any action that is performed while delivering a lecture (during a meeting), for example, when turning the camera on. Moreover, for problems such as creating a team with a similar name to an existing team, the user should be notified. In other words, Microsoft Teams should allow more notifications which have the potential to make its use easier and more effective. Microsoft Teams can also be integrated with other applications which have the potential to automate some tasks and help in achieving ease of use such as adding students to a team.

In terms of threats to its survival and existence, satisfying users' needs with competitors such as Zoom may lead to less satisfaction with MS Teams' users and accordingly threaten its survival.

Finally, the lack of notifications, tasks that are not obvious to users, and the lack of support for many languages could be considered as the weaknesses that matter most.

5. Research Insights

Significant functional and pedagogical limitations were described by the experts as factors limiting their level of satisfaction with online teaching platforms as online educators. Considering experts' suggestions for having extra features such as having more notifications could help stakeholders meet their goals smoothly and improve the interaction between educators and learners. Moreover, improving the online teaching platforms and updating them with additional features has the potential to improve the learning outcomes and the overall quality of the online educational experience.

Lecturers should relax while delivering the lectures. It is possible to discontinue using the platform if the platform does not carry out users' actions correctly or carries out some actions without making users aware that such actions are being carried out. It is evident that platforms with all of these features can enhance the effectiveness of remote teaching and yet, incorporating more features to support them might make them even better.

6. Conclusions and Future Work

To conclude, for the purpose of reviewing and evaluating online teaching platforms, the heuristic evaluation is found to be a successful method and efficient tool that was simple to apply and relatively quick. On the other hand, heuristic evaluation was criticized for only testing the thoughts of the experts who are conducting the evaluation [3]. Such an evaluation might only indicate the preferences of the experts involved, not any actual interface flaws or concerns. In order to ensure that the participating experts were qualified to make well-informed decisions on online teaching and HCI, it was particularly important to select experienced software and computer scientists who would be capable of making reliable professional judgments about pedagogy and usability. The evaluation procedure did in fact take place based on the expertise of the experts in three universities (Philadelphia University in Jordan, the University of Hull in the United Kingdom, and RWTH Aachen University in Germany). All of the experts are already educators who are using Microsoft Teams and Zoom for teaching and accordingly they are able to reliably evaluate their efficiency. Furthermore, using pre-determined scenarios that are intended to achieve a specific goal helped in achieving a consistent evaluation and helped in directing the discussion toward the issue in question. It can be observed that Microsoft Teams is an efficient and effective tool and that it does not require many resources. Furthermore, there is a potential for educators (lecturers) to perform specific tasks easily.

We concluded that Microsoft Teams provides sufficient functionality for lecturers as an online teaching platform that can be utilized to deliver lectures within a collaborative and interactive environment. Microsoft Teams can be considered user-friendly according to our results, as it did not create any form of frustration during our experiments. However, better organization of the functionality of Microsoft teams and automation of some processes has the potential to save time and improve the teaching process. For future work, we will consider evaluating Microsoft Teams from the student's perspective.

Author Contributions: Conceptualization, L.A.-Q. and O.A.S.S.; Methodology, L.A.-Q.; Analysis, L.A.-Q.; Validation, L.A.-Q., O.A.S.S. and N.G.; Writing—original draft preparation, L.A.-Q.; Data curation, L.A.-Q., O.A.S.S. and N.G.; Writing—original draft preparation, L.A.-Q.; Writing—review and editing, L.A.-Q.; Expert evaluation, L.A.-Q., O.A.S.S. and N.G. All authors have read and agreed to the published version of the manuscript.

Funding: This research was funded by the Deanship of Scientific Research at Philadelphia University.

Institutional Review Board Statement: The study was approved by the Research Ethics Committee (Faculty of Information Technology-Philadelphia University).

Informed Consent Statement: Informed consent was obtained from all subjects involved in the study.

Data Availability Statement: For data supporting reported results please contact lalqoran@philadelphia.edu.jo.

Acknowledgments: We would also like to thank Lubna Ali, a research assistant from the RWTH Aachen University in Germany, for conducting an in-depth evaluation.

Conflicts of Interest: The authors declare no conflict of interest.

Appendix A

Table A1 provides a mapping of the heuristics in the assessment carried out by the expert evaluator.

Table A1. Mapping of Nielsen's heuristics to the actual evaluation.

Heuristics	Explanation
Ensures visibility of system status	Users should always be kept up to date on developments by the design, which should provide important and relevant feedback in a timely manner.
Maximizes match between the system and the real world	The interface should be user-friendly. Instead of using internal jargon, utilize words, phrases, and ideas that the user is already familiar with. Present information in a natural and logical order, and observe real-world conventions.
Maximizes user control and freedom	Users can undo mistakes and stop unwanted actions, while also having an "emergency exit" that is marked clearly and available to them.
Consistent and matches standards	Users should not have to guess whether various expressions, circumstances, or actions mean the same thing. Operating system rules and standards are adhered to.
Prevents errors	Since concise error messages are crucial, the best designs take care to predict problems before they occur. Before users take an action, error-prone scenarios should either be avoided, detected, or provided with a confirmation option.
Supports recognition rather than recall	The amount of memory required from the user should be reduced by making elements, options, and actions visible. When users navigate between different parts of the interface, they should not need to remember a lot of information. For example, menu options should be obvious and simple to find.
Supports flexibility and efficiency of use	The design serves both inexperienced and experienced users by using shortcuts that accelerate interactions for expert users whilst such shortcuts remain hidden from novice users. The design should allow users to customize routine actions.
Uses aesthetic and minimalist design	Interface should not have unnecessary information or less frequently used functions because having such information added to an interface has the potential to reduce the visibility of core functions.
Helps users recognize, diagnose and recover from errors	Expressing error messages in simple terms where the problem is identified clearly and offering a recommendation for a fix.
Provides help and documentation	The system should be self-explanatory to enable users to carry out the tasks that they require, documentation might be needed.

References

1. World Health Organization. WHO Timeline—COVID-19, March 2020. Available online: https://www.who.int/news-room/detail/27-04-2020-who-timeline-covid-19 (accessed on 4 September 2020).
2. Robinson, C.C.; Hullinger, H. New benchmarks in higher education: Student engagement in online learning. *J. Educ. Bus.* **2008**, *84*, 101–109. [CrossRef]
3. Nielsen, J.; Molich, R. Heuristic evaluation of user interfaces. In Proceedings of the SIGCHI Conference on Human Factors in Computing Systems, Seattle, WA, USA, 1–5 April 1990.
4. International Organization for Standardization. *Ergonomic Requirements for Office Work with Visual Display Terminals (VDTs)-Part 11: Guidance on Usability*; International Organization for Standardization: Geneva, Switzerland, 1998.
5. IEEE Brand Experience. Introduction to Web Usability and Accessibility. IEEE Brand Experience. Available online: https://brand-experience.ieee.org/resources/usability/ (accessed on 26 January 2022).
6. Interaction Design Foundation. What Is Usability? The Interaction Design Foundation, UX Courses. 2014. Available online: https://www.interaction-design.org/literature/topics/usability (accessed on 26 January 2022).

7. Nielsen, J. Usability 101: Introduction to Usability. Nielsen Norman Group, 3 January 2012. Available online: https://www.nngroup.com/articles/usability-101-introduction-to-usability/ (accessed on 26 January 2022).
8. Barnum, C.M. *Usability Testing Essentials: Ready, Set . . . Test!* Morgan Kaufmann: Burlington, MA, USA, 2020.
9. Ismail, H.; Khelifi, A.; Harous, S. A Cognitive Style Based Framework for Usability Evaluation of Online Lecturing Platforms-A Case Study on Zoom and Teams. *Int. J. Eng. Pedagog.* **2022**, *12*, 104–122. [CrossRef]
10. Quiñones, D.; Rusu, C. How to develop usability heuristics: A systematic literature review. *Comput. Stand. Interfaces* **2017**, *53*, 89–122. [CrossRef]
11. Usability Evaluation Methods | Usability.Gov. Usability.gov. 2019. Available online: https://www.usability.gov/how-to-and-tools/methods/usability-evaluation/index.html (accessed on 4 February 2022).
12. Nielsen, J.; Robert, M. *Usability Inspection Methods*; John Wiley: New York, NY, USA, 1994; ISBN 0-471-01877-5-14.
13. Nielsen, J. Usability inspection methods. In Proceedings of the Conference Companion on Human Factors in Computing Systems, Boston, MA, USA, 28 April 1994; pp. 413–414.
14. Interaction Design Foundation. "What Is Heuristic Evaluation?" The Interaction Design Foundation, UX Courses. 2019. Available online: www.interaction-design.org/literature/topics/heuristic-evaluation (accessed on 27 October 2020).
15. Nielsen, J. 10 Heuristics for User Interface Design. Nielsen Norman Group, Nielsen Norman Group, 24 April 1994. Available online: https://www.nngroup.com/articles/ten-usability-heuristics/ (accessed on 24 September 2022).
16. Squires, D.; Preece, J. Predicting Quality in Educational Software: Evaluating for Learning, Usability and the Synergy between Them. *Interact. Comput.* **1999**, *11*, 467–483. [CrossRef]
17. Albion, P. Heuristic evaluation of educational multimedia: From theory to practice. In Proceedings of the ASCILITE 1999: 16th Annual Conference of the Australasian Society for Computers in Learning in Tertiary Education: Responding to Diversity, Brisbane, Australia, 5–8 December 1999; pp. 9–15.
18. Brayshaw, M.; Gordon, N.; Nganji, J.; Wen, L.; Butterfield, A. Investigating heuristic evaluation as a methodology for evaluating pedagogical software: An analysis employing three case studies. In *International Conference on Learning and Collaboration Technologies*; Springer: Cham, Switzerland, 2014.
19. Jokela, T.; Koivumaa, J.; Pirkola, J.; Salminen, P.; Kantola, N. Methods for quantitative usability requirements: A case study on the development of the user interface of a mobile phone. *Pers. Ubiquitous Comput.* **2006**, *10*, 345–355. [CrossRef]
20. Spataro, J. Microsoft Teams Reaches 13 Million Daily Active Users, Introduces 4 New Ways for Teams to Work Better Together. Microsoft 365 Blog. 2019. Available online: https://www.microsoft.com/en-us/microsoft-365/blog/2019/07/11/microsoft-teams-reaches-13-million-daily-active-users-introduces-4-new-ways-for-teams-to-work-better-together/ (accessed on 26 August 2022).
21. Foley, M. Microsoft: Teams Now has More Than 270 Million Monthly Active Users. ZDNet. 2022. Available online: https://www.zdnet.com/article/microsoft-teams-now-has-more-than-270-million-monthly-active-users/ (accessed on 21 August 2022).
22. Arora, A.K.; Srinivasan, R. Impact of pandemic COVID-19 on the teaching–learning process: A study of higher education teachers. *Prabandhan Indian J. Manag.* **2020**, *13*, 43–56. [CrossRef] [PubMed]
23. Aboagye, E.; Yawson, J.A.; Appiah, K.N. COVID-19 and E-learning: The challenges of students in Tertiary Institutions. *Soc. Educ. Res.* **2021**, *2*, 1–8. [CrossRef]
24. Bsharat, T.R.; Behak, F. The impact of Microsoft teams' app in enhancing teaching-learning English during the Coronavirus (COVID-19) from the English teachers' perspectives' in Jenin city. *Malays. J. Sci. Health Technol.* **2020**, *7*. [CrossRef]
25. Sari, T.; Nayır, F. Challenges in distance education during the (Covid-19) pandemic period. *Qual. Res. Educ.* **2020**, *9*, 328–360. [CrossRef]
26. Abushamleh, H.; Jusoh, S. Usability Evaluation of Distance Education Tools Used in Jordanian Universities. In *2021 Innovation and New Trends in Engineering, Science and Technology Education Conference (IETSEC)*; IEEE: Amman, Jordan, 2021; pp. 1–5. [CrossRef]
27. Pal, D.; Vanijja, V. Perceived usability evaluation of Microsoft Teams as an online learning platform during COVID-19 using system usability scale and technology acceptance model in India. *Child. Youth Serv. Rev.* **2020**, *119*, 105535. [CrossRef] [PubMed]

Review

Literature Review on MOOCs on Sensory (Olfactory) Learning

Pierpaolo Limone [1], Sandra Pati [2], Giusi Antonia Toto [1,*], Raffaele Di Fuccio [1], Antonietta Baiano [2] and Giuseppe Lopriore [2]

- [1] Learning Science Hub, Department of Humastic Studies, University of Foggia, Arpi Street 176, 71122 Foggia, Italy; pierpaolo.limone@unifg.it (P.L.); raffaele.difuccio@unifg.it (R.D.F.)
- [2] Department of Agriculture, Food and Environment Sciences, University of Foggia, Napoli Street 25, 71122 Foggia, Italy; sandra.pati@unifg.it (S.P.); antonietta.baiano@unifg.it (A.B.); giuseppe.lopriore@unifg.it (G.L.)
- ***** Correspondence: giusy.toto@unifg.it

Abstract: Massive Open Online Courses (MOOCs) have been described as a "next development of networked learning", and they have the potential to mediate sensory learning. To understand this phenomenon, the present systematic review examines the research techniques, subjects, and trends of MOOC research on sensory learning, in order to provide a thorough understanding of the MOOC relevant to sensory (olfactory) learning phenomena by evaluating 65 (four studies are about multisensorial learning and 61 are about multisensorial empirical MOOCs researches) empirical MOOC studies published between 2008 and 2021 by searching through databases: PubMed, Scopus, Web of Science, and Google Scholar. The results indicated that most studies were based on quantitative research methods followed by mixed research methods and the qualitative research approaches; most of the studies were surveys, followed by platform databases and interviews; almost half of the studies were conducted using at least two methods for data collection: survey and interviews; most were replicated. The most highlighted subjects included student retention, learning experience, social learning, and engagement. Implications and studies into the future have been considered in order to obtain a more evolved understanding of the acquisition of knowledge through the senses.

Keywords: MOOC; sensory learning; olfactory; smell

Citation: Limone, P.; Pati, S.; Toto, G.A.; Di Fuccio, R.; Baiano, A.; Lopriore, G. Literature Review on MOOCs on Sensory (Olfactory) Learning. *Computers* **2022**, *11*, 32. https://doi.org/10.3390/computers11030032

Academic Editors: Antonio Sarasa Cabezuelo and Covadonga Rodrigo San Juan

Received: 8 February 2022
Accepted: 18 February 2022
Published: 23 February 2022

Publisher's Note: MDPI stays neutral with regard to jurisdictional claims in published maps and institutional affiliations.

Copyright: © 2022 by the authors. Licensee MDPI, Basel, Switzerland. This article is an open access article distributed under the terms and conditions of the Creative Commons Attribution (CC BY) license (https://creativecommons.org/licenses/by/4.0/).

1. Introduction

Massive Open Online Courses (MOOCs) have been described as a "next development of networked learning" and as a platform for expanding accessibility to higher education and supporting new education methods. Coined in 2008 [1], MOOCs refer to online courses offered by colleges that draw thousands of participants, partially because they are "open", generally referring to the fact that they do not offer credit and hence are free to someone with an internet connection (Figure 1). Massive Open Online Courses (MOOCs) are courses that extend the learning process to thousands of students. These courses respond to the challenges that educational and training institutions face in critical times such as these. MOOCs, in fact, represent quality training at a low cost [2]. While there is limited official study into the nascent discipline, many fans of the format have enthusiastically embraced its implementation. The development and application of MOOCs in many fields of higher education and, more lately, health education and live science have increased dramatically [1,3].

A long-studied strategy in the realm of training is to evaluate success and effectiveness and to advise on courses improvements. However, the distinctions between teaching in MOOCs and regular face-to-face classes mean that the same standard evaluation methodologies cannot be adapted. For instance, MOOCs often do not include entry, withdrawal, or submission of assignments or assessments restrictions [4]. The approaches employed in web-based education and e-learning do not always apply to MOOCs because web-based or e-learning courses are sometimes delivered under curricula, which differ from MOOCs according to expectations of students. The low terminal completion rates of MOOCs indicate that there is a lack of self-regulation and self-motivation with respect to what is expected of students [5].

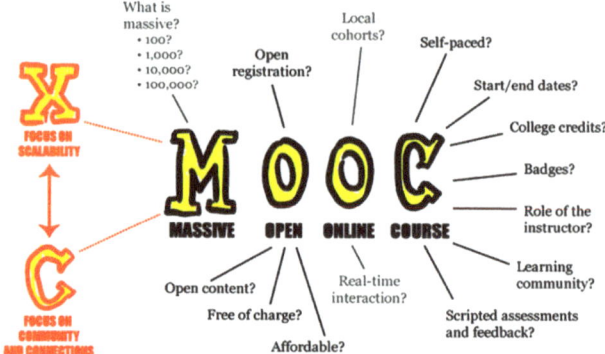

Figure 1. Evolution of the MOOC.

It is not appropriate to compare MOOCs directly with higher education courses using typical assessment standards and criteria. Our review focused on the queries highlighted in Figure 2, from which it can be seen that the research questions refer to empirical MOOCs, research referred to a multisensory approach (in the last twelve years), the research methodologies used in empirical MOOC, the analysis regarding the nations that have investigated MOOCs the most, and the diffusion of research, at a regional level, of empirical MOOCs referred to a multisensory approach.

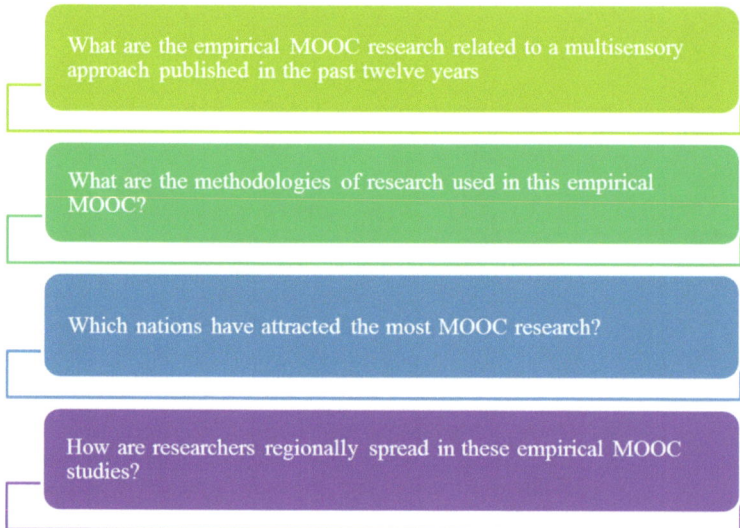

Figure 2. Research questions.

Despite the limitations in MOOC evaluation methodologies, multiple reviews of MOOC-related research methods have been undertaken without focusing especially on MOOC evaluations [6]. Two recent systemic reviews have been published summarizing methodologies and topics for MOOC research. Zhu et al. [7,8] and Bozkurt et al. (2021) [9,10]

advocated additional research on MOOC evaluation methodological techniques. This study focused little on the quality of the procedures and methodologies used. Furthermore, a considerable number of MOOC studies evaluate general pedagogic factors without assessing the course. While the broad review of MOOC education and pedagogy is valuable, it is also essential to evaluate courses [7]. The assessment of the quality of learning through MOOCs has become an "educational" variant of the Big Data problem, as it is mediated by learning analytics [11]. The application of learning analytics allows the identification of problems and potential. The dropout rate is an indicator not significantly associated with the effectiveness of MOOCs. Stracke [12] underlined that some students consider their educational objectives to be achieved even by simply downloading the materials available to pursue self-regulated learning and using them outside the time provided by the MOOC. MOOCs allow a large number of users to be reached, guaranteeing easy and immediate access to knowledge and content and mediating online communication with the teacher or among peers [12]. The online tutor is essential to favor monitoring processes in MOOCs with respect to both to the levels of completion of the course and to the management of information of a more qualitative nature, thus enhancing the relational dimension within the learning process [13]. MOOCs allow the communication of automatic and personalized feedback by placing the individual in direct comparison with his or her colleagues. Students learn by comparing themselves with more or less experienced colleagues [14]. MOOCs are offered in any different subject areas, such as STEM, art, medicine, and business, with differences in each subject area [15,16]. Studies on learning, and in particular on perceptual learning, have focused on learning stimuli consisting of a single sensory modality. However, our experience in the world involves constant multisensory stimulation. For example, visual and auditory information is integrated into the performance of many tasks that involve locating and tracking moving objects. Therefore, the human brain is likely to have evolved to develop, learn, and operate optimally in multisensory environments. Multisensory learning is determined by a multisensory stimulation that induces a unified perception. Multisensory information has been shown to facilitate learning [17]. Typically, MOOCs covers two sensory channels: sight and hearing. In this review, the authors analyze all the studies where MOOCs include a multisensory approach. One of them is the sense of smell. Smell is the greatest ally of memories: it allows us to travel through time and therefore ensures that the sense of smell is chosen as a privileged sense by memory. A smell or a perfume already smelled has the unparalleled power to rematerialize even our intimate memories, to make us present in distant events. No other sensory data is as memorable as a smell, equally resistant to the wear and tear of time, equally evocative of the past, and equally capable of stimulating all the other senses. The sense of smell demonstrates a close relationship with episodic memory. Of all the sensory stimuli, smells seem to trigger the most vivid and emotional memories: in fact, the olfactory input has direct connections via the olfactory bulb and the primary olfactory cortex (piriformis) on two key structures involved in emotion and memory (the amygdala and hippocampus), without passing through the thalamus. The strong anatomical connection between olfactory and memory structures therefore makes the sense of smell a privileged sense for accessing memories [18]. Olfaction, the sense of smell, is closely linked to learning, and certain research indicates that olfactory sensory abilities play a role in the performance of visual memory (VM). For example, the removal of the olfactory bulb inhibits visuospatial education in rats [19], and training in odor identification leads to improved visuospatial learning in rats [20]. Zelcer et al. [19] focuses on whether olfactory memory training in adult humans would have positive impacts on both VM and olfactory task performance. The olfactory system has a remarkable biological and functional flexibility [9]. The taste buds and olfactory system are a challenge to include in your eLearning course design, but it is achievable. These two senses can be mixed with vivid images and descriptive phrases. For example, when the flavor of a food or the smell in the air is described, the mind performs tricks to visualize the environment [21].

Multisensory learning through MOOCs is an important educational element for students with dyslexia. Orton Gillingham is now linked with multisensory learning. In particular, multisensory instruction involves several senses that support of the student's learning (Figure 3). This would ideally include the senses of sight, hearing, and touch or movement and enable individuals to link their learning strengths, visually, auditively, and kinesthetically, to areas of learning that are harder for them [6]. In order to address the gaps in MOOC literature evaluation methods, the objective of this systemic review was to identify and examine current MOOC assessment methodologies and their multisensory approach. This review aimed at informing the future MOOC assessment process [9].

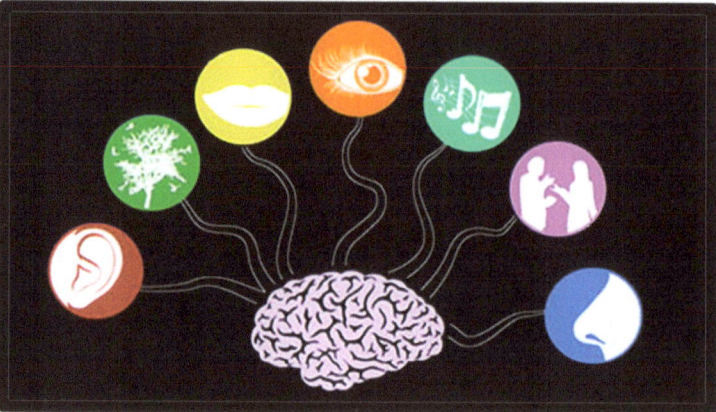

Figure 3. Multisensory learning.

Understanding the potential of sensory learning through MOOCs would allow the improvement of learning processes in response to students' needs (Figure 4). This review therefore aims to analyze the studies already conducted on the above topic to bring out the possibilities of improving practice through a more evolved understanding of knowledge acquisition through the senses.

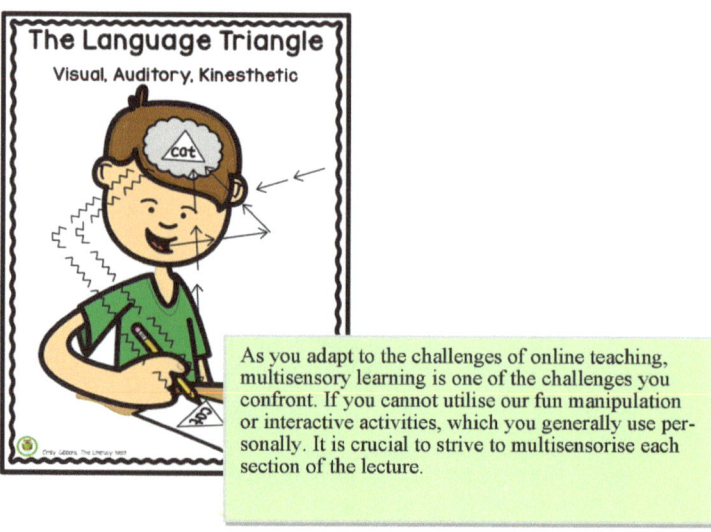

Figure 4. The language triangle.

The analysis of the state of art aims to understand how it is possible to acquire knowledge through the senses and which teaching methods can improve and make learning more efficient through MOOCs. The implications of what emerged have the potential to produce an evolution of MOOCs and inaugurate new avenues of research for training conveyed through multisensory stimulation.

2. Results

The total number of reviewed articles are 65 distributed in their publication years on MOOCs delivery, as shown in the below graph in Appendix A.

Figure 5 shows that the highest percentage of articles published is for the year 2020 followed by 2019. In addition, not taking into account the additional miscellaneous sourcing classified as "other", most of the studies are from the United States, followed by the United Kingdom (Figure 6). The nationality of the search is associated based on the context of the search. The results, emerging from the comparison of the selected studies, indicated that most studies [22,23] were based on quantitative research methods, followed by mixed research methods and qualitative research approaches [24,25]; most of the studies were surveyed, followed by platform databases and interviews [26,27]; almost half of the studies were conducted using at least two methods for data collection: survey and interview [28,29]; and most were replicated [30,31]. The most highlighted subjects included student retention, learning experience, social learning, and engagement. In particular, it emerges that the video lessons of MOOCs are a tool to increase skills, improve performance in summative assessments [32], and catalyze powerful behavioral changes [33]. Furthermore, MOOCs have the advantage of facilitating the learning process by offering materials and enabling information-sharing [34].

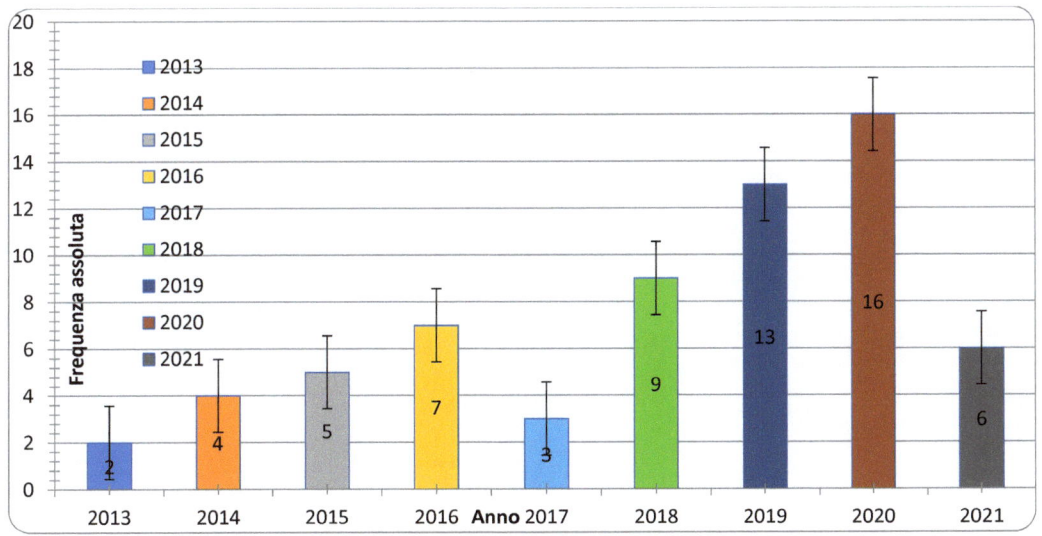

Figure 5. Distribution of MOOC publications.

The distribution of contribution on MOOCs learning worldwide is shown in the graph below.

What has been discussed is confirmed by all the selected studies, although there is a clear need to promote research in the field by presenting the evidence. In support of this, medical and healthcare students report that they are more motivated to learn through MOOCs, which allow for a beneficial sharing of digital material and a practical approach thanks to informal and transmedia learning environments [34,35]. MOOCs unlock new opportunities for training and lifelong learning by improving the safety and quality of health services in supporting patients to achieve a better quality of life [36].

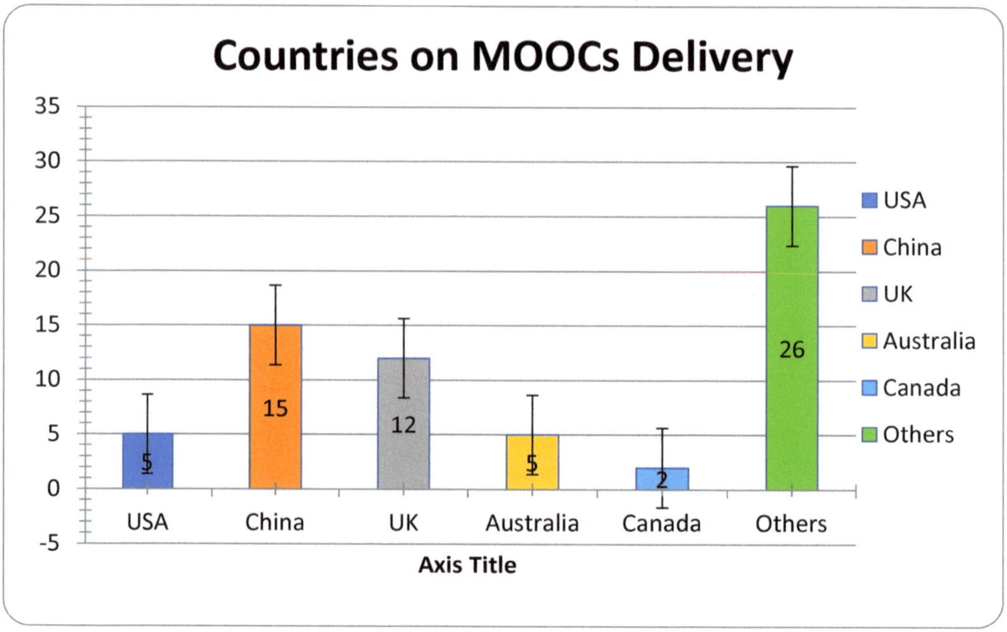

Countries on MOOCs Delivery

Country	Value
USA	5
China	15
UK	12
Australia	5
Canada	2
Others	26

Figure 6. Distribution of countries on MOOCs Delivery.

Consistent with connectivist learning theory, during a MOOC course, learners contributed their own sources of nutritional information to discussions using their own knowledge networks to teach and share information, and their information was derived primarily from websites. It emerged that nutrition professionals need to understand the principles of connectivist learning behaviors to engage course recipients [37]. A small number of articles have been published on the topic of multisensory stimulation through MOOCs, one of which illustrates the MERGO Project [38], which offers an MOOC in oenology and wine tasting combined with an olfactory experience, allowing the user to improve and train their olfactory knowledge on oenology, viticulture, and wine experimentation.

In the following, we explore what was found through these results.

3. Discussion

The motivation behind this precise audit of the examination standards and themes identified with MOOCs just as MOOC research distribution outlets and creators' topographical disseminations was to acquire a deeper comprehension of the MOOC marvel. The 65 examinations inspected in this deliberate survey uncovered a few fascinating patterns with respect to the exact exploration on MOOCs distributed between January 2008 and February 2021 [39].

3.1. Distribution Diaries for MOOC Research

The current examination investigated the distribution diaries for MOOC research just as exploration techniques directed, information assortment strategies, information examination techniques, research foci, creator's geographic data, creators' cooperation types, geographic data with respect to the conveyance of MOOCs, and the dispersion of the MOOC research by year of distribution [35,40]. Figure 5 shows that the highest percentage of published articles refer to the year 2020, followed by 2019. Furthermore, most of the studies come from the United States, followed by the United Kingdom (Figure 6).

3.2. Multimodality in the Classroom

The introduction of multimodality in the classroom requires an effort to accommodate teaching practice. Multimodal practice consists of the integration of specific modal resources: writing a recipe and then transforming it into a didactic discourse with the support of the Interactive Writing Boards (IWB); writing drafts and project texts starting from literary excerpts; debating in a reasoned way by developing a written text but then focusing on speech, its understanding, and critical analysis, as well as on the action; narrating starting from a video stimulus, transcribing spoken passages, and rewriting on the basis of a literary model [41].

3.3. Area of Cognitive Styles

Multimodality is usually considered a perceptual multimodality; it leverages the idea that learners use different sensory modalities (visual, auditory, and body mobility). The discussed area of cognitive styles, understood as a multiplicity of approaches to learning contents, is added. In other words, beyond the perceptual level, information is organized and processed according to individual modalities that are affected by one's personal history of learning [42,43].

According to the current studies, in olfactory learning and not visual learning, transfer effects are detected, while task difficulties and learning rates were equivalent in both training tasks.

Based on our findings, we anticipate that olfactory system MOOCs learning could lead to more cross-sensory transmission than is the case of the visual system (which is the dominant model for cognitive interventions). Our results also underscore that the transfer of learning is often unrelated to the extent of the gains made in the MOOCs [37,44].

3.4. Future Perspectives

Further research is needed before the value of olfactory cognitive MOOCs learning can be determined. It is not obvious if the multimodal character of the learning tasks or the unknown variations in cognitive demands were the result of this shift, rather than the commitment of olfaction per se [45,46]. This may lead to additional studies: each MOOCs learning exercise uses one type of sensory stimuli. Therefore, we consider that the sensory complexity has a great value for a new generation of MOOCs. In this direction, further study is needed where multimodal complexity of training tasks is changed [47,48]. In conclusion, the comparison of the selected articles revealed the effectiveness of MOOCs in relation to the learning achieved by students and the increase of their motivation. Furthermore, these online courses facilitate the sharing and democratization of knowledge and the acquisition of practical skills in university and training environments. The new frontier is represented by the multisensory stimulation mediated by MOOCs to facilitate learning.

We believe that the outcomes of our study will motivate more research on cognitive MOOCS learning based on odors [49]. Such operations could be advantageous for elderly people because olfactory deficits are the early indicators of cognitive impairment and dementia related to age [50–52].

4. Materials and Methods

The Search Strategy

The search was performed according to the guidelines recommended by the PRISMA statement for systematic reviews and meta-analyses [13]. This paper intends to carry out a systematic review analyzing the state of the art on the topic of MOOCs in association with sensory learning. Literature was searched for the appropriate studies from the online databases of the PubMed, Scopus, Web of Science, and Google Scholar published from 2008 until February 2021 (Figure 7). The combinations of key words used for the search were as follows: "MOOC", "Massive open online course", "olfactory", "sensory", "gustatory", and "learning". The articles were selected based on three guiding principles: "MOOC facilitates sensory learning", "olfactory learning is a rapidly developing sector", and "gustatory learning has had more space in experimentation until 2019", because, until the pandemic, it was easier to combine online learning with face-to-face experimentation with experts. During the COVID-19 phase, the course became fully online. Regarding the inclusion and exclusion criteria, the articles were selected from peer-reviewed English journals that aimed to describe or evaluate the dimensions and variables expressed with respect to the research topics mentioned above (screening). The publications unrelated to the topic, and the concerned age group were excluded, as well as those for which the complete text (relevance) was not available. Book chapters, books, news articles, and legal reports were also excluded. A qualitative synthesis of the most relevant information was also conducted with comparisons between the various publications.

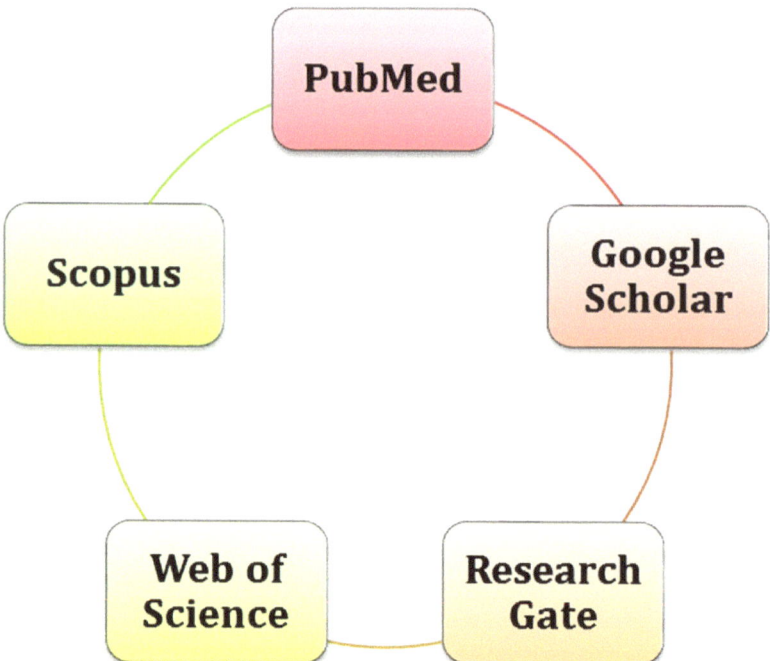

Figure 7. Databases research.

The process for including studies in the systematic review is described in Figure 8.

No filters were adopted, which is why all products such as papers, books, reviews, documents, etc., were included. Furthermore, all results were accepted without any constraints regarding the type of data analysis, measurement, sample, and tools used.

A total of 239 results emerged after searching through the various databases, of which 100 were duplicates. Of the 139 results, 57 were excluded because they consisted of reviews and meta-analyses. Of the 82 articles selected through the previous steps, 17 were excluded because they were incomplete or irrelevant (irrelevant articles $n = 10$; other reasons = 7). In conclusion, 65 studies were included (Figure 8). The AMSTAR 2 guidelines were followed for the critical appraisal of the methods adopted in the review (Beverley et al., 2017). The 16 items of the instrument were adhered to by engaging two practitioners, who were responsible for item collection and selection and operated independently.

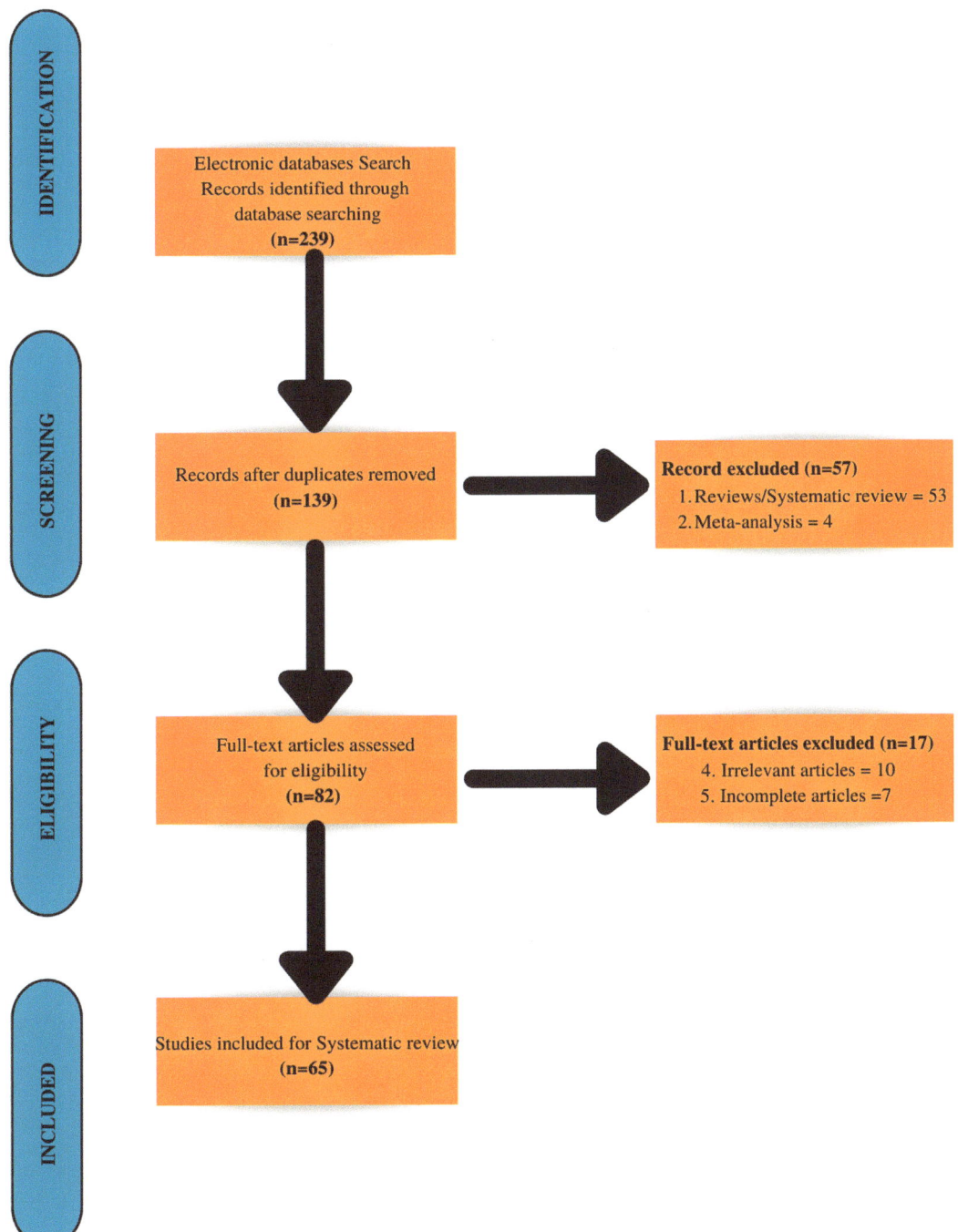

Figure 8. Prisma flow diagram.

All study participants synthesized and compared the selected studies. The method used to synthesize the results consisted of defining for each study the following characteristics: title, author, country, keywords, and results (Figure 5).

The information in this examination was gathered from Scopus and companion explored diaries and needed to meet the accompanying rules for the determination (see additionally Zhu et al. [53] Ebben 2014 [40]). To begin with, given that MOOCs previously arose in 2007 and 2008 [54–56], the investigations of this audit were distributed somewhere in the range of 2008 and 2021. Second, the investigations must be experimental examinations. Third, the investigations inspected MOOCs from instructive viewpoints and were not just about specialized issues or plans of action [57]. Fourth, we utilized catchphrases "MOOC" and "Huge Online Open Course(s)" to screen titles, abstracts, and the writing chosen. Fifth, the investigations were distributed in scholastic diaries instead of as book parts, websites, magazines, and so forth, and were distributed in English. We just included friend surveyed diaries on the grounds that such papers commonly address better expectations of exploration thoroughness and believability (Utah State University Library 2020) [54].

To accomplish proficiency and improve the dependability of this examination, the authors performed the underlying inquiry in an equivalent division of diary sources Ebben 2014 [40]. One specialist looked through articles from five key diaries in Scopus, which would in general distribute articles identified with MOOCs (for example, PCs and Education, British Journal of Educational Technology, The International Review of Research in Open and Distance Learning, Distance Education, and Educational Media International). She additionally led a hunt in a few different diaries not filed by Scopus yet have been known to distribute MOOC research. as we can see in Table 1 (e.g., Online Learning, the International Journal on E-Learning, Journal of Interactive Media in Education, Journal of Online Learning Research, and the Journal of Open Flexible and Distance Learning). The subsequent analyst looked through the remainder of the articles found in the Scopus search [55].

The relevant literature correlated with the sensory learning is depicted below.

Massive Open Online Courses (MOOCs) represent a large-scale learning modality that is changing the higher education landscape. Yu and collaborators (2017) [58] highlight the role that artificial intelligence (AI) assumes in the design and delivery of MOOCs. In particular, the authors highlight how virtual learning accompanied by human characteristics, such as curiosity and emotion, can improve the learning experience. It is also highlighted that, through artificial intelligence techniques, the learning sequence can be customized according to the needs of each student. Furthermore, qualitative and quantitative analyses carried out in a study on the delivery of a MOOC on behavioral medicine showed that the participating students were enthusiastic about interacting with virtual patients and, therefore, about experimenting; they were excited to apply the new knowledge they had acquired. The study also suggested incorporating several interactive cases with many varied levels of complexity [59].

In this particular historical moment, the COVID-19 pandemic has caused enormous difficulties in the world of education. Virtual resources have, therefore, assumed a key role, and previously developed MOOCs have received a positive reception by learners and a net increase in use, guaranteeing learning in a way that is completely innovative for many [60]. Currently, some developing countries, such as Malaysia, are adopting mass open online courses (MOOCs) in higher education. Related to this implementation is the need to make the monitoring of MOOCs easier. Asli [39] highlighted that a key component of these courses is the design of the interactive visualization: the detailed characterization and abstraction of the domain problem help the designer to derive the design requirements to generate an appropriate visualization solution.

A statistical sensitivity analysis was carried out for the many studies (in Figure 5, [1,6,12,18,20,33,36,45,54]) containing missing data with respect to the research hypothesis, which is common in each research study. The data were analyzed excluding the missing values; thus, only the complete data were analyzed; then, the missing values were imputed through single or multiple imputations and, eventually, the analyses were traced back to the imputed data. The research hypothesis in the latter case has been confirmed.

Table 1. Sensory learning results.

	Title	Author	Year	Country
1	Problem characterization for visual analytics in MOOC learner's support monitoring: A case of Malaysian MOOC	Asli et al.	2020	Malaysia
2	Virtual Patients in a Behavioral Medicine Massive Open Online Course (MOOC): A Qualitative and Quantitative Analysis of Participants' Perceptions	Berman et al.	2017	Sweden
3	Participation in an existing massive open online course in dentistry during the COVID-19 pandemic	France et al.	2020	USA
4	Towards AI-powered personalization in MOOC learning	Yu et al.	2017	Singapore

The literature review provides access to a deeper understanding of the sensory learning process mediated by MOOCs. Selected studies are identified above.

5. Conclusions

Most MOOC exploration, particularly on sensory learning, to date has zeroed in on student issues, for example, the student experience, social learning, commitment, self-controlled learning, inspiration, execution, and MOOC finish.

Instead, research on MOOC teachers has a minor impact [34,61]. To address this hole, MOOC specialists later on might target educators or plan more extensive investigations of different MOOC partners such as students, teachers, educational originators, or program heads. More examinations of MOOC teachers' plan cycle and discernments would enhance the comprehension of MOOC wonder. Such exploration could advance a more profound comprehension of the nature of MOOCs, social affectability in MOOCs, MOOC instructional methods including course intuitiveness and commitment, and evaluation rehearsals from MOOC educators' points of view [61,62].

We suggest that training protocols employing a single sensory stimulus regime do not involve multisensory learning mechanisms and, therefore, may not be optimal for learning [9].

The senses mediate knowledge, but they do not mediate it univocally, and, in any case, knowledge itself, once it is acquired through the senses, frees itself from them and is defined according to amodal values, substantially devoid of references to sensitivity. The vicarious process is proposed as the main guarantee of the didactic values of learning mediated by the different sensory systems; therefore, the use of a multisensory approach in the construction of knowledge is legitimized [52,63]. There are numerous design hypotheses for a consistent and as structured as possible use of MOOCs at the national university level, an important analysis also aimed at identifying further innovative ways of quality training in our country.

It emerges that the participants in the MOOCs of the study by An et al. [8] wanted to gamify their MOOCs to increase social interactions and student retention. The need to ensure that the themes of social learning democracy apply to content areas outside the social sciences emerges from the Paek study [64]. The perspective concludes with suggestions for the future of research on the applicability and adequacy of MOOCocracy in K–12 contexts and the knowledge and skills that learners may need to participate in and benefit from a democracy of social learning. The increasing aging of the population and the increasing prevalence of non-communicable diseases require innovation and professional skills mastered in the health sector [65,66]. MOOCs in the nursing sector open up new opportunities for training and lifelong learning, improving the safety and quality of health services in supporting patients to achieve a better quality of life.

Limitation

This review was subject to some limitations. Firstly, the review cannot draw definitive conclusions due to the heterogeneity of the interventions and the small number of available articles that focus on sensory stimulation. The second limitation is applicable to all systematic reviews; the search results are limited by the search terms and refinements used (for example, included journals and publication period). While the systematic review may not accurately reflect all of the existing literature relevant to this study, it does provide insight into current research findings and the impact of sensory stimulation in MOOCs.

The last limitation is that, despite the PRISMA quality criteria and the authors' adherence to the AMSTAR 2 guidelines to ensure a certain methodological rigor, the authors cannot fully control publication biases and therefore cannot guarantee full access to data within this systematic review.

Since our results are positive, we hope that the literature will soon be enriched with new studies investigating the efficacy of multisensory stimulation in more specific and larger populations.

Author Contributions: Conceptualization, P.L. and S.P.; methodology, G.A.T.; validation, R.D.F.; writing—original draft preparation, A.B.; writing—review and editing, G.L. All authors have read and agreed to the published version of the manuscript.

Funding: This research was funded by MERGO Erasmus Plus Progect grant number 2020-1-IT02-KA203-080040 and The APC was funded by Department of Humanistic studies of University of Foggia.

Institutional Review Board Statement: Not applicable.

Informed Consent Statement: Not applicable.

Data Availability Statement: Data is contained within the article.

Conflicts of Interest: The authors declare no conflict of interest.

Appendix A

Table A1. Data Review.

	Title	Author	Year	Country	Keywords
1	Measuring growth in students' proficiency in MOOCs: Two component dynamic extensions for the Rasch model	Abbakumov et al.	2018	Belgium	psychometrics; item response theory; cross-classification multilevel logistic model; learning effects
2	Psychometrics of MOOCs: Measuring Learners' Proficiency	Abbakumov et al.	2020	Belgium	psychometrics; item response theory; massive open online courses; learning analytics
3	Massive open online nutrition and cooking course for improved eating behaviors and meal composition	Adam et al.	2015	USA	nutrition; cooking; online education; eating behaviors; meal composition
4	Using the Internet: Nutrition Information-Seeking Behaviours of Lay People Enrolled in a Massive Online Nutrition Course	Adamski et al.	2020	Australia	nutrition education; information-seeking behavior; nutrition misinformation; online learning; social media
5	Applying MOOCocracy learning culture themes to improve digital course design and online learner engagement	Akinkuolie and Shortt	2021	USA	massively open online courses; MOOC; MOOCocracy; Online learning culture; online course design

Table A1. Cont.

	Title	Author	Year	Country	Keywords
6	Massive Open Online Courses (MOOCs): Data on higher education	Al-Rahmi et al.	2018	Malaysia	Massive Open Online Courses (MOOCs); higher education; systematic literature review
7	Data Collection Approaches to Enable Evaluation of a Massive Open Online Course About Data Science for Continuing Education in Health Care: Case Study	Alturkistani et al.	2019	United Kingdom	education, distance; education; teaching; online learning; online education; MOOC; massive open online course
8	Principles of synthetic biology: a MOOC for an emerging field	Anderson et al.	2019	USA	synthetic biology; massive open online course (MOOC); edX; education; curriculum building
9	Lessons learned on teaching a global audience with massive open online courses (MOOCs) on health impacts of climate change: a commentary	Barteit et al.	2019	Germany	health; climate change; global health; global education; global audience; capacity building; massive open online course; MOOC
10	Genomic Education at Scale: The Benefits of Massive Open Online Courses for the Healthcare Workforce	Bishop et al.	2019	United Kingdom	workforce development; genomic medicine; Massive Open Online Course; evaluation; genomic education; multi-disciplinary education; online learning
11	Stepping back and stepping in: Facilitating learner-centered experiences in MOOCs	Blum-Smith et al.	2021	USA	distance education and online learning; pedagogical issues; teaching/learning strategies; cooperative/collaborative learning; adult learning
12	One Health education in Kakuma refugee camp (Kenya): From a MOOC to projects on real world challenges	Bolon et al.	2020	Switzerland	One Health; global health; MOOC; blended learning; project-based learning; refugee camp
13	Self-regulated spacing in a massive open online course is related to better learning	Carvalho et al.	2020	USA	MOOC; learning
14	Researching for better instructional methods using AB experiments in MOOCs: results and challenges	Chen et al.	2016	USA	technology; learning; MOOC
15	Teachers' networked professional learning with MOOCs	Chen et al.	2020	USA	technology; learning; MOOC
16	Twelve tips for integrating massive open online course content into classroom teaching	de Jong et al.	2019	Netherlands	learning; MOOC; teaching
17	Application of PBL Mode in a Resident-Focused Perioperative Transesophageal Echocardiography Training Program: A Perspective of MOOC Environment	Dong et al.	2020	China	residents training; TEE; MOOC; PBL; LBL
18	Deep Learning for Discussion-Based Cross-Domain Performance Prediction of MOOC Learners Grouped by Language on Future Learn	Duru et al.	2021	Turkey	MOOCs; deep learning; English as a second language; FutureLearn; predictive models; natural language processing

Table A1. Cont.

	Title	Author	Year	Country	Keywords
19	Transformation of the mathematics classroom with the internet	Engelbrecht et al.	2020	South Africa	humans-with-media; learning environments; blended learning; mathematics teaching; mathematics teacher education; MOOC; hyper-personalization; collaboration; learning management system
20	Do Individual Differences in Cognition and Personality Predict Retrieval Practice Activities on MOOCs?	Fellman et al.	2020	Sweden	retrieval practice; test-enhanced learning; e-learning; MOOC; personality; cognition
21	Making MOOCs meaningful and locally relevant? Investigating IDCourserians—an independent, collaborative, community hub in Indonesia	Firmansyah and Timmis	2016	United Kingdom	MOOCs; learning community; communities of practice; collaborative learning; globalisation; self-regulated learning
22	Could a massive open online course be part of the solution to sport-related concussion? Participation and impact among 8368 registrants	Fremont et al.	2020	Canada	MOOC
23	Promoting Evidence Based Nutrition Education Across the World in a Competitive Space: Delivering a Massive Open Online Course	Gibson et al.	2020	Australia	distance education; global education; health promotion; internet; nutrition misinformation; online learning; social media
24	Structural limitations of learning in a crowd: communication vulnerability and information diffusion in MOOCs	Gillani et al.	2014	United Kingdom	MOOC; distance learning; learning
25	Relationship between participants' level of education and engagement in their completion of the Understanding Dementia Massive Open Online Course	Goldberg et al.	2015	Australia	dementia; online learning; MOOC; level of education; engagement
26	Symposium report on "Examining the Changing Landscape of Course Delivery and Student Learning": Experimental Biology 2017	Halpin et al.	2018	United Kingdom	Massive Open Online Course; online teaching; webcasting
27	A Massive Open Online Course for teaching physiotherapy students and physiotherapists about spinal cord injuries	Harvey et al.	2014	Australia	MOOC; learning; physiotherapy
28	Teaching modes and social-epistemological dimensions in medical Massive Open Online Courses: Lessons for integration in campus education	Hendriks et al.	2019	Netherlands	MOOC; medical MOOC; learning
29	Instructional design quality in medical Massive Open Online Courses for integration into campus education	Hendriks et al.	2019	Netherlands	MOOC; medical MOOC; learning; education

Table A1. Cont.

	Title	Author	Year	Country	Keywords
30	Uncovering motivation and self-regulated learning skills in integrated medical MOOC learning: a mixed methods research protocol	Hendriks et al.	2020	Netherlands	medical MOOC; learning; MOOC; research
31	Design for now, but with the future in mind: a "cognitive flexibility theory" perspective on online learning through the lens of MOOCs	Hu and Spiro	2021	USA	cognitive flexibility theory (CFT); MOOC; adaptive worldview; online learning
32	The utilization of data analysis techniques in predicting student performance in massive open online courses (MOOCs)	Hughes and Dobbins	2015	United Kingdom	open learning; prediction; data analysis
33	The Practitioner's Guide to Global Health: an interactive, online, open-access curriculum preparing medical learners for global health experiences	Jacquet et al.	2018	USA	global health; international; MOOC; online; curriculum
34	Twelve tips for teaching medical students online under COVID-19	Jiang et al.	2020	China	COVID-19; medical MOOC; e-learning; SPOC; assessment
35	How to make a MOOC With forethought and support, science instructors can design effective massive open online courses.	Kellogg	2013	USA	digital learning; MOOC; technology
36	Training Primary Health Professionals in Breast Cancer Prevention: Evidence and Experience from Mexico	Magaña-Valladares et al.	2016	Mexico	face-to-face learning; blended learning; MOOC; breast cancer; Mexico; training courses; virtual education and multidisciplinary training; health promoters
37	Massive Open Online Courses: Concept and Implications	Mahajan et al.	2019	India	e-learning; life-long learner; open courses; ubiquitous learning
38	Protocol for a mixed-methods evaluation of a massive open online course on real world evidence	Meinert et al.	2018	United Kingdom	digital learning; MOOC; technology; e-learning
39	Real-world evidence for postgraduate students and professionals in healthcare: protocol for the design of a blended massive open online course	Meinert et al.	2018	United Kingdom	digital learning; MOOC; technology; e-learning; blended learning
40	How health professionals regulate their learning in massive open online courses	Milligan and Littlejohn	2016	United Kingdom	massive open online courses; self-regulated learning; professional learning
41	Continuing Medical Education: MOOCs (Massive Open Online Courses) and Their Implications for Radiology Learning	Murphy and Munk	2013	Canada	continuing medical education (CME); MOOC; learning
42	MOOC Learning Assessment in Clinical Settings: Analysis from Quality Dimensions	Olivares et al.	2021	Mexico	educational assessment; clinical teaching; online education; massive open online course; faculty development

Table A1. *Cont.*

	Title	Author	Year	Country	Keywords
43	Massive Open Online Course for Health Informatics Education	Paton et al.	2014	United Kingdom	distance education; medical informatics; professional education; social media; computer-assisted instruction
44	Delivering a medical school elective with massive open online course (MOOC) technology	Robinson	2016	USA	MOOC; medical education; medical school elective; business
45	First 'Global Flipped Classroom in One Health': From MOOCs to research on real world challenges	de Castañeda et al.	2018	Switzerland	One Health; global health; MOOC; e-learning; flipped-classroom; project-based learning
46	Leveraging massive open online courses to expand quality of healthcare education to health practitioners in Rwanda	Scott et al.	2019	USA	MOOC; education
47	Blended learning in medical physiology improves nursing students' study efficiency	Shang and Liu	2018	China	blended learning; China; MOOC; physiology education; teaching reform
48	Leveraging Digital Platforms to Scale Health Care Workforce Development: The Career 911 Massive Open Online Course	Simon et al.	2019	USA	workforce development; health disparities; community-based participatory research; massive open online course; research training; health professions; education technology
49	Study design and protocol for a comprehensive evaluation of a UK massive open online course (MOOC) on quality improvement in healthcare	Smith-Lickess et al.	2019	United Kingdom	MOOC; learning; healthcare
50	Development and impact of a massive open online course (MOOC) for antimicrobial stewardship	Sneddon et al.	2017	Scotland	antimicrobial; MOOC
51	Transformation of a face-to-face workshop into a Massive Open Online Course (MOOC): A design and development case	Sommer et al.	2019	USA	instructional design; online learning; sample size; power analysis; case study; MOOC; formative evaluation
52	Beyond xMOOCs in healthcare education: study of the feasibility in integrating virtual patient systems and MOOC platforms	Stathakarou et al.	2014	Sweden	virtual patients; healthcare education; e-learning; massive open online courses; integration
53	Discover Dentistry: encouraging wider participation in dentistry using a massive open online course (MOOC)	Stokes et al.	2015	United Kingdom	dentistry; MOOC; learning
54	The contribution of a MOOC to community discussions around death and dying	Tieman et al.	2018	Australia	death attitudes; palliative care; community education; online learning; MOOC
55	An Introduction to the Inverted/Flipped Classroom Model in Education and Advanced Training in Medicine and in the Healthcare Professions	Tolks et al.	2016	Germany	inverted classroom; flipped classroom; medical education; educational video; Open Educational Resources; MOOCs; blended learning; screencasts; podcasts; E-Learning

Table A1. *Cont.*

	Title	Author	Year	Country	Keywords
56	SEPSIS. Educational and Best Practice Frontiers. Beyond the Boundaries of Fatality, Enhancing Clinical Skills and Precision Medicine	Trovato	2020	Italy	sepsis; bioinformatics; ultrasound; e-learning; MOOC; genomics; research models
57	Who will pass? Analyzing learner behaviors in MOOCs	Tseng et al.	2016	Taiwan	MOOCs; learning engagement; learning behavior; learning analytics
58	Deconstructing self-regulated learning in MOOCs: In search of help-seeking mechanisms	Vilkova and Shcheglova	2020	Russia	MOOC; self-regulated learning; education research; validation; OSLQ
59	Development and Evaluation of Affective Domain Using Student's Feedback in Entrepreneurial Massive Open Online Courses	Wu et al.	2019	Taiwan	entrepreneurship education; social entrepreneurship; affective development; MOOCs; content analysis
60	Study Partners Recommendation for xMOOCs Learners	Xu and Yang	2015	China	digital learning; MOOC; technology; e-learning
61	The Distance Teaching Practice of Combined Mode of Massive Open Online Course Micro-Video for Interns in Emergency Department During the COVID-19 Epidemic Period	Zhou et al.	2020	China	COVID-19; MOOC micro-video; intern; distance teaching; telemedicine

References

1. Bali, M. MOOC Pedagogy Gleaning Good Practice from Existing MOOCs. *MERLOT J. Online Learn. Teach.* **2014**, *10*, 44–56. Available online: https://oerknowledgecloud.org/sites/oerknowledgecloud.org/files/bali_0314.pdf (accessed on 1 October 2021).
2. Cachay-Huamán, L.; Ramírez-Hernández, D. Open, interdisciplinary and collaborative educational innovation to train in energy sustainability through MOOC: Perception of competency development. *Int. J. Interact. Des. Manuf. (IJIDeM)* **2019**, *13*, 1341–1352. [CrossRef]
3. Bulfin, S.; Pangrazio, L.; Selwyn, N. Making 'MOOCs': The construction of a new digital higher education within news media discourse. *Int. Rev. Res. Open Distrib. Learn.* **2014**, *15*, 290–304. [CrossRef]
4. Carver, L.; Harrison, L.M. MOOCs and Democratic Education. *Lib. Educ.* **2013**, *99*, 20. Available online: https://aacu.org/liberaleducation/2013/fall/carver-harrison (accessed on 1 October 2021).
5. Dang, J.; Guo, J.; Wang, L.; Guo, F.; Shi, W.; Li, Y.; Guan, W. Construction of Z-scheme $Fe_3O_4/BiOCl/BiOI$ heterojunction with superior recyclability for improved photocatalytic activity towards tetracycline degradation. *J. Alloys Compd.* **2022**, *893*, 162251. [CrossRef]
6. Chuang, I.; Ho, A.D. HarvardX and MITx: Four Years of Open Online Courses—Fall 2012–Summer 2016. 2016. Available online: https://papers.ssrn.com/sol3/papers.cfm?abstract_id=2889436 (accessed on 1 October 2021).
7. Coffrin, C.; Corrin, L.; de Barba, P.; Kennedy, G. Visualizing patterns of student engagement and performance in MOOCs. In Proceedings of the Fourth International Conference on Learning Analytics and Knowledge—LAK'14, Indianapolis, IN, USA, 24–28 March 2014; Pistilli, M., Willis, J., Koch, D., Arnold, K., Teasley, S., Pardo, A., Eds.; ACM Press: New York, NY, USA, 2014; pp. 83–92. [CrossRef]
8. An, Y.; Zhu, M.; Bonk, C.J.; Lin, L. Exploring instructors' perspectives, practices, and perceived support needs and barriers related to the gamification of MOOCs. *J. Comput. High. Educ.* **2021**, *33*, 64–84. [CrossRef]
9. Cooper, H. The structure of knowledge synthesis: A taxonomy of literature reviews. *Knowl. Soc.* **1988**, *1*, 104–126.
10. Bozkurt, A.; Zawacki-Richter, O. Trends and Patterns in Distance Education (2014–2019): A Synthesis of Scholarly Publications and a Visualization of the Intellectual Landscape. *Int. Rev. Res. Open Distrib. Learn.* **2021**, *22*, 19–45. [CrossRef]
11. Jin, C. Dropout prediction model in MOOC based on clickstream data and student sample weight. *Soft Comput.* **2021**, *25*, 8971–8988. [CrossRef]
12. Stracke, C.M. The Quality of MOOCs: How to improve the design of open education and online courses for learners? In *International Conference on Learning and Collaboration Technologies*; Springer: Cham, Switzerland, 2017; pp. 285–293.
13. Creswell, J.W.; Plano-Clark, V.L. *Designing and Conducting Mixed Methods Research*, 3rd ed.; Sage: Thousand Oaks, CA, USA, 2017.

14. Alshehri, M.; Alamri, A.; Cristea, A.I.; Stewart, C.D. Towards Designing Profitable Courses: Predicting Student Purchasing Behaviour in MOOCs. *Int. J. Artif. Intell. Educ.* **2021**, *31*, 215–233. [CrossRef]
15. Doleck, T.; Lemay, D.J.; Brinton, C.G. Evaluating the efficiency of social learning networks: Perspectives for harnessing learning analytics to improve discussions. *Comput. Educ.* **2021**, *164*, 104–124. [CrossRef]
16. Adorno, D.P.; Pizzolato, N. Teacher professional development in the context of the "Open Discovery of STEM laboratories" project: Is the MOOC methodology suitable for teaching physics? *J. Phys. Conf. Ser.* **2021**, *1512*, 012030. [CrossRef]
17. Gnaedinger, A.; Gurden, H.; Gourévitch, B.; Martin, C. Multisensory learning between odor and sound enhances beta oscillations. *Sci. Rep.* **2019**, *9*, 11236. [CrossRef]
18. Caro-Alvaro, S.; Alkasasbeh, A.A.; García-López, E.; García-Cabot, A.; Rozinaj, G.; Ghinea, G. Exploring Impact of Olfactory Stimuli on User Performance on Mobile Platforms. In *Interactive Mobile Communication, Technologies and Learning*; Springer: Cham, Switzerland, 2019; pp. 1015–1023.
19. Van Rijzingen, I.M.; Gispen, W.H.; Spruijt, B.M. Olfactory bulbectomy temporarily impairs morris maze performance: An ACTH (4–9) analog accelerates return of function. *Physiol. Behav.* **1995**, *58*, 147–152. [CrossRef]
20. Zelcer, I.; Cohen, H.; Richter-Levin, G.; Lebiosn, T.; Grossberger, T.; Barkai, E. A cellular correlate of learning-induced metaplasticity in the hippocampus. *Cereb. Cortex* **2006**, *16*, 460–468. [CrossRef] [PubMed]
21. Creed-Dikeogu, G.; Clark, C. Are you MOOC-ing yet? A review for academic libraries. *Kans. Libr. Assoc. Coll. Univ. Libr. Sect. Proc.* **2013**, *3*, 9–13. [CrossRef]
22. Gupta, R.; Sambyal, N. An understanding approach towards MOOCs. *Int. J. Emerg. Technol. Adv. Eng.* **2013**, *3*, 312–315.
23. Twiner, A.; Littleton, K.; Whitelock, D.; Coffin, C. Combining sociocultural discourse analysis and multimodal analysis to explore teachers' and pupils' meaning making. *Learn. Cult. Soc. Interact.* **2021**, *30*, 100520. [CrossRef]
24. Bateman, J.A. What are digital media? *Discourse Context Media* **2021**, *41*, 100502. [CrossRef]
25. Bjork, R.A. Being suspicious of the sense of ease and undeterred by the sense of difficulty: Looking back at Schmidt and Bjork (1992). *Perspect. Psychol. Sci.* **2018**, *13*, 146–148. [CrossRef]
26. Gašević, D.; Kovanović, V.; Joksimović, S.; Siemens, G. Where is research on massive open online courses headed? A data analysis of the MOOC research initiative. *Int. Rev. Res. Open Distrib. Learn.* **2014**, *15*, 134–176. [CrossRef]
27. Guo, S.; Zhang, G.; Guo, Y. Social Network Analysis of 50 Years of International Collaboration in the Research of Educational Technology. *J. Educ. Comput. Res.* **2016**, *53*, 499–518. [CrossRef]
28. Skoglund, L.; Brundin, R.; Olofsson, T.; Kalimo, H.; Ingvast, S.; Blom, E.S.; Glaser, A. Frontotemporal dementia in a large Swedish family is caused by a progranulin null mutation. *Neurogenetics* **2009**, *10*, 27–34. [CrossRef] [PubMed]
29. Stanciu, I.; Larsson, M.; Nordin, S.; Adolfsson, R.; Nilsson, L.G.; Olofsson, J.K. Olfactory impairment and subjective olfactory complaints independently predict conversion to dementia: A longitudinal, population-based study. *J. Int. Neuropsychol. Soc.* **2014**, *20*, 209–217. [CrossRef] [PubMed]
30. Devanand, D.P.; Lee, S.; Manly, J.; Andrews, H.; Schupf, N.; Doty, R.L.; Mayeux, R. Olfactory deficits predict cognitive decline and Alzheimer dementia in an urban community. *Neurology* **2015**, *84*, 182–189. [CrossRef] [PubMed]
31. Hew, K.F.; Cheung, W.S. Students' and instructors' use of massive open online courses (MOOCs): Motivations and challenges. *Educ. Res. Rev.* **2014**, *12*, 45–58. [CrossRef]
32. Abbakumov, D.; Desmet, P.; Van den Noortgate, W. Measuring growth in students' proficiency in MOOCs: Two component dynamic extensions for the Rasch model. *Behav. Res. Methods* **2019**, *51*, 332–341. [CrossRef]
33. Adam, M.; Young-Wolff, K.C.; Konar, E.; Winkleby, M. Massive open online nutrition and cooking course for improved eating behaviors and meal composition. *Int. J. Behav. Nutr. Phys. Act.* **2015**, *12*, 143. [CrossRef]
34. Hendriks, R.A.; De Jong, P.G.M.; Admiraal, W.F.; Reinders, M.E.J. Uncovering motivation and self-regulated learning skills in integrated medical MOOC learning: A mixed methods research protocol. *BMJ Open* **2020**, *10*, e038235. [CrossRef]
35. Scott, K.W.; Dushime, T.; Rusanganwa, V.; Woskie, L.; Attebery, C.; Binagwaho, A. Leveraging massive open online courses to expand quality of healthcare education to health practitioners in Rwanda. *BMJ Open Qual.* **2019**, *8*, e000532. [CrossRef]
36. Padilha, J.M.; Machado, P.P.; Ribeiro, A.L.; Ribeiro, R.; Vieira, F.; Costa, P. Easiness, usefulness and intention to use a MOOC in nursing. *Nurse Educ. Today* **2021**, *97*, 104705. [CrossRef] [PubMed]
37. Adamski, M.; Truby, H.; Klassen, K.M.; Cowan, S.; Gibson, S. Using the Internet: Nutrition Information-Seeking Behaviours of Lay People Enrolled in a Massive Online Nutrition Course. *Nutrients* **2020**, *12*, 750. [CrossRef] [PubMed]
38. Martiniello, L.; Borrelli, L.; Toto, G.A. Design of a MOOC for teaching and research: The innovative experience of the MERGO project. In Proceedings of the First Workshop on Technology Enhanced Learning Environments for Blended Education (teleXbe2021), Foggia, Italy, 21–22 January 2021.
39. Asli, M.F.; Hamzah, M.; Ibrahim, A.A.A.; Ayub, E. Problem characterization for visual analytics in MOOC learner's support monitoring: A case of Malaysian MOOC. *Heliyon* **2020**, *6*, e05733. [CrossRef] [PubMed]
40. Ebben, M.; Murphy, J.S. Unpacking MOOC scholarly discourse: A review of nascent MOOC scholarship. *Learn. Media Technol.* **2014**, *39*, 328–345. [CrossRef]
41. Hu, Y.; Spiro, R.J. Design for now, but with the future in mind: A "cognitive flexibility theory" perspective on online learning through the lens of MOOCs. *Educ. Technol. Res. Dev.* **2021**, *69*, 373–378. [CrossRef]
42. Hughes, G.; Dobbins, C. The utilization of data analysis techniques in predicting student performance in massive open online courses (MOOCs). *Res. Pract. Technol. Enhanc. Learn.* **2015**, *10*, 10. [CrossRef]

43. Simon, M.A.; Taylor, S.; Tom, L.S. Leveraging Digital Platforms to Scale Health Care Workforce Development: The Career 911 Massive Open Online Course. *Prog. Community Health Partnersh. Res. Educ. Action* **2019**, *13*, 123–130. [CrossRef]
44. Jacquet, G.A.; Umoren, R.A.; Hayward, A.S.; Myers, J.G.; Modi, P.; Dunlop, S.J.; Sarfaty, S.; Hauswald, M.; Tupesis, J.P. The Practitioner's Guide to Global Health: An interactive, online, open-access curriculum preparing medical learners for global health experiences. *Med. Educ. Online* **2018**, *23*, 1503914. [CrossRef]
45. Jiang, Z.; Wu, H.; Cheng, H.; Wang, W.; Xie, A.; Fitzgerald, S.R. Twelve tips for teaching medical students online under COVID-19. *Med. Educ. Online* **2021**, *26*, 1854066. [CrossRef]
46. Smith-Lickess, S.K.; Woodhead, T.; Burhouse, A.; Vasilakis, C. Study design and protocol for a comprehensive evaluation of a UK massive open online course (MOOC) on quality improvement in healthcare. *BMJ Open* **2019**, *9*, e031973. [CrossRef]
47. Kellogg, S. Online learning: How to make a MOOC. *Nature* **2013**, *499*, 369–371. [CrossRef] [PubMed]
48. Sneddon, J.; Barlow, G.; Bradley, S.; Brink, A.; Chandy, S.J.; Nathwani, D. Development and impact of a massive open online course (MOOC) for antimicrobial stewardship. *J. Antimicrob. Chemother.* **2018**, *73*, 1091–1097. [CrossRef] [PubMed]
49. Magaña-Valladares, L.; González-Robledo, M.C.; Rosas-Magallanes, C.; Mejía-Arias, M.; Arreola-Ornelas, H.; Knaul, F.M. Training Primary Health Professionals in Breast Cancer Prevention: Evidence and Experience from Mexico. *J. Cancer Educ.* **2018**, *33*, 160–166. [CrossRef] [PubMed]
50. Mahajan, R.; Gupta, P.; Singh, T. Massive Open Online Courses: Concept and Implications. *Indian Pediatr.* **2019**, *56*, 489–495. [CrossRef] [PubMed]
51. Meinert, E.; Alturkistani, A.; Car, J.; Carter, A.; Wells, G.; Brindley, D. Real-world evidence for postgraduate students and professionals in healthcare: Protocol for the design of a blended massive open online course. *BMJ Open* **2018**, *8*, e025196. [CrossRef]
52. Murphy, K.; Munk, P.L. Continuing Medical Education: MOOCs (Massive Open Online Courses) and Their Implications for Radiology Learning. *Can. Assoc. Radiol. J.* **2013**, *64*, 165. [CrossRef] [PubMed]
53. Zhou, T.; Huang, S.; Cheng, J.; Xiao, Y. The distance teaching practice of combined mode of massive open online course micro-video for interns in emergency department during the COVID-19 epidemic period. *Telemed. e-Health* **2020**, *26*, 584–588. [CrossRef]
54. Downes, S. Places to go: Connectivism & connective knowledge. *Innov. J. Online Educ.* **2008**, *5*, 1–6.
55. Fini, A. The Technological Dimension of a Massive Open Online Course: The Case of the CCK08 Course Tools. *Int. Rev. Res. Open Distrib. Learn.* **2009**, *10*, 1–26. [CrossRef]
56. Mota, R.; Scott, D. *Education for Innovation and Independent Learning*; Elsevier: Amsterdam, The Netherlands, 2014.
57. Deng, R.; Benckendorff, P. A Contemporary Review of Research Methods Adopted to Understand Students' and Instructors' Use of Massive Open Online Courses (MOOCs). *Int. J. Inf. Educ. Technol.* **2017**, *7*, 601–607. [CrossRef]
58. Yu, H.; Miao, C.; Leung, C.; White, T.J. Towards AI-powered personalization in MOOC learning. *Npj Sci. Learn.* **2017**, *2*, 1–5. [CrossRef] [PubMed]
59. Berman, A.H.; Biguet, G.; Stathakarou, N.; Westin-Hägglöf, B.; Jeding, K.; McGrath, C.; Kononowicz, A.A. Virtual patients in a behavioral medicine massive open online course (MOOC): A qualitative and quantitative analysis of participants' perceptions. *Acad. Psychiatry* **2017**, *41*, 631–641. [CrossRef] [PubMed]
60. France, K.; Hangorsky, U.; Wu, C.W.; Sollecito, T.P.; Stoopler, E.T. Participation in an existing massive open online course in dentistry during the COVID-19 pandemic. *J. Dent. Educ.* **2021**, *85*, 78–81. [CrossRef]
61. Milligan, C.; Littlejohn, A. How health professionals regulate their learning in massive open online courses. *Internet High. Educ.* **2016**, *31*, 113–121. [CrossRef]
62. Paton, C. Massive Open Online Course for Health Informatics Education. *Healthc. Inform. Res.* **2014**, *20*, 81–87. [CrossRef]
63. Robinson, R. Delivering a medical school elective with massive open online course (MOOC) technology. *PeerJ* **2016**, *4*, e2343. [CrossRef]
64. Paek, S.A. Research perspective on the concept of learning culture: MOOCs and other online contexts. *Educ. Technol. Res. Dev.* **2021**, *69*, 365–368. [CrossRef]
65. Olivares, S.L.O.; Hernández, R.I.E.; Corolla, M.L.T.; Alvarez, J.P.N.; Sánchez-Mendiola, M. MOOC Learning Assessment in Clinical Settings: Analysis from Quality Dimensions. *Med. Sci. Educ.* **2021**, *31*, 447–455. [CrossRef]
66. de Castañeda, R.R.; Garrison, A.; Haeberli, P.; Crump, L.; Zinsstag, J.; Ravel, A.; Flahault, A.; Bolon, I. First 'Global Flipped Classroom in One Health': From MOOCs to research on real world challenges. *One Health* **2018**, *5*, 37–39. [CrossRef]

Article

Learning from Peer Mistakes: Collaborative UML-Based ITS with Peer Feedback Evaluation

Sehrish Abrejo *, Hameedullah Kazi, Mutee U. Rahman, Ahsanullah Baloch and Amber Baig

Department of Computer Science, Faculty of Engineering, Science & Technology, Isra University, Hyderabad 71500, Pakistan; hkazi@isra.edu.pk (H.K.); mutee.rahman@isra.edu.pk (M.U.R.); ahsanullah.baloch@isra.edu.pk (A.B.); amber.baig@isra.edu.pk (A.B.)
* Correspondence: sehrish-abrejo@hotmail.com

Abstract: Collaborative Intelligent Tutoring Systems (ITSs) use peer tutor assessment to give feedback to students in solving problems. Through this feedback, the students reflect on their thinking and try to improve it when they get similar questions. The accuracy of the feedback given by the peers is important because this helps students to improve their learning skills. If the student acting as a peer tutor is unclear about the topic, then they will probably provide incorrect feedback. There have been very few attempts in the literature that provide limited support to improve the accuracy and relevancy of peer feedback. This paper presents a collaborative ITS to teach Unified Modeling Language (UML), which is designed in such a way that it can detect erroneous feedback before it is delivered to the student. The evaluations conducted in this study indicate that receiving and sending incorrect feedback have negative impact on students' learning skills. Furthermore, the results also show that the experimental group with peer feedback evaluation has significant learning gains compared to the control group.

Keywords: Intelligent Tutoring Systems; UML class diagrams; peer feedback evaluation; domain learning

Citation: Abrejo, S.; Kazi, H.; Rahman, M.U.; Baloch, A.; Baig, A. Learning from Peer Mistakes: Collaborative UML-Based ITS with Peer Feedback Evaluation. *Computers* **2022**, *11*, 30. https://doi.org/10.3390/computers11030030

Academic Editors: Antonio Sarasa Cabezuelo and Covadonga Rodrigo San Juan

Received: 31 December 2021
Accepted: 16 February 2022
Published: 22 February 2022

Publisher's Note: MDPI stays neutral with regard to jurisdictional claims in published maps and institutional affiliations.

Copyright: © 2022 by the authors. Licensee MDPI, Basel, Switzerland. This article is an open access article distributed under the terms and conditions of the Creative Commons Attribution (CC BY) license (https://creativecommons.org/licenses/by/4.0/).

1. Introduction

ITSs are computer-based learning systems that use Artificial Intelligence (AI) techniques to simulate human tutors to help students to improve their learning skills. Today, ITSs are in widespread use at various levels in different advanced countries and are enhancing the student learning experience [1–3]. ITSs have been successfully developed for a variety of domains including mathematics, physics, programming, databases, design tasks and learning new languages. Examples include Andes Physics Tutor (problem solving in introductory college physics) [4], Algebra Cognitive Tutor (problem solving in a high school algebra course) [5], AutoTutor (problem solving in college physics and other domains) [6,7], Sherlock (troubleshooting a large piece of simulated electrical equipment) [8], SQL-Tutor [9], COLLECT-UML (Object-Oriented software design) [10–12] and KERMIT (database design) [13–15].

With the advent of the Internet, students may now not only attend school to listen to live lectures, but they can also use Internet platforms to develop skills. To put it another way, online learning can help students study more efficiently [16]. ITSs use cutting-edge computer technologies such as the Internet, hypermedia and virtual reality to provide tutoring for individual students, and groups of students, in a collaborative learning environment [17]. Collaborative ITSs use peer feedback where the learner receives feedback from other students. Feedback can be defined as "all post-response information that is provided to a learner to inform on his or her actual state of learning or performance" [18,19]. The source of feedback can be external (peer or teacher) or internal (the learner). Peer feedback is a practice where students give feedback to each other, hence improving their learning in a particular domain. Learning of students, while providing feedback, is improved when they are involved in talking, listening, writing, reading, and reflecting on contents, ideas, and problems in the domain. Researchers have widely reported the benefits of peer tutoring and feedback in classroom settings. Refs. [20–24] present hundreds of experiences in the field. Recent literature reviews in [25–27] document the academic, social, and psychological benefits of this methodology.

In collaborative learning, students of the same learning status provide feedback to each other. The feedback can be in the form of formative assessment, which is equivalent to that of teacher's feedback [22]. In formative assessment feedback, the main difference between teacher's and peer student's feedback is that the peer is not an expert of the domain; as a result, the feedback of peers varies. Not all peer feedback results in learning gains, and the students should receive relevant feedback as guidance to revise their solutions rather than confuse them [28]. There is always a chance that the peer may not be clear about the topic and may provide wrong information. On the other hand, the student receiving inappropriate feedback can infer incorrectly, which leads to having a negative impact on students' learning. In contrast, any misinterpretation of peer feedback will cause learners to lose focus and take longer to comprehend and solve the problem. Many collaborative systems have been proposed in the literature in which one student's solution is evaluated by another student. Examples of such systems include Collab-ChiQat [29], CirCLE [30] and ITSCL [31]. In these systems, one student provides feedback on another student's solution, by rating or commenting. These ratings or comments can be misleading if they are contrary to the solution; for example, if the student has correctly solved the given problem but receives a negative rating from other students. Negative feedback can confuse students and they will not be able to solve the problem. Previous studies that allow collaboration through feedback from one student to another have revealed little or no evidence on peer feedback relevancy to correct/wrong solutions. Hence, considering the importance of peer feedback, it can be hypothesized that students receiving incorrect or irrelevant feedback from peers will have a negative impact on their domain learning. Therefore, the research question that we investigated in this study is whether there is a negative impact on students' learning if they receive incorrect feedback. To investigate and identify the effects of peer feedback on students' learning, this paper presents a Unified Modeling Language-Intelligent Tutoring System (UML-ITS) with peer feedback evaluation that focuses on improving the accuracy and relevancy of feedback in accordance with the solution. The presented ITS model not only evaluates peer feedback before delivering it, but also guides students in providing information that is correct and can be applied to the solution. The following section describes some of the ITSs that support collaboration. Next, the UML-ITS model along with its architecture and interface is discussed, before the presentation of the results. Finally, conclusions are presented.

2. Literature Review

The ITS has become increasingly common in assisting students [32]. In the literature, many tutoring systems have been proposed to support collaborative learning within ITSs to enhance students' learning. Collect-UML [12] is an ITS based on constraints that teach object-oriented (OO) analysis and design using UML. Students can use this tool to solve problems both alone and in collaboration. First, students use the system's feedback to develop UML class diagrams on their own. Then they join a group to come up with a group solution. The system compares the group solution against the individual solutions of all group members in collaboration mode. System feedback is provided on the group solution, and on the collaboration that takes place between students.

Collab-ChiQat [29] supports paired programming with a group of two students. Collab-ChiQat is designed to help students to learn linked list data structures in collaboration. One student can take a turn as a driver (the role assigned to one who writes the lines of code) at a time, and another student has to wait for his turn to write the code. The ITS provides domain hints to help the driver student to solve the given problem while another student can provide helpful feedback using a peer feedback bonus from the collaboration panel interface.

CirCLE [30] is the abbreviation for Circuitously Collaborative Learning Environment, which is designed for mathematical word problems to enhance the metacognitive awareness of the learning process. The main aim of this research was to make students rethink their solved problems after reviewing other students' solutions. Initially, all students are given a single problem which is then submitted to the system. After the first submission, the students are assigned the role of Peer Inspector to review and comment on other students' solutions. The inspector might consider rethinking their solution after receiving appropriate feedback on it and reviewing other solutions (metacognitive awareness).

ITSCL stands for Intelligent Tutoring Supported Collaborative Learning, which was proposed by [31]. It is a combination of an Intelligent Tutoring System and collaborative learning. ITSCL provides learners with three levels of interaction with the system. In the first level of interaction, the individual learner interacts with the ITS tutor without any collaboration. In this level of interaction, a single student uses the ITS on a one-on-one basis where the ITS asks questions of the student and the student has to respond. The intelligent hints are provided by ITS if the student is not able to answer or needs help. The second and third levels of interactions support learner-to-learner (two peer students) and tutor-group collaborative learning, respectively. In the second level of interaction, two students collaborate via a chat interface and share ideas to answer the questions. Hints are provided by the ITS based on their answers given. The third level of interaction allows tutor-group learning, where multiple students provide a group answer to the problem given by the ITS. In this form of interaction, each student provides an individual answer to the question given by the ITS, and the ITS displays each student's response to all other students in the group. Each student can update his/her response twice after reading other students' answers. After updating, students finalize their answers. The ITS uses natural language processing (NLP) on the finalized answers and matches the similarity with the answers stored in the database. The answer that most closely matches the stored database answer is selected as the group answer and ITS hints are then provided by the system on the selected group answer.

These systems support multiple students to collaboratively solve a problem but they do not evaluate the feedback that students send to each other while solving problems. In Collect-UML, the system does not restrict students from adding wrong elements in the collaborative group diagram. The students receiving help from the group diagram may implement wrong elements in their individual solutions. Collab-ChiQat allows the non-driver student (who is not writing the code) to comment or provide helping hints to the driver student. The feedback provided by the non-driver student can be irrelevant as they select already defined feedback from the drop-down list. ITS provides hints only when the driver student types erroneous code. In CirCLE, the inspector can disagree on students' solutions and can provide negative feedback despite all correct steps being taken. There is no support provided by the system to inform the inspector about the student's correct solution. Similarly, In ITSCL, each student can comment on the other student's answer. They can agree or disagree with the peer answer, or they can suggest changes in the peer answer. These comments are not evaluated by the ITSCL if one student provides false negative comments (the answer is correct but students comment negatively) or false positive comments (the answer is wrong but students comment positively. Moreover, textual feedback can also be helpful [33–35], but domain-related accuracy and relevance of the feedback delivered in natural language needs considerable usage of NLP techniques; otherwise, the system's ability to provide meaningful feedback would be debated. Furthermore, systems such as Collab-ChiQat and CirCLE bound students to submit feedback within the interface's boundaries, making it impossible for them to expound upon or explain their ideas. This research attempts to overcome the limitations of previous systems and proposes a peer feedback evaluation model in ITSs that examines peer feedback before it is sent to another peer. Peer feedback evaluation will not only help students to focus on providing responses that are relevant to the solution, but also help peers to rethink their feedback and avoid repeating the same mistakes while responding on similar errors.

3. System Description

Due to its complex and ill-defined nature, the UML Class Diagram was selected as a domain for the ITS design. The proposed UML-ITS is implemented to teach OO analysis and design concepts, where students collaboratively construct a UML class diagram based on some given requirements. UML-ITS creates a session between two students and assigns them roles of Tutor (the one who evaluates the solution of the other student and provides suggestions/feedback) and Tutee (the one who develops the solution). For the rest of the paper, the role names of Tutor and Tutee are used. Each action performed by the student is recorded in the log file. The students develop a solution model by drawing diagrams on the workspace area and interact with each other using the chat tool. UML-ITS provides feedback to students while solving a problem through hints. Once both students agree on the modeled solution, they can submit the final solution to the ITS. The solution is evaluated against the sample/ideal solution stored in the knowledge base. If the submitted solution has errors, the hints are generated; otherwise, a new problem scenario is displayed. Figure 1 shows the interface of UML-ITS. The same screen is displayed to both students but with different toolbar options.

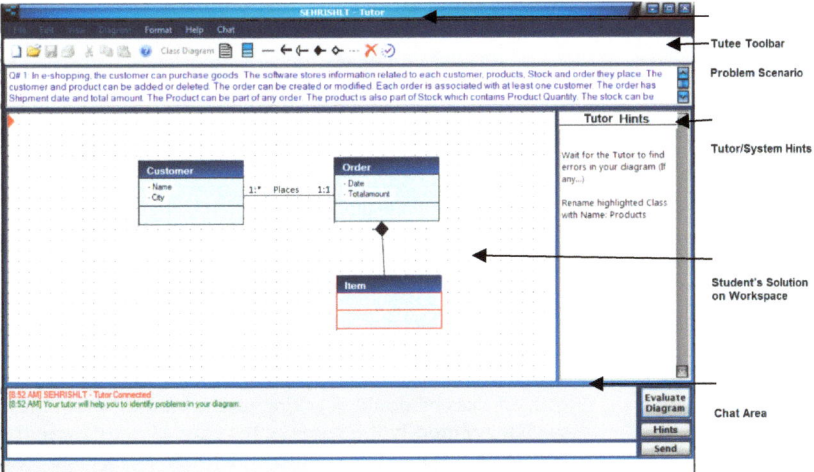

Figure 1. UML-ITS interface.

3.1. XML Solutions

XML stands for eXtensible Markup Language, which is widely being accepted as a form of information representation. XML stores information in the form of tags. In UML-ITS, all the ideal solutions of UML textual problems are stored in XML documents. All XML documents begin with an XML declaration followed by a root element, which is <ClassDiagram> in our case. Each class is defined with the <Class> tag, which includes <Name>, <Attribute>, <Method>, and <Relationship> tags as child elements. The <Relationship> tag has four attributes:

1. WithClass: Defines the name of the class that has a relationship with the current class.
2. Type: Defines the type of relationship, i.e., Association, Generalization, etc.
3. Link: Defines Start or End of the line connector. This helps in the identification of parent-child and whole-part relationships if generalization, composition, or aggregation types are used. The Link = "End" attribute value represents the "Whole" class relationship, whereas Link = "Start" represents the "Part" class relationship. For class inheritance, the parent class is represented with the End link type and child class with the Start link type.
4. Multiplicity: Defines participation constraints on association relationship types.

The student's solution is also converted to a temporary XML document that is compared against the XML solution stored in the UML-ITS's knowledge base. The temporary XML document is updated whenever the tutee student makes changes in the solution. If the temporary XML document is different from that of XML solution, the hints are generated by the UML-ITS based on the differences found. Figure 2 describes the comparison of both XML documents.

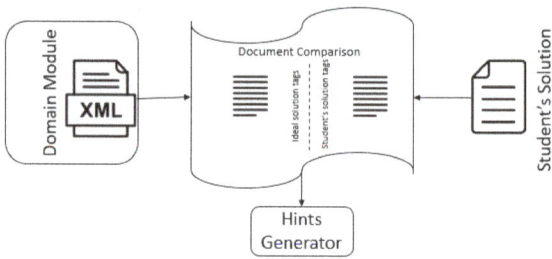

Figure 2. Ideal solution comparison with the student's solution.

3.2. Tutee Student Toolbar

The tutee student will start drawing the UML diagram by selecting the appropriate tool from the UML constructs (Figure 3).

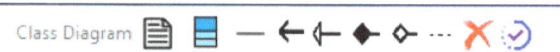

Figure 3. Tutee student toolbar.

To draw a diagram, the tutee student clicks on a specific drawing tool button, places the cursor on the desired workspace location, and presses the mouse button; for example to create a new class, the tutee clicks on the Class button (▤). An empty class component is displayed in the workspace area. The tutee then can define the name of the newly created class by double-clicking on the top portion of the class. The same method is used to change/modify the name of the class already present in the diagram. Once the class is created, its attributes and methods can be defined by double-clicking on the specific class component. The student can also change or delete class attributes/methods by right clicking and selecting required options. The relationships can be added by selecting appropriate relationship types from the toolbar.

3.3. Tutor Student Toolbar

The tutor student has the responsibility to identify tutee's misconceptions about UML class diagrams in their designed solution. Once the tutee student clicks the Evaluate Diagram button, tutor-student toolbar features are activated with the system-generated message to ask tutor to find errors in the diagram. To help tutor to find errors, some specific features are added to the tutor's toolbar, as shown in Figure 4.

Figure 4. Tutor student toolbar.

The tutor can use different toolbar features to indicate the type of error in the tutee's solution. The Suggest Missing button (💡) can be used for missing components (classes, attributes, methods or relationships), the Select Error button (■) for incorrect components, and the Delete button (✗) for extra components. If the tutor finds some errors in the diagram, then the tutor can indicate them by activating the Select Error button. The tutor can only click on specific diagram components to indicate an error. The selected component's color is changed to red, which is also visible to the tutee. Furthermore, an automatic message is generated and sent to the tutee that contains information about the error and is displayed in UML hints area on the screen.

3.4. Peer Feedback Evaluator Design

The evaluation of tutor feedback takes place before delivering it to the tutee student. The main function of the feedback evaluator module is to evaluate tutor feedback against the ideal solution. The first step in evaluating the tutor's feedback is to identify the type of feedback that the tutor is providing to the tutee student. The sub-components of the Feedback Evaluator are shown in Figure 5.

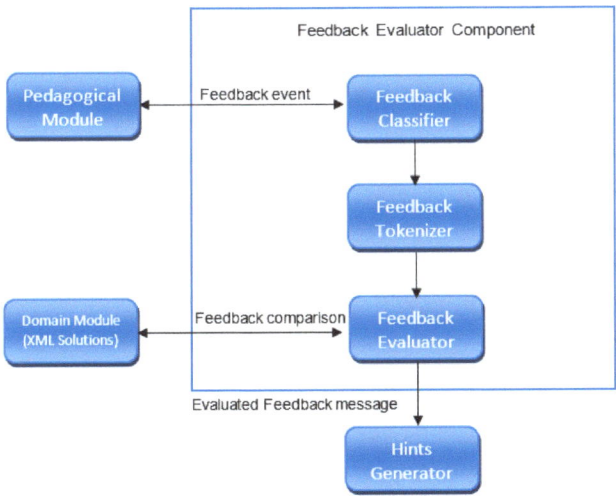

Figure 5. Sub-components of the feedback evaluator.

It can be seen in Figure 5 that the feedback classifier receives a feedback event, which is the hint that the tutor is providing to the tutee. The feedback classifier identifies whether it is related to classes, relationships, attributes, or methods. This identification is based on the tutor's actions that he/she has taken on the workspace. If the tutor clicks the class component, then it is classified as 'C', relationships as 'R', attributes as 'A', and methods as 'M'. For example, if the tutor finds an error in the solution related to classes, then the tutor clicks on that particular class. As soon as the tutor clicks on the class, the following message is generated:

C ClassName = "Items"

The message indicates that the tutor has clicked on the class component and its name is 'Items'. Once the component on which the tutor is providing feedback has been identified, then further classification takes place to see if the response is related to a wrong component, a missing component, or extra classes in the tutee's solution. This classification is based on the button activated from the tutor's toolbar. If Suggest Missing is activated, then a token related to the missing component is added to the feedback; if the Error button is selected, then a token for the wrong component is added; and if the Delete button is activated, then an extra component token is added to the feedback message. The feedback tokenizer assigns tokens based on their classification, as shown in the following example, which indicates that the 'Items' class is an incorrect class in the tutee's solution.

WrongC ClassName = "Items"

For attributes and methods, WrongA and WrongM tokens are used, respectively. Along with the class name in which the wrong attribute or method is defined, the attribute and method names are also appended in the feedback message. For example, the following feedback messages indicate that the tutor has marked the attribute with the name 'id' in the class 'Items' as a wrong attribute. Similarly, the method with name 'Show' in the class 'Items' has been marked as a wrong method.

WrongA ClassName = "Items" Attribute = "id"

WrongM ClassName = "Items" Method = "Show"

For errors in relationships, more information is added in the message to indicate the endpoints' directions along with the type of relationships. For example, if the tutor finds an error in the composition relationship type, then the following feedback message is generated:

WrongR ClassName = "Items" WithClass = "Orders" Type = "Composition" Link = "Start"

The above message indicates that the relationship of the type Composition between the Items and Orders classes is wrong. The endpoints of relationships are identified through the Link attribute. If the endpoints of the relationship are drawn incorrectly, then it is also considered to be an error in the relationship, which is tokenized similarly, as described above. Table 1 shows the list of tokens that are assigned to feedback messages.

Table 1. List of Tokens.

Token	Description	Token	Description
WrongC	Wrong Class in Tutee's solution		Name of
MissingC	Missing Class in Tutee's solution	ClassName	Wrong/Missing/Extra class
ExtraC	Extra Class in Tutee's solution		
WrongA	The wrong attribute in Class		Name of
MissingA	Missing attribute in Class	Attribute	Wrong/Missing/Extra
ExtraA	Extra attribute in Class		attribute
WrongM	Wrong Method in Class		Name of
MissingM	Missing Method in Class	Method	Wrong/Missing/Extra method
ExtraM	Extra Method in Class		
WrongR	Wrong Relationship b/w classes	With	Second class name
MissingR	Missing Relationship b/w classes	Class	Name of relationship
ExtraR	Extra Relationship b/w classes	TypeLink	End connectors of relationship

The feedback evaluator compares the tokenized feedback message with an ideal solution to see if the tutor is responding correctly to the tutee. This comparison is based on following conditions:

- A missing class diagram component is present in the ideal solution but not in the tutee's solution.
- A wrong class component is present in the tutee's solution but not in the ideal solution.
- An extra class diagram component is present in the tutee's solution but not in the ideal solution. This condition also checks if the total number of classes present in the tutee's solution is greater than the total number of class components in the ideal solution. If the number is greater, then the selected component is considered to be extra; otherwise, it is considered to be wrong.

Once the feedback evaluator compares the feedback with the ideal solution, extra information is added in the feedback message. If the tutor has correctly marked an incorrect class diagram component as the wrong class, then a plus (+) sign is added at the beginning of the message, which indicates that the feedback from the tutor is correct. Conversely, if the tutor has marked a correct class diagram component as the wrong class, then a minus (−) sign is added at the beginning of the feedback message to indicate incorrect feedback from tutor.

Table 2 shows some of the examples of correct and incorrect feedback message identification. The feedback message along with token and sign is delivered to the Hints generator to produce hints accordingly.

Table 2. Correct/incorrect feedback messages.

Correct Tutor Feedback
+WrongC ClassName = "Items"
+ExtraA ClassName = "Items" attribute = "id"
+MissingM ClassName = "Items" method = "Show"
+WrongR ClassName = "Items" WithClass = "Orders" type = "Composition" Link = "Start"
Incorrect Tutor Feedback
−MissingC ClassName = "Orders"
−ExtraA ClassName = "Items" attribute = "id"
−MissingA ClassName = "Items" attribute = "Price"
−ExtraR ClassName = "Items" WithClass = "Products" type = "Association" Link = "Start"

3.5. Tutor Feedback Evaluation Model

Tutor feedback in the UML-ITS is evaluated by the feedback evaluation component, which evaluates all feedback coming from the tutor before it is delivered to the tutee. This evaluation is beneficial for both the tutor and tutee during their learning process in many ways. Firstly, the tutors can reflect on their own knowledge about the domain when their mistakes are notified by the system. During their tutoring process, if tutors receive the same type of tutee mistake on which they provided wrong feedback, the tutors will recall and try to avoid responding incorrectly. Secondly, the tutors have an opportunity to correct themselves before their feedback is delivered to the tutee, hence upholding their faith in teaching, and preventing them from thinking of themselves as inept tutors. Thirdly, the tutor's image in the tutee's perceptions is retained since the tutee always expects to receive the required feedback. Lastly, the tutee receives relevant feedback and models the solution without recording extra misconceptions in their log.

Figure 6 illustrates the overall problem-solving flow, and the roles of each student and the system as a whole. Bold parts in the flow diagram are related to tutor feedback evaluation. The feedback evaluation process starts when the tutor sends a response to the tutee student. The tutee student can take any one action: they can take step to design a solution (i.e., creating a class or modifying some properties, etc.), they can indicate that they have completed the solution by clicking the Evaluate button, or they can ask for the tutor's help by clicking the Hints button. The tutor can respond at any time after the tutee clicks the Evaluate button or Hints button. The main function of the feedback evaluator module is to evaluate the tutor feedback against the ideal solution and generate hints depending on the tutor's error. If the tutor has marked a correct mistake/error in the solution, then positive feedback from the system is generated to appreciate the tutor. In the opposite case, where the tutor marks a correct component as a mistake/error, negative feedback is displayed to the tutor indicating that the selected component is the correct one. Once the tutor marks the correct mistake/error, then the tutor needs to suggest the changes that are not present in tutee's solution. The feedback evaluator evaluates tutor's feedback regarding classes, attributes, methods, and relationships in the same ways as described above.

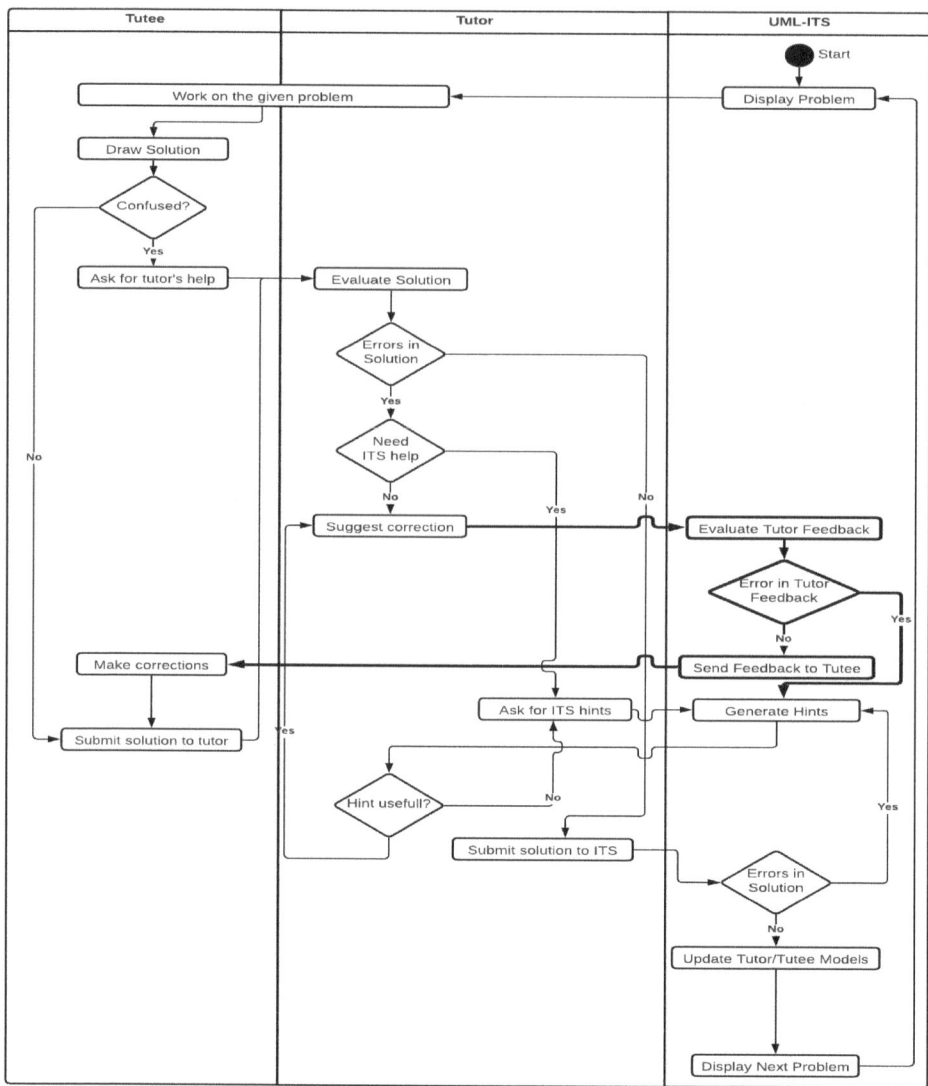

Figure 6. Swimlane diagram of the UML-ITS with peer feedback evaluation.

4. Evaluations

4.1. Experimental Design

To investigate our research questions and to determine the effects of the proposed model on a student's learning, an experimental study was conducted in which 100 students (57 female and 43 male) from different universities of Pakistan participated. All students were enrolled in different degree programs of Computer Science and they participated voluntarily. Fifty students used the UML-ITS without peer feedback evaluation (control group, in which tutors communicated erroneous feedback and suggestions to the tutee), and the other 50 students tutored each other using the UML-ITS with peer feedback evaluation (experimental group, in which tutors sent relevant and domain-related feedback to tutee students). The roles of tutor and tutee students were assigned randomly in both groups.

The study was conducted in two streams of three-hour laboratory sessions over two weeks, one week for each group. The students completed a pre-test (Supplementary S1) and then interacted with the UML-ITS, where each pair of tutor and tutee students worked on different UML class diagram scenarios. The students were seated in the same laboratory on different sides depending on their roles, and they were only allowed to communicate with one another via a chat tool provided with the system. After laboratory experimental sessions, students were asked to attempt a post-test (Supplementary S2), which was utilized to compare their results to their pre-test performance. The whole experimental design is depicted in Figure 7.

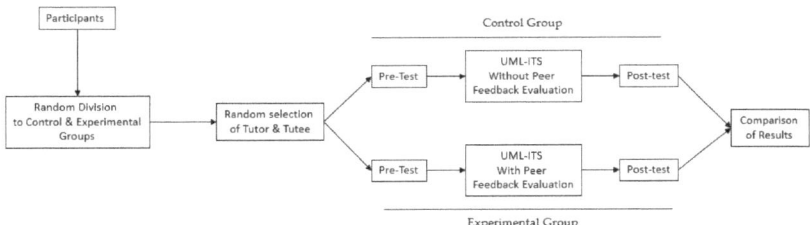

Figure 7. Experimental design.

4.2. Outcome Measures

In order to assess the performance of each student, pre- and post-tests were conducted. Each of these two tests contained a total of eight questions of 22 total marks. In the first question, students were asked to design a UML class diagram for the given problem scenario. In the second question, students were asked to write a description of the UML Class diagram. The remaining six questions were multiple-choice questions related to classes, attributes, and relationship types. All tests were administered on paper. The scores related to each question in both tests were calculated based on the number of correct class diagram components designed in the solution, the number of class attributes and relationships explained in the description, and the correct multiple-choice answers marked.

The findings of the pre- and post-tests were used to evaluate the students' performance. To monitor the difference between the pre-test and the post-test, the mean and standard deviation were calculated. Furthermore, the Normalized Learning Gain of each group was also calculated, which is the rough estimate of how efficient the prototype is at promoting the conceptual understanding of the subject. The formula presented in [36] was used and is shown in Equation (1):

$$\text{NLG} = \frac{PostTestScore - PreTestScore}{100 - PreTestScore} \quad (1)$$

4.3. Problem-Solving Measures

To examine the student's problem-solving collaboration process in Control and Experimental groups, all actions taken by the tutee, tutor, and UML-ITS were recorded in log files. The following is the list of actions included in the log file:
- Number of problems solved by each group;
- Time taken to solve each problem;
- Whether each problem was successfully completed or not;
- Correct and incorrect problem-solving steps taken by each student;
- The number of times hints were requested or provided by UML-ITS.

5. Results

The assessment of the research hypothesis regarding peer feedback evaluation started with the comparison of pre-test and post-test results respective to both conditions, including the control group and experimental group. Then, log files that were generated during the experimental study were carefully analyzed to link individual student's actions with their own and their partner's learning gains. In short, the similarities and differences of domain learning pathways that students took in both conditions were made clear upon completion of this analysis.

5.1. The Effects of the Prototype on Student's Domain Learning

The most important measure of ITS effectiveness is the improvement in a student's domain knowledge. Table 3 contains absolute pre-test and post-test scores of students who participated in both conditions. It is worth noting that, despite student's prior domain familiarity, their pre-test scores were the lowest. To explore the differences between pre-test and post-test results across both conditions, an independent sample t-test and Mann–Whitney z-test were performed. It was observed that students in both groups showed improvement in their learning after prototype intervention and there was significant difference in pre-test and post-test results ($t = 5.067$, $p = 0.000$) ($z = 7.644$, $p = 0.000$). The effects of different conditions on students' learning were also investigated and their NLGs were compared with each other; see the last row of Table 3.

Table 3. Pre-test and post-test results.

Test Data	Mean	s.d.	t/z-Value	p-Value
Control Group				
Pre-test	9.2	3.4	5.067	0.000
Post-test	13	4.0		
Experimental Group				
Pre-test	9.1	4.3	7.644	0.000
Post-test	18.2	2.8		
NLG Difference in both Conditions				
Control Group NLG	0.04	0.05	4.967	0.000
Experimental Group NLG	0.09	0.04		

Interestingly, there was significant difference between students' NLGs in both conditions ($z = 4.967$, $p = 0.000$). This reveals that the student's domain learning was affected by the conditions in which they were treated.

5.2. Total Number of Problem Scenarios Completed

To further investigate, the paths students took during the intervention were further explored by comparing the total number of questions or problem scenarios completed during the experimental session. It may be expected that each circumstance could have a similar problem-solving rate because of the significant difference between pre-test and post-test results, as explained in the above section. However, students in the control group attempted fewer problems (avg = 3.28) compared to students in the experimental group (avg: 7.26) (Table 4) since students in the control group had less relevant domain support.

Table 4. Total questions completed in two conditions.

Test Data	Mean	s.d.
Control Group	3.28	1.8
Experimental Group	7.26	1.29

In order to determine if problems completed were related to learning, the correlation of total problems successfully completed by each student with their normalized learning gain scores was calculated. Indeed, in the experimental group, problems successfully completed were marginally correlated with students' learning on NLG ($r = 0.695$, $p = 0.000$). However, the problems completed in the control group were also correlated with NLG results, but insignificantly ($r = 0.176$, $p = 0.221$), as shown in Table 5. Students in the control group received less domain support, due to which the rate of successful questions completed was lower than that of the other group. It can be inferred that if students attempt more problem scenarios, they have a chance to go through many concepts related to UML class diagrams. Those students who attempted fewer questions missed out some important concepts about which students were unclear, hence causing students to achieve a lower score in the post-test.

Table 5. Correlation—Total no. of questions completed vs. NLG.

Test Data	r	p
Control Group	0.176	0.221
Experimental Group	0.695	0.000

5.3. Problem-Solving Steps

In the above section, the difference between the total number of questions completed successfully in each condition was discussed. Although the questions completed in both conditions were correlated with student's NLG scores, students in the control group completed fewer problems compared to students of the other group. This is because the ITS did not provide them with the same support level. Furthermore, it can be hypothesized that students in the control group might appear to make more mistakes compared to those in the experimental group, again because of the lack of appropriate domain-level support from the ITS. To investigate this hypothesis, the total number of errors made by tutor and tutee students were compared in both conditions. According to the analysis results shown in Table 6, there was significant difference between tutees' errors made in both conditions ($t = 7.798$, $p = 0.003$), indicating that tutees in the control group made more errors during experimental intervention compared to tutee students in the experimental group. Interestingly, the tutor students in both conditions made identical errors as there is no significant difference ($t = 1.440$, $p = 0.157$), despite providing more domain-related help in the experimental group.

Table 6. No. of tutee and tutor errors in both conditions.

Test Data	Statistical Test	t	p
No. of Tutee errors	Independent Sample t test	7.798	0.003
No. of Tutor errors	Independent Sample t test	1.440	0.157

To investigate the effects of tutors' errors on the tutees' learning path, as hypothesized in previous sections, the correlation between the total number of errors made by the tutees was compared with the total number of errors made by the tutors in both conditions. As shown in Table 7, the errors made by the tutors in the control group were positively correlated with the total number of errors made by the tutees. This is because the tutors' wrong suggestions/mistakes were given to the tutees and the tutees followed those erroneous suggestions, which resulted in the higher rate of the tutees' errors. The errors made by the tutors in the experimental group were negatively correlated with the total number of errors made by the tutees.

Table 7. Correlation—total number of tutor and tutee errors in both conditions.

	Control Group		Experimental Group	
Test Data	r	p	r	p
No. of Tutor errors vs. Tutee errors	0.469	0.018	−0.060	0.776
No. of errors as Tutee vs. NLG	−0.270	0.191	−0.083	0.693
No. of errors viewed as Tutor vs. NLG	−0.289	0.161	0.362	0.010

It was also found that if the tutees made errors and they were viewed by the tutors, it was related to the tutors' learning in both conditions. The total number of errors made by the tutees in both conditions was negatively correlated to NLG. The total number of errors viewed by the tutors in the control group was also negatively correlated to the student's NLG. However, the viewing errors of the tutors in the experimental group were positively correlated to their NLG. It appeared that tutors who observed their tutees' inability to progress (when tutees made mistakes) was in fact connected to learning from tutoring. The overall correlation results imply that tutor students are indeed taking advantage of the ITS's peer feedback evaluation feature to reflect on their erroneous suggestions and rectifying them before sending then to the tutee.

5.4. Effects of Collaboration and Peer Feedback

At this level, the interaction between tutors, tutees, and the Intelligent Tutoring System was investigated. The first step in this analysis was to determine the effects of tutees' help-seeking behavior on their learning gains. It is believed that the students who ask for help when it is needed tend to learn more. As explained earlier, the errors viewed by tutors were correlated with their learning, but errors made by tutees were negatively correlated to their learning gains. To further explore the elements that affected tutees' learning, hints requested, correct feedback received, and incorrect feedback received were correlated with tutees' learning gains (Table 8).

Table 8. Correlation—collaboration and peer feedback.

	Control Group		Experimental Group	
Test Data	r	p	r	p
Hints Requested	0.490	0.00	0.386	0.003
Correct Feedback Received	0.558	0.000	0.783	0.000
Incorrect Feedback Received	−0.460	0.000	0.201	0.161
Hint Request Received	0.505	0.000	0.781	0.000
Incorrect Feedback Sent	−0.392	0.002	0.669	0.000

It can be observed that hints requested in both conditions were correlated to tutees' learning gains ($r = 0.490$, $p = 0.000$) ($r = 0.386$, $p = 0.003$). Correct feedback received by tutees in both conditions was also correlated to tutees' learning gains ($r = 0.558$, $p = 0.000$) ($r = 0.783$, $p = 0.000$). This indicates that correct feedback from tutors on tutees' solutions do have a positive effect on tutees' domain learning. Moreover, the incorrect feedback received from tutors in both conditions did not contribute to tutees' learning gains, which addresses our research question.

The next stage was to determine the factors that influenced the tutors' learning gains, because if tutees' hint-taking is linked to their learning, it is likely that receiving hint requests as a tutor will also contribute to their domain learning. Receiving hint requests as a tutor in both conditions was positively correlated to the tutor's learning gain ($r = 0.505$, $p = 0.000$) ($r = 0.781$, $p = 0.000$). It can be inferred that tutors learn more when they receive more hint requests from a tutee, because when tutors receive hints, they try to overcome the errors present in the tutee's solutions; hence, receiving hint requests encourages them to study more about the solutions.

Taking into account the opposite side of the story, when tutors receive hint requests, their learning improves. This depends on whether they send domain-related feedback that is in accordance with the solution, i.e., the feedback contains accurate information about the tutee's errors/mistakes in the diagram, or they send incorrect responses based on incorrect assumptions about the tutee's solutions. To explore this, incorrect feedback sent was correlated to tutors' learning gains. As shown in Table 8, the incorrect feedback provided by tutors in the control group to tutees was negatively correlated to their learning gains ($r = -0392$, $p = 0.005$). Here, because the tutors did not receive domain-level help from the UML-ITS, it is probable that they misinterpreted the tutee's solutions and replied with erroneous suggestions, resulting in a reduction in the tutee's learning gains. On the other hand, the tutor's incorrect feedback was correlated to their learning gains in the experimental group ($r = 0.669$, $p = 0.000$). The UML-ITS prevented tutors from sending incorrect feedback and provided them with domain level hints so that tutors could rethink the suggestions they were trying to send. Receiving domain level hints from the system allowed tutors to reflect on their own learning first and then send correct responses to the tutee. Furthermore, as previously mentioned, correct feedback received by tutees from a tutor was also linked to their learning improvements. In conclusion, both tutor and tutee students benefited from the UML-ITS by sending and receiving proper feedback on solutions.

5.5. Regression Analysis

As a last step, regression analysis was carried out to evaluate the abilities of the variables described in the previous sections to predict students' learning gains. The six factors of the students as tutors and tutees were considered to build a model for domain learning prediction in both conditions (control and experimental groups). The model contains the total number of questions completed, hints requested, correct feedback received, incorrect feedback received, hints requests received, and incorrect feedback sent. The model explained about 51% of the variation in learning gain as a whole ($R^2 = 0.511$, $F = 9.548$, $p = 0.000$) in the control group (Table 9). Of the six variables, three significantly predicted students' leaning gains, correct feedback received ($\beta = 0.415$, $t = 3.497$, $p = 0.001$), hint requests received ($\beta = 0.387$, $t = 2.119$, $p = 0.040$), and number of questions completed ($\beta = 0.252$, $t = 2.496$, $p = 0.016$). The remaining variables were either negatively predicted by the model or did not provide a significant prediction. While the three variables were significantly correlated to learning gains in control group, it appears that receiving a correct domain-related response from a tutor helped tutee students to overcome their learning gaps. On the other hand, receiving hint requests from a tutee also encouraged tutors to locate and correct errors in tutees' solutions, hence predicting the learning gains. It also appears that students receiving or sending incorrect feedback had a negative impact on their learning gains which, in this case, was due to the lack of appropriate system domain-level support.

Table 9. Regression analysis to predict student's learning gains.

Variables	Control Grout			Experimental Group		
	β	t	p	β	t	p
Questions Completed	0.252	2.496	0.016	0.186	2.086	0.043
Hints Requested	−0.055	−0.286	0.776	−0.147	−1.666	0.103
Correct Feedback Received	0.415	3.497	0.001	0.478	4.245	0.000
Incorrect Feedback Received	−0.022	−0.170	0.866	−0.070	−1.016	0.315
Hint Request Received	0.387	2.119	0.040	0.298	3.043	0.004
Incorrect Feedback Sent	−0.296	−2.634	0.012	0.241	2.920	0.006

Another type of regression analysis was conducted to predict the learning gains of the experimental group. The model contains the same six variables that were used to predict the learning gains of the control group, including the total number of questions completed, hints requested, correct feedback received, incorrect feedback received, hints requests received, and incorrect feedback sent. A significant percentage of the variance in the learning gain was explained by the model ($R^2 = 0.799$, $F = 33.557$, $p = 0.000$) (Table 9), although due to the small sample size it is likely that this value is inflated [37].

It can be observed from the regression analysis of the experimental group that two variables that do not significantly predict the gain in students' learning: hints requested ($\beta = -0.147$, $t = -1.666$, $p = 0.103$) and incorrect feedback received ($\beta = -0.070$, $t = -1.016$, $p = 0.315$). Interestingly, hints requested in both models does not predict students' learning gains, although, as mentioned in the previous section, hints made was positively correlated to students' learning gains. In general, this is because students may have requested help when it actually was not needed or before drawing components on the workspace. On the other hand, the tutor students who received hint requests in that way indeed provided wrong feedback. In this case, the wrong feedback was recorded when tutors suggested something through chat conversations. Apart from these two factors, every other variable substantially predicted students' learning gains, showing that the dual roles of tutor and tutee benefitted the students.

6. Discussion

This study proposed an ITS design with peer feedback evaluation and investigated its usage effects on students' learning. It was hypothesized that tutee students who receive erroneous feedback from their peer tutors would have poorer learning and overall performance than those who receive correct and domain-related feedback. It can be observed from the findings that students in both groups had improvements in their post-test results, but there was a significant difference in their learning gains in each group. This was due to the paths students took during the experimental period and certain design elements that had unique effects on students' learning in both conditions. The UML-ITS, for example, did not support tutors in the control group when they were requested to assist tutees. As a result, the tutor students gave erroneous hints, which UML-ITS evaluated when tutee students included them in their solutions. Under such situations, tutor and tutee students made more mistakes and scored less in their post-test as compared to the other group. On the other hand, students in the experimental group showed a significant improvement in their post-tests results because of receiving and sending domain-related feedback. Again, this was due to the proper domain level support from the UML-ITS. When tutors were not able to locate the mistakes in tutees' solutions or provided incorrect feedback, the UML-ITS generated hints, after evaluating the tutors' feedback, which helped tutors to revise the solution and go through it again. Furthermore, tutee students also received correct solution-related feedback from the tutors.

After the evaluation study and outcomes, it was possible to respond to the research question addressed by this paper. Some evidence was discovered in this study that suggested that receiving wrong responses had a detrimental influence on students' learning gains. For example, if tutee students followed tutors' wrong suggestions, they experienced a significant increase in their errors made (tutees' errors plus tutors' wrong suggestions that were implemented by the tutees in solutions). Not only did their number of total errors made increased, but students in those groups were also not able to attempt more problem scenarios compared to those who received domain-related responses from tutors. The tutors who were not notified about their incorrect feedback, on the other hand, also did not have the opportunity to reflect on their suggestions. Furthermore, attempting fewer problems, making more mistakes, and sending/receiving incorrect responses were all not correlated to their learning gains. Hence, receiving incorrect responses from tutors has a negative impact on tutees' learning gains. Nevertheless, based on the findings of this study, it seems that the benefits of peer feedback evaluation will grow as its quality improves.

7. Conclusions

Intelligent Tutoring Systems are computerized systems that help students in learning different subjects. These systems are gaining popularity due to the fact that they are available all the time and are easy to access and use. This paper presented UML-ITS, an intelligent tutoring for teaching UML with a peer feedback evaluation component. The empirical study included control and experimental groups (with and without peer feedback evaluation) to determine the effects of the ITS model on students' domain learning. While teaching the design of UML class diagrams, the experimental group also received support from the UML-ITS to evaluate peer feedback for its correctness and relevancy against an ideal solution. The system's peer feedback evaluation component double-checks all feedback from tutors before delivering it to the tutee student, which not only improved tutees' learning skill, but also helped peer tutors to rethink their own solutions, indicating a better influence on learning from both sides. In short, the students in both conditions showed an improvement in their domain knowledge, but students with peer feedback evaluation performed significantly better on their post-test after UML-ITS session, indicating that they gained greater expertise in UML modeling. Hence, it can be concluded that peer feedback evaluation in the ITS appears to be a promising advancement and should be implemented with enhancements in future ITS tools.

Supplementary Materials: The following supporting information can be downloaded at: https://www.mdpi.com/article/10.3390/computers11030030/s1, Supplementary S1: Pre-Test; Supplementary S2: Post-Test.

Author Contributions: Conceptualization, methodology, S.A., H.K. and A.B. (Amber Baig); software, S.A., M.U.R. and A.B. (Amber Baig); validation, formal analysis, investigation, resources, H.K., M.U.R. and A.B. (Ahsanullah Baloch); writing—original draft preparation, S.A., M.U.R. and A.B. (Amber Baig); writing—review and editing, visualization, H.K., M.U.R. and A.B. (Ahsanullah Baloch); supervision, H.K., M.U.R. and A.B. (Ahsanullah Baloch). All authors have read and agreed to the published version of the manuscript.

Funding: Research received no external funding.

Institutional Review Board Statement: Not applicable.

Informed Consent Statement: Informed consent was obtained from all subjects involved in the study.

Data Availability Statement: The data presented in this study are available in article.

Conflicts of Interest: The authors declare no conflict of interest.

References

1. Baker, R.S.; D'Mello, S.K.; Rodrigo, M.M.T.; Graesser, A.C. Better to be frustrated than bored: The incidence, persistence, and impact of learners' cognitive–affective states during interactions with three different computer-based learning environments. *Int. J. Hum.-Comput. Stud.* **2010**, *68*, 223–241. [CrossRef]
2. Chrysafiadi, K.; Virvou, M. Student modeling approaches: A literature review for the last decade. *Expert Syst. Appl.* **2013**, *40*, 4715–4729. [CrossRef]
3. VanLehn, K. The relative effectiveness of human tutoring, intelligent tutoring systems, and other tutoring systems. *Educ. Psychol.* **2011**, *46*, 197–221. [CrossRef]
4. Ma, W.; Adesope, O.O.; Nesbit, J.C.; Liu, Q. Intelligent tutoring systems and learning outcomes: A meta-analysis. *J. Educ. Psychol.* **2014**, *106*, 901. [CrossRef]
5. Woolf, B.P. *Building Intelligent Interactive Tutors: Student-Centered Strategies for Revolutionizing e-Learning*; Morgan Kaufmann: Burlington, MA, USA, 2010.
6. Graesser, A.C. Conversations with AutoTutor help students learn. *Int. J. Artif. Intell. Educ.* **2016**, *26*, 124–132. [CrossRef]
7. Graesser, A.C.; Dowell, N.; Hampton, A.J.; Lippert, A.M.; Li, H.; Shaffer, D.W. Building intelligent conversational tutors and mentors for team collaborative problem solving: Guidance from the 2015 Program for International Student Assessment. In *Building Intelligent Tutoring Systems for Teams*; Emerald Publishing Limited: Bingley, UK, 2018.
8. Katz, S.; Aronis, J.; Creitz, C. Modeling pedagogical interactions with machine learning. *Kognitionswissenschaft* **2000**, *9*, 45–49. [CrossRef]

9. Tahir, F.; Mitrovic, A.; Sotardi, V. Investigating the effects of gamifying SQL-Tutor. In Proceedings of the 28th International Conference on Computers in Education, Virtual, 23–27 November 2020; Asia-Pacific Society for Computers in Education: Taiwan, 2020.
10. Baghaei, N.; Mitrovic, A. A Constraint-Based Collaborative Environment for Learning UML Class Diagrams. In Proceedings of the International Conference on Intelligent Tutoring Systems, Jhongli, Taiwan, 26–30 June 2006; pp. 176–186.
11. Baghaei, N.; Mitrovic, A. Evaluating a collaborative constraint-based tutor for UML class diagrams. In Proceedings of the 13th International Conference on Artificial Intelligence in Education, Los Angeles, CA, USA, 9–13 July 2007; pp. 533–535.
12. Holland, J.; Baghaei, N.; Mathews, M.; Mitrovic, A. The effects of domain and collaboration feedback on learning in a collaborative intelligent tutoring system. In *International Conference on Artificial Intelligence in Education*; Springer: Berlin, Heidelberg, 2011; pp. 469–471.
13. Eid, M.I. A learning system for entity relationship modeling. In Proceedings of the PACIS 2012 Proceedings, Paper 152, Ho Chi Minh City, Vietnam, 11–15 July 2012.
14. Suraweera, P.; Mitrovic, A. KERMIT: A Constraint-based Tutor for Database Modeling. In Proceedings of the 6th International Conference on Intelligent Tutoring Systems 2002, San Sebastian, Spain, 2–7 June 2002; pp. 377–387.
15. Suraweera, P.; Mitrovic, A. An Intelligent Tutoring System for Entity Relationship Modelling. *Int. J. Artif. Intell. Educ.* **2004**, *14*, 375–417.
16. Tan, P.J. Applying the UTAUT to understand factors affecting the use of English e-learning websites in Taiwan. *Sage Open* **2013**, *3*, 2158244013503837. [CrossRef]
17. Liu, L.; Chen, L.; Shi, C.; Chen, H. The Study of Collaborative Learning Grouping Strategy in Intelligent Tutoring System. In Proceedings of the 14th International Conference on Computer Supported Cooperative Work in Design CSCWD 2010, Shanghai, China, 14–16 April 2010; pp. 642–646.
18. Narciss, S. Feedback strategies for interactive learning tasks. In *Handbook of Research on Educational Communications and Technology*; Spector, J.M., Merrill, M.D., van Merrieboer, J., Driscoll, M.P., Eds.; Taylor & Francis Group: New York, NY, USA, 2010; pp. 125–143.
19. Gielen, S.; Peeters, E.; Dochy, F.; Onghena, P.; Struyven, K. Improving the effectiveness of peer feedback for learning. *Int. J. Learn. Instr.* **2010**, *20*, 304–315. [CrossRef]
20. Jahin, J.H. The effect of peer reviewing on writing apprehension and essay writing ability of prospective EFL teachers. *Aust. J. Teach. Educ.* **2012**, *37*, 65–89. [CrossRef]
21. Wankiiri-Hale, C.; Maloney, C.; Seger, N.; Horvath, Z. Assessment of a student peer-tutoring program focusing on the benefits to the tutors. *J. Dent. Educ.* **2020**, *84*, 695–703. [CrossRef]
22. Dioso-Henson, L. The effect of reciprocal peer tutoring and non-reciprocal peer tutoring on the performance of students in college physics. *Res. Educ.* **2012**, *87*, 34–49. [CrossRef]
23. Evans, M.J.; Moore, J.S. Peer tutoring with the aid of the Internet. *Br. J. Educ. Technol.* **2013**, *44*, 144–155. [CrossRef]
24. Worley, J.; Naresh, N. Heterogeneous peer-tutoring: An intervention that fosters collaborations and empowers learners: Key features of an intervention peer-tutoring program highlight the cognitive and social benefits of this collaborative approach. *Middle Sch. J.* **2014**, *46*, 26–32. [CrossRef]
25. Alegre, F.; Moliner, L.; Maroto, A.; Lorenzo-Valentin, G. Peer tutoring in algebra: A study in middle school. *J. Educ. Res.* **2019**, *112*, 693–699. [CrossRef]
26. Alegre-Ansuategui, F.J.; Moliner, L.; Lorenzo, G.; Maroto, A. Peer tutoring and academic achievement in mathematics: A meta-analysis. *Eurasia J. Math. Sci. Technol. Educ.* **2018**, *14*, 337–354. [CrossRef]
27. Leung, K.C. Compare the moderator for pre-test-posttest design in peer tutoring with treatment-control/comparison design. *Eur. J. Psychol. Educ.* **2019**, *34*, 685–703. [CrossRef]
28. Hardavella, G.; Aamli-Gaagnat, A.; Saad, N.; Rousalova, I.; Sreter, K.B. How to give and receive feedback effectively. *Breathe* **2017**, *13*, 327–333. [CrossRef]
29. Harsley, R.; Green, N.E.; di Eugenio, B.; Aditya, S.; Fossati, D.; Al Zoubi, O. Collab-ChiQat: A Collaborative Remaking of a Computer Science Intelligent Tutoring System. In Proceedings of the 19th ACM Conference on Computer Supported Cooperative Work and Social Computing Companion—CSCW '16 Companion, San Francisco, CA, USA, 26 February–2 March 2016.
30. Duangnamol, T.; Suntisrivarporn, B.; Supnithi, T.; Ikeda, M. Circuitously Collaborative Learning Environment to Enhance Metacognition. In Proceedings of the International Conference on Computers in Education, Nara, Japan, 30 November–4 December 2014; Asia-Pacific Society for Computers in Education: Nara, Japan, 2014; pp. 1–4.
31. Haq, I.U.; Anwar, A.; Basharat, I.; Sultan, K. Intelligent Tutoring Supported Collaborative Learning (ITSCL): A Hybrid Framework. *Int. J. Adv. Comput. Sci. Appl.* **2020**, *11*, 523–535. [CrossRef]
32. Sychev, O.; Penskoy, N.; Anikin, A.; Denisov, M.; Prokudin, A. Improving Comprehension: Intelligent Tutoring System Explaining the Domain Rules When Students Break Them. *Educ. Sci.* **2021**, *11*, 179. [CrossRef]
33. Polito, G.; Temperini, M. A gamified web based system for computer programming learning. *Comput. Educ. Artif. Intell.* **2021**, *2*, 100029. [CrossRef]
34. Kumar, A.N. Allowing Revisions While Providing Error-Flagging Support: Is More Better? In Proceedings of the 21st International Conference on Artificial Intelligence in Education, Ifrane, Morocco, 6–10 July 2020; Springer International Publishing: Cham, Switzerland, 2020; pp. 147–151.

35. Kumar, A.N. Limiting the Number of Revisions while Providing Error-Flagging Support during Tests. In Proceedings of the 11th International Conference on Intelligent Tutoring Systems, Chania, Greece, 14–18 June 2012; Cerri, S.A., Clancey, W.J., Papadourakis, G., Panourgia, K., Eds.; Springer: Berlin/Heidelberg, Germany, 2012; pp. 524–530.
36. Abbasi, S.; Kazi, H.; Kazi, A.W.; Khowaja, K.; Baloch, A. Gauge Object Oriented Programming in Student's Learning Performance, Normalized Learning Gains and Perceived Motivation with Serious Games. *Information* **2021**, *12*, 101. [CrossRef]
37. Whitehead, A.L.; Julious, S.A.; Cooper, C.L.; Campbell, M.J. Estimating the sample size for a pilot randomized trial to minimize the overall trial sample size for the external pilot and main trial for a continuous outcome variable. *Stat. Methods Med. Res.* **2016**, *25*, 1057–1073. [CrossRef] [PubMed]

Article

Enriching Mobile Learning Software with Interactive Activities and Motivational Feedback for Advancing Users' High-Level Cognitive Skills

Christos Troussas *, Akrivi Krouska and Cleo Sgouropoulou

Department of Informatics and Computer Engineering, University of West Attica, 12243 Athens, Greece; akrouska@uniwa.gr (A.K.); csgouro@uniwa.gr (C.S.)
* Correspondence: ctrouss@uniwa.gr

Abstract: Mobile learning is a promising form of digital education to access learning content through modern handheld devices. Through mobile learning, students can learn using smartphones, connected to the Internet, without having restrictions posed by time and place. However, such environments should be enriched with sophisticated techniques so that the learners can achieve their learning goals and have an optimized learning experience. To this direction, in this paper, presents a mobile learning software which delivers interactive activities and motivational feedback to learners with the aim of advancing their higher level cognitive skills. In more detail, the mobile application employs two theories, namely Bloom's taxonomy and the taxonomy of intrinsic motivations by Malone and Lepper. Bloom's taxonomy is used for the design of interactive activities that belong to varying levels of complexity, i.e., remembering, understanding, applying, analyzing, evaluating, and creating. Concerning motivational feedback, the taxonomy of intrinsic motivations by Malone and Lepper is used, which identifies four major factors, namely challenge, curiosity, control, and fantasy, and renders the learning environment intrinsically motivating. As a testbed for our research, the presented mobile learning system was designed for the teaching of a primary school course; however, the incorporated taxonomies could be adapted to the tutoring of any course. The mobile application was evaluated by school students with very promising results.

Keywords: Bloom's taxonomy; learning activities; mobile learning; Malone and Lepper's taxonomy; motivational feedback; taxonomy of intrinsic motivations

Citation: Troussas, C.; Krouska, A.; Sgouropoulou, C. Enriching Mobile Learning Software with Interactive Activities and Motivational Feedback for Advancing Users' High-Level Cognitive Skills. *Computers* **2022**, *11*, 18. https://doi.org/10.3390/computers11020018

Academic Editors: Antonio Sarasa Cabezuelo and Covadonga Rodrigo San Juan

Received: 1 December 2021
Accepted: 24 January 2022
Published: 25 January 2022

Publisher's Note: MDPI stays neutral with regard to jurisdictional claims in published maps and institutional affiliations.

Copyright: © 2022 by the authors. Licensee MDPI, Basel, Switzerland. This article is an open access article distributed under the terms and conditions of the Creative Commons Attribution (CC BY) license (https://creativecommons.org/licenses/by/4.0/).

1. Introduction

Recently, significant interest has been placed on the inclusion of digital technologies in education. The rise of information and communication technology has brought new and considerable changes in many research areas, and particularly, in education. For example, several expert e-learning systems have been developed to help students advance their knowledge [1–3].

The modernization of education is now imperative and requires the use of digital tools [4], which has become profound especially during the COVID-19 pandemic. In this way, multidimensional education and cultivation, constant cognitive vigilance, and development of critical thinking can be further promoted. Students can also adapt to the continuous flow of information. Therefore, the ever-increasing need for digital education, overcoming the barriers posed by space and time, has led to mobile learning (m-learning), which supports learning in multiple contexts using personal electronic devices [5].

Learning through mobile phones is beneficial as it allows learners to learn from wherever they are, always according to their individual needs and preferences. It is a hot topic in the relevant scientific literature, as it promotes learning in an entertaining way and encourages student motivation, therefore, increasing their involvement in the educational process [6]. Therefore, it can improve the learning process and student participation.

On the one hand, learning activities, incorporated in mobile learning environments, are pedagogically useful [7] but they should be designed properly to provide best results in learners' knowledge advancement. On the other hand, motivating learners can be a powerful tool for advancing users' high-level cognitive skills [8].

In the related scientific literature, there have been several efforts that explore the delivery of learning activities and motivational messages to users. In particular, the topic of learning activities has been examined in several works [7,9–14]. In most of these works, the authors have used learning management systems and they have focused on providing example-based or collaborative learning activities. Moreover, the delivery of motivational messages has been researched in many works [8,15–20]. In most of these works, the authors have mainly focused on the motivation types of learners. The novelty of our approach is, firstly, that the user interface is a mobile learning environment which requires greater focus both on the design of learning activities and on the way of motivational messages delivery, due to its capacity. Secondly, another novelty is the blending of two taxonomies, namely Bloom's taxonomy [21] and the taxonomy of intrinsic motivations by Malone and Lepper [22], to optimize the delivery of learning activities and motivational messages to users. Analyzing the presented literature, it needs to be noted that different theories and/or models have not been sufficiently employed in combination yet to support the process of mobile learning. However, as stated in a recent review work [23], incorporating such techniques into a learning environment can have important pedagogical potential and offer learner-centered education in the context of adaptive and personalized learning.

Regarding the instructional system design, it involves the creation of learning experiences in ways that leads to the acquisition and application of cognitive and thinking skills (https://www.td.org/talent-development-glossary-terms/what-is-instructional-design, accessed on 30 November 2021). In light of the foregoing, learning solutions that have been adopted in instructional design have involved the incorporation of theories and/or taxonomies for a better eLearning plan, and the employment of instructional design models (e.g., ADDIE, Merrill's First Principles of Instruction, Dick and Carey Model, Kemp Design Model, Agile and iterative approaches, etc.) [24]. There have been several research works that deal with the field of instructional design modeling [25–31]. In this paper, the aim is to adopt an adequate instructional design in mobile learning through focusing on the incorporation of two taxonomies and employing agile modeling.

In view of the above, this paper presents a novel approach for the provision of interactive learning activities and motivational feedback to learners in a mobile environment. To preserve the pedagogical affordance of the application, two taxonomies have been employed, as mentioned above. Bloom's taxonomy is used for the design of interactive activities belonging to varying levels of complexity, i.e., remembering, understanding, applying, analyzing, evaluating, and creating. The taxonomy of intrinsic motivations by Malone and Lepper is used to identifying four major factors, namely challenge, curiosity, control, and fantasy. As a testbed for our research, a mobile learning software is developed for a primary school course. The mobile software is evaluated in a public primary school and the results are very encouraging, as presented in Section 4.

The remainder of the paper is organized as follows: In Section 2, the method and procedures of this research is presented as well as the logical architecture of the application is explained; in Section 3, the application's modules are described, namely interactive learning activity delivery using Bloom's taxonomy and motivational feedback delivery using Malone and Leeper's taxonomy; the evaluation of the mobile application is showed in Section 4; finally, in Section 5, the conclusions are drawn and future research plans are presented.

2. Methods and Procedures

This section presents important aspects of this research. The purpose of the research is to improve online learning environments by enriching mobile learning applications with effective cognitive theories. The blending of different theories (Figure 1), namely

Bloom's and Malone and Leeper's taxonomies, serves to further enhance the delivery of learning activities and motivational feedback, respectively; these two learning ingredients can booster the personalized experience of learners.

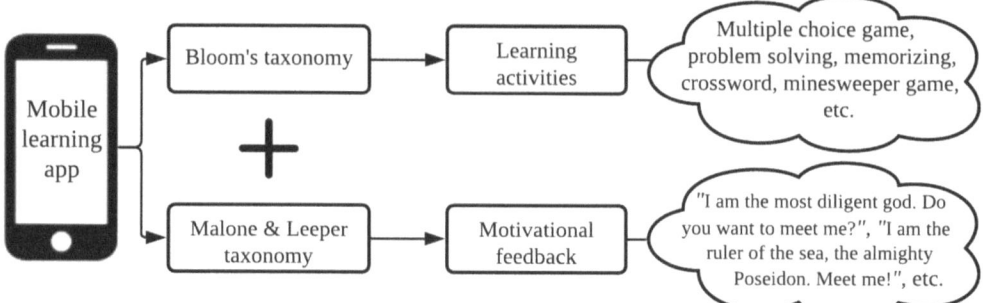

Figure 1. Logical architecture of the mobile learning application.

The steps that we followed in this research included the literature review, the design and implementation of the mobile application, the utilization of the application by school students, and the evaluation. The mobile learning software was developed for tutoring of a third-year primary school course in History, specifically, the chapter on Greek Mythology. The application was used by students, and was evaluated using techniques, such as interviews and a Likert scale questionnaire survey which was based on an established framework.

3. Modules Analysis and Presentation of the Application

In this section, the application modules are described, namely the modules on interactive learning activities delivery and motivational feedback delivery. In addition, an overview of the application is provided.

3.1. Interactive Learning Activities Delivery

The delivery of the interactive learning activities to learners is based on Bloom's taxonomy [21] (Figure 2). According to Bloom's taxonomy, the educational goals are ranked in a hierarchical form with remembering being the first tier (Figure 3a).

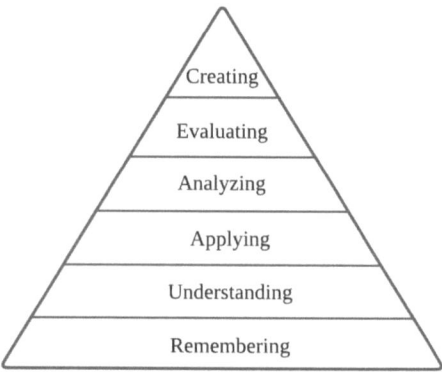

Figure 2. Bloom's taxonomy levels.

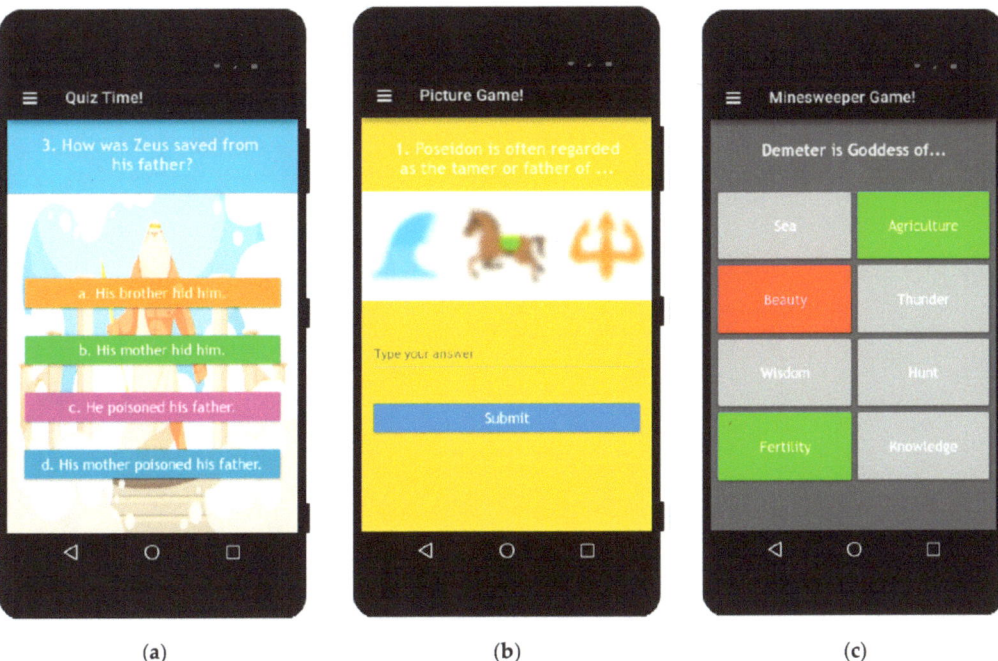

Figure 3. (**a**) Level of remembering (quiz game); (**b**) level of understanding (picture game); (**c**) level of applying (minesweeper game).

During the process of remembering, the learners should be able to recall, restate, or make use of the information they have learned. In our case, the first activity is a simple knowledge game, which aims to retrieve the knowledge acquired by students when studying the theory. More specifically, users can interact with a multi-query game environment, where students are asked to choose the correct answers and, at the end, all the questions and the answers are displayed in order, with the indication "right" or "wrong". As such, in this level, the skill of remembering can be improved since the students should recollect the theory.

In the understanding phase, it must be checked whether the student, in addition to simply memorizing words, concepts, and theories, is able to classify categories, distinguish similar objects, and find what is required, in order to finally lead to certain conclusions. Hence, at the level of understanding (Figure 3b), in the application, students can first see an image which is somewhat blurred. This image is related to a question on the same screen. The students should be able to distinguish the vague object and, by also using their previous knowledge, can record it in the specially designed field. In this way, they can further improve their skill of understanding.

At the level of applying (Figure 3c), a concept or generalization is used in new situations and contexts, therefore, applying knowledge from school to other areas. Students can solve a problem, use principles in real situations, and predict result. The third level in Bloom's classification requires both knowledge and understanding by the learner. At this level, the ability to use knowledge is examined; the knowledge that was not only memorized, but also understood, can serve as a tool for the student to solve requested situations. In view of the above, at this level, students are asked to utilize information that they have been provided to produce a practical solution to a problem.

The next activity is related to the levels of analyzing and evaluating (Figure 4). More specifically, students should be able to distinguish objects that are not included in a particular image. Next, students are required to design them. In addition, at these levels, students can test their abilities to discern situations, intentions, and implications that are not listed, and often modify their original perceptions. In more detail, at the level of analyzing, students are asked to identify patterns to solve problems. They should distinguish between objective and subjective information in order to explore and draw conclusions using their point of view. At the level of evaluating, students should utilize particular facts to make predictions or produce new theories. This requires them to apply skills to synthesize this information before drawing conclusions.

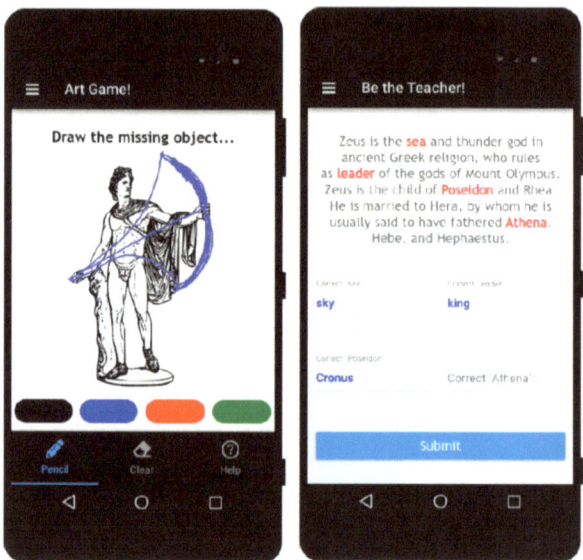

Figure 4. Levels of analyzing (art game) and evaluating (Be the Teacher! game).

Finally, students pass to the final level of creating. According to Bloom, at this level, a student is asked to put elements together in order to form a new coherent pattern or structure. Mobile learning software provides students with activities requiring them to know how to develop new knowledge and make special judgments.

3.2. Motivational Feedback Delivery

Malone and Lepper's motivation theory [22] was used for the design of the mobile learning software. This taxonomy divides the motivating factors of students' interests into four main categories: motivations that come from challenge, curiosity, control, and fantasy (Figure 5).

The taxonomy is described as follows:

- **Motivation through challenge** More specifically, this motivation concerns messages that are challenging for the student to advance their knowledge. By presenting only part of the information that is quite provocative, students are challenged to look for the remaining unknown concepts (Figure 6a). The motivational message shows part of the information, rendering students who are interested in learning more. The characteristics of this element involve goals, uncertain outcomes with different difficulty levels, and the ability to gain self-esteem and self-efficacy.
- **Motivation through control** The messages promote a sense of control towards the student, meaning that learning outcomes are determined by the student's actions (Figure 6b). Students receive additional information, take control, and decide whether

they wants to learn more through a motivating interaction. The characteristics of this element involve a reactive learning environment, choice, and learners' power.
- **Motivation through fantasy** These motivations promise students a fantasy world, i.e., the "mental images" that the learners create based on their interaction with the environment (Figure 7a). The characteristics of this element involve an appeal to emotional needs and relationships to material that was previously learned.
- **Motivation through curiosity** According to Malone and Lepper, motivation through curiosity is achieved through various audiovisual media (Figure 7b). The characteristic of this element involves interactivity between learner and environment, which should intrigue the learner.

Figure 5. Malone and Leeper's taxonomy categories.

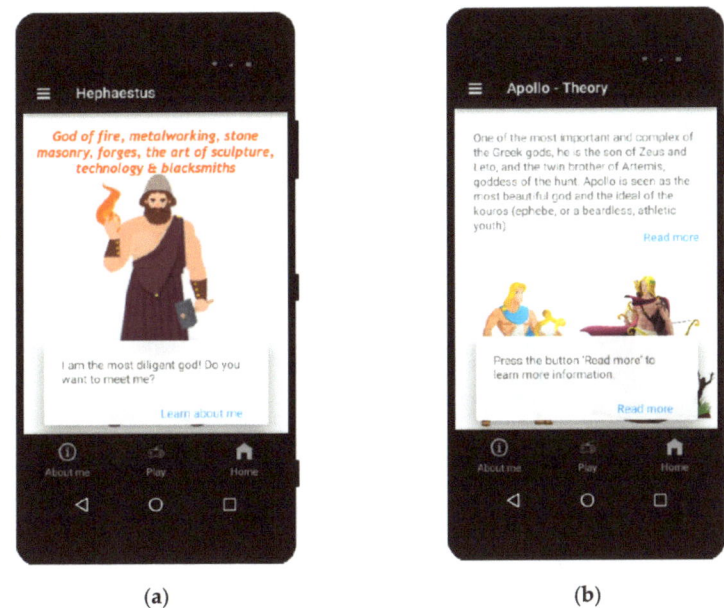

Figure 6. (**a**) Motivation through challenge; (**b**) motivation through control.

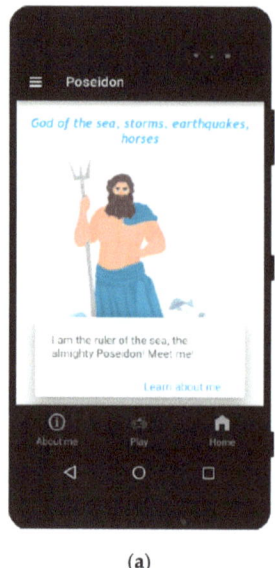 

(a) (b)

Figure 7. (a) Motivation through fantasy; (b) motivation through curiosity.

4. Evaluation

A user-based evaluation was conducted in order to assess the effectiveness and acceptance of the presented mobile learning software regarding the innovative interactive activities and motivational messages, which were incorporated. The aim of the evaluation was to assess the presented mobile learning approach, which merged Bloom's and Malone and Lepper's taxonomies. The mobile application was developed as a testbed for the mobile learning procedure.

4.1. Methods and Materials

The evaluation of the mobile learning application was based on four dimensions, namely the user experience, the effectiveness of interactive activities, the effectiveness of motivational feedback and the impact on learning [32]. The evaluation technique, which was used, included a 5-point Likert scale questionnaire survey delivered to the population after completion of the course. The questionnaire items were designed so that information about the user experience, the effectiveness of learning strategies adopted, and their impact on learning, could be gathered. Table 1 illustrates the questionnaire survey for the system evaluation. Furthermore, an interview method was used; the population was asked open-ended questions concerning the user friendliness and pleasantness of the system. In the interview process, two teachers of the students (population) helped the evaluators by conversing with respondents in order to collect and elicit data about the aforementioned subjects.

Table 1. System evaluation survey questions.

Dimension	#	Questions
User experience	1	The interface of the system is pleasant. (1–5)
	2	I am satisfied with how easy to use the system is. (1–5)
	3	I enjoy interacting with the system. (1–5)

Table 1. *Cont.*

Dimension	#	Questions
Effectiveness of interactive activities	4 5 6	The activities are creative and innovative. (1–5) The activities engage me in higher-order thinking. (1–5) I am satisfied with the quality of the activities. (1–5)
Effectiveness of motivational feedback	7 8 9	The feedback helps me redefine my learning path. (1–5) The motivational messages are insightful. (1–5) My interest in the course is stimulated by the system. (1–5)
Impact on learning	10 11 12	The system helps me achieve higher-order cognitive skills. (1–5) The feedback provided is effective in engaging me in the learning process. (1–5) I believe the system helps me understand better lesson's concepts. (1–5)

4.2. Evaluation Process and Population

The population of the evaluation included 40 students at a Greek public primary school. Students' age, computer skills, and knowledge were approximately equal, as all of them were at the same grade. The students were separated into two groups of 20 members, namely Group 1 and Group 2. The experiment took place during the COVID-19 quarantine, when the school was closed and students were attending school remotely via Internet. As mentioned in Section 2, the lesson, which was taught using the mobile learning system, belonged to the "History" course, and the learning process had a duration of six didactic hours. The course is compulsory in primary schools. In addition, the goals of the instruction are for the students to: gain knowledge of historical facts as well as mythological figures; understand ancient society and develop a sense of the cultural heritage in current society; and develop new skills, such as enquiry, investigation, analysis, evaluation and presentation.

In particular, Group 1 was taught the section solely using the presented mobile learning software, incorporating interactive activities and motivational feedback; Group 2 used a conventional system, including mainly multiple-choice activities and simple motivational messages provided randomly to students. Using this conventional system in the evaluation process, the potential of designing mobile learning software according to learning theories, namely Bloom's taxonomy and Malone and Lepper's taxonomy, could be investigated. After completion of the section taught, the students were asked to answer the aforementioned questionnaire survey.

4.3. Results and Discussion

Regarding students' acceptance of the presented system, the answers given by Group 1 were assessed. Figure 8 and Table 2 illustrate the evaluation results. Analyzing these results, it is observed that there is a high rating of satisfaction and acceptance.

Considering user experience, 85% of the students found that the system interface was pleasant and stimulated them to use it further. Moreover, based on the interview results, almost all of the students stated that the system was very easy to use (95%) and they enjoy interacting with it (90%). These factors both play an important role in students' intention to use this system and in avoiding dropouts.

Regarding the effectiveness of the interactive activities incorporated into the system, 85% of the students found them creative and innovative, as well, an equally high percentage of them indicated their high quality (90%). These results illustrate the acceptance of the proposed approach and the proper activities' design made during the system development phase. Furthermore, the vast majority of the participants (90%) reported that the activities engaged them in higher order thinking skills, strengthening the choice of adopting Bloom's taxonomy in the activities' design.

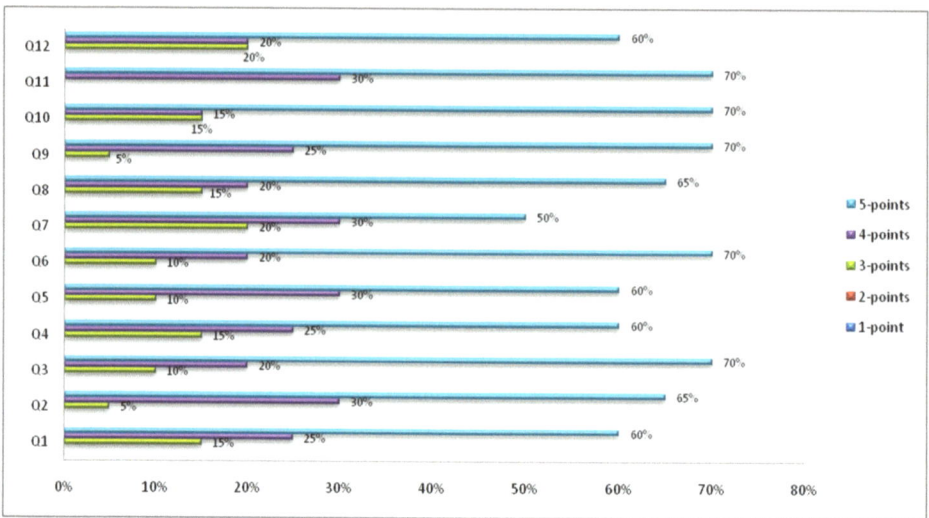

Figure 8. Bar chart for questionnaire survey results.

Table 2. Questionnaire survey results (scores, mean, standard deviation, and variance).

		1-Point	2-Points	3-Points	4-Points	5-Points	Mean	St. Deviation	Variance
User Experience	Q1	0%	0%	15%	25%	60%	4.45	0.7399	0.5475
	Q2	0%	0%	5%	30%	65%	4.6	0.5831	0.34
	Q3	0%	0%	10%	20%	70%	4.6	0.6633	0.44
Effectiveness of interactive activities	Q4	0%	0%	15%	25%	60%	4.45	0.7399	0.5475
	Q5	0%	0%	10%	30%	60%	4.5	0.6708	0.45
	Q6	0%	0%	10%	20%	70%	4.6	0.6633	0.44
Effectiveness of motivational feedback	Q7	0%	0%	20%	30%	50%	4.3	0.781	0.61
	Q8	0%	0%	15%	20%	65%	4.5	0.7416	0.55
	Q9	0%	0%	5%	25%	70%	4.65	0.5723	0.3275
Impact on Learning	Q10	0%	0%	15%	15%	70%	4.55	0.7399	0.5475
	Q11	0%	0%	0%	30%	70%	4.7	0.4583	0.21
	Q12	0%	0%	20%	20%	60%	4.4	0.8	0.64

In view of the motivational feedback that was provided to students, the evaluation results show that it was found to be very useful to redefine their learning path (80%), as well as the messages were very insightful (85%). The system stimulated students' interests to a very high degree (95%). These facts indicate the effectiveness of the motivational messages used and, by extension, the effectiveness of Malone and Lepper's taxonomy adopted for this purpose.

Regarding the impact of the presented system on learning, approximately 85% of the students stated that it helped them to achieve higher order thinking skills and to better understand the lesson's concepts. This high degree of rating in these questions can be explained by the use of Bloom's taxonomy which focuses on increasing knowledge and developing skills. In addition, 80% of the students reported that the feedback provided influenced their learning positively by engaging them in the educational process. A possible reason why this happened is because the messages were designed based on the principles of Malone and Lepper's taxonomy.

It needs to be noted that Values 1 and 2 received no responses. This fact was anticipated, since the younger generation is very keen on using smartphones and is acquainted with mobile applications.

In order to further investigate the potential of the approaches used for activities and feedback as comparing with conventional ones, a two-sample *t*-Test between Group A and Group B was applied in the aggregation of Questions 4–6, which referred to the effectiveness of the interactive activities, and of Questions 7–9, which referred to the effectiveness of the motivational feedback. As shown in Table 3, there is a statistically significant difference between the means of the two groups regarding the two learning strategies. Considering the activities used in both systems, the presented system outperforms the conventional one, indicating that designing interactive activities based on a learning theory, such as Bloom's taxonomy, and not using simply multiple-choice activities can enhance learning and lead to the acquisition of higher order cognitive skills. Regarding the feedback to students, the findings show that the presented system which adopts the Malone and Lepper's taxonomy for designing the motivational messages outperforms the conventional one. As such, the adopted approach can be characterized as a suitable one which properly motivates the students to be more active and engages them into the learning process, helping them to improve their learning outcomes.

Table 3. *t*-Test results.

	Effectiveness of Interactive Activities		Effectiveness of Motivational Feedback	
	Group A	Group B	Group A	Group B
Mean	4.65	3.2	4.45	3.15
Variance	0.345	0.8	0.576	0.45
Observations	20	20	20	20
Pooled variance	0.572		0.513	
Hypothesized mean difference	0		0	
df	38		38	
t Stat	6.06		5.739	
P(T <= *t*) two-tail	4.7×10^{-7}		1.3×10^{-6}	
t Critical two-tail	2.024		2.024	

5. Conclusions and Future Work

This paper presents a novel approach for delivering interactive learning activities and motivational feedback. To achieve this, Bloom's taxonomy and the taxonomy of intrinsic motivations by Malone and Lepper are utilized. In more detail, Bloom's taxonomy is used for the design of interactive activities belonging to varying levels of complexity, i.e., remembering, understanding, applying, analyzing, evaluating, and creating. Concerning the motivational feedback, the taxonomy of intrinsic motivations by Malone and Lepper is used, identifying four major factors, namely challenge, curiosity, control, and fantasy, rendering the learning environment intrinsically motivating. This approach has been incorporated in a mobile learning software for teaching a primary school course.

The mobile learning application were evaluated in a public primary school and the results showed that it could contribute positively to the advancement of learners' higher level cognitive skills. It needs to be noted that the presented approach can be incorporated in any mobile learning software, designed for learners of different grades and in different courses.

Based on the evaluation results, the significance of this study emerges from the incorporation of the two taxonomies in a mobile learning software, which can push the boundaries of virtual learning environments and further enhance online education by providing student-centered instruction.

Future research should include a more extensive evaluation in terms of the population. In addition, we plan to consider more learners' characteristics in the modeling process in terms of their types of misconceptions and emotional states.

Author Contributions: Conceptualization, C.T. and A.K.; methodology, C.T. and A.K.; software, C.T. and A.K.; validation, C.T. and A.K.; formal analysis, C.T. and A.K.; investigation, C.T. and A.K.; resources, C.T. and A.K.; data curation, C.T. and A.K.; writing—original draft preparation, C.T. and A.K.; writing—review and editing, C.T. and A.K.; visualization, C.T. and A.K.; supervision, C.S. All authors have read and agreed to the published version of the manuscript.

Funding: This research received no external funding.

Institutional Review Board Statement: Not applicable.

Informed Consent Statement: Not applicable.

Data Availability Statement: The data has been presented in main text.

Conflicts of Interest: The authors declare no conflict of interest.

References

1. Troussas, C.; Virvou, M.; Alepis, E. Comulang: Towards a collaborative e-learning system that supports student group modeling. *SpringerPlus* **2013**, *2*, 387. [CrossRef] [PubMed]
2. Rodríguez, M.E.; Guerrero-Roldán, A.-E.; Baneres, D.; Noguera, I. Students' Perceptions of and Behaviors toward Cheating in Online Education. *IEEE J. Lat.-Am. Learn. Technol.* **2021**, *16*, 134–142. [CrossRef]
3. Chrysafiadi, K.; Troussas, C.; Virvou, M. A Framework for Creating Automated Online Adaptive Tests Using Multiple-Criteria Decision Analysis. In Proceedings of the IEEE International Conference on Systems, Man, and Cybernetics (SMC), Miyazaki, Japan, 7–10 October 2018; pp. 226–231. [CrossRef]
4. Krouska, A.; Troussas, C.; Virvou, M. Social networks as a learning environment: Developed applications and comparative analysis. In Proceedings of the 8th International Conference on Information, Intelligence, Systems & Applications (IISA), Larnaca, Cyprus, 27–30 August 2017; pp. 1–6. [CrossRef]
5. Moldovan, A.-N.; Muntean, C.H. DQAMLearn: Device and QoE-Aware Adaptive Multimedia Mobile Learning Framework. *IEEE Trans. Broadcast.* **2021**, *67*, 185–200. [CrossRef]
6. Li, X.; Heng, Q. Design of Mobile Learning Resources Based on New Blended Learning: A Case Study of Superstar Learning APP. In Proceedings of the IEEE 3rd International Conference on Computer Science and Educational Informatization (CSEI), Xinxiang, China, 18–20 June 2021; pp. 333–338. [CrossRef]
7. Wang, C.; Li, Q.; Hu, X. Minority college students' engagement in learning activities and its relationships with learning outcomes. In Proceedings of the International Conference on Advanced Learning Technologies (ICALT), Tartu, Estonia, 12–15 July 2021; pp. 173–175. [CrossRef]
8. Simonova, I.; Faltynkova, L.; Kostolanyova, K. Learners' Motivation Types in the Smart Instruction of English for Specific Purposes. In Proceedings of the 6th IEEE Congress on Information Science and Technology (CiSt), Agadir–Essaouira, Morocco, 5–12 June 2021; pp. 225–230. [CrossRef]
9. Venditti, A.; Fasano, F.; Risi, M.; Tortora, G. The importance of interaction mechanisms in blended learning courses involving problem solving e-tivities. In Proceedings of the Thirteenth International Conference on Digital Information Management (ICDIM), Berlin, Germany, 24–26 September 2018; pp. 124–129. [CrossRef]
10. Troussas, C.; Krouska, A.; Sgouropoulou, C. A Novel Teaching Strategy Through Adaptive Learning Activities for Computer Programming. *IEEE Trans. Educ.* **2021**, *64*, 103–109. [CrossRef]
11. Weerasinghe, T.A. An Evaluation of Different Types of Blended Learning Activities in Higher Education. In Proceedings of the IEEE 18th International Conference on Advanced Learning Technologies (ICALT), Mumbai, India, 9–13 July 2018; pp. 42–45. [CrossRef]
12. Recke, M.P.; Perna, S.; Pereira, T.G. Designing Narratively Driven Learning Activities for Blended Learning Experiences. In Proceedings of the 9th International Conference on Information and Education Technology (ICIET), Okayama, Japan, 27–29 March 2021; pp. 171–177. [CrossRef]
13. Krouska, A.; Troussas, C.; Virvou, M. Computerized Adaptive Assessment Using Accumulative Learning Activities Based on Revised Bloom's Taxonomy. In *Knowledge-Based Software Engineering: 2018, Proceedings of the JCKBSE 2018: Joint Conference on Knowledge-Based Software Engineering, Corfu, Greece, 27–30 August 2018*; Virvou, M., Kumeno, F., Oikonomou, K., Eds.; Smart Innovation, Systems and Technologies; Springer: Cham, Switzerland, 2019; Volume 108.
14. Supic, H. Case-Based Reasoning Model for Personalized Learning Path Recommendation in Example-Based Learning Activities. In Proceedings of the IEEE 27th International Conference on Enabling Technologies: Infrastructure for Collaborative Enterprises (WETICE), Paris, France, 27–29 June 2018; pp. 175–178. [CrossRef]
15. Beardsley, M.; Gutierrez, N.; Hernandez-Leo, D. Examining university students' motivation, abilities and preferences related to learning to learn. In Proceedings of the IEEE 20th International Conference on Advanced Learning Technologies (ICALT), Tartu, Estonia, 6–9 July 2020; pp. 346–348. [CrossRef]

16. Troussas, C.; Krouska, A.; Virvou, M. Using a Multi Module Model for Learning Analytics to Predict Learners' Cognitive States and Provide Tailored Learning Pathways and Assessment. In *Machine Learning Paradigms*; Virvou, M., Alepis, E., Tsihrintzis, G., Jain, L., Eds.; Intelligent Systems Reference Library; Springer: Cham, Switzerland, 2020; Volume 158.
17. Merzdorf, H.E.; Douglas, K.A. Surveying Motivation and Learning Outcomes of Advanced Learners in Online Engineering Graduate MOOCs. In Proceedings of the IEEE Frontiers in Education Conference (FIE), Uppsala, Sweden, 21–24 October 2020; pp. 1–4. [CrossRef]
18. Troussas, C.; Krouska, A.; Alepis, E.; Virvou, M. Intelligent and adaptive tutoring through a social network for higher education. *New Rev. Hypermedia Multimed.* **2020**, *26*, 138–167. [CrossRef]
19. D'Aniello, G.; De Falco, M.; Gaeta, M.; Lepore, M. A Situation-aware Learning System based on Fuzzy Cognitive Maps to increase Learner Motivation and Engagement. In Proceedings of the IEEE International Conference on Fuzzy Systems, Glasgow, UK, 19–24 July 2020; pp. 1–8. [CrossRef]
20. Virvou, M.; Troussas, C.; Caro, J.; Espinosa, K.J. User Modeling for Language Learning in Facebook. In *Text, Speech and Dialogue, Proceedings of the TSD 2012: International Conference on Text, Speech and Dialogue, Brno, Czech Republic, 3–7 September 2012*; Sojka, P., Horák, A., Kopeček, I., Pala, K., Eds.; Lecture Notes in Computer Science; Springer: Berlin/Heidelberg, Germany, 2012; Volume 7499.
21. Bloom, B.S. Taxonomy of Educational Objectives. In *Handbook I: The Cognitive Domain*; David McKay Co Inc.: New York, NY, USA, 1956.
22. Malone, T.W.; Lepper, M.R. Making Learning Fun: A Taxonomy of Intrinsic Motivations for Learning. In *Aptitude, Learning, and Instruction: Conative and Affective Process Analyses*; Snow, R., Farr, M.J., Eds.; Lawrence Erlbaum Associates Publishers: Hillsdale, NJ, USA, 1987.
23. Krouska, A.; Troussas, C.; Virvou, M. A Literature Review of Social Networking- Based Learning Systems Using a Novel ISO-based Framework. *Intell. Decis. Technol.* **2019**, *13*, 23–39. [CrossRef]
24. Stefaniak, J.; Xu, M. An Examination of the Systemic Reach of Instructional Design Models: A Systematic Review. *TechTrends* **2020**, *64*, 710–719. [CrossRef]
25. Kloos, C.D.; Alario-Hoyos, C. Educational Pyramids Aligned: Bloom's Taxonomy, the DigCompEdu Framework and Instructional Designs. In Proceedings of the IEEE World Engineering Education Forum/Global Engineering Deans Council (WEEF/GEDC), Madrid, Spain, 15–18 November 2021; pp. 110–117. [CrossRef]
26. Troussas, C.; Krouska, A.; Sgouropoulou, C. Improving Learner-Computer Interaction through Intelligent Learning Material Delivery Using Instructional Design Modeling. *Entropy* **2021**, *23*, 668. [CrossRef] [PubMed]
27. Kannan, V.; Gouripeddi, S.P. Enhancement in Critical Thinking Skills Using the Peer Instruction Methodology. In Proceedings of the IEEE 18th IEEE International Conference on Advanced Learning Technologies (ICALT), Mumbai, India, 9–13 July 2018; pp. 307–308. [CrossRef]
28. Venkatalakshmi, B.; Balakrishnan, R.; Saravanan, V.; Renold, A.P. Impact of simulation software as teaching tools in engineering learning—An instructional design choice. In Proceedings of the IEEE Global Engineering Education Conference (EDUCON), Abu Dhabi, United Arab Emirates, 10–13 April 2016; pp. 868–873. [CrossRef]
29. Troussas, C.; Krouska, A.; Virvou, M.; Sougela, E. Using Hierarchical Modeling of Thinking Skills to Lead Students to Higher Order Cognition and Enhance Social E-Learning. In Proceedings of the 9th International Conference on Information, Intelligence, Systems and Applications (IISA), Zakynthos, Greece, 23–25 July 2018; pp. 1–5. [CrossRef]
30. Nolen, S.B.; Koretsky, M.D. Affordances of Virtual and Physical Laboratory Projects for Instructional Design: Impacts on Student Engagement. *IEEE Trans. Educ.* **2018**, *61*, 226–233. [CrossRef]
31. Sun, Z.; Wang, K.; Li, Z.; Li, Z. Development of CDIO-Based SPOC Model in Facilitating Learning Instructional Design. In Proceedings of the IEEE International Joint Conference on Information, Media and Engineering (ICIME), Osaka, Japan, 12–14 December 2018; pp. 236–239. [CrossRef]
32. Alepis, E.; Troussas, C. M-learning programming platform: Evaluation in elementary schools. *Informatica* **2017**, *41*, 471–478.

Article

A Cognitive Diagnostic Module Based on the Repair Theory for a Personalized User Experience in E-Learning Software

Akrivi Krouska, Christos Troussas * and Cleo Sgouropoulou

Department of Informatics and Computer Engineering, University of West Attica, 12243 Athens, Greece; akrouska@uniwa.gr (A.K.); csgouro@uniwa.gr (C.S.)
* Correspondence: ctrouss@uniwa.gr

Abstract: This paper presents a novel cognitive diagnostic module which is incorporated in e-learning software for the tutoring of the markup language HTML. The system is responsible for detecting the learners' cognitive bugs and delivering personalized guidance. The novelty of this approach is that it is based on the Repair theory that incorporates additional features, such as student negligence and test completion times, in its diagnostic mechanism; also, it employs a recommender module that suggests students optimal learning paths based on their misconceptions using descriptive test feedback and adaptability of learning content. Considering the Repair theory, the diagnostic mechanism uses a library of error correction rules to explain the cause of errors observed by the student during the assessment. This library covers common errors, creating a hypothesis space in that way. Therefore, the test items are expanded, so that they belong to the hypothesis space. Both the system and the cognitive diagnostic tool were evaluated with promising results, showing that they offer a personalized experience to learners.

Keywords: adaptive content; diagnostic model; error diagnosis; learner experience; personalized guidance; repair theory; student bug

Citation: Krouska, A.; Troussas, C.; Sgouropoulou, C. A Cognitive Diagnostic Module Based on the Repair Theory for a Personalized User Experience in E-Learning Software. *Computers* **2021**, *10*, 140. https://doi.org/10.3390/computers10110140

Academic Editors: Antonio Sarasa Cabezuelo and Covadonga Rodrigo San Juan

Received: 29 September 2021
Accepted: 28 October 2021
Published: 29 October 2021

Publisher's Note: MDPI stays neutral with regard to jurisdictional claims in published maps and institutional affiliations.

Copyright: © 2021 by the authors. Licensee MDPI, Basel, Switzerland. This article is an open access article distributed under the terms and conditions of the Creative Commons Attribution (CC BY) license (https://creativecommons.org/licenses/by/4.0/).

1. Introduction

During the last decades, Adaptive Educational Hypermedia Systems (AEHS) have prevailed in the field of online learning, since they can form a depiction of each unique user's objectives, interests, and cognitive ability [1]. Moreover, they can be utilized to tailor the learning environment to their needs and preferences. Usually, the students' goal is to learn all the learning material or at least a significant part of it. That means that students' knowledge level is a determinant for their interaction with the system and it can alter based on their performance [2]. For instance, the knowledge level of a user can vary greatly in comparison to others, but also in other cases, it can increase quickly. As such, the same educational material can be vague for a beginner learner and at the same time trivial and boring for an advanced learner. Moreover, especially for beginners, it needs to be noted that they start using the system knowing nothing about the specific subject being taught, and most of the material will lead to subjects that are completely new to them. These users need guidance to find the "right" educational path. The guidance can take the form of diagnosis of misconceptions and/or errors.

As mentioned earlier, the knowledge of the users on the subject seems to be the most important characteristic for error diagnosis in most AEHSs. Almost all adaptive presentation techniques, e.g., fuzzy weights [3,4], artificial neural networks [5,6], multiple-criteria decision analysis [7,8], are based on user knowledge as the main source of personalization. User knowledge is a variable for each user. This means that an AEHS, being based on user knowledge, must recognize changes in the user knowledge state updating the user model accordingly.

One possible way for depicting the knowledge of students in comparison to the knowledge held by the system is the approach of the overlay modeling. The overlay model is one of the most often used and popular student models. It has been proposed by Stansfield et al. [9] and incorporated in several different learning technology systems. The overlay model is based on the idea that a learner's knowledge of the domain may be partial, yet valid. As a result, the student model is a subset of the domain model [10], which shows expert-level knowledge of the subject [11], according to overlay modeling. The discrepancies between the student's and expert's sets of knowledge are thought to be due to the student's lack of skills and knowledge, and the instructional goal is to minimize these differences.

A disadvantage of the overlay model is its inability to represent possible misunderstandings (misconceptions) of the user [12]. For this purpose, the buggy model has been proposed representing the user's knowledge as the union of a subset of the field of knowledge and a set of misunderstandings. The buggy model helps to better correct the user's mistakes since the existence of an image for the wrong knowledge is very useful from a pedagogical point of view.

In the bug catalog model, there is a large library of predefined misinterpretations that are used to add the relevant misinterpretations to the user model. A disadvantage of this model is the difficulty of creating the library of misinterpretations. The user's misinterpretations are detected during the assessment process. Usually the library contains symbolic rules—conditions and actions that are performed when they are activated.

Analyzing the related literature, there is strong evidence that the field of error diagnosis in e-learning software has been poorly researched for the learning of different concepts, the most prevalent of which are language learning and computer programming. Concerning language learning, there have been several research efforts that present the error diagnosis process can diagnose, among others, grammatical, syntactic, vocabulary mistakes by using techniques, such as approximate string matching, convolutional sequence to sequence modeling, context representation, etc. [13–19]. For example, the work of [19] proposes a sequence-to-sequence learning approach using recurrent neural networks for conducting error analysis and diagnosis. The main idea is that errors may hinder in specific words and with this approach, the error correction can happen successfully. Another example is the work of [13]. The authors employed a context representation approach to detect grammatical errors emerging from the vagueness problems of words. In the work of [14], the authors used the Clause Complex model to analyze the learners' errors emerging from grammatical differences in language learning. The work of [15] proposes a framework of hierarchical tagging sets to perform annotation of grammatical mistakes in language learning. Finally, the authors of [16] performed classification on spelling mistakes in two categories, i.e., orthographic and phonological errors. Concerning computer programming, the researchers perform error diagnosis for identifying either syntax or logic errors, by employing different intelligent techniques, such as fuzzy logic, periodical advice delivery about program's behavior, concept maps, highlighting similarities [20–26]. It must be noted that all the aforementioned mistakes (e.g., grammatical or vocabulary in language learning systems, and syntax or logical in programming learning systems) may emerge from different causes, such as negligence or incomplete knowledge [27–29].

From the presented literature review, it can be inferred that researchers fail to adequately blend theories and models with intelligent techniques to support the process of error diagnosis. In our approach, we employed the Repair theory [30,31] to explain how students can learn with specific attention to the learning way and the reasons of their misconceptions. To extend the efficiency of the presented module, we incorporated a buggy model, associated to the assessment process. This model holds several possible reasons for learners' misconceptions, such as carelessness or knowledge deficiency. The novelty of our approach is not only the use of buggy modeling based on the Repair theory, but also the exploitation of the exported diagnosis for recommending the optimal learning path to students. In particular, the system using the diagnostic mechanism detects the possible reason of students' misconceptions and provides tailored descriptive feedback about the score achieved, the test duration, and the learning path that should be followed in order for the students to improve their learning outcomes and knowledge bugs detected.

2. Diagnosis of Student Cognitive Bugs and Personalized Guidance

When evaluating the student performance, the e-learning systems mainly consider only the number of incorrect answers and based on the score achieved, they construct the student profile [32]. However, this score is not representative of the actual student knowledge and skills, since an incorrect answer does not always imply a cognitive gap, but it may occur due to student carelessness [33]. As such, the reason why students fail to answer correctly in tests is of great importance in order to provide them the proper guidance for increasing their learning outcomes.

To this direction, the paper presents an integrated student bugs diagnostic mechanism, embodied into an e-learning system, for detecting the student cognitive bugs and providing personalized guidance. The novelty of this approach is that not only is it based on Repair theory incorporating additional features, such as student carelessness and completion time of tests, in its diagnostic mechanism, but it also recommends to students the optimal learning path according to their misconceptions using descriptive feedback on the test and adapting learning content.

Considering the Repair Theory, the presented diagnostic mechanism uses a buggy rule library to explain the causes of students' bugs, observed during the assessment process. This library includes the common bugs, creating a hypothesis space in that way. Hence, the test items are developed in order that they appertain to the hypothesis space. The buggy rules were constructed by 10 computer science professors in Greek Universities, who have taught the HTML language for at least three years. In particular, they were asked through interviews to describe the most usual misconceptions the students made during the instruction of the course. Their answers were recorded and classified, producing a draft version of the buggy rules. In the second round of interviews, the experts were asked to update and/or confirm the rules. This process was repeated one more time. After that, the final version of the buggy rules was produced, including 96 potential misconceptions.

The diagnostic mechanism utilizes a repository of tests associated with the course lessons. Each test consists of a set of questions; each of which is related to a certain concept of the lesson. Every question's answer is characterized by the degree of student carelessness ranging from 0 (indicating a possible knowledge gap) to 1 (suggesting a choice by mistake) and the buggy rule explaining the student misconception. Thus, when students give an incorrect answer, the system can detect if there is a misconception and in which part of the lesson. Every question item of a test has an alternative one referred to the same concept. Hence, when a student, taking a test, gives a wrong answer that has a high degree of carelessness, the system delivers the alternative question. If the student answers this question correctly, then the system supposes that the first wrong answer was due to student carelessness. In this case, the mistake is not calculated to the final score and the system just informs the student to be more careful. If the student answers incorrectly in the second chance he/she has, then the system assumes that there is a knowledge gap on the concept to which the questions are referred, regardless of their degree of student carelessness. Moreover, the system considers the final score and the completion time of the test in order to provide to students a full report of hints for improving their learning outcomes. Figure 1 illustrates the entity–relationship model of the diagnostic mechanism. The algorithmic representation of diagnostic mechanism is shown in Algorithm 1.

Algorithm 1 Diagnostic Mechanism

1: student test time = 0
2: mistakes = 0
3: start time = time
4: **do**
5:     Display question(test)
6:     Get answer
7:     **if** is in correct(answer) AND degree of carelessness (answer) < 0.5 **then**
8:         Display alternative question in same concept(test, question)
9:         **if** is correct (answer) **then**
10:            Print "Be careful with your answers!"
11:        **else**
12:            Get concept, buggy rule related to answer
13:            Store concept, buggy rule in student profile
14:            mistakes + = 1
15:        **endif**
16:    **endif**
17:    **if** last question (test) **then**
18:        Student test time = time—start time
19:    **endif**
20: **until** student test time <> 0
21: student test score = Calculate score (mistakes)
22: Print report on score (student test score)
23: Print report on test duration(student test time)
24: Print report on concepts(student profile)
25: Print report on bugs(student profile)

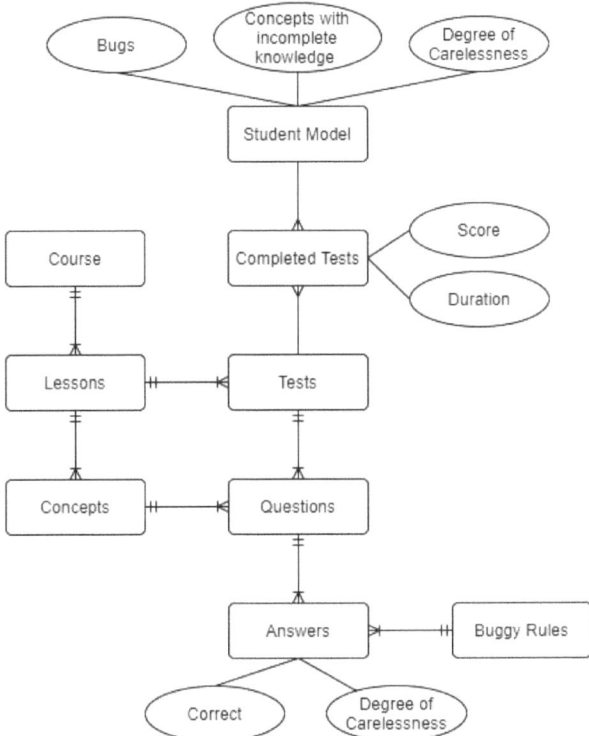

Figure 1. Entity-Relationship model.

At the end of a test, the system provides personalized guidance, which constitutes the optimal learning path that can lead the student to improve his/her performance. This descriptive feedback reports on the following:
- Success rate on the test, giving a corresponding motivation message.
- Time taken for completing the test, which is compared to the average time all students needed to fill in the test.
- Concepts in which the student had made a mistake that indicated a misconception.
- The misconceptions detected by the diagnostic mechanism.

Table 1 depicts the structure and rationale behind the personalized guidance.

Table 1. The structure and rationale of the personalized guidance.

Score Feedback	Score < 50%	50% ≤ Score < 70%	70% ≤ Score < 85%	Score ≥ 85%
Icon	☹	😐	🙂	😄
Motivation message on the score	You have made many mistakes. You must study the lesson again from scratch to be better prepared for the test. Your score is xx%	You are close to success. Study harder to improve your skills. Your score is xx%	Bravo! You are very good. Keep up the good work. Your score is xx%	Congratulations! Excellent job. Continue like this. Your score is xx%
Comment on test duration	\multicolumn{4}{l}{Average duration of all student to complete the test < Completion time of the student: The test was completed in Xm Xs. This duration is greater than the average one. Try to be more confident of your answers. Average duration of all student to complete the test ≥ Completion time of the student: The test was completed in Xm Xs. This duration reflects a satisfactory completion of the test.}
Lesson's Concepts	\multicolumn{4}{l}{The system recommends to student to study again the sub-units of the lesson where was detected a bug.}
Student Bugs	\multicolumn{4}{l}{The systems delivers the detected misconceptions according to the buggy rule library.}

3. Examples of Operation

The course that has been chosen for learning through the presented system is the HTML language. The reason for this choice is that although this language can be characterized as quite easy to learn and to use, it has many peculiarities emerging from the pages' structure and plenty of tags. The HTML elements are blocks, namely tags, written using angle brackets, and may include other tags as sub-elements. Moreover, each element may consist of a number of attributes related to the type of tag. These markups may make the understanding of the language difficult, leading to several misconceptions. These bugs in student cognitive state were documented by the experts, based on their experience in teaching the HTML language. A sample of the buggy rules emerged from this process is illustrated in Table 2.

Table 2. A sample of buggy rules.

	Buggy Rules
1	You have misunderstood the tag "<" with "#".
2	You have confused the body section with the head section.
3	You are confused about the i tag and the b tag.
4	You have misunderstood the attribute face of font tag.
5	You have confused the p tag with the paragraph tag.
6	You have confused the <ol> tag with the <ul> tag.
7	You are confused about the start attribute and the type attribute of <ol> tag.
8	You are confused about the <ul> tag.

In order to better understand the functionality of the diagnostic module and the adaptive feedback delivered, an example of operation is provided comparing the interaction of two users with the system. In particular, Student A and Student B took the third Test which corresponds to the "HTML Lists" lesson. Figures 2 and 3 illustrates their results on the test. Both students reached a score of 68%; however, they received different feedback. The system stimulates Student A to study further the "Ordered Lists" and suggests that it might be useful a revision on <li> tag. Student A bugs concern the <ul> and <ol> tags, as well as the start and type attributes of <ol> tag. On the other hand, the system recommends that Student B should study "Nested Lists" and "Description Lists"; while his misconceptions refer to the <dl>, <dt>, and <dd> tags, as well as the elements that can be included in <li> tag.

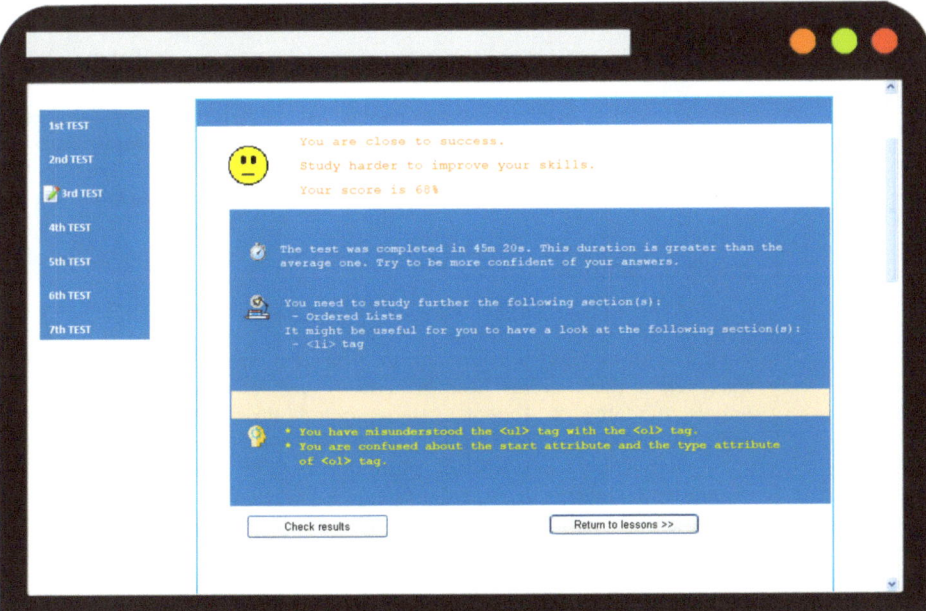

Figure 2. Feedback to Student A on third Test.

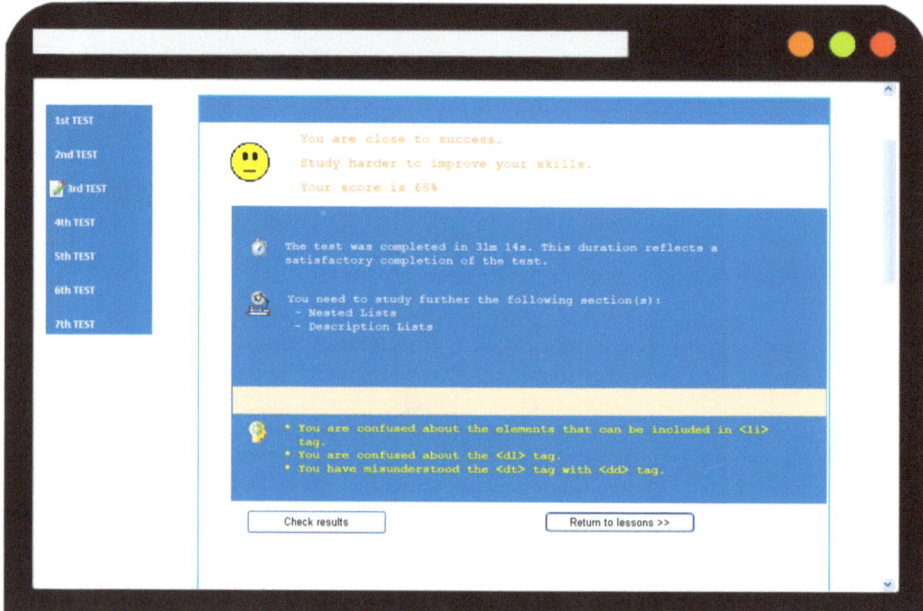

Figure 3. Feedback to Student B on third Test.

The reason why the reports to students are different is that although they made the same number of mistakes, they either gave different incorrect answers on the same question or made mistakes in different questions, referred to different sections of the lessons. As such, the system diagnosed different misconceptions and incomplete knowledge in sections for each student, providing individualized guidance regarding the learning path that should be followed. Moreover, it informed them about the bugs detected, helping them on their better handling.

4. System Evaluation

For evaluating the presented system, 80 undergraduate computer science students at a public university in Greece participated. Students' age ranged from 20 to 21 years old, having approximately equal computer skills and knowledge, as all of them were at the third year of their studies. Moreover, the sample consists of 44 (55%) male and 36 (45%) female students. The students were separated into two groups of 40 members with the same number of males and females, i.e., Group A and Group B.

The evaluation process took place during the tutoring of the "Web Programming" course, for a semester. In particular, Group A was taught the section concerned the "HTML Language" solely using the presented personalized e-learning system; while Group B used a conventional one without diagnosis of student bugs or personalization for this purpose. The reason of using the conventional system in the evaluation process is for assessing the potential of the cognitive diagnosis and personalized guidance used in our system in comparison to conventional approaches. All the students reacted passively to this new learning experience, completing successfully the required tasks/tests without dropouts.

Firstly, the system evaluation pertains to three dimensions, namely the user experience, the effectiveness of personalization and the impact on student learning [34]. Hence, a 10-point Likert scale questionnaire was conducted, including three questions for the assessment of the two first dimensions and four questions for the last dimension (Table 3). The questionnaire was delivered to students after the completion of the course and all of them answered it.

Table 3. Questionnaire of system evaluation.

Dimension		Questions
User Experience	1	Rate the user interface of the system. (1–10)
	2	Rate your learning experience. (1–10)
	3	Did you like the interaction with the system? (1–10)
Effectiveness of personalization	4	Did the system detect appropriately your misconceptions? (1–10)
	5	Rate the way the personalized guidance was presented. (1–10)
	6	Rate the learning content relevance to your personal profile. (1–10)
Impact on Learning	7	Would you like to use this platform in other courses as well? (1–10)
	8	Did you find the software helpful for your lesson? (1–10)
	9	Would you suggest the software to your friends to use it? (1–10)
	10	Rate the easiness in interacting with the software. (1–10)

The 10-point Likert scale answers were converted into three categories, namely Low ranging from 1 to 3, Average ranging from 4 to 7, and High ranging from 8 to 10; and, they were aggregated in the three dimensions. Figure 4 illustrates the evaluation results of Group A, concerned its interaction with the presented system, in comparison with Group B, which was interacting with the conventional system. The results reveal that the presented system is superior to the conventional one, regarding the three dimensions of the evaluation.

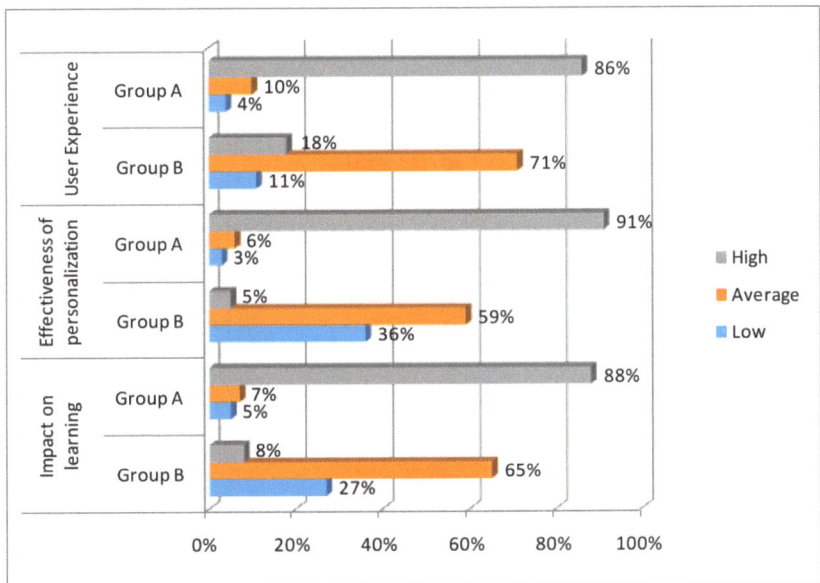

Figure 4. Evaluation results.

The "User Experience" of the presented system had 86% of high rating, indicating that students had a positive learning experience; whereas, the conventional one was rated 18% for high scores. In addition, 91% of Group A students declared the personalization mechanism was extremely helpful in establishing a learner-centered environment, as emerged by the results of the category "Effectiveness of Personalization". On the other hand, the low rating of Group B in this category indicates the lack of personalization in the conventional system. Finally, unlike the conventional version, the findings for the category "Impact on Learning" of the presented system are quite encouraging, demonstrating a 88% success rate for our software's pedagogical affordance. Analyzing the results of the evaluation research, there is strong evidence that our presented method can further improve the adaptivity and personalization of e-learning software by incorporating error diagnosis mechanisms, laying the groundwork for more individualized tutoring systems.

Secondly, in order to determine whether the personalization mechanisms used in the presented system have an effect on students comparing to conventional systems, the two-sample t-test between Group A and Group B was applied in questions 4–6.

Based on the t-test findings (Table 4), it can be concluded that there is a statistically significant difference between the means of the two trials when it comes to the aforementioned questions (Q4, Q5, Q6). In further detail, the system used by Group A was found to detect significantly more appropriately students' misconceptions than the conventional one used by Group B (Q4: $t(39) = 16.19$, $p < 0.05$). Moreover, there was a significant difference in the rating of the personalized guidance for Group A (Mean: 8.73, Variance: 2.72) and Group B (Mean: 5.45, Variance: 1.38), where $t(39) = 10.78$ and $p = 2.92 \times 10^{-13}$ (Q5); as well as, in the relevance of learning content delivered for Group A (Mean: 8.48, Variance: 3.18) and Group B (Mean: 5.6, Variance: 1.89), where $t(39) = 10.81$ and $p = 2.7 \times 10^{-13}$ (Q6). These results suggest that the proposed system outperforms its conventional version in terms of appropriate detection of learners' misconceptions, personalized guidance and delivery of learning content. These outcomes were anticipated, given that the presented system, based on buggy model and Repair theory, provides tailored feedback to students about their misconceptions and the actions they should take in order to improve them. As a result, a student-centered learning environment is provided, with enhanced knowledge acquisition and learning outcomes. On the other hand, the conventional system only delivers the final score, lacking in descriptive analysis of test results and thus, students are totally helpless regarding the learning path they should follow.

Table 4. T-test results on Q4, Q5, and Q6.

	Q4		Q5		Q6	
	Group A	Group B	Group A	Group B	Group A	Group B
Mean	8.65	5.23	8.73	5.45	8.48	5.6
Variance	3.36	2.18	2.72	1.38	3.18	1.89
Observations	40	40	40	40	40	40
Pooled Variance	0.69		0.11		0.46	
Hypothesized Mean Difference	0		0		0	
Degree of Freedom	39		39		39	
t Stat	16.19		10.78		10.81	
P(T ≤ t) two-tail	6.58×10^{-19}		2.92×10^{-13}		2.7×10^{-13}	
t Critical two-tail	2.023		2.023		2.023	

Finally, for evaluating the leaning outcomes, the final score of the course, emerged from the average of all chapters' tests, was calculated for each student in Group A and Group B, and the two-sample t-test between the final scores of these two groups was applied. The goal of this experiment is to investigate whether the students who used the presented system achieved higher performance than those who used the conventional version.

Analyzing the t-test results on learning outcomes (Table 5), it can be observed that there is a statistically significant difference between the means of the two groups. In particular, students who used the presented system had higher final scores (Mean: 82.45, Variance: 167.99) than did those using the conventional one (Mean: 70.05, Variance: 170.05), $t(78) = 4.27$ and $p = 5.55 \times 10^{-5}$. These results suggest that the approaches used for detecting students' misconceptions and for providing the tailored descriptive feedback can enhance learning process and lead students to achieve higher performance.

Table 5. *T*-test results on learning outcomes.

	Learning Outcomes	
	Group A	Group B
Mean	82.45	70.05
Variance	167.99	170.05
Observations	40	40
Pooled Variance	169.02	
Hypothesized Mean Difference	0	
Degree of freedom	78	
t Stat	4.27	
P(T ≤ t) two-tail	5.55×10^{-5}	
t Critical two-tail	1.99	

5. Conclusions

This paper describes a novel cognitive diagnostic module that has been included in an e-learning program for HTML instruction. The technology is responsible for identifying the learners' cognitive flaws and providing tailored instruction. This approach is unique in that it is based on the Repair theory and incorporates additional features into its diagnostic mechanism, such as student negligence and test completion times; it also employs a recommender module that suggests students optimal learning paths based on their misconceptions using descriptive test feedback, as well as the flexibility of learning materials. Using the Repair theory, the diagnostic mechanism explains the source of errors, noticed by the student during the assessment. This library covers typical blunders, effectively generating a hypothesis space. As a result, the test items are enlarged to include the hypothesis space. The buggy rules were developed by a group of computer science academics with a great experience in teaching HTML. They were specifically asked through interviews to characterize the most common misconceptions that learners had, during the course's training.

Our approach was fully evaluated using a well-known model and student's *t*-test. The results are very promising, showing that the system assisted students in a high degree to better understand their misconceptions. Based on the evaluation results, our approach was reported to have a positive impact on learning, to create a personalized learning environment for students and offer an optimal user experience.

Future work includes the extension of the buggy modeling so that the e-learning software can cope with different misconceptions and reasons of learners' mistakes. Moreover, future research plans include the alteration of recommendations to learners in terms of level of detail. Finally, part of our future work is to further evaluate the efficiency and acceptance of our system using qualitative techniques, such as interviews, and additional quantitative ones, such as pretest-posttest design.

Author Contributions: Conceptualization, A.K. and C.T.; methodology, A.K. and C.T.; validation, A.K. and C.T.; formal analysis, A.K. and C.T.; investigation, A.K. and C.T.; resources, A.K. and C.T.; data curation, A.K. and C.T.; writing—original draft preparation, A.K. and C.T.; writing—review and editing, A.K. and C.T.; visualization, A.K. and C.T.; supervision, C.S. All authors have read and agreed to the published version of the manuscript.

Funding: This research received no external funding.

Institutional Review Board Statement: Not applicable.

Informed Consent Statement: Informed consent was obtained from all subjects involved in the study at the time of original data collection.

Data Availability Statement: The data used to support the findings of this study have not been made available because they contain information that could compromise research participant privacy/consent.

Conflicts of Interest: The authors declare no conflict of interest.

References

1. Somyürek, S. The new trends in adaptive educational hypermedia systems. *Int. Rev. Res. Open Distrib. Learn.* **2015**, *16*. [CrossRef]
2. Somyürek, S.; Brusilovsky, P.; Guerra, J. Supporting knowledge monitoring ability: Open learner modeling vs. open social learner modeling. *Res. Pract. Technol. Enhanc. Learn.* **2020**, *15*, 1–24. [CrossRef]
3. Troussas, C.; Krouska, A.; Sgouropoulou, C. Collaboration and fuzzy-modeled personalization for mobile game-based learning in higher education. *Comput. Educ.* **2020**, *144*, 103698. [CrossRef]
4. Cuong, B.C.; Lich, N.T.; Ha, D.T. Combining Fuzzy Set—Simple Additive Weight and Comparing with Grey Relational Analysis For Student's Competency Assessment in the Industrial 4.0. In Proceedings of the 2018 10th International Conference on Knowledge and Systems Engineering (KSE), Ho Chi Minh City, Vietnam, 1–3 November 2018; pp. 294–299.
5. Saad, M.B.; Jackowska-Strumillo, L.; Bieniecki, W. ANN Based Evaluation of Student's Answers in E-tests. In Proceedings of the 2018 11th International Conference on Human System Interaction (HSI), Gdansk, Poland, 4–6 July 2018; pp. 155–161.
6. Troussas, C.; Krouska, A.; Virvou, M. A multilayer inference engine for individualized tutoring model: Adapting learning material and its granularity. *Neural Comput. Appl.* **2021**, 1–15. [CrossRef]
7. Troussas, C.; Krouska, A.; Sgouropoulou, C. Improving Learner-Computer Interaction through Intelligent Learning Material Delivery Using Instructional Design Modeling. *Entropy* **2021**, *23*, 668. [CrossRef] [PubMed]
8. Huang, Y.-M.; Hsieh, M.Y.; Usak, M. A Multi-Criteria Study of Decision-Making Proficiency in Student's Employability for Multidisciplinary Curriculums. *Mathematics* **2020**, *8*, 897. [CrossRef]
9. Stansfield, J.C.; Carr, B.; Goldstein, I.P. *Wumpus Advisor I: A First Implementation of a Program that Tutors Logical and Probabilistic Reasoning Skills*; Massachusetts Institute of Technology: Cambridge, MA, USA, 1976.
10. Martins, A.C.; Faria, L.; de Carvalho, C.V.; Carrapatoso, E. User modeling in adaptive hypermedia educational systems. *Educ. Technol. Soc.* **2008**, *11*, 194–207.
11. Liu, Z.; Wang, H. A Modeling Method Based on Bayesian Networks in Intelligent Tutoring System. In Proceedings of the 2007 11th International Conference on Computer Supported Cooperative Work in Design, Melbourne, Australia, 26–28 April 2007; pp. 967–972.
12. Qodad, A.; Benyoussef, A.; El Kenz, A.; Elyadari, M. Toward an Adaptive Educational Hypermedia System (AEHS-JS) based on the Overlay Modeling and Felder and Silverman's Learning Styles Model for Job Seekers. *Int. J. Emerg. Technol. Learn.* **2020**, *15*, 235–254. [CrossRef]
13. Zhao, J.; Li, M.; Liu, W.; Li, S.; Lin, Z. Detection of Chinese Grammatical Errors with Context Representation. In Proceedings of the 2018 International Conference on Network Infrastructure and Digital Content (IC-NIDC), Guiyang, China, 22–24 August 2018; pp. 25–29.
14. Lin, X.; Ge, S.; Song, R. Error analysis of Chinese-English machine translation on the clause-complex level. In Proceedings of the 2017 International Conference on Asian Language Processing (IALP), Singapore, 5–7 December 2017; pp. 185–188.
15. Lee, L.-H.; Chang, L.-P.; Tseng, Y.-H. Developing learner corpus annotation for Chinese grammatical errors. In Proceedings of the 2016 International Conference on Asian Language Processing (IALP), Tainan, Taiwan, 21–23 November 2016; pp. 254–257.
16. Haridas, M.; Vasudevan, N.; Nair, G.J.; Gutjahr, G.; Raman, R.; Nedungadi, P. Spelling Errors by Normal and Poor Readers in a Bilingual Malayalam-English Dyslexia Screening Test. In Proceedings of the 2018 IEEE 18th International Conference on Advanced Learning Technologies (ICALT), Mumbai, India, 9–13 July 2018; pp. 340–344.
17. Troussas, C.; Chrysafiadi, K.; Virvou, M. Machine Learning and Fuzzy Logic Techniques for Personalized Tutoring of Foreign Languages. In Proceedings of the International Conference on Artificial Intelligence in Education, London, UK, 27–30 June 2018; pp. 358–362.
18. Khodeir, N.A. Constraint-based and Fuzzy Logic Student Modeling for Arabic Grammar. *Int. J. Comput. Sci. Inf. Technol.* **2020**, *12*, 35–53. [CrossRef]
19. Li, S.; Zhao, J.; Shi, G.; Tan, Y.; Xu, H.; Chen, G.; Lan, H.; Lin, Z. Chinese Grammatical Error Correction Based on Convolutional Sequence to Sequence Model. *IEEE Access* **2019**, *7*, 72905–72913. [CrossRef]
20. Henley, A.Z.; Ball, J.; Klein, B.; Rutter, A.; Lee, D. An Inquisitive Code Editor for Addressing Novice Programmers' Misconceptions of Program Behavior. In Proceedings of the 2021 IEEE/ACM 43rd International Conference on Software Engineering: Software Engineering Education and Training (ICSE-SEET), Madrid, Spain, 25–28 May 2021; pp. 165–170.
21. Lai, A.F.; Wu, T.T.; Lee, G.Y.; Lai, H.Y. Developing a web-based simulation-based learning system for enhancing concepts of linked-list structures in data structures curriculum. In Proceedings of the 2015 3rd International Conference on Artificial Intelligence, Modelling and Simulation (AIMS), Kota Kinabalu, Malaysia, 2–4 December 2015; pp. 185–188.
22. Chang, J.-C.; Li, S.-C.; Chang, A.; Chang, M. A SCORM/IMS Compliance Online Test and Diagnosis System. In Proceedings of the 2006 7th International Conference on Information Technology Based Higher Education and Training, Ultimo, Australia, 10–13 July 2006; pp. 343–352.

23. Barker, S.; Douglas, P. An intelligent tutoring system for program semantics. In Proceedings of the International Conference on Information Technology: Coding and Computing (ITCC'05), Las Vegas, NV, USA, 4–6 April 2005; Volume 1, pp. 482–487.
24. Khalife, J. Threshold for the introduction of programming: Providing learners with a simple computer model. In Proceedings of the 28th International Conference on Information Technology Interfaces, Cavtat, Croatia, 19–22 June 2006; pp. 71–76.
25. Troussas, C.; Krouska, A.; Virvou, M. Injecting intelligence into learning management systems: The case of adaptive grain-size instruction. In Proceedings of the 2019 10th International Conference on Information, Intelligence, Systems and Applications (IISA), Patras, Greece, 15–17 July 2019; pp. 1–6.
26. Krugel, J.; Hubwieser, P.; Goedicke, M.; Striewe, M.; Talbot, M.; Olbricht, C.; Schypula, M.; Zettler, S. Automated Measurement of Competencies and Generation of Feedback in Object-Oriented Programming Courses. In Proceedings of the 2020 IEEE Global Engineering Education Conference (EDUCON), Porto, Portugal, 27–30 April 2020; pp. 329–338.
27. Almeda, M. Predicting Student Participation in STEM Careers: The Role of Affect and Engagement during Middle School. *J. Educ. Data Min.* **2020**, *12*, 33–47.
28. Sumartini, T.S.; Priatna, N. Identify student mathematical understanding ability through direct learning model. *J. Phys. Conf. Ser.* **2018**, *1132*, 012043. [CrossRef]
29. Troussas, C.; Krouska, A.; Sgouropoulou, C. A Novel Teaching Strategy Through Adaptive Learning Activities for Computer Programming. *IEEE Trans. Educ.* **2021**, *64*, 103–109. [CrossRef]
30. Brown, J.; VanLehn, K. Repair Theory: A Generative Theory of Bugs in Procedural Skills. *Cogn. Sci.* **1980**, *4*, 379–426. [CrossRef]
31. Brown, J.S.; Burton, R.R. Diagnostic models for procedural bugs in basic mathematical skills. *Cogn. Sci.* **1978**, *2*, 155–192. [CrossRef]
32. Rashid, T.; Asghar, H.M. Technology use, self-directed learning, student engagement and academic performance: Examining the interrelations. *Comput. Hum. Behav.* **2016**, *63*, 604–612. [CrossRef]
33. Krouska, A.; Troussas, C.; Sgouropoulou, C. Fuzzy Logic for Refining the Evaluation of Learners' Performance in Online Engineering Education. *Eur. J. Eng. Res. Sci.* **2019**, *4*, 50–56. [CrossRef]
34. Alepis, E.; Troussas, C. M-learning programming platform: Evaluation in elementary schools. *Informatica* **2017**, *41*, 471–478.

Article

Motivation, Stress and Impact of Online Teaching on Italian Teachers during COVID-19

Giusi Antonia Toto * and Pierpaolo Limone

Department of Humanistic Studies, University of Foggia, 71100 Foggia, Italy; pierpaolo.limone@unifg.it
* Correspondence: giusi.toto@unifg.it

Abstract: The use of digital technology as the only communication and relationship channel in work, school and social contexts is bringing out dynamics that are sometimes in contrast with each other. The purpose of this article is to investigate the impact of digital technology on teachers' school practices in the context of COVID-19. This impact was studied in relation to the constructs of motivation, perceived stress, sense of self-efficacy and resistance to/acceptance of technologies. This study examined the role played by the massive and coercive use of digital technologies (and the relationship with innovation and change) in predicting motivation and perceived stress among teachers. To this end, the impact of digital technologies on motivation and perceived stress were explored in the sample. A questionnaire consisting of three scales was administered to 688 Italian school teachers of all educational levels (from childhood to upper-secondary school), who completed a socio-demographic section, a section on the scale of the impact of technology and distance learning, a perceived stress scale and items on motivation and professional development. Descriptive and inferential analyses were applied to the data. Key findings indicated that the impact of digital technologies during the pandemic negatively correlates with both perceived stress and motivation. Practical implications were suggested to help teachers develop functional coping styles to cope with technological changes in work and life contexts.

Keywords: professional vision; motivation; stress; digital learning; COVID-19

Citation: Toto, G.A.; Limone, P. Motivation, Stress and Impact of Online Teaching on Italian Teachers during COVID-19. *Computers* **2021**, *10*, 75. https://doi.org/10.3390/computers10060075

Academic Editors: Antonio Sarasa Cabezuelo, Covadonga Rodrigo San Juan and Santi Caballé

Received: 30 April 2021
Accepted: 4 June 2021
Published: 11 June 2021

Publisher's Note: MDPI stays neutral with regard to jurisdictional claims in published maps and institutional affiliations.

Copyright: © 2021 by the authors. Licensee MDPI, Basel, Switzerland. This article is an open access article distributed under the terms and conditions of the Creative Commons Attribution (CC BY) license (https://creativecommons.org/licenses/by/4.0/).

1. Introduction

Themes of the perception and professional vision of teachers have been consolidated as a specific realm of study in the last 30 years [1]. In the European context, the demand for digital skills within school contexts is determined by the development of the eight key skills (including digital literacy) and the DigCompEdu model for educators, which encourages the acquisition of meta-skills (learning to feel professional or learning to act with the media) that mediate their relationship with pupils [2,3]. This theoretical model involves the development of three fundamental components—awareness, reflexivity and cooperation—in the digital and pedagogical vision. The initial training of teachers is increasingly oriented and consolidated towards the use of information and communication technology (ICT) in contemporary teaching and teaching practice [4]. In fact, media education provides three possible applications of digital technology at school: (1) full online teaching, (2) hybrid teaching and (3) digitally mediated teaching. The first model is linked to distance training and e-learning, which were strongly implemented during the COVID-19 pandemic [5]. The second is still experimental in an Italian context (expected to be adopted in the post-COVID phase) and involves the use of moments and models of in-person teaching suitably alternated with those of online teaching [6]. The third is the more traditional model of digital technologies at school, which involves the instrumental use of technology that supports and enriches the frontal lesson [7] (essentially designed face-to-face). The scientific evidence reported in the meta-analysis by Bernard [8] shows that blended learning produces greater effects on students in terms of interactions with teachers, peers and with the content of the lesson taught in the classroom. Subsequent and application studies [9] have shown that the use of a mixed teaching model (online and face-to-face) is significantly associated with higher learning performance of students in the Science, Technology, Engineering and Mathematics (STEM) disciplines than traditional classroom practice. The contemporary debate stimulated by the COVID-19 pandemic has expanded research into unique full-online teaching practices during the pandemic (with a huge development of trials) and the future of this practice post-COVID that could result in a teaching hybrid. In the European context, the most unexpected scenarios are emerging. For example, English universities are experimenting with alternative solutions for students who do not have access to the Internet at home and the Charles III University of Madrid will carry out practical lessons in person and theoretical lessons online. Distance teaching for many universities, including those in Italy, has marked the loss of many economic gains [10]. The change of perspective described here manifests the need to move towards a social analysis of the impact of technology on the working life of the subjects and to describe the change taking place that determines the effects on professional well-being/malaise. Although paradigmatically discordant, the succession of different models is a testament to the construction of a professional paradigm oriented towards professional competence and well-being [11]. The five constituent components of well-being, in fact, turn out to be self-esteem, self-determination, positive emotions, optimism and resilience, which will characterise and direct subsequent research developments. The theme of teacher motivation is deeply felt by school governance boards and leadership because the motivation of teachers is reflected in the motivation of students [12,13]. These approaches are intended to encourage greater interaction with students and enhance self-determination, promote structured collaborative learning processes and reduce the number of traditional lessons. One of teachers' main concerns is to keep students' motivation high. However, education has one of the highest levels of stress compared to other professional groups and educators [14] often declare that they want to leave their profession. The context of the pandemic has made educational relationships with students even more intangible and has complicated this dynamic. A thriving field of study concerns the stress related to the use of digital technologies caused by a lack of training in the use of the technologies or by teachers' resistance to adopting them [15].

Influenced by Bandura's [16] social cognitive theory, and dissatisfied with previous models, Compeau and Higgins [17] developed a theory of human behaviour applied to the use of new technologies. Although in the first place the theory was devised to test acceptance of the use of the PC, subsequent studies [18] have shown that it is also easily usable in the field of communication technologies in general (Figure 1). The dimensions investigated concern the expectations of results in terms of both performance and interiority. The former refers to the consequences of one's behaviour in terms of professional results (outcome expectations); the latter, on the other hand, affects self-esteem and the sense of personal fulfilment. The dimension of computer self-efficacy, which crosses all socio-cognitivist interpretative models, represents the subject's own assessment of the use of technology to skilfully accomplish a specific task. Affect is the individual's preference to experience a certain behaviour, and finally, anxiety, i.e., the induction of strong anxious or emotional reactions, is a reaction to the use of a specific technology [19]. The antecedents of outcome expectations and self-esteem are found in the encouragement of others, other uses and support. The process described in the model is aimed at the use of digital technology.

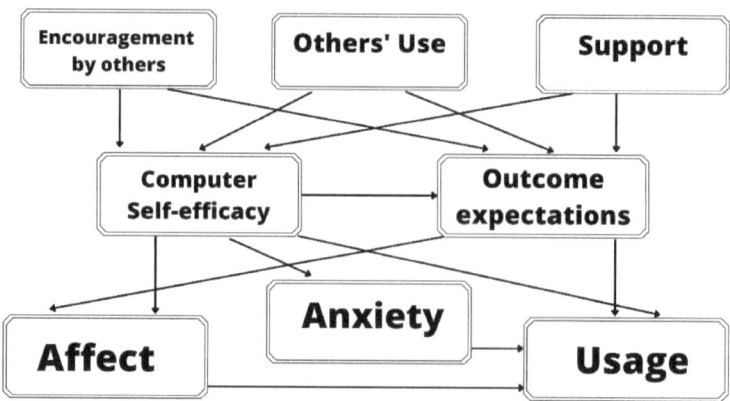

Figure 1. Social Cognitive Theory. Adapted with permission from ref. [17]. Copyright 2021 M I S Quarterly.

Bandura (and socio-cognitivist theorists in general) argues that, even in work contexts, subjects build their beliefs of self-efficacy by interpreting multiple inputs; experience of well-developed skills are one of the main sources of information for subjects to feel self-effective (and competent). In fact, teachers engage in training and didactic activities, interpret the results obtained and develop beliefs that will guide their choices and future actions. Usually, they persevere in activities in which they perceive themselves to be most effective and abandon those at which they consider themselves to be unsuccessful [20].

2. The Study and Its Contexts

The purpose of this research work was to analyse the motivation, stress perceived and impact and performance expectation of teachers in distance learning. The research hypothesis concerns the relationship and mutual influence between these three variables, especially in relation to the effects on the professional vision and the professionalism of teachers. The continuation of the COVID-19 pandemic in 2021 has made digital education the privileged channel for providing teaching in schools of all levels worldwide. An educational and social phenomenon of this magnitude has stimulated the interest of psychologists and pedagogues on learning problems related to distance learning and the motivation and professional competence of teachers working in this area. Experiments in online, hybrid and mixed training have been carried out for years, with the focus aimed at measuring their positive and negative effects on students in terms of learning effectiveness [21]. The COVID-19 pandemic has caused a profound change in the professional modality of teachers, as well as perceptions of self-efficacy and motivation in the use of online teaching. In this context, the University of Foggia has experimented with a work model that facilitates the first-person experimentation (by teachers) of innovative teaching methodologies linked to media education, gamification and knowledge transfer in the context of their daily professional practice. The monitoring of these three dimensions represents a fundamental step for the future of online and hybrid teaching within schools. The research is developed in the Italian context, where the specialisation course of teachers is online and groups teachers on a national scale; students therefore belong to all areas of Italy (67% from southern Italy). The 10-year-old University of Foggia is a leader in distance learning and has provided all teacher training completely online (including workshops and internships) since March 2020, proposing for the third time a specialisation course for teachers ($n = 688$).

The interviewed teachers actually received a dual treatment: (1) trainers who delivered lessons, each in their own grade of school, and (2) students of a specialisation course carried out completely online (lessons, workshops and internships). This study was developed in relation to a questionnaire built on three scales: a scale on the impact of online teaching, a scale of stress perceived by students in the virtual room (validated in the context of COVID-19) and the expectation of performance and professional development of teachers. The interviewees were an adult population, coming from different areas of Italy, with an extensive training course behind them, and intrinsically motivated by the specificity of the care profession they were about to undertake and extrinsically by their attendance of a course that 'rewards' them with direct access to the profession and employability.

The data were broken down by demographic profile, response processing and educational level (childhood, primary school, lower-secondary school or upper-secondary school). The data was provided via Google Forms in March 2021 during the third wave of the COVID-19 state of emergency. Using the online form made it possible to receive results in real time and quickly view a summary.

The final version of the questionnaire, in addition to demographic questions about gender, school level, years of teaching, experience, work situation and others, also presented 26 Likert-type questions regarding the previous three scales with which the user could express various levels of agreement or disagreement (a copy of the questionnaire in Italian is available in Supplementary Materials).

An initial demographic analysis confirms research on gender differences that demonstrates that in the lower levels of education (childhood, primary), males represent only 1.1% of respondents for primary education and 4.4% for childhood. The percentage reaches 28–30% in lower and upper secondary schools. The average age was over 42 for kindergarten, over 40 for primary, 36.1 for middle school, and 37.9 in high school.

Participants were administered a self-report survey, including a sociodemographic scale and the following questionnaires:

(i) The online teaching–learning questionnaire measures the challenges faced in online teaching–learning, teacher-trainees' proposals for effective online teaching–learning and students' preferred way of conducting the course [22]. Background information provided by respondents measured variables including gender and the curriculum. The learning impact of online teaching and the challenges of online teaching learning was measured through items that contained Likert scales of 1 = strongly agree (SA), 2 = agree (A), 3 = undecided (U), 4 = disagree (D), and 5 = strongly disagree (SD). The alpha values of 0.82 and 0.78 were found for the two constructs with Likert scales. There was internal consistency reliability test of items on the two constructs with the Likert scales using the Cronbach's Alpha (α) reliability analysis measures. However, Ghazali [23] indicated that the alpha value of 0.60 is also considered acceptable. This study attained the alpha values of 0.82 and 0.78 on the two constructs with the Likert Scales.

(ii) The Perceived Stress Scale (PSS) of Sheldon Cohen [24]. The scale consists of ten questions that are used to measure the perception of stress experienced by the participants over the past month. It includes a 5-point Likert scale that capture responses ranging from never to very often [25]. Total mean scores of 0–13 are considered to be low stress, 14–26 indicate moderate stress and 27–40 indicate high stress. The PSS is an easily and widely used tool with acceptable psychometric properties [26]. Across diverse conditions, researchers report relatively satisfactory reliability estimates for scores on the 14- and 10-item forms. For example, Roberti et al. [27] reported reliability estimates of 0.85 and 0.82 in a university sample for scores on the perceived helplessness and perceived self-efficacy scales, respectively.

(iii) The teacher motivation scale section, career development, consists of twelve items scored on a five-point Likert scale (from 1 = not at all true of me to 5 = very true of me) [28]. Sample items are: "When reading for a course, I make up questions to help focus my reading"; "I try to change the way I study in order to fit the course requirements and the lecturer's teaching style". In the current study, the scales showed adequate levels of reliability (Cronbach's alpha = 0.66). From the Teacher Motivation Framework of Analysis described in Section 3, a 98-question questionnaire was created and sent to 19 SC COs. The19 SC COs were not selected randomly, but rather on the basis of the type of SC Basic Education programming they were involved in. The survey was opened 15 April and closed on 29 April. Cos were given the option of completing the survey online via SurveyMonkey or via Microsoft Word attachment. Of the 19 COs contacted, 16 responded: from Afghanistan, Bangladesh, Bolivia, Egypt, El Salvador, Ethiopia, Haiti, Kyrgyzstan, Malawi, Mali, Mozambique, Nepal, Nicaragua, the Philippines, Tajikistan and Uganda.

In this study, forward translation of all questionnaires, from English into Italian, was performed by an English native speaker. The discrepancies existing in the Italian and in the back-translations were then discussed with the authors until consensus was reached.

3. The Triadic Model

All data were processed in IBM's statistical software SPSS, version 25. Before the main analysis, data were screened for univariate and multivariate outliers. Z-scores were used as the criterion for detection of univariate outliers. More precisely, all participants that had z-score higher than +3 or lower than −3 on one or more target variables were removed from further analyses. Seven univariate outliers were detected and removed from the data set. The criterion for detection of multivariate outliers was the Mahalanobis distance. No multivariate outliers were detected in the data set. The final sample had 688 participants.

In the next step, skewness and kurtosis of all target variables was inspected in order to determine whether the data were normally distributed. The results have shown that both skewness and kurtosis of all target variables (impact on online teaching, stress and motivation) were in the −1 to +1 range; hence, we may conclude that all variables were normally distributed (Table 1).

Table 1. Descriptive statistics.

	Descriptives		Statistic	Std. Error
Impact on Online Teaching Total	Mean		12.7674	0.15742
	95% Confidence Interval for Mean	Lower Bound	12.4584	
		Upper Bound	13.0765	
	5% Trimmed Mean		12.6059	
	Median		12.0000	
	Variance		17.049	
	Std. Deviation		4.12907	
	Minimum		6.00	
	Maximum		26.00	
	Range		20.00	
	Interquartile Range		5.00	
	Skewness		0.555	0.093
	Kurtosis		0.027	0.186
Stress Total	Mean		27.2049	0.30936
	95% Confidence Interval for Mean	Lower Bound	26.5975	
		Upper Bound	27.8124	
	5% Trimmed Mean		27.0287	
	Median		26.0000	
	Variance		65.846	
	Std. Deviation		8.11455	
	Minimum		10.00	
	Maximum		48.00	
	Range		38.00	
	Interquartile Range		12.00	
	Skewness		0.323	0.093
	Kurtosis		−0.652	0.186

Table 1. *Cont.*

	Descriptives		Statistic	Std. Error
Motivation Total	Mean		28.9331	0.15983
	95% Confidence Interval for Mean	Lower Bound	28.6193	
		Upper Bound	29.2470	
	5% Trimmed Mean		29.0061	
	Median		29.0000	
	Variance		17.576	
	Std. Deviation		4.19241	
	Minimum		17.00	
	Maximum		39.00	
	Range		22.00	
	Interquartile Range		6.00	
	Skewness		−0.262	0.093
	Kurtosis		−0.053	0.186

3.1. Reliability Analysis of the Questionnaires

The initial questionnaire that measured the impact on online teaching consisted of seven items, and the Cronbach's alpha coefficient for complete scale was $\alpha = 0.78$. However, the results of reliability analysis showed that the removal of one item from the questionnaire would improve the internal consistency of the scale. Item number one was removed because it was the only item in the scale that had a significantly lower item-total correlation in comparison to the item-total correlations of other items. When item number one was removed, the alpha coefficient increased to $\alpha = 0.83$.

The initial questionnaire that measured stress consisted of 10 items, and the Cronbach's alpha coefficient for complete scale was $\alpha = 0.88$. None of the items were removed from the scale because they all had approximately equal and optimal item-total correlation, and because the removal of any item would have lowered the alpha coefficient.

The initial questionnaire that measured motivation consisted of seven items, and the Cronbach's alpha coefficient for complete scale was $\alpha = 0.66$. However, the results of reliability analysis showed that the removal of one item from the questionnaire would improve the internal consistency of the scale. The item that was named "item 22" was removed because it was the only item in the scale that had a significantly lower item-total correlation in comparison to the item-total correlations of other items. When the item named as "item 22" was removed, alpha coefficient increased to $\alpha = 0.67$.

3.2. Correlation

Pearson's correlations were computed in order to test the significance of the relationships between impact on online teaching, stress and motivation (Table 2). The results of correlation analyses showed that the impact on online teaching was significantly correlated to motivation $r = -0.17$, $r^2 = 0.03$, $p < 0.001$ and to stress $r = 0.24$, $r^2 = 0.06$, $p < 0.001$. The correlation between the impact on online teaching and motivation was negative, which means that when motivation was lower, the impact on online teaching tended to be higher. On the other hand, the correlation between the impact on online teaching and stress was positive, which means that higher stress was associated with the higher impact on online teaching. However, it must be emphasized that both correlation coefficients were very low. More precisely, impact on online teaching and motivation shared only 3% of variance, while impact on online teaching and stress shared only 6% of variance. Hence, it is highly probable that both correlations were significant only because the sample was large. Therefore, it is highly probable that both correlations were actually spurious.

Table 2. Correlation among dimensions.

	Correlations	Motivation Total	Impact_on_Online_Teaching_Total	Stress Total
Motivation Total	Pearson Correlation Sig. (2-tailed) N	1 688	−0.173 ** 0.000 688	−0.216 ** 0.000 688
Impact on Online Teaching Total	Pearson Correlation Sig. (2-tailed) N	−0.173 ** 0.000 688	1 688	0.235 ** 0.000 688
Stress Total	Pearson Correlation Sig. (2-tailed) N	−0.216 ** 0.000 688	0.235 ** 0.000 688	1 688

** Correlation is significant at the 0.01 level (2-tailed).

From the results reported in the two proposed tables, this study explores an important aspect of the use of technology in teaching, specifically the effects of distance learning on Italian teachers in terms of motivation and perceived stress. Compeau and Higgins's socio-cognitive model of professional use and acceptance of technology within work contexts identifies anxiety, affect, self-efficacy and performance expectation as competing factors for digital technology use in teaching. The tool used in this study instead demonstrates (in the specific context of the COVID-19 pandemic) how motivation, stress and the impact of technology on learning and teaching have a significant value in the perceptions of Italian teachers. The construct of motivation is investigated in relation to professional development both in terms of skills acquisition and career progression. Perceived stress is measured in relation to teacher/student activities within the classroom, and the third scale investigates the advantages/disadvantages of web-enhanced (online) courses.

SEM (structural equation modelling) allows us to examine the relationships between the three independent variables with the dependent variable. In the case of the indirectly measured considerations observed in this study, the latent (i.e., indirectly measured) variables can be seen in the scheme proposed in Figure 2. The structural equation model (SEM) combines two tools within a single framework: confirmatory factor analysis and multivariate regression analysis. The CFA (confirmatory factor analysis) aims to build a model suitable for studying the relationships between the observed variables and the latent variables; that is, those constructs that are not observed but are derived from a combination of the observed variables. Regression analysis, on the other hand, aims to explain the random relationships between constructs. From the data, a triadic model of the professional vision of teachers in COVID-19 emerges, where motivation, stress and digital teaching are mediators, respectively, between career progression, perceptions and advantages/stress and the same professional vision. Compeau and Hiddigs' socio-cognitive theory model has also recently been associated with a line of studies on the acceptance of digital technology in teachers' school practice (UTAUT) [29]. Specifically, the intrinsic and extrinsic motivation factors of support from others (encouragement, use and support), stress (anxiety and emotion in general) and digital performance in general have strengthened the idea of using online teaching in school lessons. Individually analysed data collected by the three scales indicates that the interviewed sample showed high scores in all three dimensions: career desire, stress and the benefits of digital technologies (Figure 2). At the same time, the negative correlation between motivation and stress was confirmed (−0.216 **). As the impact of digital technologies increased, perceived stress also increased (0.235 **), and the original data of this research concerned the increase in the impact of technology, which decreased the motivation of the interviewees (−0.173 **).

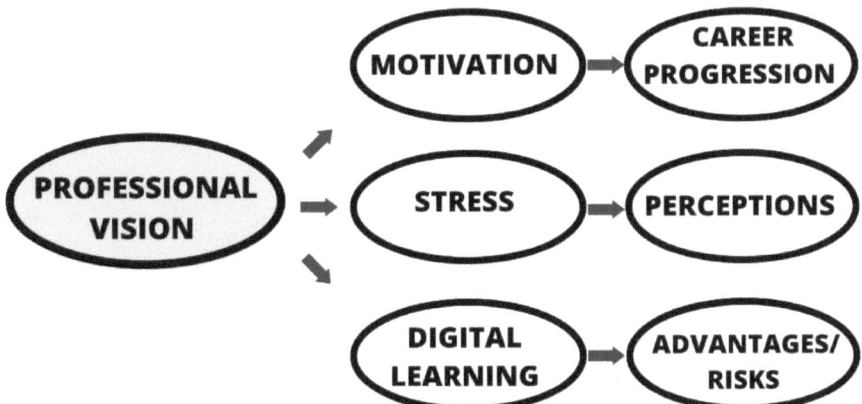

Figure 2. Model of professional vision in COVID-19.

Although online teaching was the only possible communication channel during the pandemic, the teachers on the course continued to practice it one year after its exclusive use; they experienced it as a demotivator and a source of stress and therefore, there is evidence of a possible refusal in the future use of online teaching. In higher education, learning environments are transforming to respond to new demands in the field of teaching methodologies. Everything is happening through the integrated use of technologies in educational paths, redesigning the space–time boundaries of learning thanks to the application of flexible teaching methodologies [30].

In the current historical period, it has been highlighted how the rapid transition from face-to-face teaching to DDA has strongly influenced teaching methods. Research on learning design has always emphasized the importance of developing teachers' skills related to devising pedagogically sound interventions on the basis of designed and sustainable teaching methodologies [31,32]. Therefore, there is a clear need for training interventions aimed at teachers to strengthen a design capacity that will guarantee quality teaching through the application of the most recent digital technologies [33,34]. In fact, in this initial phase of exploring technological tools, many educators have neglected the principles of collaborative teaching that require planning and organisation skills at work. Above all, these components are strategic for promoting social interactions and strengthening cooperative learning. Given that the world of digital didactic technologies is equipped with dialogic tools, teacher training should be aimed at better consolidation of the network affordances for quality technological didactic planning [35].

4. Discussion and Conclusions

The socio-cognitive model applied to digital technology in the professional practice of teachers is described as influencing three fundamental factors: personal, behavioural and socio-environmental. In this study, the three factors of motivation, stress and impact of the technology were operationalized. These factors influence each other, but contemporary research must understand their influences on teaching and learning. The factor of motivation investigated in this study is linked to the dimension of self-determination and the career prospects of teachers [36]. Perceived stress becomes a fundamental element in the analysis because it is linked both to the specificity of the COVID-19 period, which forced social isolation, and to the exclusive use of digital technology as a training and work channel [37].

The arduous process of integrating technologies into formal learning environments has rapidly accelerated during the COVID-19 pandemic. Virtual and immersive learning environments were the solution to the emergency phase for all levels of training. The slow integration process, however, requires a degree of digital competence on the part of teachers to guide policies and procedures in their own school. The process must be supported by planning and designing the training and education of teachers for the use of technology in their classrooms [38]. In the present study, the category of "students" captures participants in their double role as students in the training course and as teachers in their everyday professional practice. In the school and academic context, the emergency situation has had significant repercussions; prolonged closures and the sudden transmission and construction of content in online mode has had an impact on various levels. Onyema et al. [39] listed as major repercussions the renewed learning methods with the relative activation difficulties, the danger of social isolation and the increase in socio-economic inequalities deriving from the existing digital divide [40]. The consequences have been twofold for education professionals: on the one hand, the need for a quick transformation of teaching practices and personal styles of instruction has caused stress, and on the other, learning new teaching methods that will be useful in the future has provided motivation.

Teachers are among the key actors involved in academic rehabilitation. A study conducted by the Italian Society of Didactic Research (SIRD) found that their main problems were a perceived lack of preparation in dealing with this new modality, as well as the required total reorganisation of the didactics, which is associated with an excessive workload, both in terms of construction and timing. However, a study by Ardizzoni [41] highlighted that the use of educational technologies played a supportive role in the management of relational dynamics with students. Nevertheless, difficulties with devices and reaching all students, especially those in a fragile condition, remain unchanged.

On the other hand, it is hypothesised that the implementation of digital technologies has allowed educators to understand the potential associated with their use. It emerges that instruction through digital platforms motivates students to learn and optimises the classroom environment [42]. Teachers, therefore, have gradually reinvented the already consolidated teaching methods, and the most highly motivated teachers have taken part in training courses with a view to lifelong learning.

The process of including technology within the classroom context is never exhausted but goes hand in hand with technological evolution. In this picture, two competing dynamics emerge: the first, motivation, oscillates, according to socio-cognitive theory, between the expectation of performance and the attribution of value and self-efficacy. In fact, the self-determined teacher pursues the need for competence (since he/she is an expert and master of carrying out his/her task), the need for autonomy (his/her actions emerge from intrinsic motivation) and the need for a relationship (establish close emotional ties and attachment to significant subjects, i.e., colleagues and students) [43].

If it is true that motivation, stress and digital learning have direct effects on the professional vision of teachers, it is also true that the desire (and perspectives) of career development, the perceptions (and personal beliefs) of teachers and the knowledge of the risks and benefits of technologies within the teaching process have a secondary (and latent) effect on the profession of teaching. The importance of this second implication of the study allows us to reflect on what dimensions are necessary to act for a general improvement of professional vision. Although career prospects are linked to leadership and school governance, personal beliefs and knowledge of the risks/benefits of technologies require in-service training interventions that enhance performance in these areas [44].

When this process does not follow a linear development like that shown due to limiting beliefs, low self-esteem, limited sense of self-efficacy and lack of social support, it can become a source of stress for teachers, students and the whole social context. A maladaptive response to the change triggered by technologies in work (and school) contexts produces perceived stress on the part of teachers. The perceived stress more specifically concerns the lack of control and unpredictability rather than a relationship with real stressful events. The subjects are focused on what might happen and decide that a change to horrible conditions is inevitable. Among the negative effects of perceived stress in relation to technology (in addition to those related to psycho–physical well-being), is the structuring of dysfunctional coping mechanisms. The most evident phenomenon is represented by the resistance and non-acceptance of digital technology in teaching practice [45]. The COVID-19 pandemic has prompted the reinvention of university teaching. Academic institutions have had to reset their teaching practices so as to incorporate digital technologies, some of them for the first time. This sudden change has led to a number of problems in the use of an emergency type of distance learning, including technological infrastructure weakness, teacher inexperience and a perceived invasion of privacy in the home environment [46]. Furthermore, research by Bao [47] revealed that students were more concerned about the quality of internet connectivity, which is essential for both participation in synchronous lessons and exams. The teachers involved in this research declared that they preferred online lessons in asynchronous mode. The main problem is not related to the use of technological tools but to the lack of both structural and didactic preparation of the teachers themselves. Therefore, in many cases, remote teaching has resulted in the transfer of traditional frontal lessons to an online mode with little awareness of the design required to ensure effective learning in virtual teaching environments.

Future research perspectives could investigate precisely this dynamic linked to the construction of increasingly valid and effective tools for investigating motivation and perceived stress in relation to digital technologies and all the main changes affecting the world of education. In addition, it would be necessary to build intervention and prevention models in relation to the stress perceived by teachers that would lead to the educational success of their students and greater well-being within the classroom.

Supplementary Materials: The following are available online at https://www.mdpi.com/article/10.3390/computers10060075/s1.

Author Contributions: Conceptualization, and The Study and Its Contexts: P.L.; The Triadic Model and Discussion and Conclusions: G.A.T. All authors have read and agreed to the published version of the manuscript.

Funding: This research received no external funding.

Institutional Review Board Statement: The study was conducted according to the guidelines of the Declaration of Helsinki and ap-proved by the Institutional Review Board of PhD trials, protocol code 30216-III.11 and approved on 30 January 2021.

Informed Consent Statement: Informed consent was obtained from all subjects involved in the study.

Data Availability Statement: The data presented in this study are available in article.

Conflicts of Interest: The authors declare no conflict of interest.

References

1. Keppens, K.; Consuegra, E.; De Maeyer, S.; Vanderlinde, R. Teacher beliefs, self-efficacy and professional vision: Disentangling their relationship in the context of inclusive teaching. *J. Curric. Stud.* **2021**, *53*, 314–332. [CrossRef]
2. Caena, F.; Redecker, C. Aligning teacher competence frameworks to 21st century challenges: The case for the European Digital Competence Framework for Educators (Digcompedu). *Eur. J. Educ.* **2019**, *54*, 356–369. [CrossRef]
3. Boccioni, S.; Earp, J.; Panesi, S. *DigCompEdu. Il quadro di Riferimento Europeo Sulle Competenze Digitali dei Docenti*; Istituto per le Tecnologie Didattiche, Consiglio Nazionale delle Ricerche (CNR), 2018. Available online: https://www.itd.cnr.it/doc/DigCompEduITA.pdf (accessed on 7 June 2021).
4. Schmid, M.; Brianza, E.; Petko, D. Self-reported technological pedagogical content knowledge (TPACK) of pre-service teachers in relation to digital technology use in lesson plans. *Comput. Hum. Behav.* **2021**, *115*, 106586. [CrossRef]
5. Marek, M.W.; Chew, C.S.; Wu, W.C.V. Teacher experiences in converting classes to distance learning in the COVID-19 pandemic. *Int. J. Distance Educ. Technol.* **2021**, *19*, 40–60. [CrossRef]
6. Limone, P. Towards a hybrid ecosystem of blended learning within university contexts. In *CEUR Workshop*; Elsevier: Amsterdam, The Netherlands, 2021; p. 2817.
7. Tejasvee, S.; Gahlot, D.; Poonia, R.; Kuri, M. Digital Learning: A Proficient Digital Learning Technology Beyond to Classroom and Traditional Learning. In *Advances in Information Communication Technology and Computing*; Springer: Singapore, 2021; pp. 303–312.
8. Bernard, R.M.; Borokhovski, E.; Schmid, R.F.; Tamim, R.M.; Abrami, P.C. A meta-analysis of blended learning and technology use in higher education: From the general to the applied. *J. Comput. High. Educ.* **2014**, *26*, 87–122. [CrossRef]
9. Vo, H.M.; Zhu, C.; Diep, N.A. The effect of blended learning on student performance at course-level in higher education: A meta-analysis. *Stud. Educ. Eval.* **2017**, *53*, 17–28. [CrossRef]

10. Semenzato, A. Alma mater- how the great European universities are trying to deal with the consequences of the pandemic. In *Linkiesta*; Linkiesta.it S.r.l.: Milan, Italy, 2020.
11. Toto, G.A.; Limone, P. New Perspectives for Using the Model of the Use and Acceptance of Technology in Smart Teaching. In *International Workshop on Higher Education Learning Methodologies and Technologies Online*; Springer: Cham, Switzerland, 2020; pp. 115–125.
12. Wang, H.; Hall, N.C.; Rahimi, S. Self-efficacy and causal attributions in teachers: Effects on burnout, job satisfaction, illness, and quitting intentions. *Teach. Teach. Educ.* **2015**, *47*, 120–130. [CrossRef]
13. Lin, M.-H.; Chen, H.-C.; Liu, K.-S. A Study of the Effects of Digital Learning on Learning Motivation and Learning Outcome. *Eurasia J. Math. Sci. Technol. Educ.* **2017**, *13*, 3553–3564. [CrossRef]
14. Abou-Khalil, V.; Helou, S.; Khalifé, E.; Chen, M.A.; Majumdar, R.; Ogata, H. Emergency Online Learning in Low-Resource Settings: Effective Student Engagement Strategies. *Educ. Sci.* **2021**, *11*, 24. [CrossRef]
15. Fernández-Batanero, J.M.; Román-Graván, P.; Reyes-Rebollo, M.M.; Montenegro-Rueda, M. Impact of Educational Technology on Teacher Stress and Anxiety: A Literature Review. *Int. J. Environ. Res. Public Health* **2021**, *18*, 548. [CrossRef] [PubMed]
16. Bandura, A. *Social Foundations of Thought and Action*; Prentice-Hall: Englewood Cliffs, NJ, USA, 1986; pp. 23–28.
17. Compeau, D.R.; Higgins, C.A. Computer self-efficacy: Development of a measure and initial test. *MIS Q.* **1995**, *19*, 189–211. [CrossRef]
18. Venkatesh, V.; Bala, H. Technology acceptance model 3 and a research agenda on interventions. *Decis. Sci.* **2008**, *39*, 273–315. [CrossRef]
19. Compeau, D.; Higgins, C.A.; Huff, S. Social cognitive theory and individual reactions to computing technology: A longitudinal study. *MIS Q.* **1999**, *23*, 145–158. [CrossRef]
20. Barak, M. Science teacher education in the twenty-first century: A pedagogical framework for technology-integrated social constructivism. *Res. Sci. Educ.* **2017**, *47*, 283–303. [CrossRef]
21. Wu, J.Y.; Nian, M.W. The dynamics of an online learning community in a hybrid statistics classroom over time: Implications for the question-oriented problem-solving course design with the social network analysis approach. *Comput. Educ.* **2021**, *166*, 104120. [CrossRef]
22. Tsitsia, B.Y. Assessing Teacher-Trainees' Perceptions Regarding the Online teaching-learning mode of the Agricultural Science Course. *Int. J. Educ. Res.* **2020**, *8*, 111–124.
23. Ghazali, D. Kesahan dan Kebolehpercayaan Dalam Kajian Kuantitatif dan Kualitatif. *J. Inst. Perguru. Islam* **2008**, 61–82.
24. Cohen, S. Psychosocial vulnerabilities to upper respiratory infectious illness: Implications for susceptibility to coronavirus disease 2019 (COVID-19). *Perspect. Psychol. Sci.* **2021**, *16*, 161. [CrossRef] [PubMed]
25. Deemah, A.A.; Sumayah, A.; Dalal, A. Perceived stress among students in virtual classrooms during the COVID-19 outbreak in KSA. *J. Taibah Univ. Med Sci.* **2020**, *15*, 398–403.
26. Taylor, J.M. Psychometric analysis of the ten-item perceived stress scale. *Psychol. Assess* **2015**, *27*, 90–101. [CrossRef]
27. Roberti, J.W.; Harrington, L.N.; Storch, E.A. Further Psychometric Support for the 10-Item Version of the Perceived Stress Scale. *J. Coll. Counseling* **2006**, *9*, 135–147. [CrossRef]
28. Guajardo, J. *Teacher Motivation: Theoretical Framework, Situation Analysis of Save the Children Country Offices, and Recommended Strategies*; Save the Children: Fair-Field, CT, USA, 2011.
29. Tan, P.J.B. Applying the UTAUT to understand factors affecting the use of English e-learning websites in Taiwan. *Sage Open* **2013**, *3*, 2158244013503837. [CrossRef]
30. Heilporn, G.; Lakhal, S.; Bélisle, M. An examination of teachers' strategies to foster student engagement in blended learning in higher education. *Int. J. Educ. Technol. High. Educ.* **2021**, *18*, 1–25. [CrossRef]
31. Linn, M.; Eylon, B.; Kidron, A.; Gerard, L.; Toutkoushian, E.; Ryoo, K.; Bedell, K.D.; Swearingen, A.; Clark, D.; Virk, S.; et al. Knowledge Integration in the Digital Age: Trajectories, Opportunities and Future Directions. In *Rethinking Learning in the Digital Age: Making the Learning Sciences Count, 13th International Conference of the Learning Sciences (ICLS) 2018*; International Society of the Learning Sciences: London, UK, 2018; Volume 2.
32. Canlon, E.; Anastopoulou, S.; Conole, G.; Twiner, A. Interdisciplinary Working Methods: Reflections Based on Technology-Enhanced Learning (TEL). *Front. Educ.* **2019**, *4*, 134. [CrossRef]
33. Hodges, C.; Moore, S.; Lockee, B.; Trust, T.; Bond, A. The difference between emergency remote teaching and online learning. *Educ. Rev.* **2020**, *27*, 1–12.
34. Williamson, B.; Eynon, R.; Potter, J. Pandemic politics, pedagogies and practices: Digital technologies and distance education during the coronavirus emergency. *Learn. Media Technol.* **2020**, *45*, 107–114. [CrossRef]
35. Pérez-Paredes, P.; Guillamón, C.O.; Van de Vyver, J.; Meurice, A.; Jiménez, P.A.; Conole, G.; Hernández, P.S. Mobile data-driven language learning: Affordances and learners' perception. *System* **2019**, *84*, 145–159. [CrossRef]
36. Panisoara, I.O.; Lazar, I.; Panisoara, G.; Chirca, R.; Ursu, A.S. Motivation and Continuance Intention towards Online Instruction among Teachers during the COVID-19 Pandemic: The Mediating Effect of Burnout and Technostress. *Int. J. Environ. Res. Public Health* **2020**, *17*, 8002. [CrossRef]
37. Salikhova, N.R.; Lynch, M.F.; Salikhova, A.B. Psychological Aspects of Digital Learning: A Self-Determination Theory Perspective. *Contemp. Educ. Technol.* **2020**, *12*, ep280. [CrossRef]

38. Toto, G.; Limone, P. From Resistance to Digital Technologies in the Context of the Reaction to Distance Learning in the School Context during COVID-19. *Educ. Sci.* **2021**, *11*, 163. [CrossRef]
39. Onyema, E.M.; Eucheria, N.C.; Obafemi, F.A.; Sen, S.; Atonye, F.G.; Sharma, A.; Alsayed, A.O. Impact of Coronavirus Pandemic on Education. *J. Educ. Pract.* **2020**, *11*, 108–121.
40. Cucco, B.; Gavosto, A.; Romano, B. How to Fight Against Drop Out and Demotivation in Crisis Context: Some Insights and Examples from Italy. In *Radical Solutions for Education in a Crisis Context*; Springer: Singapore, 2021; pp. 23–36.
41. Ardizzoni, S.; Bolognesi, I.; Salinaro, M.; Scarpini, M. *Didattica a Distanza con le Famiglie: L'esperienza di Insegnanti e Genitori, in Italia e in Cina, Durante L'emergenza Sanitaria 2020. Uno Studio Preliminare. Infanzia, Famiglie, Servizi Educativi e Scolastici nel Covid-19*; University of Bologna: Bologna, Italy, 2020; p. 71. (In Italian)
42. Tan, P.J.B.; Hsu, M.H. Developing a system for English evaluation and teaching devices. In Proceedings of the 2017 International Conference on Applied System Innovation (ICASI), Sapporo, Japan, 13–17 May 2017; pp. 938–941.
43. Sprenger, D.A.; Schwaninger, A. Technology acceptance of four digital learning technologies (classroom response system, classroom chat, e-lectures, and mobile virtual reality) after three months' usage. *Int. J. Educ. Technol. High. Educ.* **2021**, *18*, 1–17. [CrossRef]
44. Fan, R.-J.D.; Tan, P.J.B. Application of Information Technology in Preschool Aesthetic Teaching from the Perspective of Sustainable Management. *Sustainbility* **2019**, *11*, 2179. [CrossRef]
45. Bolatov, A.K.; Seisembekov, T.Z.; Askarova, A.Z.; Baikanova, R.K.; Smailova, D.S.; Fabbro, E. Online-Learning due to COVID-19 Improved Mental Health Among Medical Students. *Med Sci. Educ.* **2021**, *31*, 183–192. [CrossRef] [PubMed]
46. Bao, W. COVID-19 and online teaching in higher education: A case study of Peking University. *Hum. Behav. Emerg. Technol.* **2020**, *2*, 113–115. [CrossRef] [PubMed]
47. Liu, X.; Liu, J.; Zhong, X. Psychological State of College Students during COVID-19 Epidemic (3/10/2020). Available online: https://ssrn.com/abstract=3552814 (accessed on 7 June 2021).

Article

Educational Challenges for Computational Thinking in K–12 Education: A Systematic Literature Review of "Scratch" as an Innovative Programming Tool

Hugo Montiel * and Marcela Georgina Gomez-Zermeño

School of Humanities, Tecnologico Monterrey, Monterrey 64849, Mexico; marcela.gomez@tec.mx
* Correspondence: a00600529@itesm.mx; Tel.: +52-812-354-4705

Abstract: The use of information and communications technologies (ICTs) has emerged as an educational response amidst the COVID-19 pandemic, providing students the technological tools that enable them to acquire or strengthen the necessary digital skills to develop computational knowledge. The purpose of this study was to analyze Scratch, a programming language used to foster the teaching of computational thinking, particularly in K–12 education. A systematic literature review (SLR) was conducted, identifying 30 articles on the topic of Scratch and computational thinking in the database ProQuest Central from January 2010 to May 2020. These articles were analyzed to identify the use of Scratch worldwide and the educational impact it has on computational thinking, specifically in K–12 education. The results highlight the following: (1) countries which incorporated Scratch into their teachers' study plans (curricula); (2) the transformation of learning environments that Scratch promotes; and (3) the importance of incorporating tools like Scratch in the current curricula and, more importantly, developing the framework for innovative ICTs capable of transforming education.

Keywords: computational thinking; educational innovation; K–12 education; project-based research; Scratch; teacher training; higher education

Citation: Montiel, H.; Gomez-Zermeño, M.G. Educational Challenges for Computational Thinking in K–12 Education: A Systematic Literature Review of "Scratch" as an Innovative Programming Tool. *Computers* **2021**, *10*, 69. https://doi.org/10.3390/computers10060069

Academic Editors: Antonio Sarasa Cabezuelo, Covadonga Rodrigo San Juan and Santi Caballé

Received: 14 April 2021
Accepted: 17 May 2021
Published: 21 May 2021

Publisher's Note: MDPI stays neutral with regard to jurisdictional claims in published maps and institutional affiliations.

Copyright: © 2021 by the authors. Licensee MDPI, Basel, Switzerland. This article is an open access article distributed under the terms and conditions of the Creative Commons Attribution (CC BY) license (https://creativecommons.org/licenses/by/4.0/).

1. Introduction

It is a reality that the COVID-19 pandemic brought socioeconomic disruptions and technological changes worldwide. Political, social, religious, and sporting events were canceled to promote social distancing and prevent the virus from spreading widely. The educational sector is no exception, and institutions had to take measures based on their human capabilities and technological resources. Some institutions decided to finish their ongoing school terms abruptly, while others adapted their operations to the sanitary requirements forced by the pandemic. In general, the coronavirus pandemic presents a significant challenge to teachers at all educational levels. This hurdle demands the development of new competencies in using computational tools and the continuous adaptation of digital pedagogical strategies to meet the students' needs.

As this digital transformation has advanced, the skills that students must possess have been changing along with emerging technologies. Countries feel the need to make changes to their educational systems to ensure that students acquire these new skills [1]. In K–12 education, computational thinking (CT) is an important part of cultivating students' key abilities [2]. Lonka mentions "that students should learn to identify the central principles and practices of programming and understand how it affects everyday life" [3]. Despite its recent acclaim, there have been some drawbacks and uncertainty surrounding CT regarding teacher training and development for understanding the aims and intentions of CT education [4].

Contributions such as Zhang and Nouri's SLR on Scratch have laid the foundation for the relationship between Scratch, problem solving, computing, and programming at the K–9 level [5]. Other studies, like the systematic literature review on computational thinking with Scratch by Fagerlund et al. [4], emphasize the concepts associated with CT and CT fostering in primary education while acknowledging the importance of refining and validating meaningful ways to assess CT in students' projects and programming processes. Moreno-León and Robles's review [6] presents studies on the use of Scratch for enhancing and developing not only CT skills, but competencies and capabilities beyond programming or coding skills. Considering the aforementioned reviews as a springboard, this study intends to review and summarize the literature about the use of Scratch as a digital tool to promote CT in K–12 education. The analysis can serve as one of the catalysts for the digital transformation that has been forced by COVID-19.

The results of this review intend to show how countries around the world have incorporated CT not only into their students' curricula but, more importantly, into formative plans for teachers. Understanding what features make Scratch a feasible tool to teach CT while innovating and renewing the traditional learning environment is of the utmost importance, given the disruption in the educational setting. Motivated by the shift in pedagogical strategies and the introduction of computational thinking as an essential skill to be developed in primary education, we aim to evaluate the impact Scratch has on learning environments and how it could possibly encourage the development of teacher training frameworks to support CT learning. The study also strives for answers to the questions concerning whether Scratch could serve as a digital answer to the challenges and difficulties presented by COVID-19, supporting the idea of the development of technological competencies among educators to be better prepared for future contingencies or disruptions to education.

1.1. Computational Thinking as an Educational Challenge

Information and communications technologies (ICTs) are more present than ever in the educational setting, although this was not always the case. At the end of the 1970s, an official report emphasized the importance of differentiating between informatics as a subject and informatics as a teaching and learning tool [7]. This report prompted, at the time, the creation of an elective informatics course, whose goal was not to teach programming languages but to promote an algorithmic way of thinking that would be useful for other subjects [8]. This way of thinking led to the belief that informatics should not be taught as a discrete subject; rather, it should be learned and mastered in different disciplines supported by the integration of ICT tools. Programming, which had long been a major concern in the world of computational education, was no longer considered accessible for everyone [9].

The 21st century brought initiatives that acknowledged the need for informatics skills to be taught and assessed in the learning environment. Associations like Public Education and Informatics, which brings together educators, researchers, and activists, have been stressing the urgent need to include informatics as a subject in schools from an early age [8]. This approach allowed new ICT tools and skills to emerge, with multiple benefits to the achievement of learning objectives [10].

One of these skills is CT which, according to Wing, "involves solving problems, designing systems, and understanding human behavior by drawing on the concepts fundamental to computer science" [11]. Fundamentally, CT involves breaking down complex problems into familiar and manageable subproblems, using a sequence of steps or instructions to provide a solution to set problems, reviewing the solution's transferability to similar problems, and finally, determining if a computer process is able to help solve those problems more efficiently [12]. In summary, the idea of CT is to allow students to develop an understanding of computing and programming competencies, thus allowing them to move from being users of technology to producers of information technology [13]. As this view had been accepted by many, in 2016, the International Society for Technology in Education (ISTE) [14], which developed the standards for teachers and students to use technology in teaching–learning processes, included CT in the basic skills to be acquired by students. Aiming for emancipation through training is undoubtedly a laudable goal, but it is very difficult to achieve. Technologies, in the guise of openness, too often reinforce social silos [10].

1.2. Scratch Used as an Innovative Educational Response

Scratch is a programming language that provides students with the means to create stories, animations, games, and music and to share projects on the web [15]. It is one of the emerging technologies that can be applied to interactive game design, storytelling, animation, and multimedia projects in the classroom [16].

Scratch scripts are created by putting together blocks that represent programming statements, expressions, and control structures. The shapes of the blocks suggest how they fit together, and the drag-and-drop system does not allow connecting blocks in ways that would have no effect on the programming logic [17]. This approach, known as block-based programming, is easy to understand because the blocks are described in common language which, combined with the aforementioned drag-and-drop interactions and the convenience of browsing programming languages, makes its mastery attainable [2]. Scratch's trial and error design allows students to play with situations, modify parameters on the fly, and tinker, all while coding without having to write an algorithm [18]. Scratch builds on the constructionist ideas of Logo and Etoys and provides a bridge to Brennan and Resnick's framework, which is likely to be suitable for CT in the programming contexts of K–12 education [19–25]. Scratch's popularity and userbase make it one of the predominant ITC tools to start teaching computational thinking (CT) to students from a young age.

It is not farfetched to assume that, given Scratch's features and capabilities, institutions would include it in their formative plans for teachers. Surprisingly, that is not the case, as mentioned by Fagerlund [4], who stated that there have been some shortcomings and uncertainty surrounding CT in terms of teacher training needs and the aims and intentions of CT education. There is a present need for frameworks and guides like Csizmadia's [26], which supports teaching CT concepts, approaches, and techniques in the classroom.

1.3. Project-Based Research to Develop Computational Thinking in Grades K–12

Moving toward the education of the future involves an extensive modernization of all educational processes. Such modernization includes the introduction of smart technologies, systems, and devices that create new opportunities for training organizations to have higher standards and employ innovative solutions. Education should be transformed rather than reformed to confront the digital challenges successfully. The key to this transformation is not to standardize education but to personalize it, discover the individual talents of each child, and place the students in an environment where they want to learn and naturally discover their true passions [27–29]. To perform such a transformation, educators have launched many initiatives to promote computer sciences and programming among the population, especially among children. Learning how to program a computer has many benefits for those who practice it, but the best one is that it helps people think about solving problems [28].

In France, the National Research Agency (ANR) promotes project-based research to stimulate innovation by promoting collaborative, multidisciplinary projects between the public and private sectors. Through the IE-CARE project, it was proposed to "set up sustainable modalities for informatics curricula in compulsory education" [30]. One of the main interests is to know how to articulate different content throughout the first three French school cycles progressively. This research project has "a multidisciplinary character, bringing together researchers in the humanities, social sciences, and informatics" [30]. It employs three main axes that depict a transversal task aimed at ensuring convergence in the research [30]. The first axis identifies teachable concepts and pedagogical practices. The second axis aims at designing, testing, and validating pedagogical scenarios and resources both in primary school and junior high school. The third axis "focuses on building a framework that supports teachers and trainers in informatics" [30].

The IE-CARE project "aims to develop a culture in informatics as well as a technical culture that includes professional development for primary school teachers and people in charge of supervising the teachers' actions" [30]. During the transversal task of the first and second axes for the extraction of teachable content and proposals for curricula and instruments, a systematic literature review (SLR) was conducted to identify studies related to Scratch being used as a tool to facilitate CT teaching in K–12 or K–9 educational settings. The following research question was proposed: Which elements should be considered in a teacher training framework to support learning computational thinking through Scratch in K–9 or K–12?

Before following the methodology of Brereton et al. [31] pertaining to SLRs, we divided our main objective into three sub-objectives which would guide our study. These sub-objectives are later addressed in the methods and materials section. It is pertinent to mention this, as these subjects of interest will serve as inclusion and exclusion criteria while reviewing the existing literature. The following section introduces the findings for each of the sub-objectives within the selected literature.

2. Results

As part of the Brereton et al. [31] methodology, the document review phase pertains to the creation and validation of a written report with the findings of the study, which are presented as the results related to the proposed research questions presented in the previous phase. The tools used for the illustrated figures were Vosviewer and Tableau.

2.1. RQ1: Scratch around the World in Formative Plans for Teachers in K–12 and K–9 Education as a Means to Develop Computational Thinking (CT)

Given the acceptance of CT as a necessary skill in the educational setting, we sought to find within the studies the countries that incorporated Scratch in the development and formative plans for their teachers [2]. Having these lessons incorporated into the curricula would raise the question of whether the teachers or students have the skills necessary to apply them.

The first study found was in Italy, where an empirical experiment was carried out with 141 Italian preservice teachers who attended a programming course. Demir reports that the program had the following aims: (1) use Scratch 2.0 to provide them the main coding concepts, (2) offer practical advice on how to design educational applications to be used in the school context, and (3) assess their applications by applying an already existing methodology for giving them feedback on their programming expertise and CT skills [32].

The impact Scratch has had in Turkey is evident because there are 484,137 users of Scratch in this country, which comprises 1.44 percent of Scratch users around the world (as of 20 February 2019). Turkey is second only to the USA in Scratch usage, according to Scratch's worldwide map [33]. The developments in coding education have positively contributed to the coding education in Turkey, and consequently, a course titled Information Technologies and Software has been incorporated in the curricula of grades five and above since the 2012–2013 academic year [33]. One of the studies selected was Uzunboylu et al. [34], which aimed to analyze the countries where coding training was integrated into their curricula and compare them to studies on coding training, particularly in Turkey.

Initiatives in the United Kingdom, New Zealand, and Denmark suggest an imperative movement toward training young minds in computing. The fact that countries are implementing more and more programs does not help the problem of the shortage of teachers to teach introductory computing [35]. Such is the case of the VELA project, implemented in a diverse urban district in the United States of America. The purpose of this project was to introduce four concepts to students, namely variables (V), expressions (E), looping (L), and abstraction (A) in a new pedagogical approach toward computational understanding. This project required teachers to participate in two days of professional development. Teachers learned about the VELA rationale and the principles guiding the curriculum design. They participated in roleplaying during the curriculum's enactment, engaged in hands-on activities to experience using the curriculum and reviewing lesson plans [36].

Israel, to assess whether creating games proved to be compelling for learning computational concepts and practices, conducted a study among seventh- to ninth-grade students in middle school for three years (2011–2013). The students were in a new CS curriculum that used Scratch. The results of that study led to changes in the teaching methods for loop concepts [37].

Greece decided to implement a program to help primary and secondary education teachers acquire a solid comprehension of the basic programming concepts which are common in all programming languages [29,38]. They decided to use Scratch because it is effective for introducing programming concepts. Trainee evaluations for this project were positive; the trainees indicated that they would like to participate in another learning activity with more advanced topics [39].

Many internationally funded programs can be found among the studies that include "Code Week", "Hour of Code", and "Computer Science for All" [40]. These programs intend to reinforce the coding skills of students and teachers using a mixture of pedagogical approaches and technologies [39,41,42]. Figure 1 and Table 1 illustrate the countries and initiatives that incorporate Scratch in their formative plans, as well as the occurrence of mentions for each country throughout the studies.

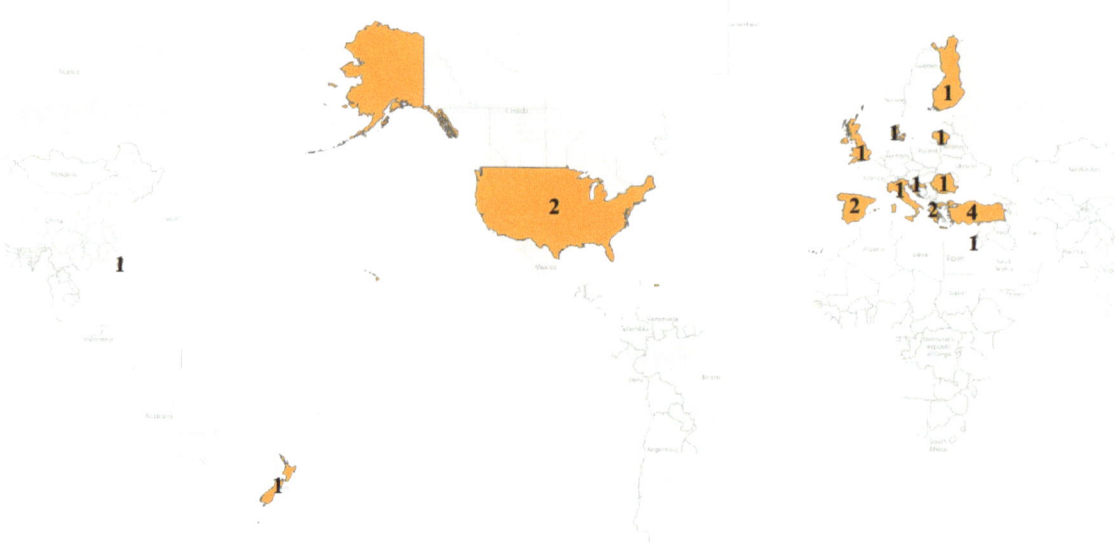

Figure 1. Countries that incorporate Scratch in formative plans.

2.2. RQ2: Features of Scratch to Assist in Teaching CT in K–12 and K–9 Education

The second aspect we considered in the study pertained to identifying the features mentioned in the literature that described Scratch as a feasible tool for CT instruction. We decided to organize the different elements of Scratch mentioned in the studies into categories.

The most prominent category among the studies concerned the problem solving, logical thinking approach that Scratch uses. The Scratch members learn their problem solving and project design skills (e.g., logical reasoning and debugging problems), along with specific programming concepts (e.g., sequence, looping, conditional statements, variables, arrays, and Boolean logic) as they create digital media in Scratch [6,16,43–45]. This approach allows students to acquire programming skills, as Ali Oluk et al. [1] stated that individuals need to find different solutions to problems and select the fastest path. Finding the fastest path requires understanding the logic of the algorithm well. Çakıroğlu et al. [46] concurred with Hagge [43] and stated that "researchers believe students should acquire procedural, conditional, and analogical thinking skills in the programming process, which will allow students to assess the thought process of the problem as well".

Table 1. Countries' initiatives regarding CT and Scratch.

Country	Description
Turkey	Information technologies and Software incorporated into fifth grade curricula. Second biggest Scratch user in the world.
Italy	Scratch was incorporated into programming courses to assess programming expertise and CT skills of preservice teachers.
United Kingdom	Formulated computing curriculum as a result of the Royal Society policy charter.
New Zealand	Implemented the Computer Science Unplugged project, which included Scratch activities.
United States	VELA project targeted teachers to introduce programming concepts and computational understanding.
Israel	Introduced CT into school curriculum to further develop Israeli high-tech industry.
Greece	Program based on Scratch to introduce basic programming concepts to educators.

The second commonality we discovered among the studies concerned the social dynamic that Scratch provides. With over 21 million registered users, Scratch is the largest online programming community for youth [43]. Therefore, Scratch can provide students a social platform to share their creations. The "do it yourself" (DIY) culture embodied in Scratch is reflective of a trend in the literacy practices of youth to shift toward DIY media [47]. This increase in DIY media aligns with the "maker movement" defined by Halverson and Sheridan [48]. A growing number of people who engage in the creative production of artifacts find physical and digital forums to share their processes and products with others. The idea of "computational participation" is compelling as a social motivator to learn computing, especially for younger learners [35,38,41,42,49].

Block-based programming was another common denominator in the studies analyzed. As fifth- and sixth-grade students are mostly still in the pre-formal phase of cognitive development, programming games in visual programming languages offer them real experience in learning complex programming concepts [6,35,44]. Visual programming blocks allow syntax problems to be eliminated, thus permitting students to focus on algorithms [2,50]. Lee [51] even compared visual programming blocks to "putting together jigsaw puzzles or LEGO pieces, using a computer mouse instead of typing program-language constructs on a computer keyboard" [16,37,50,51]. These ideas compliment Traylor's statement of new technologies having a "low floor" and a "high ceiling", making it easy for people to get started while also allowing advanced users to do more complex things as well [25,41]. Although some authors like Hagge and Deng think that this approach limits the coding schema required for children to create projects, they acknowledge that one key goal should be to increase accessibility to coding concepts [2,43].

Some other concepts were mentioned throughout the studies, but the three described above were the most numerous.

2.3. RQ3: Scratch and Its Impact on the Design of Learning Environments and Teaching Resources in K–12 and K–9 Education

Our last research question aims to collect information regarding how Scratch helps in the design of learning environments in K–12 and K–9 education. Scratch was used in different ways throughout the studies as a tool to strengthen lesson plans and educational resources. Lee states that Scratch can provide an excellent platform for education researchers and practitioners to develop creative, enjoyable, interdisciplinary curriculum materials, becoming a creative medium for students to express their imagination and making school subjects considered boring and difficult more meaningful and engaging [41,42,51]. Scratch helps elementary learners create projects such as animations, games, and simulations amusingly, turning programming into a pleasurable, visual learning experience rather than a textual struggle [50,52].

Scratch is also found to foster subskills of computational thinking skills, namely creative thinking, algorithmic thinking, critical thinking, collaborative learning, and communication skills, which are similar to the skills expected from today's students [6,38,49,53]. The task-based learning environments provided by Scratch enhance motivation and cognitive outcomes [54]. As an example, the progression of early computational thinking model by Seiter and Foreman [55] can be considered useful for establishing age-appropriate curricula and defining lesson plans aligned with the students' cognitive development stages [32,55].

Some studies showed that teachers had positive experiences while incorporating Scratch and were eager to find ways to integrate CT into their lesson plans seamlessly [40]. There are several benefits to incorporating programming and simulations in the classroom. Simulations are effective at promoting scientific understanding. Many students are visual learners, and allowing them to visualize what they are being taught can help them remember it [43,56,57].

Specifics about the social features of Scratch mentioned in the studies include different tasks that involve creating a project, testing it, demonstrating it to the entire class, documenting and writing reflections on it, and playing with each other's games in the online studio [35]. Scratch emerged with an implicit belief that if learners could share and show some of their accomplishments, they would learn well and learn more. No longer merely recipients of knowledge, children create and publish an array of texts as they interact in virtual social spaces. As youths explore new ways to communicate and engage in an increasingly globalized world, the ways they find to make meaning expand [40,43].

Nowadays, educators lean toward designing active and dynamic learning environments based on instructional methodologies centered around the student. This new environment should be aligned with the availability and use of technologies in the classroom [58]. One common thought shared in the studies was the idea that the implementation of tools like Scratch motivates institutions to rethink and redesign instructional approaches and plans.

To further strengthen the findings on the studies, a density visualization of the most-mentioned concepts amongst the articles is illustrated in Figure 2. The concepts were limited to no less than 100 occurrences in all 30 articles. Entries such as student (1358), problem (646), programming (665), skill (500), process (348), computational thinking (328), program (280), block (259) were among the most mentioned concepts. The most-mentioned concepts are presented in Table 2.

Table 2. Concepts mentioned throughout the studies.

No.	Concept	Mentions
1	Student	1358
2	Problem	646
3	Programming	665
4	Skill	500
5	Process	348
6	Computational Thinking	328
7	Program	280
8	Block	259
9	Variable	178
10	Instruction	124

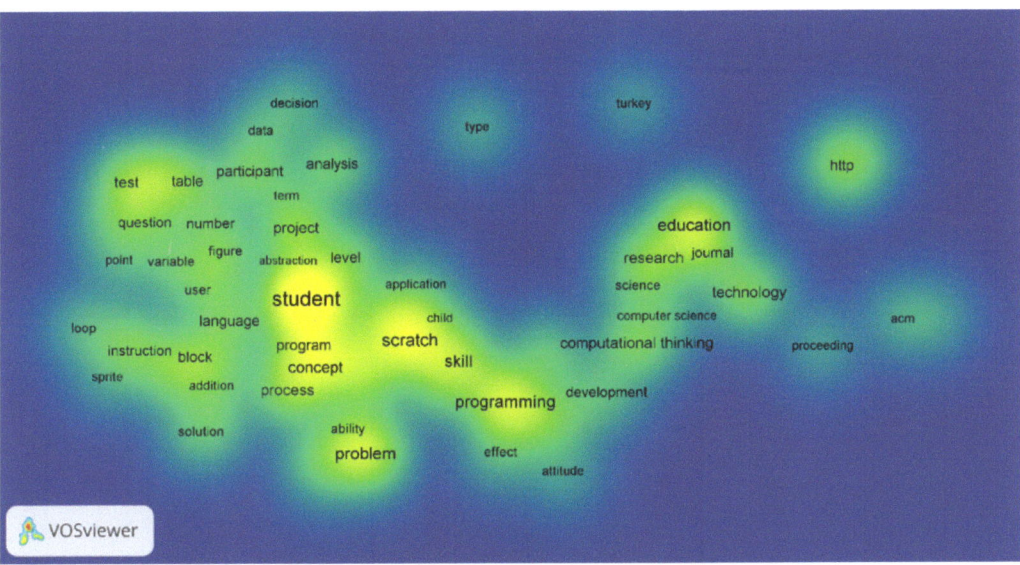

Figure 2. Density visualization of the frequency of concepts on Scratch (threshold of 100 occurrences, displaying 54 concepts).

3. Discussion

As the SLR was conducted, information was generated to answer the research question: Which elements should be considered in a teacher training framework to support learning computational thinking through Scratch in K–9 and K–12 education?

The rising popularity today of CT as a requisite skill for students has pushed countries to design, implement, and incorporate CT in the formative plans of the teachers' curricula as an element to be considered. The SLR results showed that the evaluation phase some countries conducted to determine Scratch's feasibility to teach CT concluded with leading the way into the implementation phase, where long-term formative assessments were designed to cope with the students' need for CT. Therefore, there is a need to provide teachers an understanding of the role CT plays not only in problem solving but also in other cognitive domains. The implementation of teacher training programs should create an educational path to teach, include, and assess CT abilities [32].

Scratch's features, reviewed throughout the SLR, suggest that the symbiotic relationship with the ever-changing educational paradigms and settings is another element to be considered. The shift in learning environments toward a DIY approach correlates with the self-paced dynamic Scratch presents. This, in turn, helps transition the role of the teacher into a more passive facilitator who guides the student into acquiring knowledge through the use of technology. Scratch nurtures the creation of such environments by incorporating technology in a gamified environment that results in students learning and fostering skills other than just CT. Creating inspiring and motivational learning environments for students has become of paramount importance and needs to be considered in a teacher training framework.

Some studies, like Hagge's [43], concur that "the vacuum-controlled environment Scratch provides limits the ways students can solve a problem and restricts their creativity; nonetheless, most studies agree that at these stages of primary education, it is more important to introduce coding concepts at the expense of flexibility". It is necessary to consider that, restricted or not, Scratch encourages the development of creativity and problem solving via the implementation of different routes or solutions to the same problem. It is also necessary to carefully consider how teachers use the affordances of computing tools and not merely put them in front of their students [44]. These observations bolster the argument that classroom management and course design by the teachers are crucial. Teachers should apply CT environments in their multidisciplinary teaching practice and guide students to transfer this thinking into multiple fields [2].

4. Materials and Method

An SLR was conducted to provide insights for a teacher training framework to support learning computational thinking through Scratch in K–12 and K–9 educational settings. Following the principles stated by Brereton et al. [31], this review will serve as a means of evaluating and interpreting all available research relevant to a particular research question, topic area, or phenomenon of interest. We grouped the SLR activities into three main phases (see Figure 3): (1) plan review, (2) conduct review, and (3) document review. [31,59].

Figure 3. SLR phases, as suggested by Brereton et al. [31].

4.1. Plan Review

The first phase of the SLR methodology described by Kitchenham et al. [56] allowed us to develop and validate a strategy that revolved around specific research questions. Before stating these questions, an exploratory review was conducted to identify possible gaps in the subject of computational thinking and K–12 or K–9 education. Consequently, as part of our plan review phase, the research questions, search engine (database), keywords, and inclusion and exclusion criteria for document selection were stated. As suggested by the authors, the research questions were based on knowledge gaps identified in the field of study for a specific period [60,61].

4.1.1. Research Question and SLR Protocol

To generate the relevant information to answer the research question, three questions were established:

RQ1. Which countries incorporate Scratch in the formative plans for teachers in K–12 or K–9 education as a means to develop computational thinking (CT)?
RQ2. Which features of Scratch assist in teaching CT in K–12 and K–9 education?
RQ3. How does Scratch encourage the design of learning environments and teaching resources in K–12 and K–9 education?

4.1.2. Database and Search Terms

To include academic publications for this review, we selected the *ProQuest Central* database. We created a search string for each of the proposed questions (see Table 3). The three major terms were "Computational Thinking," "Scratch," and "K–12 or K–9 Education." The search strings were constructed using a Boolean "AND" to join the main terms and "OR" to include synonyms [31].

Table 3. Search strings in ProQuest Central.

No.	Research Question	Keywords	Results
RQ1	(AB(Scratch) AND ((Computational Thinking OR CT) OR (Programming OR Computer) Logic) AND (K–12 OR K–9) AND (Training OR Development OR Teaching OR Skills)) AND (stype.exact("Scholarly Journals") AND pd(20100426-20200426))	Scratch, Computational Thinking, CT, Programming Logic, Computer Logic, K–12, K–9, Training, Development, Teaching, Skills	38
RQ2	(AB(Scratch) AND ((Computational Thinking OR CT) OR (Programming OR Computer) Logic) AND (K–12 OR K–9) AND (Teaching OR Skills)) AND (stype.exact("Scholarly Journals") AND pd(20100426-20200426))	Scratch, Computational Thinking, CT, Programming Logic, Computer Logic, K–12, K–9, Teaching, Skills	36
RQ3	(AB(Scratch) AND (Learning Environment OR Educational Resources OR Facilities) AND (K–12 OR K–9) AND (Development OR Teaching OR Learning OR Learn OR Teach)) AND (stype.exact("Scholarly Journals") AND pd(20100426-20200426))	Scratch, Learning Environment, Educational Resources, Facilities, K–12, K–9, Training, Development, Teaching, Skills, Learning, Learn, Teach	37

4.1.3. Inclusion and Exclusion Criteria

Following Ramírez-Montoya's work [62], a set of detailed inclusion and exclusion criteria (see Table 4) was designed to identify whether a study could help answer the specified research questions [31]. The word Scratch by itself presented an issue, because the idiom "start from Scratch" is commonly used to refer to something or someone starting from the beginning or with no aid or help. We decided to include all studies that mentioned the word "scratch" in their "Abstract" sections. We did this intentionally to avoid any studies that mentioned Scratch merely as an example of a visual programming environment or as part of the idiom. Even with this condition, some studies mentioned Scratch simply as an example of a visual programming environment or idiom. The conduct review phase later addressed these studies by selecting only the ones that centered their research around the programming language Scratch. The scope of this review considered academic publications no older than ten years (2010).

Table 4. Inclusion and exclusion criteria.

Inclusion Criteria	Exclusion Criteria
Academic publications	Studies mention Scratch only as an example of a visual programming environment
Publishing date no older than 2010	Non-academic publications
Studies that focus on Scratch and computational thinking	The word "scratch" used as part of an idiom
Studies that center around K–12 or K–9 education	

4.1.4. Limitations of the Study

Possible limitations of this study include the use of ProQuest Central as the primary source used to conduct the study, and the use of additional databases to further complement the review for future works is encouraged. There are examples in the literature such Zhao's, which suggested that multiple database engines should be used for a valid systematic review. However, there is evidence offered by Bramer et al. regarding single database publications [63,64]. This is an ongoing debate among systematic literature review authors and a potential critique of this study, depending on the reader's point of view. In light of Scratch's young age (launched in 2007), the review was limited to publications no older than a 10 years (2010–present). This fact creates a methodological debate for future work, we suggest that the date selection for articles be reviewed, given that programming tools, programming paradigms, and processing power are constantly evolving at a rapid pace.

Another limitation of this study was the primary focus on Scratch's impact on K–9 and K–12 education. There is no doubt that computational thinking extends beyond primary education, and thus future work should consider analyzing the impact tools like Scratch have on middle and higher education. Publication bias should be another factor to consider, as Kitchenham and Charters [65] stated that studies with positive results are more likely to be published than negative ones, resulting in an overly positive review of the use of Scratch rather than a full spectrum of views. In an effort to diminish validity threats posed to the study, we addressed each of the validity threats identified in Feldt and Magazinius's work [66]. We considered the external validity and transferability of our findings by stating the limitations of our work and presenting a general overview of the use of Scratch in the educational setting in different contexts. This was done to avoid wrongful generalization by only analyzing the use of Scratch in a particular setting. Regarding dependability, the methodology used for this study was stated in detail by presenting each of the steps taken to elaborate the report. The inclusion and exclusion criteria for document selection were included to enable the results to be consistent and replicable. As stated by Ramirez-Montoya, it is the nature of an SLR to introduce the findings of a specific subject from the existing literature. We are confident the reviewed publications are reliable sources of information, thus diminishing any credibility threats to our study [60].

4.2. Conduct Review

During this phase, studies that fulfilled the search terms for each research question were listed and input into a spreadsheet (link: https://figshare.com/s/3386a37cff72deee02ce (accessed on 4 January 2021). The search produced 111 results, which were then filtered to eliminate duplicates. Once the duplicates were removed, a detailed review was conducted to assess the relevance of the studies to the proposed research questions. This review discarded 81 studies as either duplicates or not having relevance to the research questions for this review, thus returning a total of 30 studies (see Table 5), that met the protocol developed in the first phase of the methodology. Figure 4 illustrates the process that took place for selection of the studies.

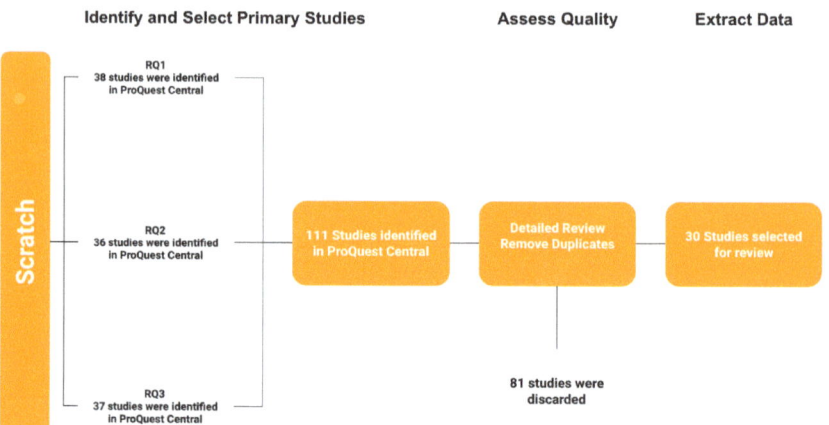

Figure 4. SLR conduct review phase.

Table 5. Studies selected for the review.

#	Authors	Item Type	Title
1	Halverson, E.; Sheridan, K.	Journal Article	The Maker Movement in Education
2	Burke, Q.	Book Section	DIY zones for Scratch design in class and club
3	Traylor, S.	Journal Article	Scratch that: MIT's Mitchel Resnick Says Kids Should Do It for Themselves
4	Demir, Ö.; Seferoglu, S.	Journal Article	Developing a Scratch-based coding achievement test
5	Moreno-León, J.; Robles, G.	Conference Paper	Code to learn with Scratch? A systematic literature review
6	Yadav, A.; Cooper, S.	Journal Article	Education fostering creativity through computing
7	Haduong, P.	Journal Article	"I like computers. I hate coding": a portrait of two teens' experiences
8	Gross, K; Gross, S	Journal Article	TRANSFORMATION: Constructivism, Design Thinking, and Elementary STEAM
9	Grover, S.; Jackiw, N.; Lundh, P.	Journal Article	Concepts before coding: non-programming interactives to advance learning of introductory programming concepts in middle school
10	Erümit, A.	Journal Article	Effects of different teaching approaches on programming skills
11	Deng, W. et al.	Journal Article	Pencil Code improves learners' computational thinking and computer learning attitude
12	Pellas, N.; Vosinakis, S.	Journal Article	The effect of simulation games on learning computer programming: A comparative study on high school students' learning performance by assessing computational problem-solving strategies
13	Oluk, A.; Korkmaz, Ö.; Oluk, H.	Journal Article	Effect of Scratch on 5th Graders' Algorithm Development and Computational Thinking Skills
14	Tang, K.; Chou, T.; Tsai, C.	Journal Article	A Content Analysis of Computational Thinking Research: An International Publication Trends and Research Typology
15	Yildiz Durak, H.	Journal Article	The effects of using different tools in programming teaching of secondary school students on engagement, computational thinking and reflective thinking skills for problem solving
16	Hagge, J.	Journal Article	Coding to Create: A Subtext of Decisions as Early Adolescents Design Digital Media
17	Mladenović, M.; Boljat, I.; Žanko, Ž.	Journal Article	Comparing loops misconceptions in block-based and text-based programming languages at the K–12 level
18	Lee, Y.J.	Journal Article	Scratch: Multimedia Programming Environment for Young Gifted Learners
19	Grover, S.; Pea, R.; Cooper, S.	Journal Article	Designing for deeper learning in a blended computer science course for middle school students
20	Chang, C.	Journal Article	Effects of Using Alice and Scratch in an Introductory Programming Course for Corrective Instruction
21	Sáez-López, J.; Cózar-Gutiérrez, R.	Journal Article	Programación visual por bloques en Educación Primaria: Aprendiendo y creando contenidos en Ciencias Sociales
22	Martin, C.	Journal Article	Libraries as Facilitators of Coding for All
23	Uzunboylu, H.; Kinik, E.; Kanbul, S.	Journal Article	An Analysis of Countries which have Integrated Coding into their Curricula and the Content Analysis of Academic Studies on Coding Training in Turkey
24	Lazarinis, F. et al.	Journal Article	A blended learning course for playfully teaching programming concepts to school teachers
25	Çakiroğlu, Ü. et al.	Journal Article	Exploring perceived cognitive load in learning programming via Scratch
26	Gabriele, L. et al.	Journal Article	Lesson Planning by Computational Thinking Skills in Italian Pre-Service Teachers
27	Adler, R.; Kim, H.	Journal Article	Enhancing future K–8 teachers' computational thinking skills through modeling and simulations
28	Romero, M.; Lepage, A.; Lille, B.	Journal Article	Computational thinking development through creative programming in higher education
29	Oluk, A.; Korkmaz, Ö.	Journal Article	Comparing Students' Scratch Skills with Their Computational Thinking Skills in Terms of Different Variables
30	Seiter, L.; Foreman, B.	Conference Paper	Modeling the learning progressions of computational thinking of primary grade students

5. Conclusions

Today, project-based research on developing a culture in informatics and a technical culture that includes professional development for primary teachers and people in charge of supervising teachers' actions is needed more than ever. The tools of ICT develop at an accelerated rate, creating a pressing need for curricular frameworks that can cope with their velocity. Research projects, like that of IE-CARE, must be set in motion to generate the knowledge required to rise to the challenges of whatever impact the pandemic might have on educational outcomes.

The theoretical contribution of this study is to provide elements to be considered in a teacher training framework to support learning computational thinking through Scratch in K–9 and K–12 education. Scratch is an innovative tool to help younger-aged students learn introductory programming concepts. The reviewed features of Scratch suggest that it not only has the potential to teach CT skills but also competencies in subjects that are not related to ICT. Its ease of use, accessibility, and trial-and-error approach make it an appealing tool for educators to implement, creating a bridge between the complex programming syntax and playful storytelling and animated scene creation. The ability to use Scratch for creativity and problem solving should inspire teachers to design and implement activities and resources that cater to students' academic needs.

This framework may also serve to support other disciplinary programs where technology plays an important role in the response to the COVID-19 educational disruption. A culture focused on the development of competencies among primary school teachers will prepare them for any future contingencies that disrupt or change education. An imperative need in our society is to prepare teachers with skills to design and deliver content efficiently, and this requires adequate experience with curricula and a reasonable time of practice. There are still significant issues to be addressed in the design and implementation of CT in educational curricula. Long gone are the days when research focused on whether technology in the educational setting would benefit the students. We need to move past that era and embrace the reality that technology is inherent in the learning processes and environments, especially in the context of educational disruptions like the one imposed by the COVID-19 pandemic. Future research should center on how and when technology should be incorporated into the classroom rather than discuss why and if it should be in educational settings. The COVID-19 disruption brought undesired challenges to the continuity of education. These must be addressed with the appropriate design and implementation of digital pedagogy and technological tools to ensure that the disruption in education is limited.

Author Contributions: Conceptualization, H.M. and M.G.G.-Z.; data curation, H.M. and M.G.G.-Z.; formal analysis, H.M. and M.G.G.-Z.; funding acquisition, H.M. and M.G.G.-Z.; investigation, H.M. and M.G.G.-Z.; methodology, H.M. and M.G.G.-Z.; project administration, H.M. and M.G.G.-Z.; resources, H.M. and M.G.G.-Z.; software, H.M. and M.G.G.-Z.; supervision, H.M. and M.G.G.-Z.; validation, H.M. and M.G.G.-Z.; visualization, H.M. and M.G.G.-Z.; writing—original draft, H.M. and M.G.G.-Z.; writing—review & editing, H.M. and M.G.G.-Z. Both authors have read and agreed to the published version of the manuscript.

Funding: This research received no external funding.

Data Availability Statement: Authors can confirm that all relevant data are included in the article.

Acknowledgments: The authors acknowledge the contributions of Eric Brouillard and George-Luis Baron from Laboratoire EDA of the Université René Descartes, members of the IE-CARE project supported by the French National Research Agency (ANR). The authors would also like to acknowledge the financial support of Writing Lab, Institute for the Future of Education, Tecnologico de Monterrey, Mexico, in the production of this work.

Conflicts of Interest: The authors declare no conflict of interest.

References

1. Oluk, A.; Korkmaz, Ö.; Oluk, H.A. Effect of Scratch on 5th Graders' Algorithm Development and Computational Thinking Skills. *Turk. J. Comput. Math. Educ. (TURCOMAT)* **2018**, *9*, 1. [CrossRef]
2. Deng, W.; Pi, Z.; Lei, W.; Zhou, Q.; Zhang, W. Pencil Code improves learners' computational thinking and computer learning attitude. *Comput. Appl. Eng. Educ.* **2020**, *28*, 90–104. [CrossRef]
3. Hair, J.F.; Anderson, R.E.; Tatham, R.L.; Black, W.C. *Análisis Multivariante*; Prentice Hall: Madrid, Spain, 1999; ISBN 9788578110796.
4. Fagerlund, J.; Häkkinen, P.; Vesisenaho, M.; Viiri, J. Computational thinking in programming with Scratch in primary schools: A systematic review. *Comput. Appl. Eng. Educ.* **2021**, *29*, 12–28. [CrossRef]
5. Zhang, L.; Nouri, J. A systematic review of learning computational thinking through Scratch in K-9. *Comput. Educ.* **2019**, *141*, 103607. [CrossRef]
6. Moreno-Leon, J.; Robles, G. Code to learn with Scratch? A systematic literature review. In Proceedings of the 2016 IEEE Global Engineering Education Conference (EDUCON), Abu Dhabi, United Arab Emirates, 10–13 April 2016; pp. 150–156.
7. Simon, J.-C. *L'éducation et l'informatisation de La Société*. Documentation Francaise, 1980. Available online: https://www.epi.asso.fr/revue/histo/h80simon2.htm (accessed on 24 August 2020).

8. Baron, G.-L.; Drot-Delange, B.; Grandbastien, M.; Tort, F. Computer Science Education in French Secondary Schools. *ACM Trans. Comput. Educ.* **2014**, *14*, 1–27. [CrossRef]
9. Baron, G.-L.; Bruillard, E. Information technology, informatics and pre-service teacher training. *J. Comput. Assist. Learn.* **1994**, *10*, 2–13. [CrossRef]
10. Bruillard, E. Sesame Street et l'évaluation Des Technologies Éducatives. Available online: https://adjectif.net.shs.parisdescartes.fr/spip.php?article533 (accessed on 25 August 2020).
11. Wing, J.M. Computational thinking. *Commun. ACM* **2006**, *49*, 33–35. [CrossRef]
12. Yadav, A.; Hong, H.; Stephenson, C. Computational Thinking for All: Pedagogical Approaches to Embedding 21st Century Problem Solving in K-12 Classrooms. *TechTrends* **2016**, *60*, 565–568. [CrossRef]
13. Yadav, A.; Mayfield, C.; Zhou, N.; Hambrusch, S.; Korb, J.T. Computational Thinking in Elementary and Secondary Teacher Education. *ACM Trans. Comput. Educ.* **2014**, *14*, 1–16. [CrossRef]
14. Hsu, T.-C.; Chang, S.-C.; Hung, Y.-T. How to learn and how to teach computational thinking: Suggestions based on a review of the literature. *Comput. Educ.* **2018**, *126*, 296–310. [CrossRef]
15. MIT Scratch—About. Available online: https://scratch.mit.edu/about/ (accessed on 6 September 2020).
16. Chang, C.-K. Effects of Using Alice and Scratch in an Introductory Programming Course for Corrective Instruction. *J. Educ. Comput. Res.* **2014**, *51*, 185–204. [CrossRef]
17. Maloney, J.; Resnick, M.; Rusk, N.; Silverman, B.; Eastmond, E. The Scratch Programming Language and Environment. *ACM Trans. Comput. Educ.* **2010**, *10*, 1–15. [CrossRef]
18. Baron, G.-L.; Voulgre, E. Initier à La Programmation Des Étudiants de Master de Sciences de l'éducation? {Un} Compte Rendu d'expérience. In Proceedings of the Sciences et Technologies de L'information et de la Communication en Milieu Éducatif: {Objets} et Méthodes D'enseignement et D'apprentissage, de la Maternelle à L'université, Patras, Greece, 24–26 October 2011.
19. Lye, S.Y.; Koh, J.H.L. Review on teaching and learning of computational thinking through programming: What is next for K-12? *Comput. Hum. Behav.* **2014**, *41*, 51–61. [CrossRef]
20. Salvo, M.J. *Constructionism in Practice: Designing, Thnking, and Learning in a Digital World—ProQuest*; Routledge: London, UK, 1998; Volume 7, ISBN 0805819843.
21. Dean, P.G.; Papert, S. Mindstorms: Children, Computers and Powerful Ideas. *Math. Gaz.* **1981**, *65*, 298. [CrossRef]
22. Kay, A. Squeak Etoys, Children & Learning. Available online: https://docs.huihoo.com/smalltalk/Squeak-Etoys-Children-and-Learning.pdf (accessed on 24 August 2020).
23. Steinmetz, J. Computers and squeak as environments for learning. In *Squeak: Open Personal Computing and Multimedia*; Guzdial, M., Rose, K., Eds.; Prentice-Hall, Inc.: Upper Saddle River, NJ, USA, 2002; pp. 453–482.
24. Brennan, K.; Resnick, M. New Frameworks for Studying and Assessing the Development of Computational Thinking. In Proceedings of the annual American Educational Research Association meeting, Vancouver, BC, Canada, 16 April 2012; Volume 1, pp. 1–25.
25. Traylor, S. Scratch That: MIT's Mitchel Resnick Says Kids Should Do It for Themselves. *Technol. Learn.* **2008**, *29*, 27.
26. Csizmadia, A.; Curzon, P.; Dorling, M.; Humphreys, S.; Ng, T.; Selby, C.; Woollard, J. Computational Thinking A Guide for Teachers. Available online: http://computingatschool.org.uk/computationalthinking (accessed on 25 August 2020).
27. Robinson, K. *The Element: How Finding Your Passion Changes*; Ken, R., Lou, A., Eds.; Penguin Books: London, UK, 2009; ISBN 978-0143116738.
28. Segredo, E.; Miranda, G.; León, C. Hacia la educación del futuro: El pensamiento computacional como mecanismo de aprendizaje generativo. *Educ. Knowl. Soc. (EKS)* **2017**, *18*, 33. [CrossRef]
29. Troussas, C.; Krouska, A.; Sgouropoulou, C. Collaboration and fuzzy-modeled personalization for mobile game-based learning in higher education. *Comput. Educ.* **2020**, *144*, 103698. [CrossRef]
30. ANR. ANR Computer Sciences at School: Conceptualizations, Accompanying, Resources. Available online: https://anr.fr/Project-ANR-18-CE38-0008 (accessed on 31 December 2020).
31. Brereton, P.; Kitchenham, B.A.; Budgen, D.; Turner, M.; Khalil, M. Lessons from applying the systematic literature review process within the software engineering domain. *J. Syst. Softw.* **2007**, *80*, 571–583. [CrossRef]
32. Gabriele, L.; Bertacchini, F.; Tavernise, A.; Vaca-Cárdenas, L.; Pantano, P.; Bilotta, E. Lesson Planning by Computational Thinking Skills in Italian Pre-service Teachers. *Informatics Educ.* **2019**, *18*, 69–104. [CrossRef]
33. Demir, Ö.; Seferoğlu, S.S. Developing a Scratch-based coding achievement test. *Inf. Learn. Sci.* **2019**, *120*, 383–406. [CrossRef]
34. Uzunboylu, H.; Kinik, E.; Kanbul, S. An Analysis of Countries Which Have Integrated Coding into Their Curricula and the Content Analysis of Academic Studies on Coding Training in Turkey. *TEM J.* **2017**, *6*, 783–791. [CrossRef]
35. Grover, S.; Pea, R.; Cooper, S. Designing for deeper learning in a blended computer science course for middle school students. *Comput. Sci. Educ.* **2015**, *25*, 199–237. [CrossRef]
36. Grover, S.; Jackiw, N.; Lundh, P. Concepts before coding: Non-programming interactives to advance learning of introductory programming concepts in middle school. *Comput. Sci. Educ.* **2019**, *29*, 106–135. [CrossRef]
37. Mladenović, M.; Boljat, I.; Žanko, Ž. Comparing loops misconceptions in block-based and text-based programming languages at the K-12 level. *Educ. Inf. Technol.* **2018**, *23*, 1483–1500. [CrossRef]

38. Troussas, C.; Krouska, A.; Virvou, M.; Sougela, E. Using Hierarchical Modeling of Thinking Skills to Lead Students to Higher Order Cognition and Enhance Social E-Learning. In Proceedings of the 2018 9th International Conference on Information, Intelligence, Systems and Applications (IISA), Zakynthos, Greece, 23–25 July 2018; pp. 1–5. [CrossRef]
39. Lazarinis, F.; Karachristos, C.V.; Stavropoulos, E.C.; Verykios, V.S. A blended learning course for playfully teaching programming concepts to school teachers. *Educ. Inf. Technol.* **2018**, *24*, 1237–1249. [CrossRef]
40. Martin, C. Libraries as Facilitators of Coding for All. *Knowl. Quest* **2017**, *45*, 46–53.
41. Haduong, P. "I like Computers. I Hate Coding"': A Portrait of Two Teens' Experiences. *Inf. Learn. Sci.* **2019**, *120*, 349–365. [CrossRef]
42. Gross, K.; Gross, S. TRANSFORMATION: Constructivism, Design Thinking, and Elementary STEAM. *Art Educ.* **2016**, *69*, 36–43. [CrossRef]
43. Hagge, J. Coding to Create: A Subtext of Decisions as Early Adolescents Design Digital Media. *Technol. Knowl. Learn.* **2018**, *23*, 247–271. [CrossRef]
44. Yadav, A.; Cooper, S. Fostering creativity through computing. *Commun. ACM* **2017**, *60*, 31–33. [CrossRef]
45. Tang, K.-Y.; Chou, T.-L.; Tsai, C.-C. A Content Analysis of Computational Thinking Research: An International Publication Trends and Research Typology. *Asia-Pacific Educ. Res.* **2019**, *29*, 9–19. [CrossRef]
46. Çakiroğlua, Ü.; Suiçmez, S.S.; Kurtoğlu, Y.B.; Sari, A.; Yildiz, S.; Öztürk, M. Exploring perceived cognitive load in learning programming via Scratch. *Res. Learn. Technol.* **2018**, *26*, 26. [CrossRef]
47. Burke, Q. DIY zones for Scratch design in classand club. In *Creating the Coding Generation in Primary Schools*; Routledge India: New Delhi, India, 2017; pp. 81–100.
48. Halverson, E.R.; Sheridan, K. The Maker Movement in Education. *Harv. Educ. Rev.* **2014**, *84*, 495–504. [CrossRef]
49. Romero, M.; Lepage, A.; Lille, B. Computational thinking development through creative programming in higher education. *Int. J. Educ. Technol. High. Educ.* **2017**, *14*, 42. [CrossRef]
50. Pellas, N.; Vosinakis, S. The effect of simulation games on learning computer programming: A comparative study on high school students' learning performance by assessing computational problem-solving strategies. *Educ. Inf. Technol.* **2018**, *23*, 2423–2452. [CrossRef]
51. Lee, Y.-J. Scratch: Multimedia Programming Environment for Young Gifted Learners. *Gift. Child. Today* **2011**, *34*, 26–31. [CrossRef]
52. Erümit, A.K. Effects of different teaching approaches on programming skills. *Educ. Inf. Technol.* **2020**, *25*, 1013–1037. [CrossRef]
53. Oluk, A.; Korkmaz, Ö. Comparing Students' Scratch Skills with Their Computational Thinking Skills in Terms of Different Variables. *Int. J. Mod. Educ. Comput. Sci.* **2016**, *8*, 1–7. [CrossRef]
54. Durak, H.Y. The Effects of Using Different Tools in Programming Teaching of Secondary School Students on Engagement, Computational Thinking and Reflective Thinking Skills for Problem Solving. *Technol. Knowl. Learn.* **2020**, *25*, 179–195. [CrossRef]
55. Seiter, L.; Foreman, B. Modeling the learning progressions of computational thinking of primary grade students. In Proceedings of the ninth annual international ACM conference on International computing education research—ICER '13, San Diego, CA, USA, 12–14 August 2013; pp. 59–66.
56. Adler, R.F.; Kim, H. Enhancing future K-8 teachers' computational thinking skills through modeling and simulations. *Educ. Inf. Technol.* **2018**, *23*, 1501–1514. [CrossRef]
57. Arnedo-Moreno, J.; Garcia-Solorzano, D. Programming Is Fun! A Survey of the STEAM Digital Distribution Platform. In Proceedings of the 2020 IEEE 32nd Conference on Software Engineering Education and Training, CSEE and T, Munich, Germany, 1 November 2020; pp. 325–328.
58. López, J.M.S.; Gutiérrez, R.C. Programación visual por bloques en Educación Primaria: Aprendiendo y creando contenidos en Ciencias Sociales. *Revista Complutense de Educación* **2016**, *28*, 409–426. [CrossRef]
59. Kitchenham, B.; Pretorius, R.; Budgen, D.; Brereton, O.P.; Turner, M.; Niazi, M.; Linkman, S. Systematic literature reviews in software engineering—A tertiary study. *Inf. Softw. Technol.* **2010**, *52*, 792–805. [CrossRef]
60. Ramírez-Montoya, M.-S.; García-Peñalvo, F.-J. Co-creation and open innovation: Systematic literature review. *Comunicar* **2018**, *26*, 9–18. [CrossRef]
61. Ramirez-Montoya, M. Challenges for Open Education with Educational Innovation: A Systematic Literature Review. *Sustainability* **2020**, *12*, 7053. [CrossRef]
62. Ramírez-Montoya, M.-S.; Lugo-Ocando, J. Systematic review of mixed methods in the framework of educational innovation. *Comunity* **2020**, *28*, 9–20. [CrossRef]
63. Zhao, J.-G. Combination of multiple databases is necessary for a valid systematic review. *Int. Orthop.* **2014**, *38*, 2639. [CrossRef]
64. Bramer, W.M.; Rethlefsen, M.L.; Kleijnen, J.; Franco, O.H. Optimal database combinations for literature searches in systematic reviews: A prospective exploratory study. *Syst. Rev.* **2017**, *6*, 245. [CrossRef]
65. Kitchenham, B.; Kitchenham, B.; Charters, S. Guidelines for Performing Systematic Literature Reviews in Software Engineering. Available online: https://www.bibsonomy.org/bibtex/aed0229656ada843d3e3f24e5e5c9eb9 (accessed on 29 November 2020).
66. Feldt, R.; Magazinius, A. Validity Threats in Empirical Software Engineering Research—An Initial Survey. Available online: http://www.robertfeldt.net/publications/feldt_2010_validity_threats_in_ese_initial_survey.pdf (accessed on 25 April 2021).

Article

Development of Life Skills Program for Primary School Students: Focus on Entry Programming

Nam-gyeong Gim

Department of Administration, Yuk-buk Elementary School, Yongin 17061, Korea; v-ness@daum.net

Citation: Gim, N.-g. Development of Life Skills Program for Primary School Students: Focus on Entry Programming. *Computers* **2021**, *10*, 56. https://doi.org/10.3390/computers 10050056

Academic Editors: Antonio Sarasa Cabezuelo, Covadonga Rodrigo San Juan and Santi Caballé

Received: 21 February 2021
Accepted: 21 April 2021
Published: 23 April 2021

Publisher's Note: MDPI stays neutral with regard to jurisdictional claims in published maps and institutional affiliations.

Copyright: © 2021 by the author. Licensee MDPI, Basel, Switzerland. This article is an open access article distributed under the terms and conditions of the Creative Commons Attribution (CC BY) license (https://creativecommons.org/licenses/by/4.0/).

Abstract: There are areas where the competencies obtained through computer coding activities substantially overlap with life skills components. Studies of these common competencies have suggested the possibility of including these contents in a life skills program. Therefore, the purpose of this study was to develop a program through the Entry program that elementary school students could use online to improve their life skills, given the need to increase contactless online classes due to COVID-19. Eight elementary school teachers with 20 years of experience and two curriculum experts participated in the program's development. For data collection, 360 data points were collected from eight elementary schools located in each Korean province, including urban and rural areas. SPSS 21.0 was used to analyze the data. Upon completing the 8-week program, the difference in life skills between groups was confirmed using variance analysis based on the number of implementation times, and post-hoc testing was conducted. The study's results confirmed the difference between the groups conducted for two weeks ($M = 3.22$), four weeks ($M = 3.25$), and six weeks ($M = 3.67$), and the group conducted for eight weeks ($M = 3.83$). In other words, as the number of weeks of participation in the life skills program increased, there was a difference between groups. These findings suggest a life skills program could be included as part of Entry based computer coding activities for elementary school students through a backward curriculum. In conclusion, this study showed the possibility of using contactless online classes with free Entry-based websites to improve the life skills of elementary school students struggling at home due to COVID-19. It also showed that each elementary school teacher could operate the life skills programs as a contactless learning method using a free coding platform and manual.

Keywords: life skills; Entry platform; backward curriculum; elementary school students

1. Introduction

Changes to daily life related to the Fourth Industrial Revolution are taking place at home and abroad. To keep up with the Fourth Industrial Revolution's global trend, which will further advance the so-called 'hyper-connected society' and 'super-intelligent society' through the convergence and integration of industries, nations and individuals must prepare themselves for this eventuality. This is especially true when considering the job changes the Fourth Industrial Revolution will bring. The Fourth Industrial Revolution, where 5G technology is the norm, will result in an industrial revolution in which human desires for convenience through artificial intelligence (AI) and the Internet of Things are accomplished using AI robots instead of humans performing complex tasks [1]. The Fourth Industrial Revolution, which was officially mentioned at the World Economic Forum held in Davos, Switzerland, in 2016, differs slightly according to scholars.

However, it is generally agreed that in the future, machines, artificial intelligence, the Internet of Things, and smart AI robots will replace humans, taking over most of the work that requires judgment [2]. In order to cultivate expertise in dealing with AI robots, it is necessary to understand software fundamentals. When it comes to understanding software, studies show that teaching at a younger age enhances things such as language education [3]. Enthusiasm for introducing software education, especially coding education, at a young age is increasing worldwide. Although each country's coding education has distinct characteristics and features, the goal of fostering human resource development in terms of national competitiveness is something they have in common [4].

On the other hand, these software competencies are focused on one's career and happiness from a personal perspective. Developing personal competencies for social change increases one's competitiveness in society. There are usually various types of competitiveness, such as knowledge, language, skill, physical strength, academic qualification, etc. Still, the life skills that are the psychological and physical basis of these things cannot be over emphasized. Countries and scholars define life skills in various ways. Still, many agree that creativity, empathy, problem-solving, communication, etc., are essential cognitive, emotional, and social factors for individuals to live as members of society [5].

These capabilities are still required, despite the changes brought by the Fourth Industrial Revolution [1]. Several programs promote these competencies, which are needed more now than ever before. However, there have been few studies linking software activities with life skills. At a time when public social life has become difficult due to the COVID19 pandemic, software education using a free open platform is an advantageous form of contactless online education. As a result, this study hypothesized that education centered on the Entry platform as a program to improve the life skills of elementary school students could affect a student's life skills. Therefore, this study aimed to develop a life skills program for elementary school students focusing on the Entry platform.

2. Examples of Coding Education in Several Countries

Worldwide, coding education is conducted in various ways to suit each country's national characteristics. National support and aspirations for coding education is increasing globally. According to foreign media such as The Wall Street Journal, Chinese parents spend over $1000 a year on coding classes. This is primarily influenced by the Chinese government's emphasis on IT (information technology) education. China began mandating 70 h of software education per year from the third grade of elementary school in 2001, and artificial intelligence classes are required for high school students [4].

Next, in India, where the class-based society reinforces the caste system, coding education is a way to raise one's status through employment in global IT companies. Thus, coding education's appeal is greater in India than in any other country. The Indian government views IT talent as critical to its national competitiveness. Software education has been a required subject in Indian elementary, middle, and high schools since 2010. High school students generally learn major coding languages such as C++ and Javascript. According to a 2016 Barclays report, India produces about ten times more people skilled in coding skills than the United States [6]. However, the report highlights that India's focus on the mass production of good technical coders rather than creative talent is a limitation. In India, there is a street called SAP, known as the hub of software education. The day begins with 100,000 trainees who want to learn IT technology [7]. Indian-Americans, such as Microsoft's Satya Narayana, Google's Sundar Pichai, Adobe's Shantanu Narayen, and Harman International's Dinesh Paliwal, were all born and educated in India [8]. In addition, they were all entrepreneurs who started their own companies. After larger companies acquired their companies, they led stable lives as business executives at other companies.

In the United States, coding education policies vary from state to state, but many public schools, including California, Florida, and Arkansas, have incorporated coding into their standard curriculum. These schools teach coding with free programs distributed by Silicon Valley IT companies such as Google, Facebook, Microsoft, and Apple. The coding program created by a leading IT company is close to play. It does not focus on teaching 'computing language' but instead on a process that fosters 'thinking skills to structure problems' and induces educational effects through programming activities closely related to play activities [9].

The UK, the birthplace of the Industrial Revolution, has made coding education mandatory for all grades since September 2014. Students begin writing simple programs at five years old, and from the age of 11, they learn programming languages with the same methodology used to teach foreign languages. A primary characteristic of British coding education is convergence education. In other words, coding education is composed of subjects such as science, technology, engineering, and mathematics to form convergence education. It focuses on enhancing problem-solving skills and creativity through coding and improving science mathematics-based knowledge. In the UK, the primary school app development curriculum consists of six steps. The first step is planning the app, the second is project composition and role allocation, the third is market research and idea derivation, the fourth is the composition and design of the app menu, the fifth is coding education, and the sixth is the product's market disclosure [10].

Software education for elementary students in the fifth grade was included in Korea's 2015 revised curriculum. Some units focused on improving students' coding competencies and were organized in the approved textbook. Currently, coding education is partially organized in several textbooks and is often conducted as an after-school activity. Then, what are the implications of coding education in these domestic and overseas coding education cases? Firstly, hardware and software education must be developed in a balanced manner. Secondly, fun and interest should play a role as a driving force for participation in software education. Therefore, software education should be implemented as an interesting level-specific computing activity in elementary, middle, and high school levels to increase voluntary participation. Thirdly, coding education should not involve just the screen and monitor. Instead, coding technology beyond the computer screen should be used, and educational activities must be extended to physical coding. Fourthly, an open platform with economic feasibility should be provided to introduce students' coding programs to the market. Fifth, in terms of equality in education, coding education should have a social enterprise character so that it is not proportional to the cost and should be positioned as a fair life education concept that can resolve educational inequality.

3. Entry Program Features

Elementary schools have focused on improving computing thinking through block coding, which is similar to game-based activities. In middle school, emphasis has been placed on laying the software foundation through text coding using a coding language. In high school, input coding focuses on using a robot that moves through a physical computer. This AI-related education requires individual creativity, and its creative design emphasizes open and cooperative characteristics [9]. Compared to traditional classes, learning based on innovative design increases learners' motivation for learning, giving them a sense of satisfaction and self-efficacy, motivating them to continue. It is also effective in metacognition, cooperative attitude, problem-solving, and exploration skills [11].

The Entry platform has various content that uses creative design to teach learners. 'Entry' is a non-profit coding software education platform developed by KAIST University in Korea and later acquired by Naver. Developed using a block-type language rather than the existing text coding, it consists of four main menus: Learn, Create, Share, and Community with a graphics-based program. Therefore, the design allows elementary school students and beginners to learn very quickly, as shown in Figure 1 below. The program's drag and drop method uses a mouse and is similar to assembling Lego blocks. By employing block coding, gaming and language students use daily, students in lower grades can understand the programming language. The program's advantage is the sense of accomplishment it creates because students can select their elementary or middle school level, perform coding activities, and create and share their work. Additionally, Entry is a JavaScript-based program with fairly good compatibility, and thus works with smartphones and tablet PCs without an app. Starting with a simple change of direction or movement, one can create complex games or animations, share them with friends, and receive feedback.

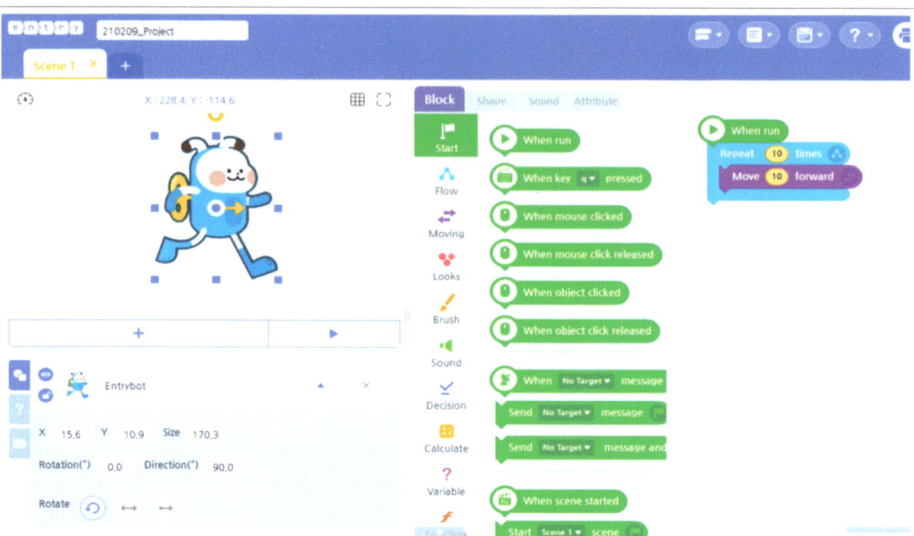

Figure 1. Screen example of Entry program.

However, the most significant advantage is that it is a free web-based platform that economically disadvantaged students can use. There are free wireless hotspots throughout Korea, including government offices, restaurants, bus stops, subways, buses, department stores, libraries, schools, hospitals, etc. As of 2018, Korea had the world's highest internet access rate per household at 99.5% (including wired and wireless), followed by Iceland (99.2%), the Netherlands (98.0%), Norway (96.0%), the United Kingdom (94.8%) and Germany (94.4%), followed by Finland (94.3%) [12]. The proliferation of free Wi-Fi zones in Korea made it attractive for content selection.

As personal computer programming skills become increasingly important in the modern world, Entry guides elementary, middle and high school students to start coding, not just for fun. Instead, by cultivating their interest, Entry eventually gives students a solid foundation in coding. It can be called a new basic AI tool.

4. Possibility of Linking Coding Education and Life Skills Programs

However, Entry's most significant advantage is that it is a free web-based platform that economically disadvantaged students can use. The dictionary defines coding as signifying something or designing a program using a specific programming language. Coding is a technology that implements an abstract algorithm as a motion of a specific object using a programming language. Coding can form the basis of programs such as games, apps, and vaccines. In other words, by engaging in programming activities, one can create games and implement robotic movements, and these activities can improve thinking and logic [13,14].

Therefore, coding education is included in the official curriculum in many countries worldwide, and it has been a regular course in Korea since 2018. Coding education promotes logical and creative thinking, and in the future, it could be one of the core competencies helping people lead independent lives. Advanced research has demonstrated coding's positive effects, including improving logical thinking, self-directed learning, problem-solving, creative thinking, cooperation, and empathy [14]. Various studies have been conducted on how SW education and Entry-based block coding activities affect students' creativity and achievement level. Studies have confirmed that entry-level programming classes using software education material for high school students positively affect metacognition, which plays a vital role in students' creative problem-solving ability. Besides, these studies confirmed that coding education enhances students' self-efficacy [13].

Elementary school students prefer hands-on learning using their bodies to theoretical learning. Thus, they may be interested in making a game and simplifying it, and they can correct misconceptions related to the program while giving and receiving feedback. A striking characteristic of students is that they can enjoy working. Students gradually develop their professionalism and feel a sense of accomplishment by enjoying their work [15]. The optimal state is when an individual's skills and abilities are balanced with challenges and tasks. Subjective satisfaction and happiness felt while maximizing one's potential while performing a task can be called a 'flow'. Through immersion in work, one experiences both joy and competence. The sense of self-efficacy acquired at this time will become an asset in challenging and overcoming complex tasks until adulthood. The many assets that can be gained through computing, thinking and other activities include self-efficacy, problem-solving skills, collaboration, communication, confidence, critical thinking, empathy, etc. [13]. Together, these can become life skills. If computing activities are organized into systematic education programs, there is a possibility that they could be linked to life skills education.

Various types of coding education need to be considered before curriculum related to AI basics can be reflected in textbooks and systematically settled. The competencies that can be obtained through education related to coding can lead to improved life skills necessary for students to live as productive members of society [14]. Elementary school students are often immersed in games. There are times when the people around you cannot hear who you are talking to, forget about the concept of time and space, and even miss a meal. According to previous studies, in order to satisfy the condition of immersion, five principles of goal setting, expectation, interest, self-determination, and challenge must be preceded [15,16]. The Entry platform provides a visual environment to motivate students to set goals, expect success, and induce interest in achieving internal and external goals. Also, it encourages self determination in achieving the goal while participating in the program [17]. The challenge of progressing to a higher level is goal-oriented rather than competition-oriented, so I chose it as a basic program for improving life skills [18].

5. Life Skills Program Factors

Life skills can be defined as skills that would be useful at any time in an individual's life. Life skills education aims to develop the communication skills, self-assertion skills, decision-making skills, problem-solving skills, abuse defense skills, and creative thinking skills necessary to cope with the dangers encountered in life [19]. UNICEF defines life skills as the ability to adapt effectively to meet the needs and challenges of everyday life and the ability to act positively [20]. Elementary school is a period of rapid emotional and physical growth. People define who they are, their likes and dislikes, and how others see themselves and are more concerned about themselves and their surroundings. Therefore, it is believed that this period is an appropriate time to acquire life skills based on various experiences. In adolescence, more than at any other time, many students struggle with interpersonal relationships and may lack the skills to make decisions or listen to others [19,20].

Suppose students learn and utilize the various life skills necessary for daily life, such as communicating with others, resisting peer pressure, refusing drugs and alcohol, cooperating with others, and being considerate. In that case, those skills will become not only lifelong assets but also help them live a happy life [21]. In the short term, life skills prevent health risks so that individuals can achieve their goals successfully. In the long run, life skills contribute to securing a job and living as a productive member of society. In particular, schools increasingly emphasize the need for life skills because schools are no longer a safe zone due to bullying [22], school violence, and suicide. There are many programs and methods for acquiring life skills, but until now, they have primarily been developed in the field of physical activity and physical education [22].

Looking at the life skills factors suggested by WHO, the core elements of life skills are divided into self-awareness, empathy, interpersonal relationships, communication, critical thinking, creative thinking, decision making, problem-solving, coping with stress, and coping with emotions [19]. UNICEF reported that an educational approach based on life skills effectively solves health problems such as smoking and drugs in adolescents [20]. The World Health Organization is encouraging life skills education through schools because life skills education improves adolescents' health [19]. According to foreign studies, positive studies show that it effectively improves academic performance, improves the relationship between students and parents, and prevents drug misuse and abuse [23]. For example, in the US, focusing on the Life Skill Training Centre, the Life Skills Program is being implemented simultaneously online and offline for elementary school students, middle school students, high school students, teachers, and parents in each state.

With the expansion of online services due to the 2020 COVID-19 pandemic, contactless digital transformation has accelerated across the planet, including politics, economy, society, culture, education, and industry. Moreover, school learning has been transformed. Depending on how the Coronavirus spread, elementary, middle, and high school classes were often held remotely [24]. For this reason, there was a period when educational programs allowing students to learn independently at home were urgently needed. After their parents went to work, students had more time to study alone with their teacher online. Thus students required skills necessary for leading their own lives. In proportion to the importance of contactless learning, life education programs such as life skills became more necessary. Life skills education is being developed through various programs in every country, but few studies exist on computer coding activities. In this study, three conditions had to be met when developing a life skills program. First, it should conform to the learning characteristics of a contactless program that could be fully accomplished independently using a simple manual. Second, it should be a free platform that anyone could access from home at any time. Third, users could share their work with others and upload it to the web. The Entry platform met all of these conditions.

6. Program Development Process

The research procedures were primarily divided into five steps. In the first step, a literature review was conducted to confirm the factors that constitute life skills. In general, it has been shown that life skills can be acquired through various activities. However, up to now, life skills have been cultivated mainly through sports [24]. In the second step, I introduced the Entry program, identifying its pros and cons. While doing various activities, we investigated the points that students might find difficult, what they needed to learn more deeply, and what knowledge they needed to acquire before starting the Entry program. In addition, we identified improvements that could be raised in the program execution stage. Methods to supplement the program's deficiencies were reflected in the program development stage. The third step was to set the program format and main topics. The opinions of curriculum experts were reflected, confirming the backward curriculum fit the life skills program's characteristics [25]. Next, in the program development stage, the Entry program's subject was aligned with the program detailed above. A simulation (mock class) and two modifications were used to develop the program. The last step was verifying the developed program. After completing two to eight weeks of contactless online class activities, life skills were measured. It was judged that a more sophisticated verification method would be to check the program's effects according to the number of participants and sessions by subdividing the group rather than simply checking the difference between the pre-and-post group after running all the programs. Therefore, the population was divided into four groups. After running the program for two weeks, four weeks, six weeks, and eight weeks, respectively, the difference in life skills was confirmed. The overall progress of the study consists of five stages, as shown in Figure 2 below. The fourth stage's program development process is shown in more detail in Figure 3 below. The detailed development of the program consists of five stages. In the first stage, the life skills factors that can be acquired through Entry activities were determined. In the second stage, the operation hours and training methods were discussed by participating in block coding using the Entry program. In the third step, the program's model, which is at the core of the study, was produced under the theoretical framework. In the fourth stage, the program was operated through a mock class for a small number of students. In the final step, modifications were made based on what was learned during the study to compensate for unexpected scenarios, such as difficulty solving problems online, time delays, and insufficient feedback. These modifications were reflected in the final program.

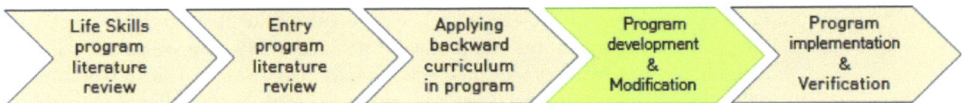

Figure 2. The overall series of research procedure.

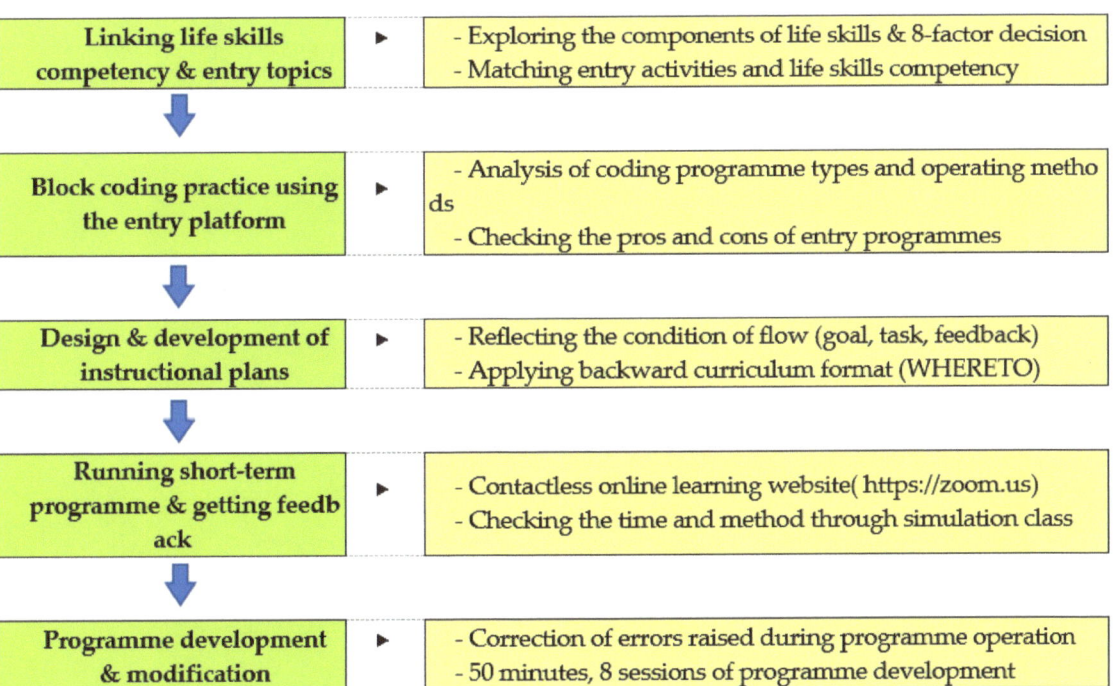

Figure 3. Life skills program development steps.

7. Summary of the 8-Session Program

Subjects were presented in order of difficulty during the eight-week Entry program. In other words, to prevent new students from experiencing problems upon beginning the Entry program, they could start with simple learning before progressing to the complicated game production sequence. In the first step, students had time to get to know and experience the Entry program and learn the meaning of block coding. In the second step, students had time to create their own stories using bubble talk. From the third class, students were guided to construct a straightforward linear motion object.

Additionally, students were asked to choose various screen backgrounds centering on block coding and practice block command by selecting and moving an object. The fourth week was guided so that two or more objects were appearing in the background. There were linear motions and repetitive motions, collisions and disappearances of moving objects mixed in the reverse direction, and motions that incorporated the effects of music and speech bubbles. The spatial concept of repetition and stop, touch, and four directional walls, including conditional language blocks, is important for these movements. This activity involves high-level block coding such as infinite repetition, random replication, and movement of east, west, north, and south coordinates. In the seventh session, they made a video of their own story using cartoons to receive friends' feedback. The final session's work did not end as a simple result. Instead, it could be linked to economic value by having students create a competitive game. In other words, when uploading their work to an open platform to determine whether it was marketable, students had time to explore the possibility of generating economic profits by participating with multiple people. These programs' superficial appearance may give the impression of simply making games, but behind them are various activities to promote life skills. In other words, they engage in activities that reinforce the core factors of life skills, such as solving problems creatively, empathizing with other people's work, and sometimes cooperating on one task while learning games, producing, and giving or receiving feedback. Eight teachers at each school conducted the program for two to eight weeks, and the program's per session duration was one week. Each teacher trained 30–50 students, and one session lasted 50 min. In addition, the researcher trained the participating teachers on the Entry program's operation and method before starting the study. Figure 4 below shows the core competencies of life skills according to the program's title for a total of eight sessions.

T: Learning Topic & Learning activity M: Access route or instruction manual	C: Life Skills Competency Q: Core Questions & A: Assessment Method
T1: Hello, Entry? & I can access the entry.	C: Critical think-ing, Self-awareness
M: 'entry' in the portal→Click to 'learn.' Entry first steps for starters	Q: Can you access the entry site? A: Whether to perform mission using blockbox.
T2: Adding an object & Create a talk bubble!	C: Empathy, Communication
M: Block-Looks-Write in, say block- Move right.	Q: Can you make a talk bubble? A: Whether to create a cartoon scene
T3: Catch zombies & Making a flying game.	C: Problem-solving, Creative thinking.
M: Using repeat infinity, clone block.	Q: Can you code to make one object move? A: Whether conditional code can be used.
T4: Creating objects that move in a straight line	C: Interpersonal relationship, Critical thinking
M: Creating moving objects using conditional, infinite repeat, and clone blocks.	Q: Can you make moving objects? A: Whether the object performs linear motion.
T5: Adding various backgrounds & object.	C: Self-awareness, Creative thinking
M: Adding sounds, backgrounds & objects using the search function.	Q: Can you add more than two objects? A: Whether the object performs linear motion.
T6: Create objects that move in reverse.	C: Communication, Decision making
M: Collaborate with friends to create cooperative works.	Q: Did you create a cooperative work? A: Whether the co-op works properly.
T7: Tell your own story	C: Interpersonal relationship, Empathy
M: Expressing one's story using objects and talk balloons.	Q: Can you make your own picture book? A: Whether you have created your own book.
T8: Olympic games	C: Coping with stress, Coping with emotions
M: Create a competitive game using timers and sound effects.	Q: Can you make a competitive game? A: Whether timers and sound effects are used.

Figure 4. Summary of the eight session program.

8. Program Format and Example

The life skill program's design method and content structure using the Entry program's contents are based on the 'flow' theory and the 'backward curriculum'. The program included three conditions necessary for students' flow: the educational goal of the day, the task to expand the scaffold, and feedback that could reflect improvement. In the program's overall flow, a backward design (WHERETO) [26] was applied to prioritize education evaluation and objectives. This design makes it convenient for teachers in the field to teach according to the manual, keeping them from deviating from the educational goal without preparing a separate evaluation when the class is over [25]. Above all, the core question presented in step 1 has the advantage of clarifying students' educational goals by structuring the content and process. Therefore, in consideration of these advantages, it was judged that the evaluation-centered curriculum of Wiggins and McThai was more suitable for the composition of this program than the generally widespread Gane and Bloom's learning method. Therefore, the program's superficial design takes the form of a backward curriculum that prioritizes teachers' availability and the conditions of students' [26].

Backward curriculum design first explores the learning content's key ideas and then selects appropriate topics [27]. Next, classes are designed in the following order: setting learning goals, establishing evaluation plans, and selecting learning experiences so that students can achieve proper understanding. The backward curriculum design model, widely used in schools and teacher training institutions in the United States, reminds teachers of the core evaluation elements of instruction [28]. In other words, it has the advantage of allowing teachers to identify desirable outcomes based on achievement standards so that teachers do not deviate significantly from their responsibilities and coordinate the class process. The reason for this design process is that first, there may be cases where the educational goal may not be reached due to distraction caused by contactless instruction, and the goal-setting necessary for the immersion environment can be naturally linked to the core evaluation factor. Second, because the design process is a three step linear model, it is not too complicated, so teachers can follow the manual well in the field. Third, it is due to the emphasis on various evaluation methods that value individual experiences to cultivate the life skills of students participating in the program.

In summary, this study's life skills program incorporates clear goals, a balance between challenges and abilities, and clear feedback, all components or prerequisites of flow [17]. Also, the program's framework was taken from the backward design method. Backward design is a concept stating teachers should plan their training based on the desired outcome. Backwards curriculum has three stages of design (1. Desired Results: what the students will learn, 2. Assessment Evidence: developing valid assessments, 3. Planning Instruction: planning learning experiences and instruction). WHERETO (Where, Hook, Explore, Rethink, Exhibit, Teacher's, Organize) encompasses the contents of the main activities the instruction must include as part of the three steps in backward design. Therefore, WHERETO is an acronym that helps design learning activities that support student acquisition, meaning-making, transfer, and feedback [27]. Figure 5 shows the backward design, and Figure 6 is an example of a life skills program based on the backward design.

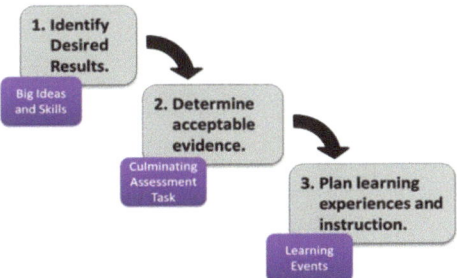

Figure 5. Wiggins, G. P, & McTighe, J. (2005). Understanding by design.

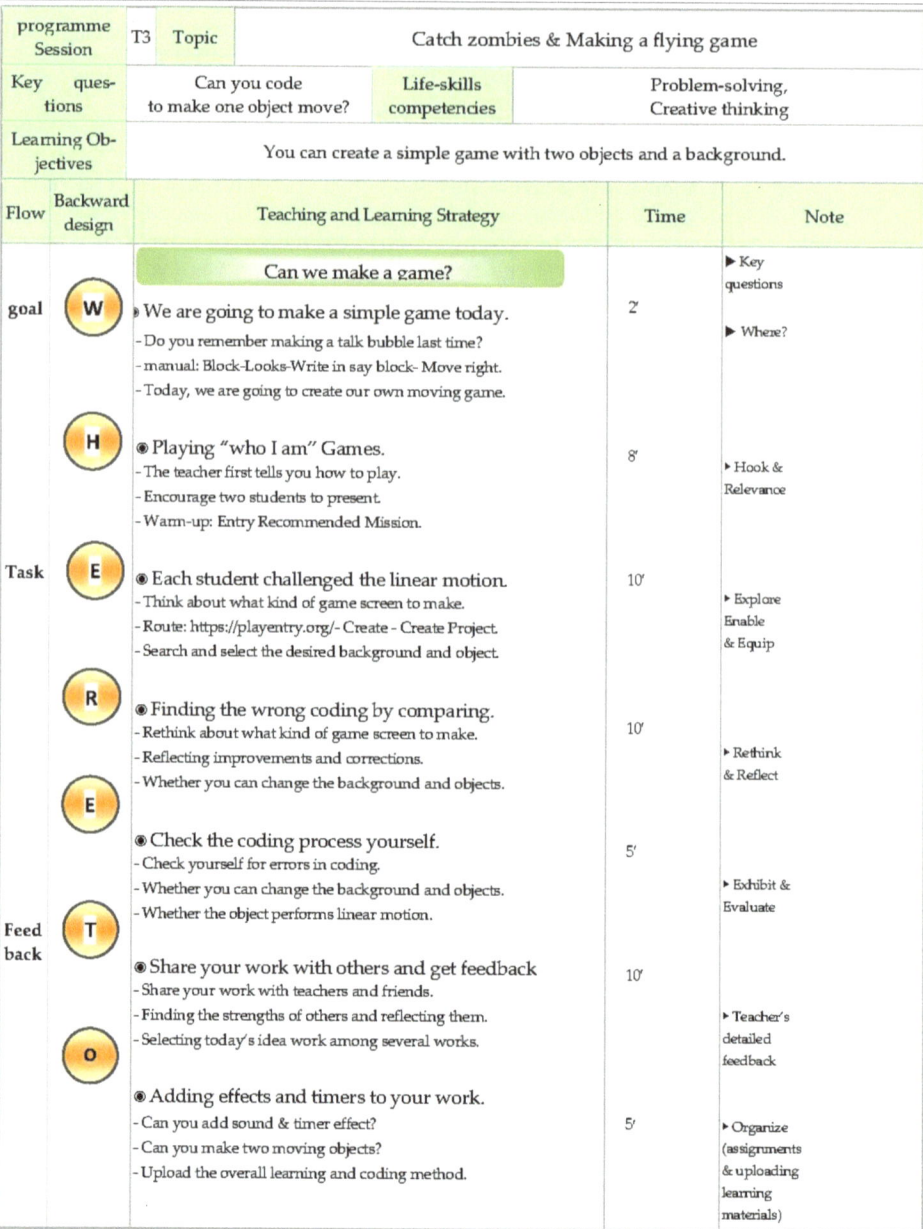

Figure 6. Example of life skills program.

9. Materials and Methods

9.1. Study Population and Sampling

The study's population is elementary school grades 5–6 nationwide. Due to the COVID-19 outbreak, Korea conducted its first nationwide contactless classes in March 2020. There were many difficulties in autonomous participation, equipment use, and timekeeping in lower elementary school grades [23]. Considering these contactless classes' trials and errors, it was judged that this program would only be appropriate for higher grades. Therefore, in this study, a non-probabilistic sampling (purposive sample or judgement sample) reflecting the researcher's intention was used [29]. To determine the program's effectiveness, the population was selected from elementary school students in higher grades nationwide. Therefore, eight elementary schools from four major Korean cities voluntarily participated in the program (Gyeong-gi, In-cheon, Busan, and Gwang-ju) and four rural areas (Gang-won, Chung-cheong, Jeolla, and Gyeon-gsang) were targeted (1 September 2020).

The study's purpose was explained to the homeroom teacher. In addition, the Entry program's pre-education was conducted in a contactless manner for a week to enhance the participating teachers' professionalism. After that, the life skills program developed based on the Entry program was implemented at each school (21 September 2020–23 November 2020). To exclude the pre- and post-test's learning effect and more closely check the programs impact according to each time, the difference in life skills according to the number of participants was attempted. Participating groups each conducted a program for 2 to 8 weeks and measured their life skills.

9.2. Measurement

Students' life skills is this study is dependent variable. LSSS (Life Skills Scale for Sport) is a life skills scale developed to measure the field of sports [30]. All eight factors (Time Management, Team Work, Goal setting, Emotional Skills, Interpersonal Communication, Social Skills, Leadership, Problem Solving, and Decision Making) consist of 47 questions. Each question is composed of a 5-point Likert scale, ranging from 1 point 'not at all' to 5 points 'very much'. As a result of conducting exploratory factor analysis, it was identified as five factors different from the original scale.

This study determined that 47 items were too many for elementary school students, so it was judged that the item response fatigue level was high. Therefore, it was necessary to reduce the number of factors and items. Emotional skills, problem-solving and decision-making, which were not clearly loaded as factors were removed. Also social skills and interpersonal communication, which are redundant factors, were integrated into social skills. In this way, the study was set as a total of five factors, and when deleted, items that increase reliability were found and removed. Cronbach's α value was calculated as the item consistency index. The question's consistency index, Cronbach's α (Leadership = 0.84, Goal setting = 0.81, Time Management = 0.80, Team Work = 0.71, Social Skills = 0.70), appeared in that order, which was relatively acceptable [31]. As a result, the measurement was simplified to 18 questions with three questions per factor and translated into words used by elementary school students in everyday life as much as possible to make it easier to understand when translating the original item. The cumulative variance (%) of five factors was found to be 65.65 in the factor analysis. As the extraction method, the Maximum Likelihood Rotation Method and oblimin rotations were used.

9.3. Data Analyses

Before the analysis of variance, the skewness and kurtosis, which were checked to verify the normality of the population, satisfied all of the criteria (skewness < |2|, kurtosis < |4|). As a result of the normality test, both Kolmogorov–Smirnov and Shapiro–Wilk were satisfied and passed normality ($p > 0.05$) [32]. One-way analysis of variance (ANOVA) was used as an analysis method to verify the mean difference between the four groups. The total number of subjects analyzed was 360 students (Agroup = 82, Bgroup = 90, Cgroup = 96, Dgroup = 92). Of these, there were 164 female students and 196 male students, 149 in the fifth grade and 211 in the sixth grade. The result of t-test analysis of life skills according to demographics showed the male average was 3.58, and that of females was 3.41. The fifth grade students' average was 3.45, and that of sixth grade students was 3.53, so there was no statistically significant difference. Group A participated in the Life Skills program for two weeks (two times). Group B participated four times for four weeks. Group

C participated six weeks and six times, and Group D participated eight times for eight weeks. First, when life skills were assumed as one factor without classifying any factors, each group's levels were compared. As a result of the analysis, it was confirmed that the C, D groups were higher than the A, B groups, as shown in Figure 7 below ($p < 0.01$). As shown in Table 1, the mean difference for each group was analyzed for five factors. As a result of testing the difference in life skills according to the number of times participated in the program over eight weeks, there were statistically significant differences between the groups in five factors. As a result of Scheffe's post-hoc test, the higher the frequency of participation in life skills, the higher the life skills score ($p < 0.01$).

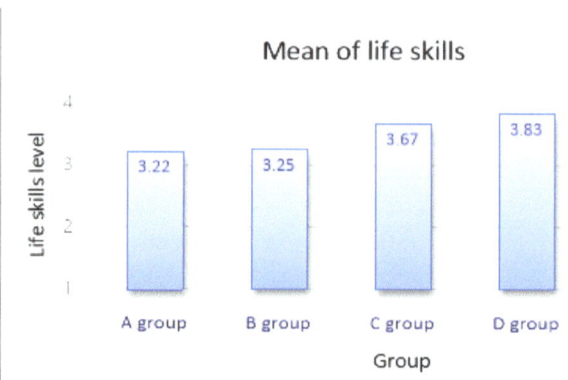

Figure 7. Mean difference of sum of life skills factors by group.

Table 1. Life skills according to the number of program participations.

	A Group (M/SD)	B Group (M/SD)	C Group (M/SD)	D Group (M/SD)	F	Post-Hoc
Leadership	3.12 −0.55	3.15 −0.51	3.41 −0.59	3.58 −0.69	5.70 ***	D > A,B
Goal Setting	3.45 −0.59	3.25 −0.64	3.76 −0.65	4.00 −0.60	19.56 ***	D > A,B C > B
Team Work	3.05 −0.71	3.33 −0.62	3.78 −0.61	3.95 −0.63	19.82 ***	C,D > A,B
Social Skills	3.48 −0.60	3.26 −0.59	3.78 −0.64	4.02 −0.62	19.44 ***	C > B D > A,B
Time Management	3.00 −0.69	3.24 −0.63	3.59 −0.71	3.63 −0.69	5.10 **	D > A,B
Life skills	3.22 −0.63	3.25 −0.60	3.67 −0.64	3.83 −0.65	14.65 ***	C,D > A,B

M = mean, SD = standard deviation. ** $p < 0.01$, *** $p < 0.001$.

As shown in the post-hoc analysis results in Table 1 below, the higher the life skills program participation based on the once-a-week entry, the more the groups differed. In other words, the groups that participated six to eight times had higher life skills scores than the groups that participated two to four times. In general, the difference in effect was revealed only after the groups had participated in the program's fourth session of four weeks or longer. The analysis is characterized by the fact that a difference appeared when the life skill program lasted more than four weeks. Therefore, it can be seen that the difference in statistical life skills must be satisfied by at least eight sessions.

10. Discussion

This study aims to develop a program that improves elementary school students' life skills through Entry-based coding activities. Among other activities, you may be wondering why we chose to study coding. In previous studies, life skills were often taught directly, but recently, there has been an increase in programs that cultivate life skills through various activities [33]. In general, coding education is highly recommended for problem-solving and creativity education. In modern society, where human resources' competitiveness is more important, countries focus on various educational activities by combining coding education with the regular curriculum [34]. This study was undertaken because the competencies acquired through coding education have a common factor in life skills, and many domains [14].

Everything that represents the Fourth Industrial Revolution era, such as artificial intelligence, big data, and the Internet of Things, is implemented through software [1]. Coding education, which is conducted as a part of software education, has the advantage of developing creativity, problem-solving, rational thinking, and career skills [14]. In particular, metacognition, which can be acquired through setting up a strategy and modifying it by participating in coding education, can be the basis of life skill competency. Life skills strengthen resilience skills, enabling students to effectively cope with substance abuse, violence, malnutrition, and other socio-economic and environmental challenges. In addition, its importance was emphasized in that it guarantees the youth's personal and social success and plays a key role in leading a successful life [35].

However, just as there is a phenomenon of cultural retardation that the law cannot keep pace with the speed of culture, program development cannot keep pace with social demands. This may be due to the misconception that life skills is a capability that can be acquired without a program, or it may be because program development experts do not have high expectations for life skill improvement. However, above all, in terms of methodology, there is no diversification of professional knowledge in the program development field, and there is regret that it continues to develop in some sports fields. A study shows that students' life skills level improved through various activities in the life skills intervention program designed for elementary school students. It can be said that these programs, which specialize in life skills competencies, suggest that the effect can be evident in younger students [36]. Looking back at the meaning of life skill, believing it only improves students' life skills, is too narrow of an interpretation. The definition of life skills also includes personal skills and the people who have a relationship with the individual and the individual's surrounding environment. Therefore, the study's implications are not that the Entry-based life skills management program has increased students' level.

The implications and features of this study are as follows. First, life skills programs need to be diversified in relation to future educational trends. In this era of the Fourth Industrial Revolution centered on artificial intelligence, it is necessary to learn and express individual creativity, problem-solving ability, interpersonal relationships, and empathy differently from before. Therefore, it is essential to consider the methodological considerations of mutual sympathy and cooperation by establishing relationships and solving problems in a contactless way rather than using the existing contact program. Entry programs only have value when students cooperate and empathize with others while releasing their creativity freely through a unique task execution method called coding [35]. Therefore, the relationship and cooperation process in the Internet space are emphasized.

Moreover, in order to participate in the contactless education program using Zoom, the habit of managing time is established to practice time management. Eventually, the results of these activities could be linked to economic value, that is, the commercial idea of merchantability. On the other hand, looking at past life skills programs, there were not many cases where life skills improvement was linked to economic value. However, this program is characterized by helping students take a leap toward perfecting their work by evaluating it from the perspective of economical merchandising on an open platform and giving it various feedback. In this part, an appropriate task, a condition of immersion, intervenes [37]. While students' competencies and tasks are balanced, scaffolding is established, and the core life skills competencies grow [38].

Second, this study combined teaching and learning theory with the Entry program. However, more studies are needed to see if synergies are produced when effective teaching and learning theory are combined with life skills programs [17]. This study verified the effect by linking the backward curriculum and immersion theory. The backward curriculum, which presents clear evaluation criteria to make up for the concentration of learning that can be distracted in contactless learning, would have helped the students 'set goals' among their life skills competencies. Third, the flow and content of educational activities provided by the program are centered on the self-competitive structure and 'cooperation and empathy'. Hence, they have a socially friendly character rather than an antisocial one. The programs intended fundamental goal is 'the expression of collaborative creativity'. In the future, it will be challenging to succeed only with creativity. Without cooperating creatively with others, it may be difficult to receive interest and economic sympathy for one's work. Entry games created by individuals will only receive objective compassion when they derive cooperation from others and are recognized for their product's economic value [39]. Fourth, it is necessary to discuss an effective free education program intended to improve life skills. When a free educational program is implemented, various research approaches are needed to see if its effectiveness can be proven. In this study, a free platform was selected in consideration of the student's ability to pay. In fact, life skills may have a more significant impact on the socially underprivileged need than the economically affluent [39]. If life skills can be improved through a free education platform, this could be a financial consideration for economically vulnerable social classes [35]. This is also why this type of free platform-centered convergence education program is needed in the future. Fifth, we learned during the pre-education of teachers while conducting this study that the level of teacher and student program guidance is not very meaningful. In other words, in the case of block coding, it does not mean that because someone is a teacher, they will find the program easy or need less time to learn the program or students will take more time to complete the program or find it more difficult. Therefore, with respect to block coding education, since there is not a large gap between adult and child learning ability, teachers and students can maintain an equal relationship while progressing through the program. Instead, there may be cases where teachers receive feedback from students. This closes the gap between instructors and learners in terms of interpersonal relationships among the life skills competencies. Thus, more active interactions are expected [40]. As mentioned above, the implications and features of the Entry-based life skill program have been listed, but this study has limitations. The study's subject was limited to 5–6 grade years, not all elementary school students. Since it was impossible to perform objective simple random sampling, the researcher's convenience method was used for the sampling method. That is why there is a limit to generalizing the study to the entire elementary school student population.

11. Conclusions

This study aims to develop an Entry-based life skills program, and the hypothesis is whether an Entry-based life skill program is effective. Life skills need to be developed within the broader framework of an environment that includes personal relationships. Therefore, we should not neglect the possibility of using a school's space because we have focused too much on how to improve life skills. This program for elementary school students was developed to emphasize activities that enhance individual creativity, problem-solving skills, and co-operation and empathy within the school environment [41]. As a result of the program operating from two weeks to eight weeks, it was confirmed that the participating students' various life skills improved. However, it has not been confirmed whether this study's results will be applied uniformly throughout countries with distinct cultural environments. From the first to the third session, teachers led the guidance without difficulty. However, when the conditional sentence appeared in the fourth session, the students became difficult. Therefore, it is necessary to create and distribute a simple workbook in advance for use with conditional sentences, which are the core of coding classes. This study received feedback from participating teachers that practice based on simple theory books was effective because coding classes are the basis of algorithms above all else. It was emphasized that teachers' selective intervention was necessary to reduce the difference in participating students' competency levels.

Teachers working in the school field should consider integrating students' core competencies demanded by the large society into the curriculum through these life skills programs [42]. From the national standpoint, it is necessary to consider a plan to systematically support how life skills' core competencies can develop into human resources. The effect of life skills does not appear in a short period, but it is desirable to form it earlier.

Life skills formed at an early age can be a powerful asset because they help individuals succeed at school, at home, or in different social fields where they live with other neighbors while living in a group [33]. Suppose these assets are cultivated at an early stage. In that case, it would be expected that one could better cope with school violence, bullying, and conflict with friends, which have recently been a problem in countries worldwide. One would also develop a sense of community that warmly embraces society [43]. Therefore, the development of teaching and learning methods for cultivating elementary school students' life skills and research exploring its effects should be pursued for younger age groups. Although research on life skills has been actively conducted in recent years, research on life skills programs for elementary school students is still insufficient.

Considering that life skills are more likely to be internalized and transferred more efficiently, the sooner they are acquired, research targeting elementary school students should be expanded. According to the WHO, there are several ways to improve life skills [19]. There are many things that teachers should do to improve students' life skills, such as the choice and consumption of school meals, integration with the subject class in the classroom, and the formation of a cooperative atmosphere. Among them, the integrated education method with the subject class can be an advantage in the school environment only.

Even if there was no official program called 'Life Skills', perhaps even today, education in schools is related to life skills. Just as various activities are supported to acquire one competency, multiple methods such as physical education, music, reading, computer, storytelling, and mathematics could be used to acquire life skills competencies. In particular, if an activity is related to making or creating games, students' interest and concentration are bound to increase. Therefore, it is expected that more educational programs aimed at improving life skills will be developed on the Internet in the future.

Funding: This research received no external funding.

Institutional Review Board Statement: According to No. 2 of the Elementary and Middle school Education Act, The ethical approval of human study related to general educational practice in official educational institutions could be exempted.

Informed Consent Statement: All subjects and their parents gave their informed consent for inclusion before they participated in the study.

Acknowledgments: The author is grateful for the advice of their colleagues at the Yuk-Buk primary school.

Conflicts of Interest: The authors declare no conflict of interest.

References

1. Schwab, K. *The Fourth Industrial Revolution*; Portfolio Penguin: Broadway, NY, USA, 2016.
2. Kurzweil, R.; Grossman, T. *Transcend: Nine Steps to Living Well Forever*; Rodal: Philadelphia, PA, USA, 2010.
3. Merrill, J.; Merrill, K. *The Interactive Class: Using Technology to Make Learning More Relevant and Engaging in the Elementary Classroom*; ElevateBook Edu: Del Mar, CA, USA, 2020.
4. Budhai, S.S.; Skipwith, K. *Best Practices in Engaging Online Learners through Active and Experiential Learning Strategies*; Routledge: London, UK, 2017.
5. Danish, S.; Forneris, T.; Hodge, K.; Heke, I. Enhancingyouth development through sport. *World Leis. J.* **2006**, *46*, 38–49. [CrossRef]

6. Barclays PLC Annual Report (Registered No: 48839). Churchill Place, London E14 5HP, UK. 2016. Available online: https://www.annualreports.com/HostedData/AnnualReportArchive/b/LSE_BARC_2016.pdf (accessed on 7 February 2021).
7. SAP News Center. How India and Its People Grow with SAP (Feature Article by Michael Zipf: 21 September 2017). Available online: https://news.sap.com/2017/09/india-grows-with-sap/ (accessed on 7 February 2021).
8. Korea IT TIMES, Global News Network (People & Interview: Harman International's Dinesh Paliwal: 18 September 2017 11:40 Approved). Yeouido, Seoul, Korea. Available online: http://www.koreaittimes.com/news/articleView.html?idxno=74021 (accessed on 6 February 2021).
9. Somma, R. *Coding in the Classroom: Why You Should Care about Teaching Computer Science*; No Starch Press: San Francisco, CA, USA, 2020.
10. Bickford, J.H.; Lawson, D.R. Examining Patterns within Challenged or Banned Primary Elementary Books. *J. Curric. Stud. Res.* **2020**, *2*, 16–38. [CrossRef]
11. Mehalik, M.M.; Doppelt, Y.; Schunn, C.D. Middle-school science through design-based learning versus scripted inquiry: Better overall science concept learning and equity gap reduction. *J. Eng. Educ.* **2008**, *97*, 71–85. [CrossRef]
12. OECD. The OECD Model Survey on ICT Access and Usage by Households and Individuals: 2nd Revision ICT. 2015. Available online: https://www.oecd-ilibrary.org/science-and-technology/data/oecd-telecommunications-and-internet-statistics/ict-access-and-usage-by-households-and-individuals_b9823565-en (accessed on 9 February 2021).
13. Romero, M.; Lepage, A.; Lille, B. Computational thinking development through creative programming in higher education. *Int. J. Educ. Technol. High Educ.* **2017**, *14*, 42. [CrossRef]
14. Chen, G.; Shen, J.; Barth-Cohen, L.; Jiang, S.; Huang, X.; Eltoukhy, M. Assessing elementary students' computational thinking in everyday reasoning and robotics programming. *Comput. Educ.* **2017**, *109*, 162–175. [CrossRef]
15. Curzon, P.; Dorling, M.; Ng, T.; Selby, C.; Woollard, J. Developing Computational Thinking in the Classroom: A Framework. 2014. Available online: https://eprints.soton.ac.uk/369594/1/DevelopingComputationalThinkingInTheClassroomaFramework.pdf (accessed on 9 February 2021).
16. Brennan, K.; Balch, C.; Chung, M. *Creative Computing*; Harvard University Press: Cambridge, MA, USA, 2014; Available online: http://scratched.gse.harvard.edu/guide/ (accessed on 9 February 2021).
17. Mihaly, C. *Flow: The Psychology of Optimal Experience*; HarperCollins: Broadway, NY, USA, 2008.
18. Ahyoung, H.; Jihyun, K.; Kwangyun, W. Entry: Visual Programming to Enhance Children's Computational Thinking. In *UbiComp/ISWC'15 Adjunct: Adjunct Proceedings of the 2015 ACM International Joint Conference on Pervasive and Ubiquitous Computing and Proceedings of the 2015 ACM International Symposium on Wearable Computers*; Association for Computing Machinery: New York, NY, USA, 2015; pp. 73–76. [CrossRef]
19. World Health Organization. *Partners in Life-Skills Education*; Department of Mental Health, World Health Organization: Geneva, Switzerland, 1999.
20. UNICEF. *Review of the Life Skills Education Program: A Report Published by UNICEF and Partners in 2016*; National Institute of Education, UNICEF: New York, NY, USA, 2016; Available online: https://www.unicef.org/maldives/reports/review-life-skills-education-programme (accessed on 19 February 2021).
21. Botvin, G.J.; Griffin, K.W.; Diaz, T.; Ifill-Williams, M. Preventing binge drinking during early adolescence: One- and two-year follow-up of a school-based preventive intervention. *Psychol. Addict. Behav.* **2001**, *15*, 360–365. Available online: https://pubmed.ncbi.nlm.nih.gov/11767269 (accessed on 9 February 2021). [CrossRef] [PubMed]
22. Arnett, J.J. Emerging adulthood: What is it and what is it good for? *Child Dev. Perspect.* **2007**, *1*, 68–73. [CrossRef]
23. Weiss, M.R.; Bolter, N.D.; Kipp, L.E. Evaluation of the First Tee in Promoting Positive Youth Development: Group Comparisons and Longitudinal Trends. *Res. Q. Exerc. Sport* **2016**, *87*, 271–283. [CrossRef] [PubMed]
24. Jeong, E.; Hagose, M.; Jung, H.; Ki, M.; Flahault, A. Understanding South Korea's Response to the COVID-19 Outbreak: A Real-Time Analysis. *Int. J. Environ. Res. Public Health* **2020**, *17*, 9571. [CrossRef]
25. Kirkpatrick, M.S.; Aboutabl, M.; Bernstein, D.; Simmons, S. Backward Design: An Integrated Approach to a Systems Curriculum. In Proceedings of the SIGCSE'15: Proceedings of the 46th ACM Technical Symposium on Computer Science Education, Kansas City, MO, USA, 4–7 March 2015; pp. 30–35.
26. Anderson, L.W.; Krathwohl, D.R.; Airasian, P.W.; Cruikshank, K.A.; Mayer, R.E.; Pintrich, P.R.; Raths, J.; Wittrock, M.C. *A Taxonomy for Learning, Teaching, and Assessing: A Revision of Bloom's Taxonomy of Educational Objectives*; Longman: New York, NY, USA, 2001.
27. Roth, D. Understanding by Design: A Framework for Effecting Curricular Development and Assessment. *CBE Life Sci. Educ.* **2007**, *6*, 95–97. [CrossRef]
28. Wiggins, G.P.; McTighe, J. *Understanding by Design*; Association for Supervision and Curriculum Development: Alexandria, VA, USA, 2005.
29. Dorofeev, S.; Grant, P. Sampling methods. In *Statistics for Real-Life Sample Surveys: Non-Simple-Random Samples and Weighted Data*; Cambridge University Press: Cambridge, UK, 2006.
30. Cronin, L.D.; Allen, J. Development and initial validation of the Life Skills Scale for Sport. *Psychol. Sport Exerc.* **2017**, *28*, 105–119. [CrossRef]
31. Garson, D.G. *Validity and Reliability: 2016 Edition (Statistical Associates Blue Book Series 12)*; Amazon.com: Kindle eBooks: Seattle, WA, USA, 2016.

32. Ghasemi1, A.; Zahediasl, S. Normality Tests for Statistical Analysis: A Guide for Non-Statisticians. *Int. J. Endocrinol. Metab.* **2012**, *10*, 486–489. [CrossRef] [PubMed]
33. Gould, D.; Carson, S. Life skills development through sport: Current status and future directions. *Int. Rev. Sport Exerc. Psychol.* **2008**, *1*, 58–78. [CrossRef]
34. Cook, M. Chapter 11—Creating Code Creatively: Automated Discovery of Game Mechanics through Code Generation. In *Video Games and Creativity*; Department of Computing, Imperial College: London, UK, 2015; pp. 225–245.
35. Reynolds, R.; Farshad, F. Urbarium A Socially-Based Game Platform. In Proceedings of the 2007 IEEE Swarm Intelligence Symposium, Honolulu, HI, USA, 1–5 April 2007; pp. 361–365.
36. Ju, H.; Choi, S. Development of Coding Education to Enhance 4Cs Competency. *Korean Soc. Cult. Converg.* **2019**, *41*, 817–846. [CrossRef]
37. Liu, E.Z.-F.; Lin, C.-H.; Liou, P.-Y.; Feng, H.-C.; Hou, H.-T. An analysis of teacher-student interaction patterns in a robotics course for kindergarten children: A pilot study. *Turk. Online J. Educ. Technol.* **2013**, *12*, 9–18.
38. Donovan, C.; Smolkin, L. Children's Genre Knowledge: An Examination of K-5Students Performance on Multiple Tasks Providing Differing Levels of Scaffolding. *Read. Res. Q. Newark.* **2002**, *37*, 428–465. [CrossRef]
39. Hermens, N.; Super, S.; Verkooijen, K.T.; Koelen, M.A. A systematic review of life skill development through sports programs serving socially vulnerable youth. *Res. Q. Exerc. Sport* **2017**, *88*, 408–424. [CrossRef] [PubMed]
40. Marta, G.K. Space and Creativity: Students' Opinions on School Space as a Component of the Creative Environment. *Creat. Theor. Res. Appl.* **2016**, *3*, ctra-2016-0006. Available online: https://content.sciendo.com/configurable/contentpage/journals$002fctra$002f3$002f1$002farticle-p84.xml (accessed on 20 February 2021).
41. Holt, N.L. *Positive Youth Development through Sport*; Routledge: New York, NY, USA, 2016.
42. Gupta, R. The Role of Pedagogy in Developing Life Skills. *Margin J. Appl. Econ. Res.* **2021**, *15*, 50–72. [CrossRef]
43. Menka, C.; Reena, R. Life skills intervention program: A worth change in level of life skills of students. *Int. J. Sci. Res.* **2019**, 8.

Article

Development of an Educational Application for Software Engineering Learning

Antonio Sarasa-Cabezuelo [1,*] and Covadonga Rodrigo [2]

[1] Department of Computer Systems and Computing, School of Computer Science, Complutensian University of Madrid, 28040 Madrid, Spain
[2] Department of Languages and Computer Systems, Computer Science Engineering Faculty, UNED, 28040 Madrid, Spain; covadonga@lsi.uned.es
* Correspondence: asarasa@ucm.es

Abstract: Software engineering is a complicated subject for computer engineering students since the explained knowledge and necessary competencies are more related to engineering as a general knowledge area than to computer science. This article describes a software engineering learning application that aims to provide a solution to this problem. Two ideas are used for this. On the one hand, to facilitate its use it has been implemented as an Android app (in this way it can be used anywhere and at any time). In addition, and on the other hand, a gamification system has been implemented with different learning paths that adapt to the learning styles of each student. In this way, the student is motivated by competing with other classmates, and on the other hand, the application adapts to the way of learning that each one has.

Keywords: eLearning; Android app; software engineering; quiz online; gamification

1. Introduction

Software engineering is a subject that generally does not motivate computer science students [1]. The theoretical and conceptual nature of the contents explained is far from the purely coding tasks [2], and is closer to the engineering tasks that are applied to execute a project [3]. For this reason, students do not show enthusiasm and often have difficulties [4] to understand the usefulness of these techniques and apply them in the development of a computer project. However, the contents and tools of software engineering are key for any computer engineer [5] in order to be able to develop and execute a project in the professional life. It is for this reason that teachers need tools to motivate them.

There are multiple options to motivate students such as actively monitoring less motivated students [6], carrying out internships [7] or curricular adaptation. In the particular case of software engineering, a very widespread technique consists of simulating the realization and execution of a computer project [8]. In this way, the student can experience the same problems and difficulties that occur when working in a company. There are variants in the implementation of this simulation [9]. The most common is to create workgroups that specify and run the same job. However, there is another variant that consists of changing [10] the roles of the students throughout the simulation so that they can play the role of analyst, designer and developer, or else they have to work with projects that have been specified by others partners.

In recent years, the usefulness of the use of gamification as a motivational element in education has been proven in different areas of knowledge [11]. Games promote competitiveness among students [12], and thus encourage them to become more involved in the study of the content [13] that the game deals with in order to obtain good results. There are quite a few studies [14,15] that support the positive effect of its use in education and its influence on a better understanding and comprehension of the contents [16], and on an improvement in academic results [17]. In this sense, different computer tools have been developed that allow the creation of games whose purpose is to show and teach the contents of a subject [18,19]. The result can be games with a significant multimedia load [20] being similar to a video game or simpler games where the important thing is the competitive nature that arises in it.

On the other hand, in the last decade, there has been a revolution in the way in which content is accessed [21]. Thus, it has moved towards digital access based on the use of mobile devices [22,23]. Most students use mobile devices as the main, and in many cases the only way, to access information and to interact with others [24]. In particular, intensive use is made for the consumption of multimedia elements [25] such as movies, video, photos and others. Mobile devices have important advantages in this regard, since they can be used at any time [26] and anywhere. This offers great flexibility as there are no restrictions in terms of schedules [27], leaving the user free to use it. Likewise, mobile devices have another advantage [28] with respect to the speed of access and updating of content. The content creator can keep the content updated in a very simple way [29], as well as report updates and news in the content immediately.

In this article, a tool is presented that aims to help a software engineering teacher to motivate students and complement their training. For this, two design principles have been considered; on the one hand, the advantages offered by using a game as a motivational element that favors the competitiveness of students and their involvement in the game. In addition, the second idea is the format of the game, for this it has been decided to implement it as an application for a mobile device [30], given the widespread use by students and the advantages it offers to be able to be used anywhere and at any time, offering great flexibility of schedules.

The structure of the paper is as follows. In Section 2, the architecture of the application, the data model used and the REST API implemented will be described. Next, in Section 3, the functionality of the application is presented according to the three types of users that can use it: administrator, student and teacher. Section 4 describes an evaluation of usability that has been carried out among a group of professors, students and non-university personnel. Finally, Section 5 presents a set of conclusions and lines of future work.

2. Architecture and Data Model

The application has been implemented using a client-server model where the client is an Android application that runs on the mobile device, which does requests to the server and waits for a response. The server implements a set of services that are used by clients. An API (application programming interface) of REST services has been implemented in the server that allows access to a specific service. When the client does requests through HTTP to the services exposed by the REST API, it retrieves the necessary data from the database, processes it and returns it to the client with the necessary structure. To use them, the client only needs to know the format and content of the response to the requested service.

The data model has been implemented using a MariaDB-type relational database consisting of nine tables:

- User table. Stores profile information and manages the three types of users present in the application.
- Topic table. Stores the information of the topics present in the application and their description.
- Question table. Stores the information of the question repository present in the application.
- NodoCA table. Represents a node in the tree that contains an exam question that will be shown to the student user. It contains information about the question, a pointer to the node with the alternative question, a pointer to the topic that the question refers to, and a pointer to the teacher user who created the question.
- Alternative node table. Describes the information that represents the "Object" defined as an alternative question in the exam, if the student fails the main question. This entity represents a node in the tree structure formed for the learning path.

- Achievements table. This describes the information represented in the Achievements table, which represents the level obtained by a student user in a certain topic, so it is related to both tables.
- Answer table. Represents the information of an answer to a specific question, so it contains a pointer to the question from which it came.
- Statistics table. It contains the information that a student has obtained in a certain exam, that is, number of correct and failed answers, average response time.
- Question_Suspended table. It contains the information that represents the information of the questions that a student has failed in a certain exam, that is, the ids of these questions.

Finally, regarding the implemented REST API, services have been defined for the following modules:

- User Module. It contains all the services related to the user's profile, login and registration, all the achievements and milestones corresponding to the students and their statistics. The base URL on which these services would be mounted would be "/user". The description of the available endpoints is shown in Table 1.
- Question module. It contains all the services related to the questions of the common repository for all teachers. The base URL on which these services will be mounted will be "/question". The description of the available endpoints is shown in Table 2.
- Topic module. It contains all the services related to the themes of the common repository for all users. The base URL on which these services will be mounted will be "/topic". The description of the available endpoints is shown in Table 3.
- NodoCA module. It contains all the services related to the nodes that together will represent a complete exam, that is, the tree corresponding to a learning path created by a teacher. The base URL on which these services will be mounted will be "/nodeca". The description of the available endpoints is shown in Table 4.

Table 1. Endpoints available in the User module.

ENDPOINT	HTTP Method	Answer	Description
/	POST	Error code (200 or 400) with msg	Insert a user in DB
/{nick}	GET	Error code (200 or 400) with user object in body	Gets a user from the DB
/	GET	Error code (200 or 400) with users	Get list of registered users
/{nick}	PUT	Error code (200 or 400) with msg	Update a user in DB
/level/{nick}/reset	PUT	Error code with msg	Update user statistics
/{nick}	DELETE	Error code with msg	Delete a user from the DB
/teachers	GET	Error code with msg and users (teachers) objects in Json	Gets all teachers who have request submitted for registration and not approved by admin
/students	GET	Error msg and users (students) objects in Json	Gets all student users sorted by percentage
/activate/{nick}	PUT	Msg with error code	Activates a teacher user
/porc/{nick}/{porcentaje}	PUT	Msg with error code	Updates a user's game completion percentage
/picture/{nick}	POST	Msg with error code	Updates a user's profile picture
/pictures	GET	User images	Get the profile images of the students

Table 1. Cont.

ENDPOINT	HTTP Method	Answer	Description
/level/{user}/{IdTema}	GET	Error msg along with user level	Gets the level of a student user in a given topic
/levels/{user}	GET	Error msg, along with array of levels per topic	Gets all levels of a user per topic
/level/increment/{nick}/{idTema}	PUT	Msg with response code	Increase the level of a user in a certain topic
/level/decrement/{nick}/{idTema}	PUT	Msg with response code	Decreases the level of a user in a certain topic
/stadistics/{nick}/{nodoCA}	PUT	Msg with response code	Updates a user's statistics based on their current level
/stadistics/{user}	GET	Msg with response code, if ok, array of user statistics	Get all user statistics for all levels
/exam/suspended/{user}	GET	Msg with response code, if ok, exam object array	Gets the failed exams of a student
/{idUsuario}/{idNodoCa}	DELETE	Msg with response code	Removing a user's statistics

Table 2. Endpoints available in the Question module.

ENDPOINT	HTTP Method	Answer	Description
/	POST	Error code (200 or 400) with msg	Insert a question in DB
/questions/{idTema}	GET	Error code (200 or 400) with question array object	Get all questions for a given topic
/questions/{idTema}/{language}	GET	Error code (200 or 400) with question array object	Get all questions for a given topic and language
/{id}	GET	Error code (200 or 400) with msg and in case of ok, object asks.	Get a question
/	PUT	Error code with msg	Update all data for a question
/{id}	DELETE	Error code with msg	Delete a question with its answers from the DB
/suspended/{userNick}/{nodoCa}	GET	Error code with msg and query object array	Get a list of failed questions in an exam

Table 3. Endpoints available in the Topic module.

ENDPOINT	HTTP Method	Answer	Description
/	GET	Error code (200 or 400) with msg and in case of ok, topic object array	Get all topics
/{id}	GET	Error code (200 or 400) with msg and in case of ok, topic object	Get a topic

Table 4. Endpoints available in the NodoCA module.

ENDPOINT	HTTP Method	Answer	Description
/	POST	Error code with msg	Insert a node in DB
/saveCA	GET	Error code with msg	Add a complete CA, that is, save an exam in the DB.
/getCA/{nick}/{tema}/{nivel}/{language}	GET	Error code (200 or 400) with question array object	Get complete random CA for a given topic at a given level (initial, bronze, silver, gold) and language that is published
/list/nopublished/{tema}/{teacher}/{language}	GET	Error code with msg and in case of ok, full nodeca object array (tree structure)	Get all unpublished CAs (Exams) from a teacher on a certain topic
/list/{tema}/{teacher}/{language}	GET	Error code with msg and in case of ok, full nodeca object array (tree structure)	Get all the CAs of a teacher in a certain topic
/{id}	GET	Error code with msg and in case of ok, CA node object without children	Get a CA node
/public/{idParent}	PUT	Error code with msg	Publish a CA or exam (Parameter id of the parent node)
/{idParent}	DELETE	Error code with msg	Delete an exam from the DB
/original/{idParent}/{idNodoASust}/{idQuestionaAn}	PUT	Error code with msg	Update a CA modifying original question {idQuestioASust} id of the question we want to replace, {idQuestionaAn} id of the question to add
/alt/{idParent}/{idNodoASust}/{idQuestionaAn}	PUT	Error code with msg	Update a CA by modifying Alternative question, {idQuestioASust} id of the question we want to replace, {idQuestionaAn} id of the question to add

3. Functionality

The functionality of the Android application will be explained below. For this, the dynamics of the game will be explained first, and then the functions of each type of user will be explained: administrator, student and teacher.

3.1. The Quizz

From the student's perspective, the application implements a game that is structured in several phases or content modules. In each module there are different topics that have a certain level of difficulty associated with them. The four levels of the game are initial, bronze, silver or gold. The objective of a student is to obtain the highest possible level in each module. To pass a level you must take an exam that consists (Figure 1) of 10 main questions and 10 alternatives for each main question. There are 30 s to answer each question so that if this time is exceeded, the system goes to the next one and it will be counted as a failure.

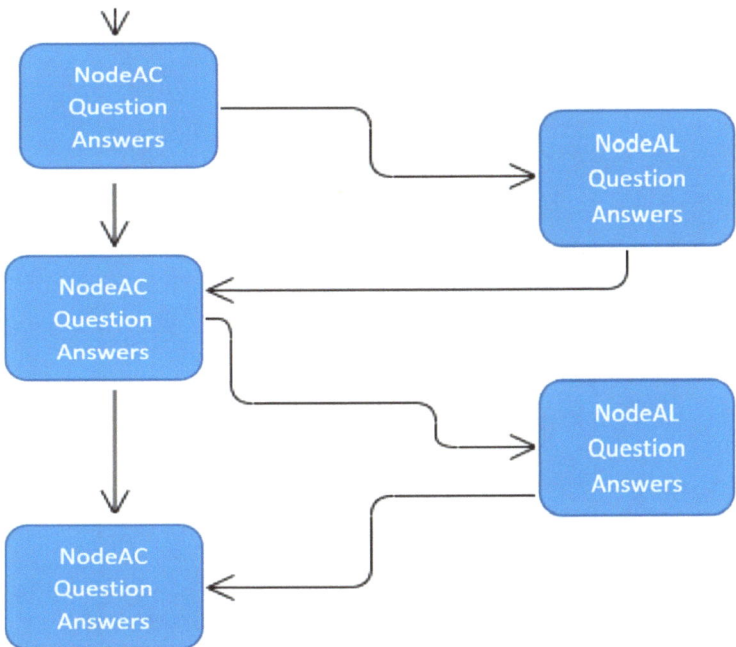

Figure 1. Tree structure containing the exam.

Structurally, each exam is represented as a question tree where in each node there is a child that represents the main question and another child that represents the alternative question. If the student fails, they lose 0.5 points, a message is displayed on the screen, and then an alternate question is displayed. If the alternative question is answered correctly then 0.5 points are added to it and if it is failed, again it is assigned 0 points. If the student answers the main question correctly, 0.5 points are added. This process continues (Figure 2) until Question 10 (in the worst case it would be necessary to answer 20 questions in total).

When the exam ends, the student is informed by a sound according to the score, whether or not they have passed the exam. If the student passes, the application adds the percentage of the game. In the case of abandoning the exam, the student will drop one level with respect to the one they have at that moment. Each exam counts a percentage of the completed game based on whether an exam is being taken for a certain level, that is, the full gold level, adds 45% of the completed game, silver level 35% and bronze level 20%. If the user is in the initial level and takes an exam on Topic 1 to go up to the bronze level (there are 16 topics available) then in case of passing it, a percentage of the game completed of $20/16 = 1.25\%$ will rise. In the same way, it is calculated for the levels of gold and silver.

The criteria to pass to the next level are as follows:

- If the user had an initial level and obtains a score ≥ 5 in the exam, they will pass to the bronze level;
- If the user was bronze level and gets a score ≥ 7 in the exam, they will pass to silver level;
- If the user had a silver level and gets a score ≥ 8 in the exam, they will pass to the gold level;

The game ends when the user reaches the gold level in all topics.

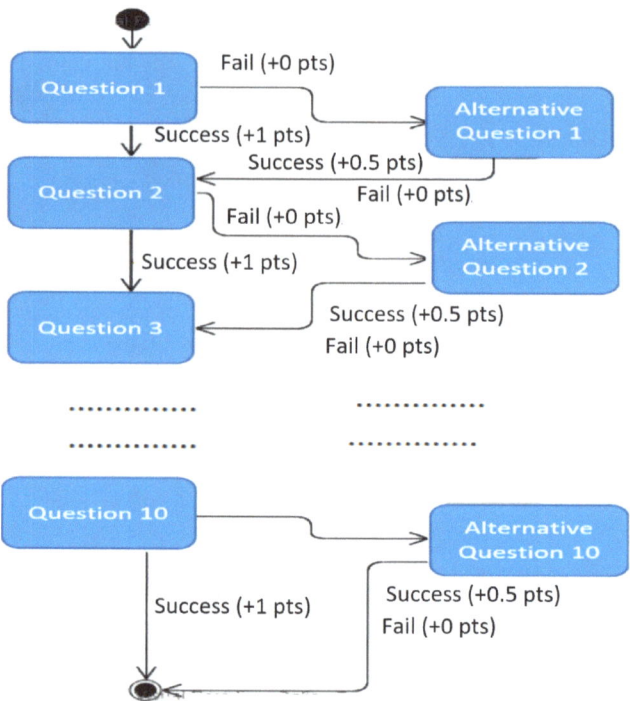

Figure 2. Game development sequence diagram.

3.2. Student

The main functions of the student user are:

- Take an exam. Figure 3 shows the screen where the different content modules appear. When clicking on a module, the user is asked if they want to take an exam to level up, and if they accept, the exam to take is shown. To do this, the student clicks on the "Game" ("Juego") menu tab, and a screen is displayed with all the available topics and the level of each one of them. Next, if it is clicked on one of the topics, then the student will be able to take an exam to obtain the next level in that particular topic. For it, the student must click on the "Play" ("Jugar") button. If there are published exams for that topic and that level, the student will be able to do the exam. Otherwise, the initial screen is returned and it is reported that there are no exams in the repository to obtain the next level.
- View statistics. Figure 4 shows the screen where the modules that a user has made appear. When you click on an exam, the statistics of each module appear, and the incorrect answers are shown for each exam performed. The user can see the statistics of the exams taken, the average response time or the level obtained in each topic. To do this, the user must go to the Ranking screen of the menu where a list of all students is displayed, and click on the own profile or that of any other student, showing the levels in each topic. Regarding statistics, only the own statistics are visible but not those of the rest of students. On the other hand, if it is clicked on the "Show Fails" ("Mostrar Suspensos") button, a screen will be displayed with a summary with the exams it has been failed, and by clicking on a specific exam; the content of the exam and the failed questions will be displayed.
- Reset state. The student can reset the game counter and clear all the statistics and tests taken. To do this, on the main screen it must be clicked on the "Reset Score and Achievements" ("Resetear Puntuación y Logros") button.

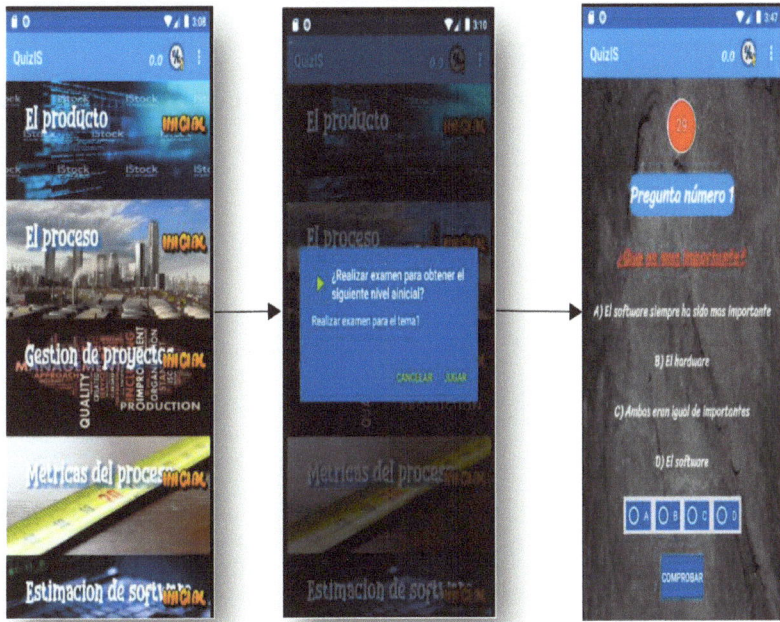

Figure 3. Take an exam.

Figure 4. View statistics.

3.3. Teacher

The main functions of the teacher user are the following:
- Check the status of a student. It is possible to view the ranking and the statistics associated with any student registered in the application.
- Manage question repository. Figure 5 shows the teacher's screen with all the content modules. When you click on a module, another screen is displayed where the teacher can create or edit exams for that module. When a teacher user accesses the menu tab called "Game" ("Juego"), it is possible to view an interface where the course topics are listed but without levels associated with each topic. If it is clicked on a topic, a screen is displayed where the next actions are shown:
    1. Add question. Figure 6b shows the teacher's screen from which a new question can be created to include in the question repository. To do this, it is necessary to click on the "Create Question" ("Crear Pregunta") button that will display a new screen where the data for the question are entered. Then, click on the "Save" ("Guardar") button, being stored in the common repository of questions for all teacher users. The questions in the repository can be modified, deleted or used to create an exam by any teacher.
    2. Create a question repository. Figure 6a shows the teacher's screen from which a question repository can be created. To do this, it is necessary to click on the "Create repository" ("Crear Repositorio") button, which will display a form where the number of questions in the repository must be indicated. The same process of creating questions is repeated as many times as the number of questions indicated.
    3. Delete a question. To do this, it is necessary to click on the "Delete Question" ("Borrar Pregunta") button, showing a screen with all the questions available in the common repository of teachers. If it is clicked on any of the questions, it will be asked if the user would like to delete that question. If it is confirmed, then it will permanently delete it from the repository. If the question is used in some exam, then it cannot be deleted and an informational message will be displayed to the user.
    4. Modify question. To do this, it is necessary to click on the "Modify Question" ("Modificar Pregunta") button and a screen will appear with all of the questions available in the common repository of teachers. If it is clicked on any of the questions, the same screen used for "Add Question" appears but with the data filled in. Next, the data is modified, and when the modification is finished, it must be clicked on "Save" ("Guardar") button.
    5. Create an exam. Figure 7a shows the screen that shows the list of exams that have not been published and Figure 7b shows the screen for creating a new exam. The process is the following. It must be clicked on the "Create CA" ("Crear CA") button, and a screen will be displayed where it must be indicated the level of the exam (bronze, silver or gold). Next, it is shown the question repository where it must be repeated 10 times: choose a main question and choose an alternate question each time. The repository must have at least 11 questions in order to create an exam.
    6. Modify exam. Figure 7c shows the screen for modifying an exam and Figure 7d shows the screen that allows you to delete a specific exam. The process is the following. It is clicked on the "Modify CA" ("Modificar CA") button, showing a screen with a summary of the exams that have not yet been published. If it is clicked on one of them, all the information of the exam will be displayed, and below the repository of questions. If one of the exam questions is selected, the application will ask if the user would like to replace the main question or the alternative. The user must then select a question from the repository to replace the previous one. Finally, it must be clicked on the "Modify" ("Modificar") button.

7. Delete exam. Figure 7d shows the screen that allows you to delete a specific exam. The process is the following. It is clicked on the "Delete CA" ("Borrar CA") button, showing a screen with a summary of all published and unpublished exams. If it is clicked on an exam, all the information of the exam will be displayed. Next, it must be clicked on "Delete" ("Borrar") button to delete it from the system.
8. Publish exam. It is clicked on the "Publish CA" ("Publicar CA") button, showing a screen with a summary of all unpublished exams. If it is clicked on an exam, all the information of the exam will be displayed. Next, it must click on "Publish" ("Publicar") button to publish it in the system.

Figure 5. Manage question repository.

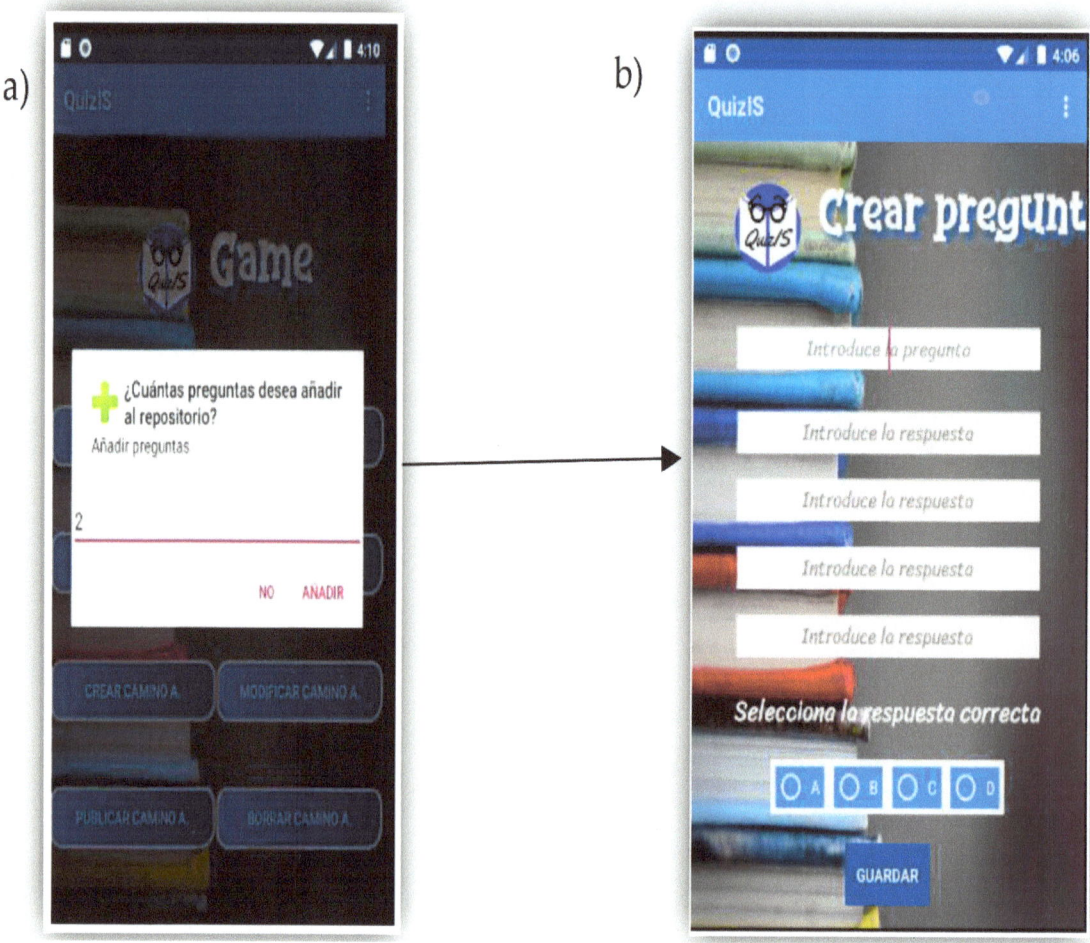

Figure 6. (**a**) Create a question repository; (**b**) add question.

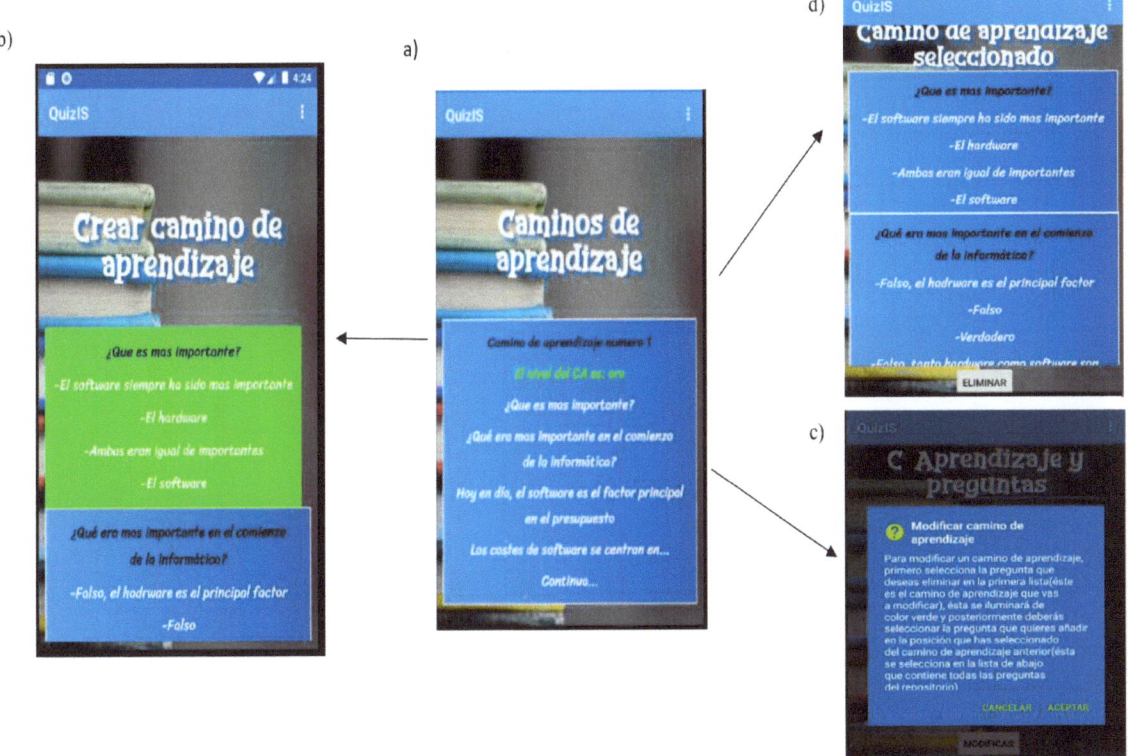

Figure 7. (**a**) Unpublished exams repository; (**b**) create exam; (**c**) modify exam; (**d**) delete exam.

3.4. Administrator

The main functions of the administrator user are the following:

- Deactivate teacher Figure 8a shows the screen where a teacher can be deactivated. The process is the following. The administrator must search for the user that it must be deactivated, select it and click on the button "Unsubscribe Users" ("Dar de baja usuarios").
- Activate teacher. Figure 8b shows how to activate a teacher. The process is the following. If there is a teacher user pending activation, when the administrator logs in a notification is displayed. Next, to activate the user, the administrator must click on the notification, and a screen appears where the activation must be confirmed by clicking "Accept" ("Aceptar").

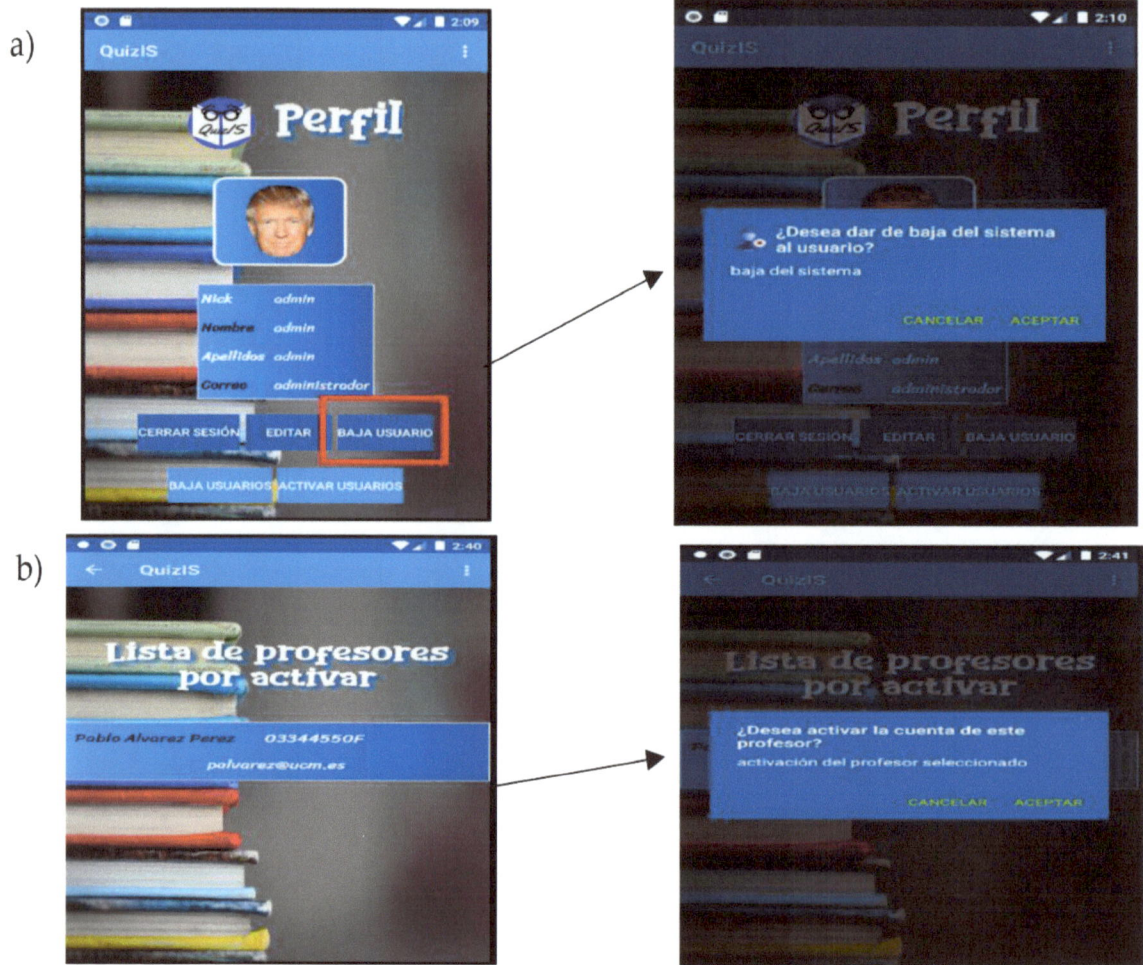

Figure 8. (**a**) Deactivate teacher; (**b**) activate teacher.

3.5. Other Common Functions

The application has a set of functions common to all users:

- Login. Figure 9a shows the login screen. The process is as follows: It is necessary to be registered in the application. In the login screen, the username and password must be entered. When the session starts, the user's home page is displayed. Always, it is possible to log out and return to the login screen using the log out ("Cerrar sesión") button.
- Register. Figure 9b shows the screen for editing a user's profile. The process is as follows: the "Register" ("Registro") button that appears on the login screen must be clicked, and the user must enter the requested data on the screen that appears. In particular, it must be indicated if the user will register as a teacher or as a student.
- Edit profile. Figure 9c shows the screen for registering. The process is the following. To do this, click on the edit button that appears on the user's home page and a screen is displayed with the user's data that can be modified: password, image and others. To confirm the changes, it must be clicked on the "Update" ("Actualizar") button.

- Unsubscribe user. Figure 10c shows the screen to unsubscribe from the application. To do this, it must be clicked on the "Unsubscribe" ("Dar de baja") button that appears on the user's home page, and confirm the action.
- Check ranking. Figure 10a shows the application options menu and Figure 10b shows the user profile edit screen. To do this, it must be clicked on the menu located at the top right of the user's home page. As a result, a list of students is shown, so that if it is selected one, then the name, nick, email and percentage of the game completed will be displayed.

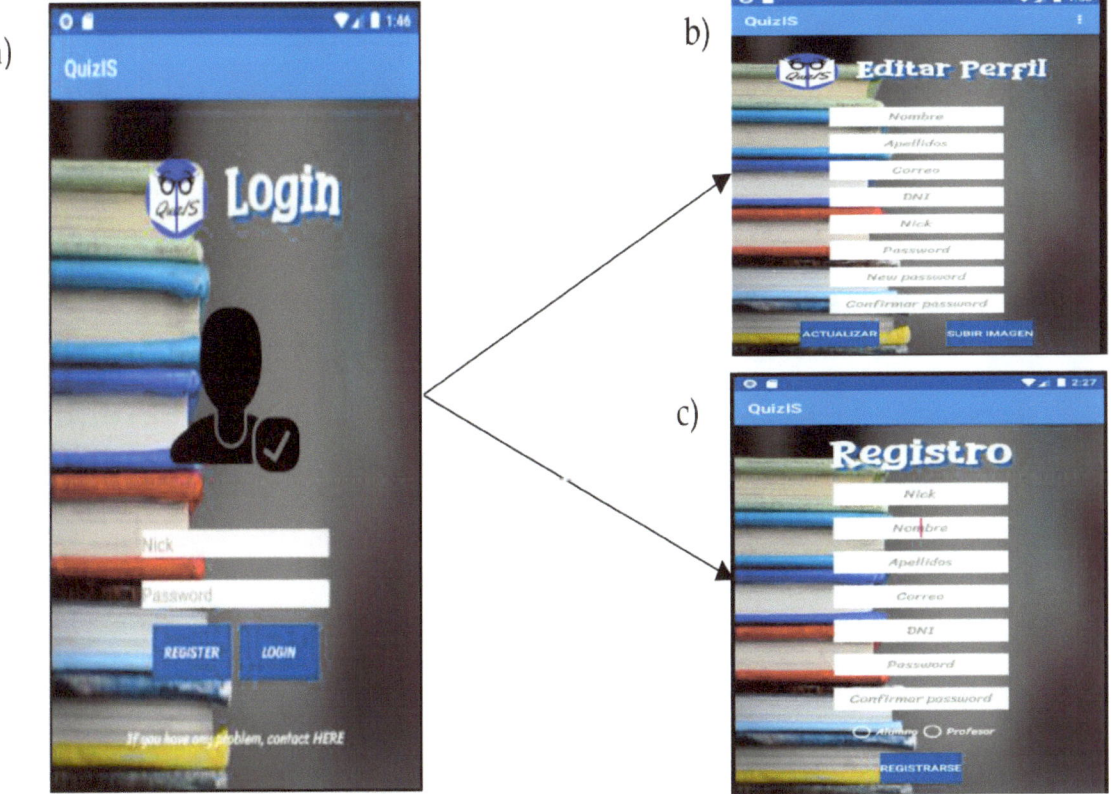

Figure 9. (**a**) Login; (**b**) edit profile; (**c**) register.

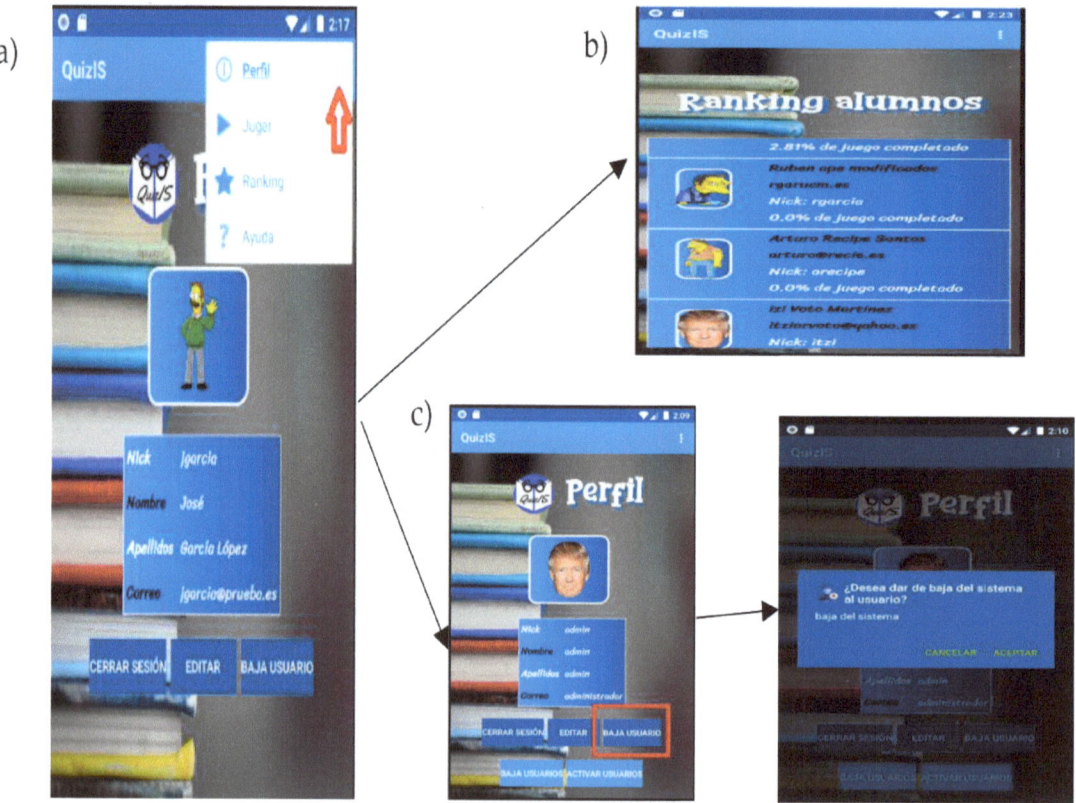

Figure 10. (**a**) Menu; (**b**) ranking; (**c**) unsubscribe process.

4. Evaluation

An evaluation of the usability of the implemented application has been carried out. For this, a study population of 43 people has been considered, made up of 13 teachers, 17 students and 13 people with no relation to the university. The administrator, student or teacher roles have been evaluated, and based on the type; one type of question or another has been shown (half of the respondents tested the application with the role of student, and the other half with the role of administrator and teacher). The questions asked in the evaluation are measured using a Likert scale between one and five where zero would be the least satisfied and five would be the most. The evaluation has been carried out using Google Forms. In each block of the survey, it is possible to see the steps to follow before asking the user the assessment question (Questions used in the assessment can be found in Appendix A). The classification of the question blocks is as follows:

- The first block of questions shows general questions related to age, relationship with university, and gender.
- The second block shows questions related to the user's role. At this point, the user must follow the steps indicated before evaluating the questions.

The third block of questions deals with the global evaluation of the application and proposals for improvements and changes where the user can freely give their opinion. The results of the evaluation have been as follows. The evaluation of the usability of the profile editing interface has been assessed in all cases with values greater than three points (Figure 11a). Likewise, the interface of the game screen that shows the study topics has been evaluated with four and five points (Figure 11b), and has a high percentage with two and three points, in terms of the process of uploading an image to the profile (Figure 11c). Finally, all the respondents evaluate with five points, the process of taking an exam (Figure 11d).

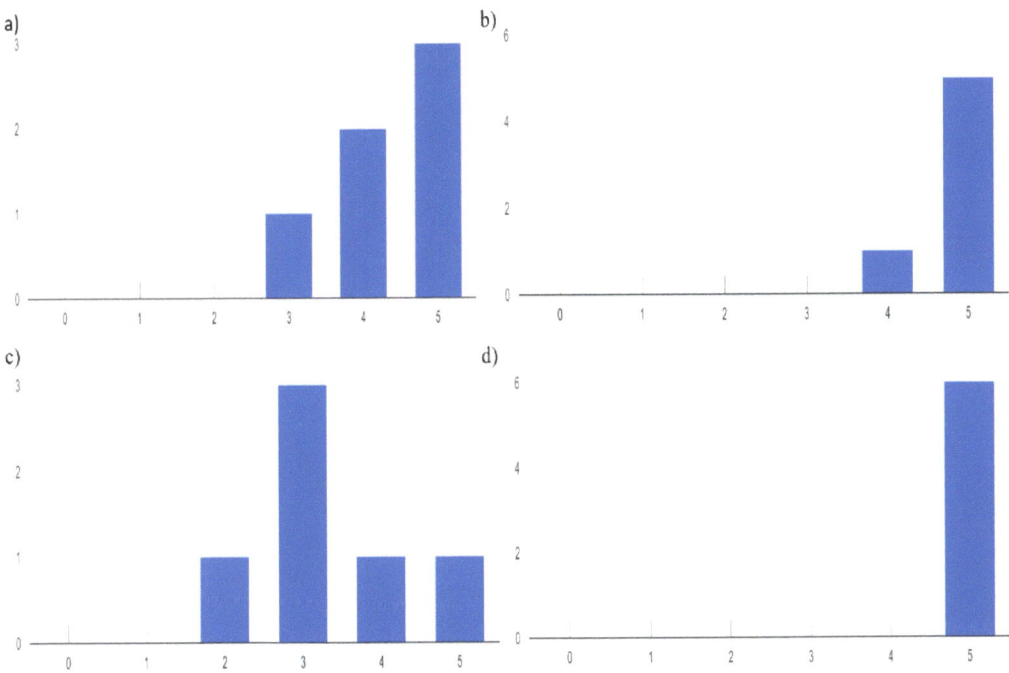

Figure 11. Student role evaluation. (**a**) Usability of the profile editing interface, (**b**) Usability of interface of the game screen, (**c**) The process of uploading an image, (**d**) The process of taking an exam.

The process of editing the profile and uploading an image of the teacher role is evaluated with two points in most cases and three points in the rest (Figure 12a,b). On the other hand, the game interface for the teacher role is evaluated in all cases with four and five points (Figure 12c). The process of creating an exam or updating a question from the repository is rated by participants above three points (Figure 12d). Finally, satisfaction with the quiz post and delete screens for users taking the survey as teachers is rated above four in all cases (Figure 12e,f).

(The usability of the interface of the role administrator has been evaluated by all participants with four points (Figure 13).

A total of 33% of those surveyed have evaluated the ease of use of the application with four points and 66% with five points (Figure 14a). Likewise, most of the participants evaluate with four and five points, the colors used in the application and the usability of the interface (Figure 14b), and only a few cases evaluate it with two and three points.

In Block 3 of the evaluation, there was a block of free response questions where the respondents have made some proposals for improvements such as:

- View the screen horizontally.
- Eliminate background sound when pressing.
- Improve the colors and design of the interface.
- Improve the editing of an exam.
- Improve the display of some texts in the application.
- Improve the color and font of some texts
- Improve the identification of possible answers in question tests.

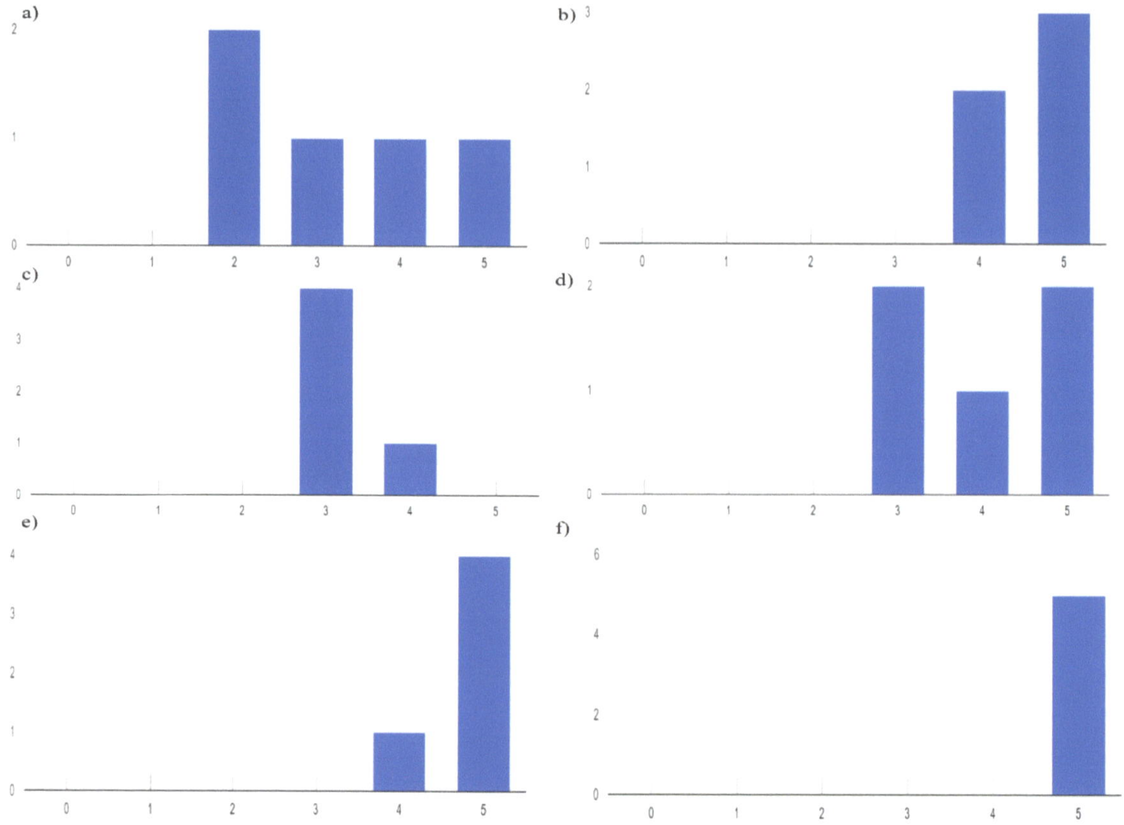

Figure 12. Teacher role evaluation. (**a**) The process of editing the profile, (**b**) The process of uploading an image, (**c**) Evaluating of interface, (**d**) The process of creating exams, (**e**) Satisfaction of the quiz post, (**f**) Satisfaction with delete screens for users.

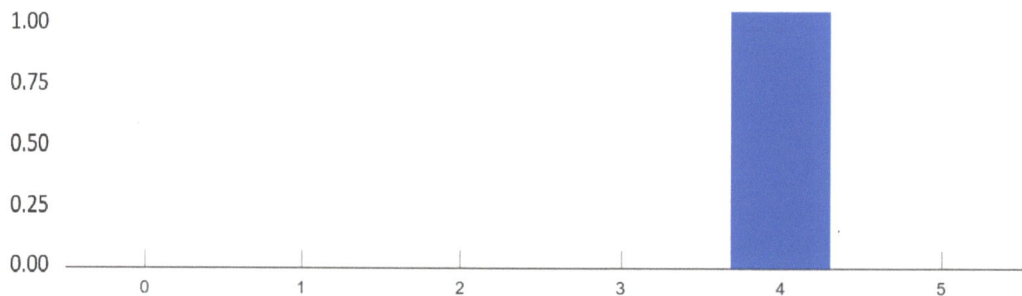

Figure 13. Administrator role evaluation.

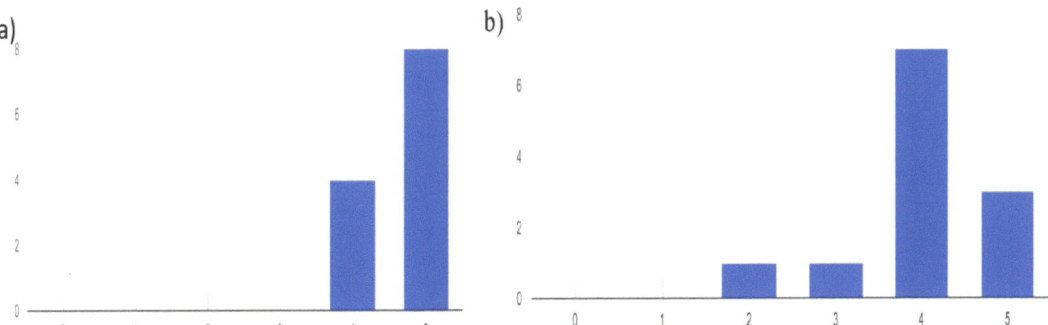

Figure 14. Overall satisfaction evaluation. (**a**) Ease of use of the application, (**b**) Usability of the interface.

5. Conclusions and Future Work

This article has described an Android application that allows complementing the training of university students in software engineering. The application implements a game of questions organized in 16 different topics with different levels of difficulty. To finish the game it is necessary to obtain the maximum level in each one of the subjects. The game consists of taking exams with questions about the corresponding topic and with the appropriate difficulty for the level at which it is being played. Each exam consists of 10 main questions and 10 alternative questions for the case of failure the main questions. For each correct answer to a main question, one point is obtained, and if it is an alternative question, one half of a point is obtained. In all other cases, zero points are obtained. The students who participate in the game are organized in a ranking according to the points they have obtained in the different exams carried out, and can consult the points of the rest of the participants. In addition to the student user, the application administrator role and the teacher role in charge of preparing the questions and exams have been defined.

The application has been evaluated among students, professors and people outside the university, obtaining a good result and a good acceptance.

The advantages of the application are the use of gamification to introduce and complement a subject that is normally complex and not very motivating for computer science students. Through play and the promotion of the competitive aspect, students are motivated and receptive to the contents explained. Likewise, another advantage is the possibility of using the application from a mobile phone, so that it is easy to access anytime, anywhere. This aspect is key, given that the habits of current students demonstrate intensive use of mobile devices. On the other hand, it is important to highlight the intuitive and simple interfaces of the application, which facilitates its use and favors its use. Finally, from the teacher's point of view, the application is interesting since it constitutes an optimal tool to complement the regular training of face-to-face classes. In addition, it serves as an instrument to better know their students and their understanding of the subject: concepts they do not understand, the level of knowledge of the students, participation and motivation of the students.

There are a wide variety of systems that offer functionalities similar to those implemented in this work. However, the described tool presents some novelties and differences. In the first place, the learning process developed is novel since it allows the creation of different learning itineraries adapted to the levels of the students. For this, a tree-shaped structure of the exams is used in which alternative questions to the main ones can be created, functioning as a Socratic tutor. Second, from a technological point of view, the application presents as a novelty the implementation of a layer of REST-type web services that allows the modification and addition of new services in a simple way since all services are independent of each other, achieving a loosely coupled, consistent and easily extensible and maintainable system. Lastly, the tool implements a "learning by doing" strategy, given that learning is carried out through practical tests where the teacher can delve into a topic through questions aimed at reinforcing learning.

However, the application has some limitations that represent future lines of work. In the first place, with regard to the exams, it would be interesting to expand the types of questions that can be used as well as the possibility of obtaining a certificate of completion of the course. Regarding the services offered to students, the application could be improved with functions such as creating groups of friends among users so that they can follow the activity of friends, implement the interface in languages other than Spanish or provide new tools, providing communication for teachers and students. In addition, with regard to the operation of the application, it could be improved by allowing competitions between the best players, expanding the application to other areas of knowledge or connecting the application with the course management system used at the university to share information about students, the activity and the grades obtained.

On the other hand, it should be noted that the evaluation carried out consisted of conducting an exploratory investigation with a non-representative sample. However, it is proposed as an improvement to consider a more significant sample and perform an evaluation in a real software engineering class with the aim of evaluating the usefulness to improve student learning. The qualitative and quantitative data obtained would be analyzed using analysis tools such as SAS Enterprise Miner.

Author Contributions: Conceptualization, A.S.-C. and C.R.; methodology, A.S.-C.; software, A.S.-C. and C.R.; validation, A.S.-C. and C.R.; investigation, A.S.-C.; writing—original draft preparation, A.S.-C. and C.R.; writing—review and editing, A.S.-C. and C.R.; supervision, C.R. All authors have read and agreed to the published version of the manuscript.

Funding: This research received no external funding.

Institutional Review Board Statement: Not applicable.

Informed Consent Statement: Not applicable.

Data Availability Statement: All data has been present in main text.

Acknowledgments: I would like to thank Rubén García Mateos for implementing the system described in the article.

Conflicts of Interest: The authors declare no conflict of interest.

Appendix A

The evaluation questions asked are shown below. There are three blocks of questions, Block 1 contained more generic questions about the respondents, Block 2 contained personal opinion about the different functionalities of the application depending on the role of the person who carried out the survey, and Block 3 contained changes proposed by the respondent and general assessment.

The first block of questions that are shown to the user are questions related to age, relationship with the university or teaching, and gender (Figure A1).

The second block shows questions related to the role of the user who has decided when taking the survey in the last question of Block 1:

(a) Assessment questions for registered student role (Figures A2–A5)

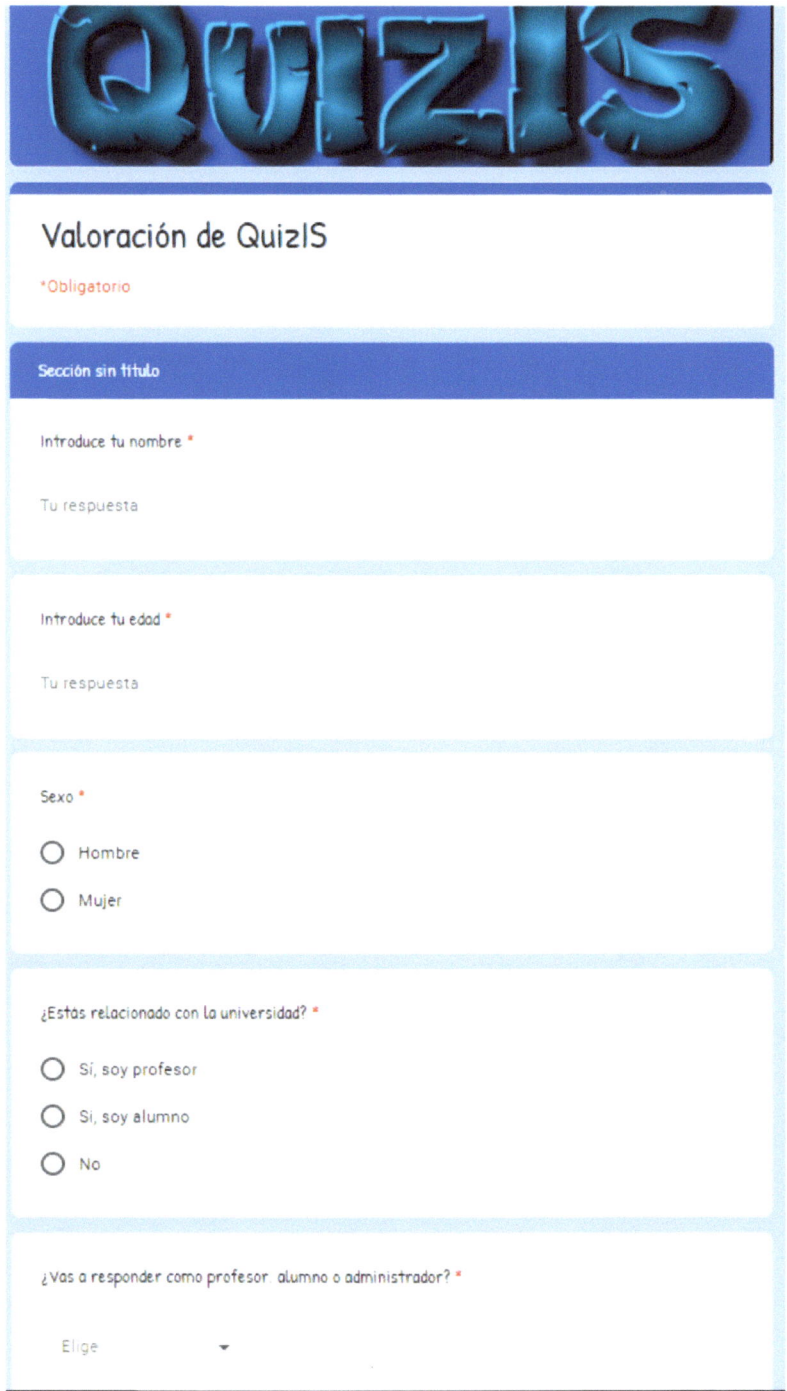

Figure A1. First block of questions.

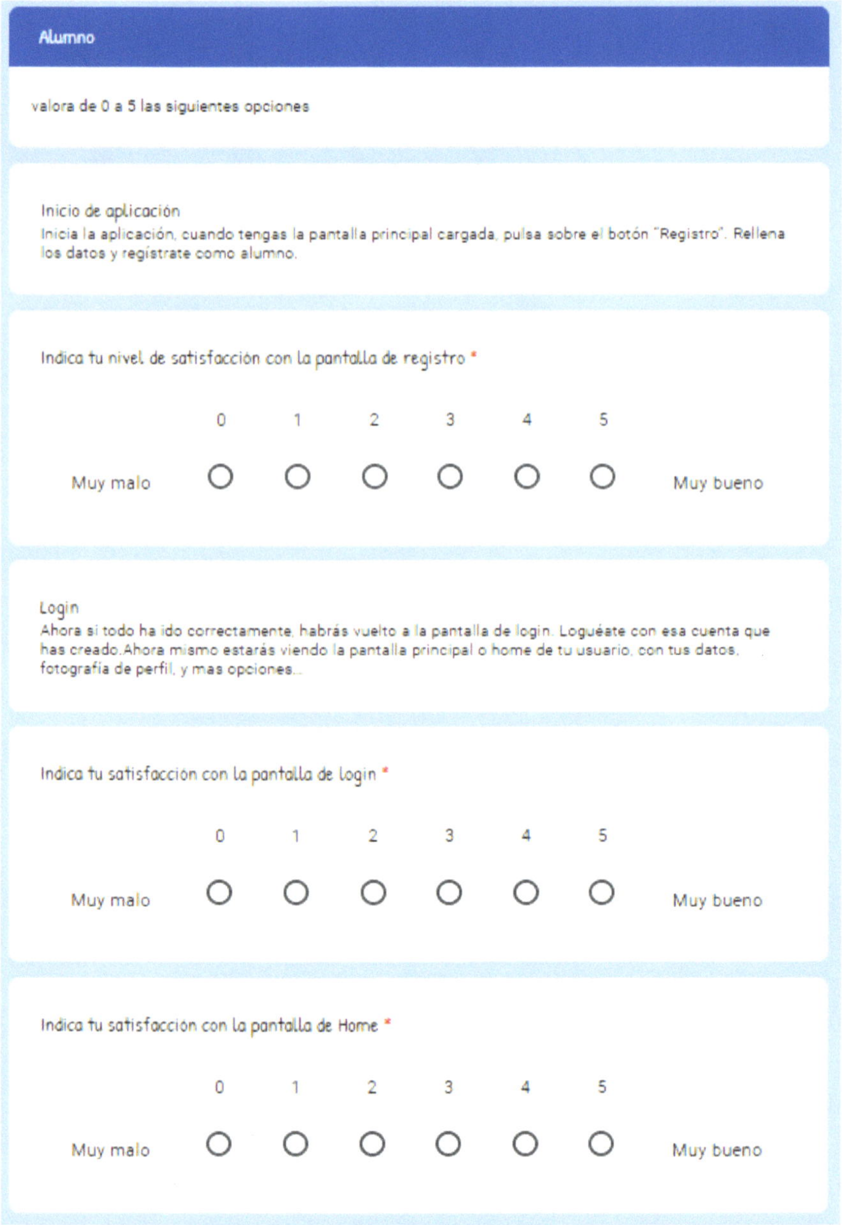

Alumno

valora de 0 a 5 las siguientes opciones

Inicio de aplicación
Inicia la aplicación, cuando tengas la pantalla principal cargada, pulsa sobre el botón "Registro". Rellena los datos y regístrate como alumno.

Indica tu nivel de satisfacción con la pantalla de registro *

	0	1	2	3	4	5	
Muy malo	○	○	○	○	○	○	Muy bueno

Login
Ahora si todo ha ido correctamente, habrás vuelto a la pantalla de login. Loguéate con esa cuenta que has creado. Ahora mismo estarás viendo la pantalla principal o home de tu usuario, con tus datos, fotografía de perfil, y mas opciones...

Indica tu satisfacción con la pantalla de login *

	0	1	2	3	4	5	
Muy malo	○	○	○	○	○	○	Muy bueno

Indica tu satisfacción con la pantalla de Home *

	0	1	2	3	4	5	
Muy malo	○	○	○	○	○	○	Muy bueno

Figure A2. Assessment questions for registered student role.

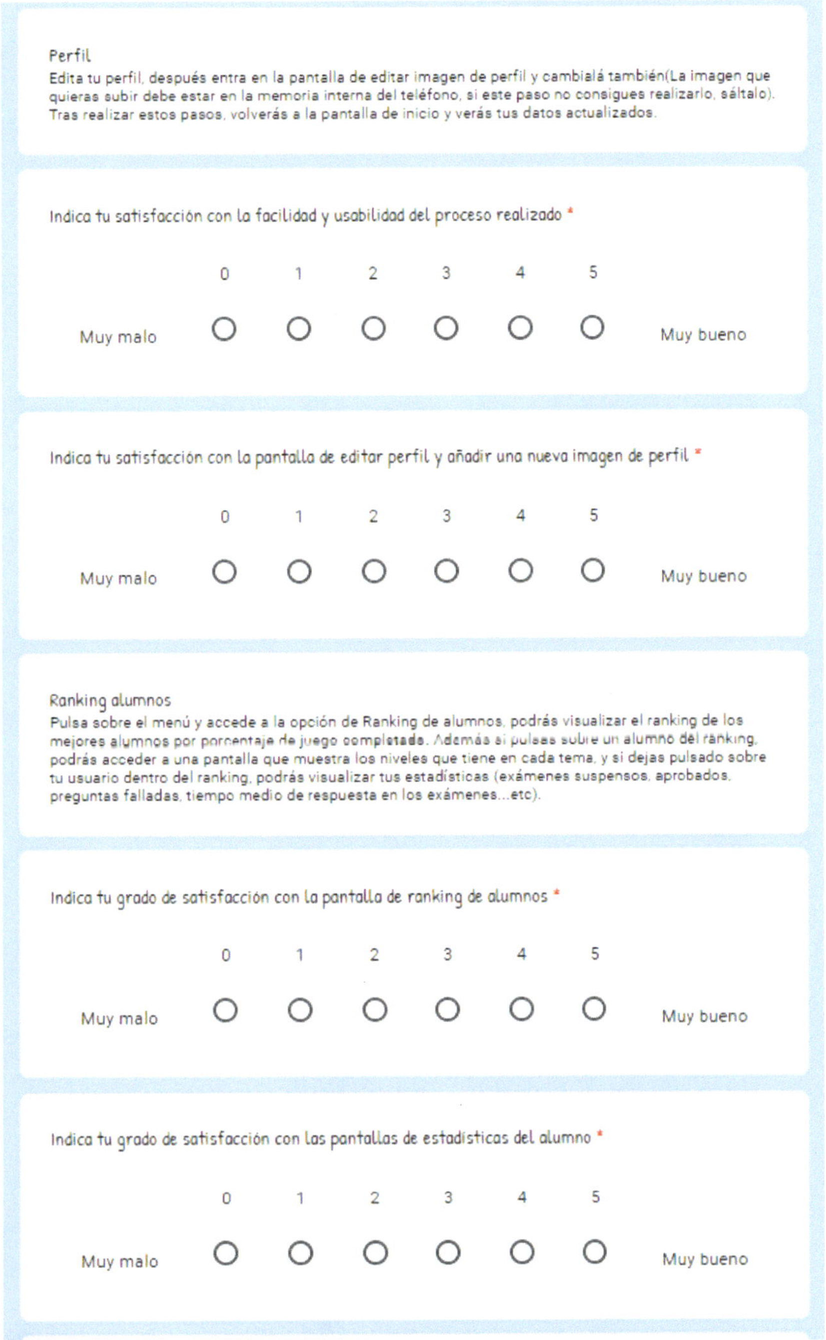

Perfil
Edita tu perfil, después entra en la pantalla de editar imagen de perfil y cambiala también(La imagen que quieras subir debe estar en la memoria interna del teléfono, si este paso no consigues realizarlo, sáltalo). Tras realizar estos pasos, volverás a la pantalla de inicio y verás tus datos actualizados.

Indica tu satisfacción con la facilidad y usabilidad del proceso realizado *

0   1   2   3   4   5
Muy malo   ○   ○   ○   ○   ○   ○   Muy bueno

Indica tu satisfacción con la pantalla de editar perfil y añadir una nueva imagen de perfil *

0   1   2   3   4   5
Muy malo   ○   ○   ○   ○   ○   ○   Muy bueno

Ranking alumnos
Pulsa sobre el menú y accede a la opción de Ranking de alumnos, podrás visualizar el ranking de los mejores alumnos por porcentaje de juego completado. Además si pulsas sobre un alumno del ranking, podrás acceder a una pantalla que muestra los niveles que tiene en cada tema, y si dejas pulsado sobre tu usuario dentro del ranking, podrás visualizar tus estadísticas (exámenes suspensos, aprobados, preguntas falladas, tiempo medio de respuesta en los exámenes...etc).

Indica tu grado de satisfacción con la pantalla de ranking de alumnos *

0   1   2   3   4   5
Muy malo   ○   ○   ○   ○   ○   ○   Muy bueno

Indica tu grado de satisfacción con las pantallas de estadísticas del alumno *

0   1   2   3   4   5
Muy malo   ○   ○   ○   ○   ○   ○   Muy bueno

Figure A3. Assessment questions for registered student role.

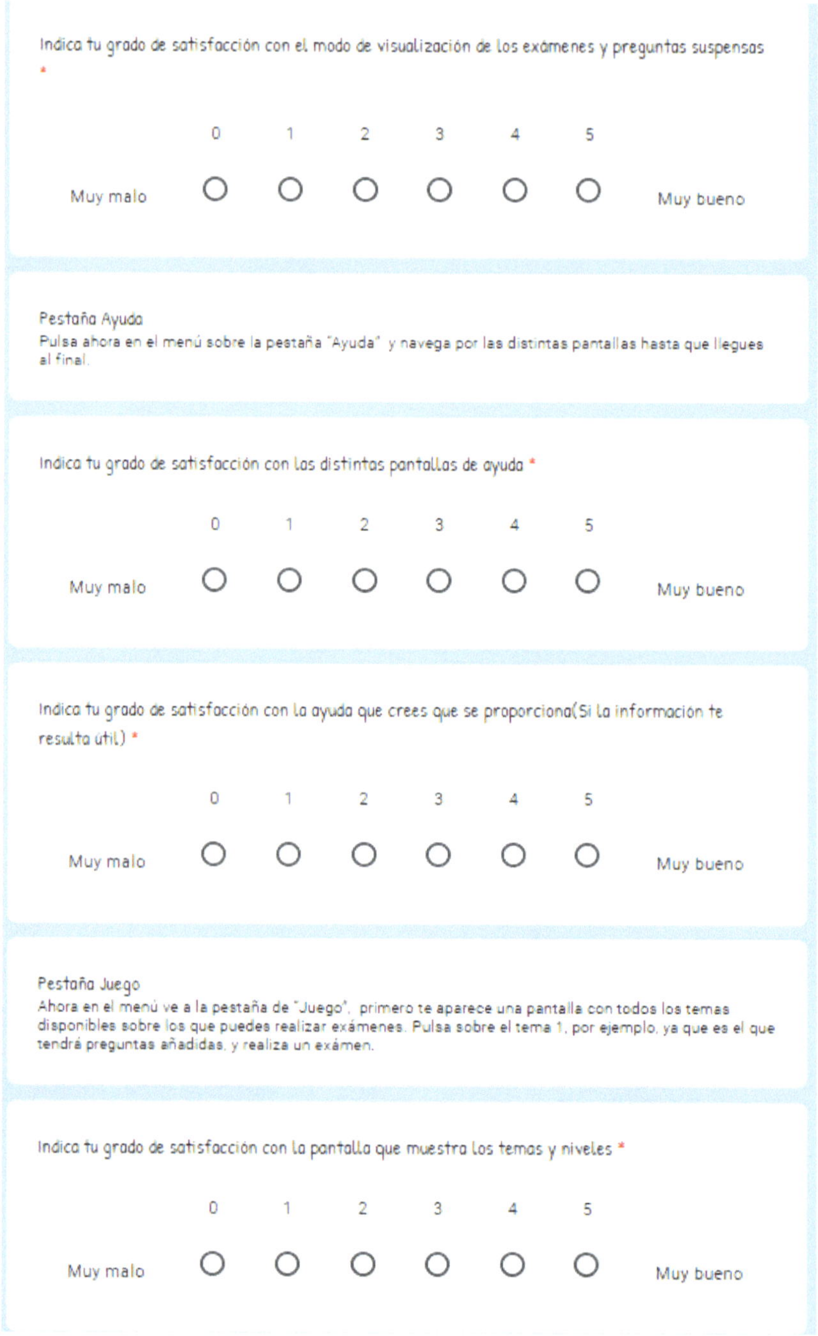

Indica tu grado de satisfacción con el modo de visualización de los exámenes y preguntas suspensas *

	0	1	2	3	4	5	
Muy malo	○	○	○	○	○	○	Muy bueno

Pestaña Ayuda
Pulsa ahora en el menú sobre la pestaña "Ayuda" y navega por las distintas pantallas hasta que llegues al final.

Indica tu grado de satisfacción con las distintas pantallas de ayuda *

	0	1	2	3	4	5	
Muy malo	○	○	○	○	○	○	Muy bueno

Indica tu grado de satisfacción con la ayuda que crees que se proporciona(Si la información te resulta útil) *

	0	1	2	3	4	5	
Muy malo	○	○	○	○	○	○	Muy bueno

Pestaña Juego
Ahora en el menú ve a la pestaña de "Juego", primero te aparece una pantalla con todos los temas disponibles sobre los que puedes realizar exámenes. Pulsa sobre el tema 1, por ejemplo, ya que es el que tendrá preguntas añadidas, y realiza un examen.

Indica tu grado de satisfacción con la pantalla que muestra los temas y niveles *

	0	1	2	3	4	5	
Muy malo	○	○	○	○	○	○	Muy bueno

Figure A4. Assessment questions for registered student role.

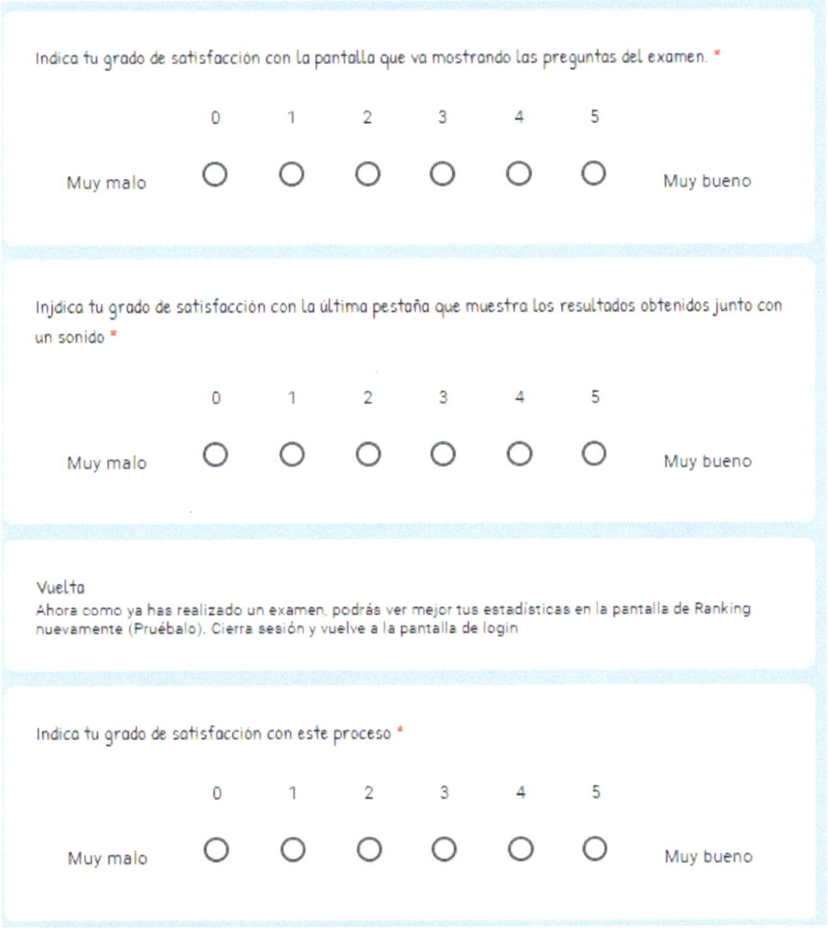

Indica tu grado de satisfacción con la pantalla que va mostrando las preguntas del examen. *

      0 1 2 3 4 5

Muy malo ○ ○ ○ ○ ○ ○ Muy bueno

Indica tu grado de satisfacción con la última pestaña que muestra los resultados obtenidos junto con un sonido *

      0 1 2 3 4 5

Muy malo ○ ○ ○ ○ ○ ○ Muy bueno

Vuelta
Ahora como ya has realizado un examen, podrás ver mejor tus estadísticas en la pantalla de Ranking nuevamente (Pruébalo). Cierra sesión y vuelve a la pantalla de login

Indica tu grado de satisfacción con este proceso *

      0 1 2 3 4 5

Muy malo ○ ○ ○ ○ ○ ○ Muy bueno

Figure A5. Assessment questions for registered student role.

(b) Assessment questions for a registered teacher role (Figures A6–A10)

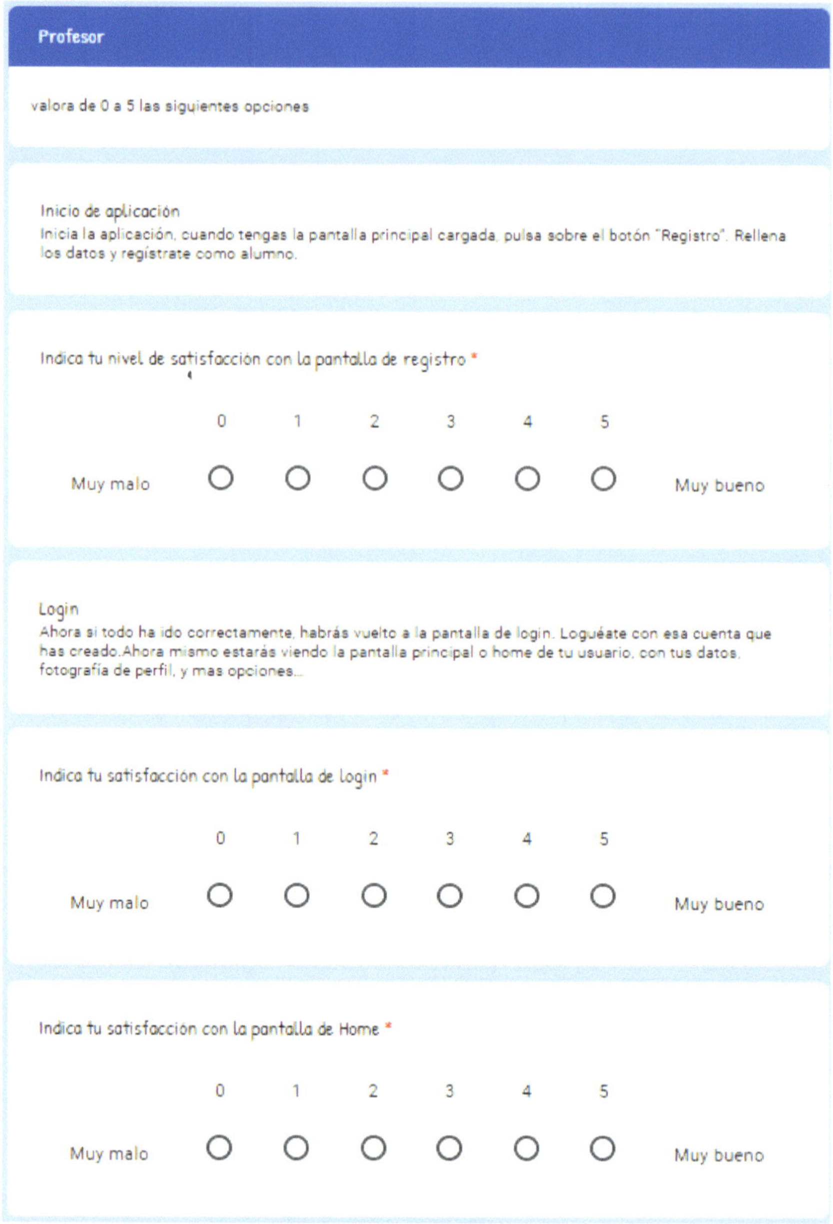

Profesor

valora de 0 a 5 las siguientes opciones

Inicio de aplicación
Inicia la aplicación, cuando tengas la pantalla principal cargada, pulsa sobre el botón "Registro". Rellena los datos y regístrate como alumno.

Indica tu nivel de satisfacción con la pantalla de registro *

	0	1	2	3	4	5	
Muy malo	○	○	○	○	○	○	Muy bueno

Login
Ahora si todo ha ido correctamente, habrás vuelto a la pantalla de login. Loguéate con esa cuenta que has creado. Ahora mismo estarás viendo la pantalla principal o home de tu usuario, con tus datos, fotografía de perfil, y mas opciones...

Indica tu satisfacción con la pantalla de Login *

	0	1	2	3	4	5	
Muy malo	○	○	○	○	○	○	Muy bueno

Indica tu satisfacción con la pantalla de Home *

	0	1	2	3	4	5	
Muy malo	○	○	○	○	○	○	Muy bueno

Figure A6. Assessment questions for a registered teacher role.

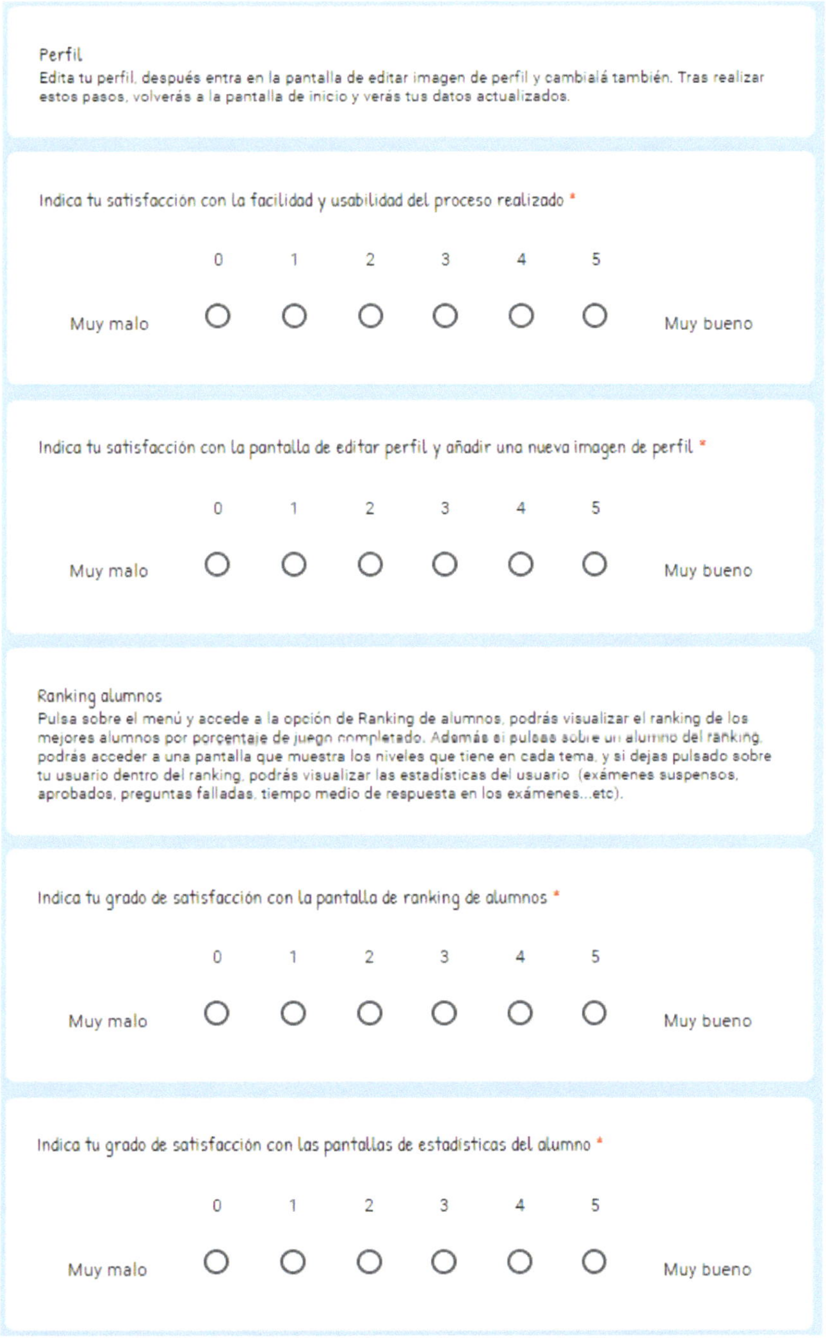

Perfil
Edita tu perfil, después entra en la pantalla de editar imagen de perfil y cambiala también. Tras realizar estos pasos, volverás a la pantalla de inicio y verás tus datos actualizados.

Indica tu satisfacción con la facilidad y usabilidad del proceso realizado *

	0	1	2	3	4	5	
Muy malo	○	○	○	○	○	○	Muy bueno

Indica tu satisfacción con la pantalla de editar perfil y añadir una nueva imagen de perfil *

	0	1	2	3	4	5	
Muy malo	○	○	○	○	○	○	Muy bueno

Ranking alumnos
Pulsa sobre el menú y accede a la opción de Ranking de alumnos, podrás visualizar el ranking de los mejores alumnos por porcentaje de juego completado. Además si pulsas sobre un alumno del ranking, podrás acceder a una pantalla que muestra los niveles que tiene en cada tema, y si dejas pulsado sobre tu usuario dentro del ranking, podrás visualizar las estadísticas del usuario (exámenes suspensos, aprobados, preguntas falladas, tiempo medio de respuesta en los exámenes...etc).

Indica tu grado de satisfacción con la pantalla de ranking de alumnos *

	0	1	2	3	4	5	
Muy malo	○	○	○	○	○	○	Muy bueno

Indica tu grado de satisfacción con las pantallas de estadísticas del alumno *

	0	1	2	3	4	5	
Muy malo	○	○	○	○	○	○	Muy bueno

Figure A7. Assessment questions for a registered teacher role.

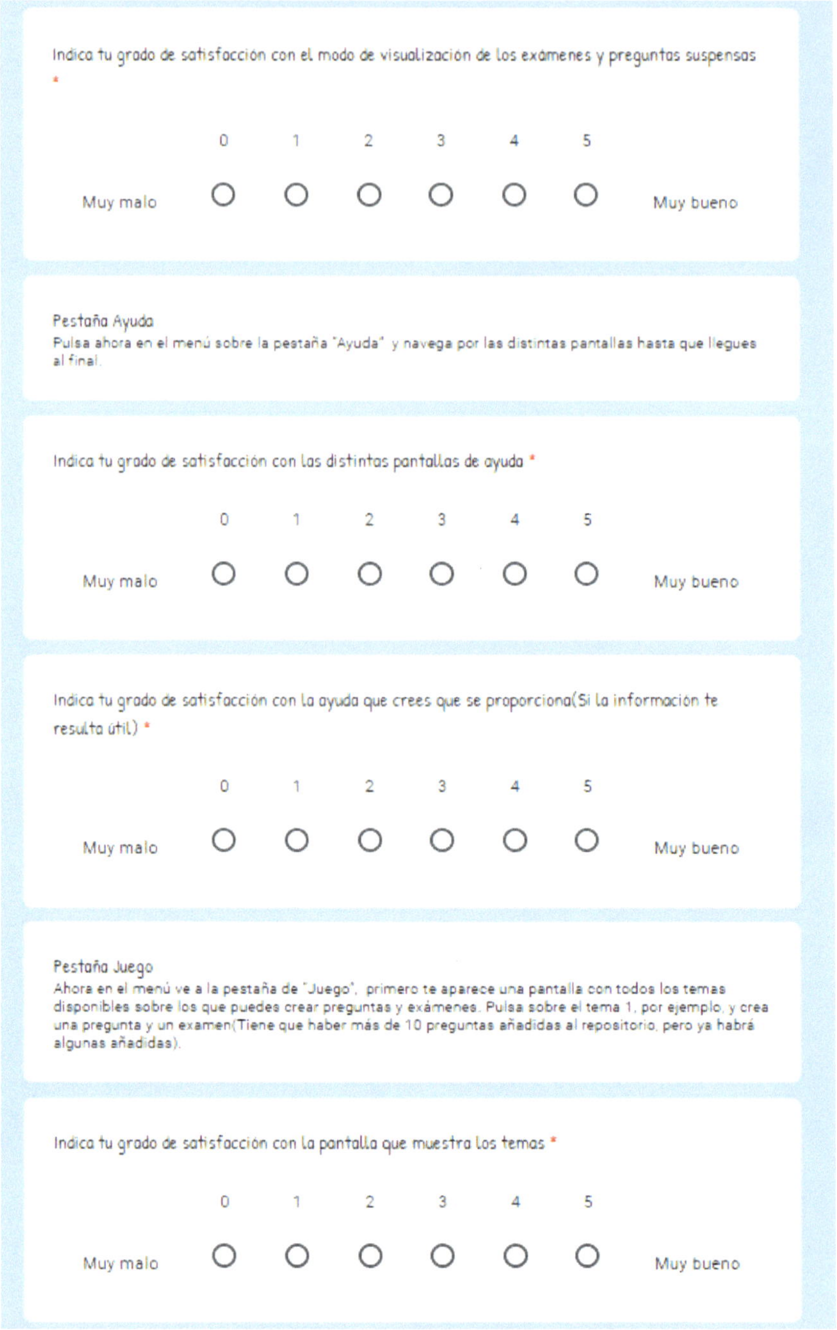

Indica tu grado de satisfacción con el modo de visualización de los exámenes y preguntas suspensas *

	0	1	2	3	4	5	
Muy malo	○	○	○	○	○	○	Muy bueno

Pestaña Ayuda
Pulsa ahora en el menú sobre la pestaña "Ayuda" y navega por las distintas pantallas hasta que llegues al final.

Indica tu grado de satisfacción con las distintas pantallas de ayuda *

	0	1	2	3	4	5	
Muy malo	○	○	○	○	○	○	Muy bueno

Indica tu grado de satisfacción con la ayuda que crees que se proporciona(Si la información te resulta útil) *

	0	1	2	3	4	5	
Muy malo	○	○	○	○	○	○	Muy bueno

Pestaña Juego
Ahora en el menú ve a la pestaña de "Juego", primero te aparece una pantalla con todos los temas disponibles sobre los que puedes crear preguntas y exámenes. Pulsa sobre el tema 1, por ejemplo, y crea una pregunta y un examen(Tiene que haber más de 10 preguntas añadidas al repositorio, pero ya habrá algunas añadidas).

Indica tu grado de satisfacción con la pantalla que muestra los temas *

	0	1	2	3	4	5	
Muy malo	○	○	○	○	○	○	Muy bueno

Figure A8. Assessment questions for a registered teacher role.

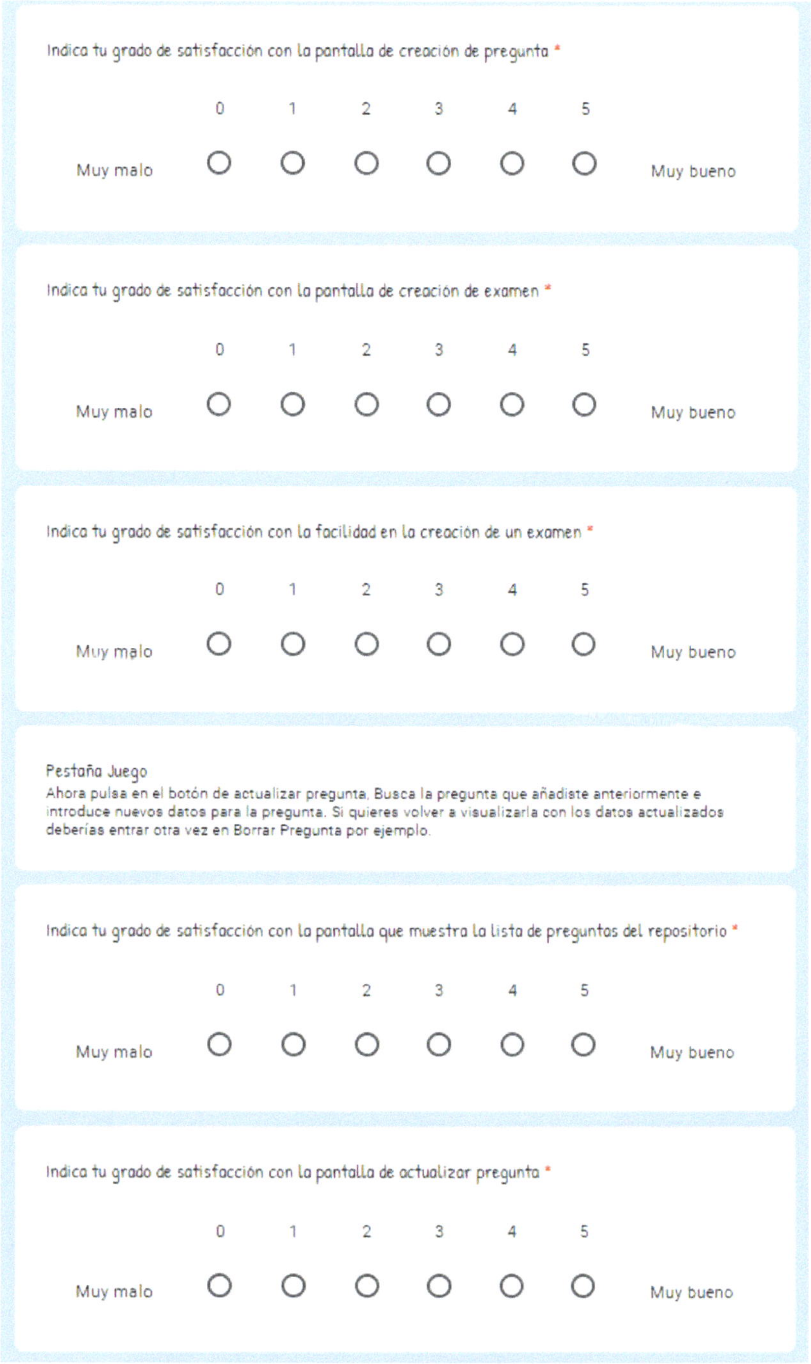

Indica tu grado de satisfacción con la pantalla de creación de pregunta *

               0   1   2   3   4   5

Muy malo   ○   ○   ○   ○   ○   ○   Muy bueno

Indica tu grado de satisfacción con la pantalla de creación de examen *

               0   1   2   3   4   5

Muy malo   ○   ○   ○   ○   ○   ○   Muy bueno

Indica tu grado de satisfacción con la facilidad en la creación de un examen *

               0   1   2   3   4   5

Muy malo   ○   ○   ○   ○   ○   ○   Muy bueno

Pestaña Juego
Ahora pulsa en el botón de actualizar pregunta. Busca la pregunta que añadiste anteriormente e introduce nuevos datos para la pregunta. Si quieres volver a visualizarla con los datos actualizados deberías entrar otra vez en Borrar Pregunta por ejemplo.

Indica tu grado de satisfacción con la pantalla que muestra la lista de preguntas del repositorio *

               0   1   2   3   4   5

Muy malo   ○   ○   ○   ○   ○   ○   Muy bueno

Indica tu grado de satisfacción con la pantalla de actualizar pregunta *

               0   1   2   3   4   5

Muy malo   ○   ○   ○   ○   ○   ○   Muy bueno

Figure A9. Assessment questions for a registered teacher role.

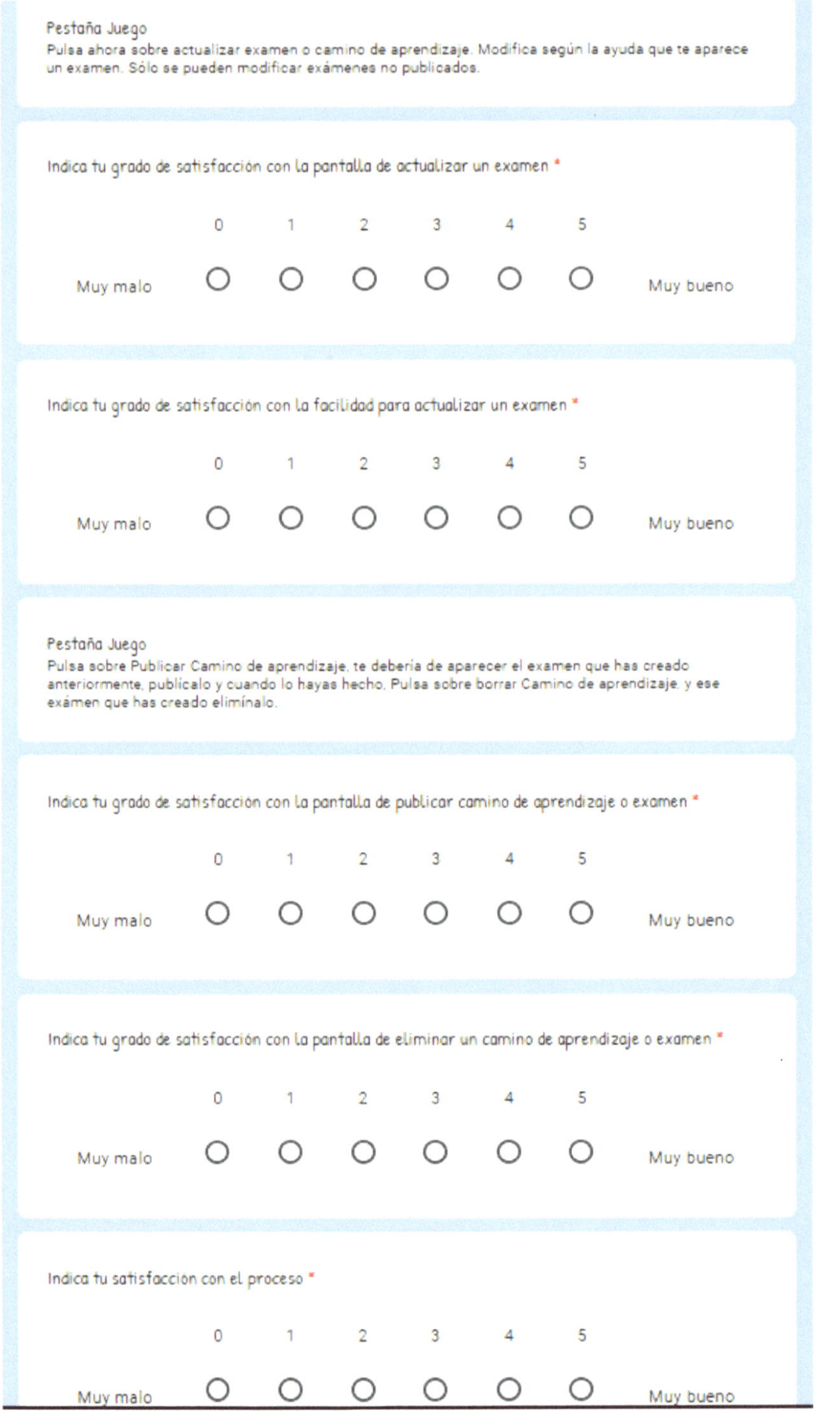

Pestaña Juego
Pulsa ahora sobre actualizar examen o camino de aprendizaje. Modifica según la ayuda que te aparece un examen. Sólo se pueden modificar exámenes no publicados.

Indica tu grado de satisfacción con la pantalla de actualizar un examen *

                              0   1   2   3   4   5

Muy malo   ○ ○ ○ ○ ○ ○   Muy bueno

Indica tu grado de satisfacción con la facilidad para actualizar un examen *

                              0   1   2   3   4   5

Muy malo   ○ ○ ○ ○ ○ ○   Muy bueno

Pestaña Juego
Pulsa sobre Publicar Camino de aprendizaje, te debería de aparecer el examen que has creado anteriormente, publícalo y cuando lo hayas hecho, Pulsa sobre borrar Camino de aprendizaje, y ese examen que has creado elimínalo.

Indica tu grado de satisfacción con la pantalla de publicar camino de aprendizaje o examen *

                              0   1   2   3   4   5

Muy malo   ○ ○ ○ ○ ○ ○   Muy bueno

Indica tu grado de satisfacción con la pantalla de eliminar un camino de aprendizaje o examen *

                              0   1   2   3   4   5

Muy malo   ○ ○ ○ ○ ○ ○   Muy bueno

Indica tu satisfacción con el proceso *

                              0   1   2   3   4   5

Muy malo   ○ ○ ○ ○ ○ ○   Muy bueno

Figure A10. Assessment questions for a registered teacher role.

(c) Assessment questions for an administrator role (Figures A11 and A12).

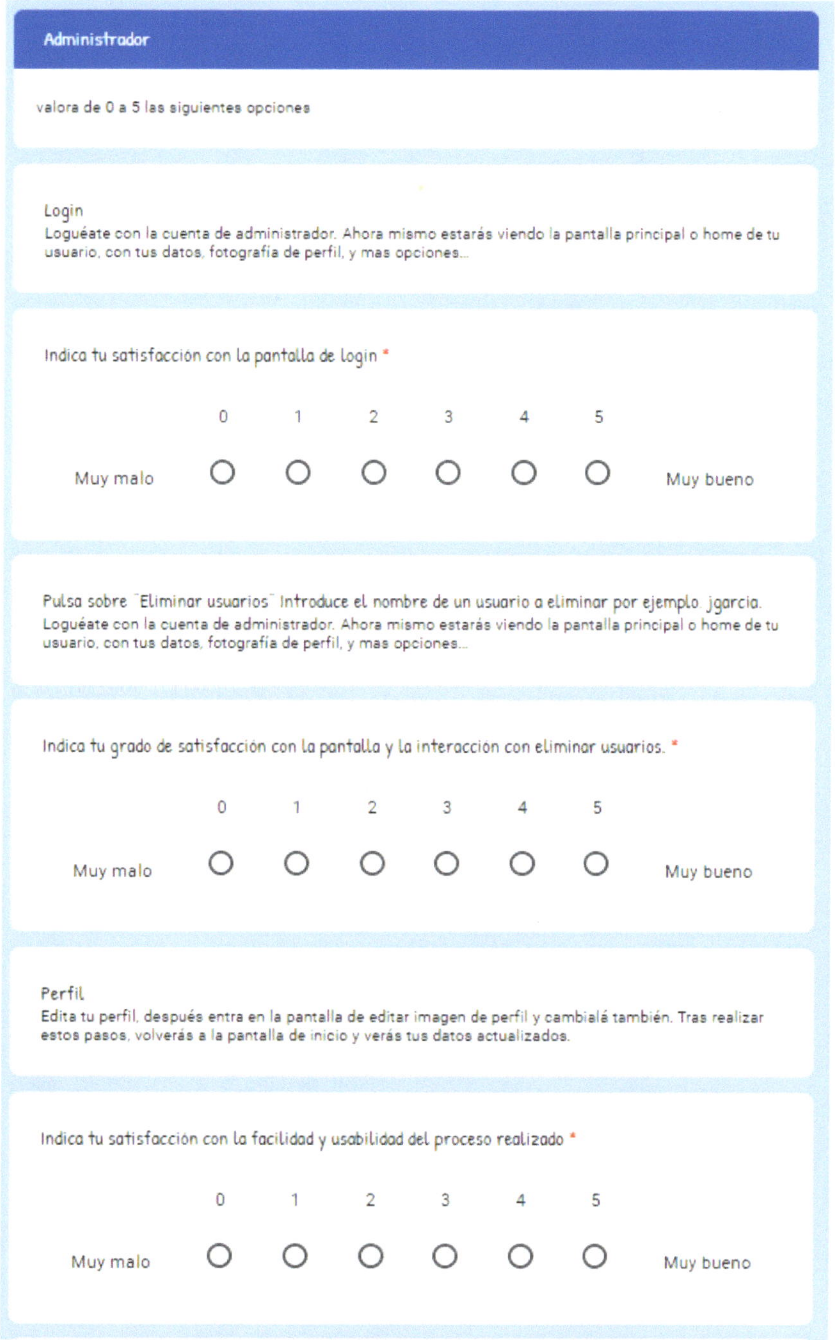

Administrador

valora de 0 a 5 las siguientes opciones

Login
Loguéate con la cuenta de administrador. Ahora mismo estarás viendo la pantalla principal o home de tu usuario, con tus datos, fotografía de perfil, y mas opciones...

Indica tu satisfacción con la pantalla de login *

	0	1	2	3	4	5	
Muy malo	○	○	○	○	○	○	Muy bueno

Pulsa sobre "Eliminar usuarios" Introduce el nombre de un usuario a eliminar por ejemplo, jgarcia. Loguéate con la cuenta de administrador. Ahora mismo estarás viendo la pantalla principal o home de tu usuario, con tus datos, fotografía de perfil, y mas opciones...

Indica tu grado de satisfacción con la pantalla y la interacción con eliminar usuarios. *

	0	1	2	3	4	5	
Muy malo	○	○	○	○	○	○	Muy bueno

Perfil
Edita tu perfil, después entra en la pantalla de editar imagen de perfil y cambiala también. Tras realizar estos pasos, volverás a la pantalla de inicio y verás tus datos actualizados.

Indica tu satisfacción con la facilidad y usabilidad del proceso realizado *

	0	1	2	3	4	5	
Muy malo	○	○	○	○	○	○	Muy bueno

Figure A11. Assessment questions for administrator role.

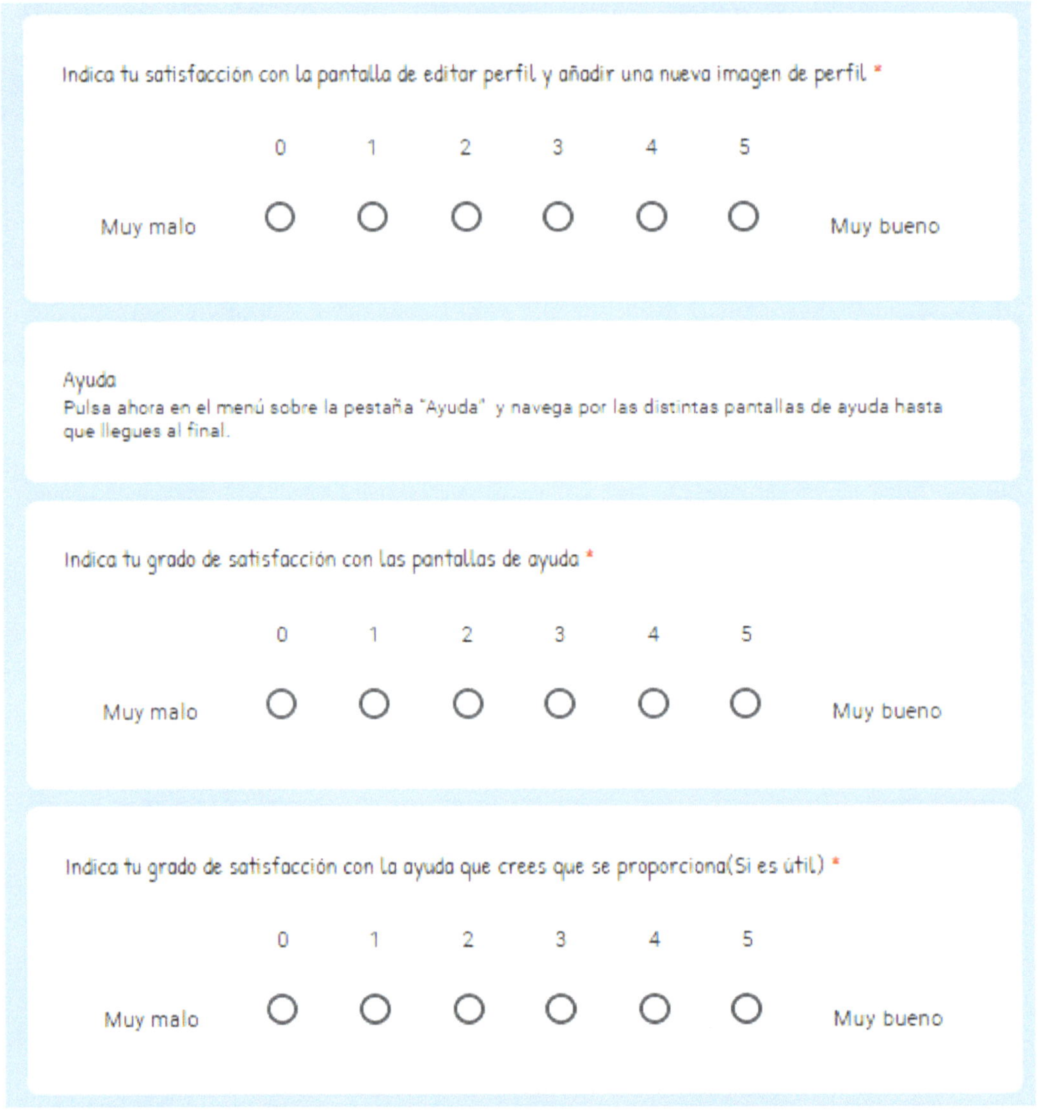

Indica tu satisfacción con la pantalla de editar perfil y añadir una nueva imagen de perfil *

        0   1   2   3   4   5
Muy malo O   O   O   O   O   O   Muy bueno

Ayuda
Pulsa ahora en el menú sobre la pestaña "Ayuda" y navega por las distintas pantallas de ayuda hasta que llegues al final.

Indica tu grado de satisfacción con las pantallas de ayuda *

        0   1   2   3   4   5
Muy malo O   O   O   O   O   O   Muy bueno

Indica tu grado de satisfacción con la ayuda que crees que se proporciona(Si es útil) *

        0   1   2   3   4   5
Muy malo O   O   O   O   O   O   Muy bueno

Figure A12. Assessment questions for an administrator role.

The third block of questions consists of a series of questions on the global evaluation of the application and proposals for improvements and changes (Figure A13).

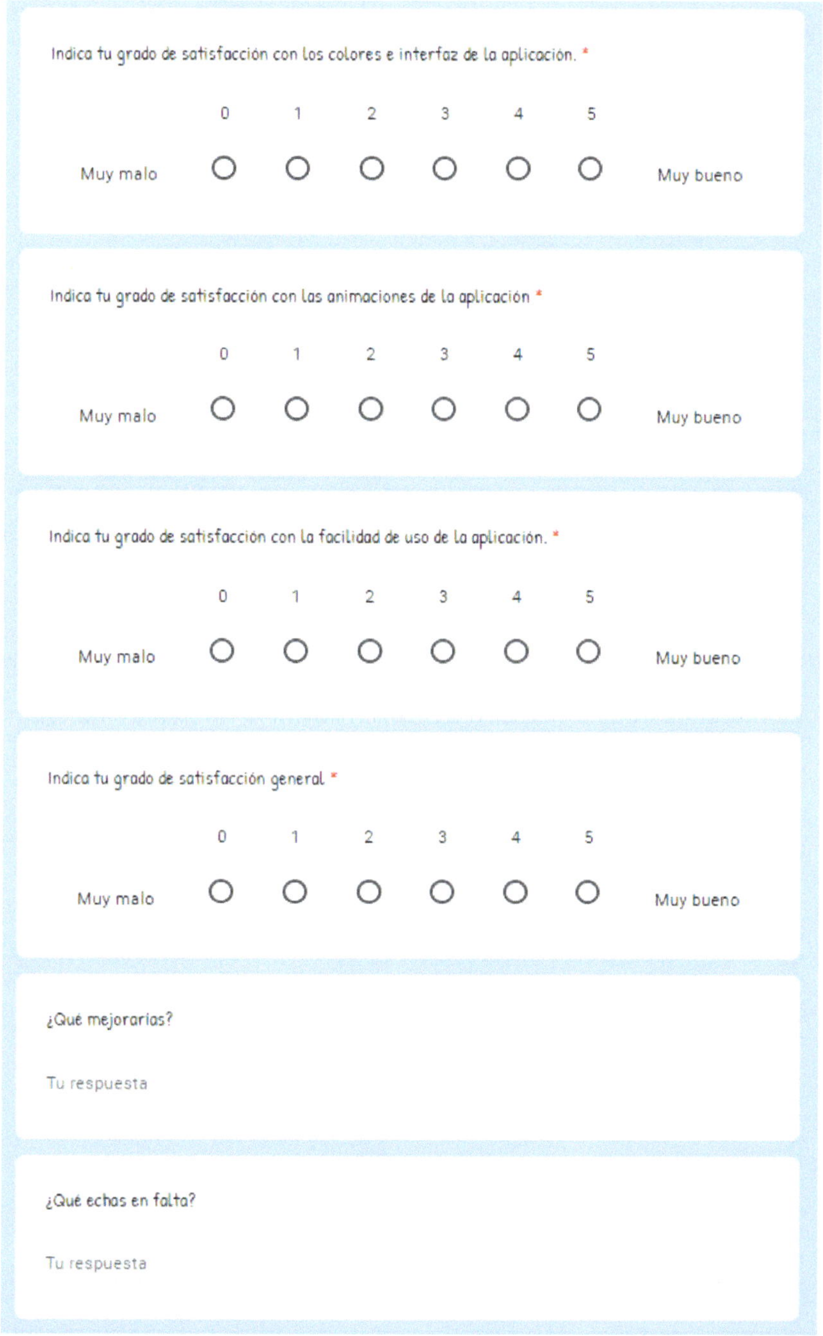

Indica tu grado de satisfacción con los colores e interfaz de la aplicación. *

	0	1	2	3	4	5	
Muy malo	○	○	○	○	○	○	Muy bueno

Indica tu grado de satisfacción con las animaciones de la aplicación *

	0	1	2	3	4	5	
Muy malo	○	○	○	○	○	○	Muy bueno

Indica tu grado de satisfacción con la facilidad de uso de la aplicación. *

	0	1	2	3	4	5	
Muy malo	○	○	○	○	○	○	Muy bueno

Indica tu grado de satisfacción general *

	0	1	2	3	4	5	
Muy malo	○	○	○	○	○	○	Muy bueno

¿Qué mejorarías?

Tu respuesta

¿Qué echas en falta?

Tu respuesta

Figure A13. Third block of questions.

References

1. Ouhbi, S.; Pombo, N. Software engineering education: Challenges and perspectives. In Proceedings of the IEEE Global Engineering Education Conference (EDUCON), Porto, Portugal, 27–30 April 2020; IEEE: Piscataway, NJ, USA; pp. 202–209.
2. Streveler, R.A.; Pitterson, N.P.; Hira, A.; Rodriguez-Simmonds, H.; Alvarez, J.O. Learning about engineering education research: What conceptual difficulties still exist for a new generation of scholars? In Proceedings of the IEEE Frontiers in Education Conference (FIE), El Paso, TX, USA, 21–24 October 2015; IEEE: Piscataway, NJ, USA; pp. 1–6.
3. Cheah, C.S. Factors contributing to the difficulties in teaching and learning of computer programming: A literature review. *Contemp. Educ. Technol.* **2020**, *12*, ep272. [CrossRef]
4. Bosse, Y.; Gerosa, M.A. Why is programming so difficult to learn? Patterns of Difficulties Related to Programming Learning Mid-Stage. *ACM SIGSOFT Softw. Eng. Notes* **2017**, *41*, 1–6. [CrossRef]
5. Jaccheri, L.; Morasca, S. On the importance of dialogue with industry about software engineering education. In Proceedings of the 2006 International Workshop on Summit on Software Engineering Education, Shanghai, China, 20 May 2006; IEEE: Piscataway, NJ, USA; pp. 5–8.
6. Barkley, E.F.; Major, C.H. *Student Engagement Techniques: A Handbook for College Faculty*; John Wiley & Sons: Hoboken, NJ, USA, 2020; pp. 167–205.
7. Hodges, C.B. Designing to motivate: Motivational techniques to incorporate in e-learning experiences. *J. Interact. Online Learn.* **2004**, *2*, 1–7.
8. Verner, J.M.; Babar, M.A.; Cerpa, N.; Hall, T.; Beecham, S. Factors that motivate software engineering teams: A four country empirical study. *J. Syst. Softw.* **2014**, *92*, 115–127. [CrossRef]
9. Sarasa-Cabezuelo, A. Desarrollo de competencias mediante la realización de proyectos informáticos. Experiencia en la asignatura de Ingeniería del Software. In *Actas del Congreso Virtual: Avances en Tecnologías, Innovación y Desafíos de la Educación Superior (ATIDES 2020)*; Servei de Comunicació i Publicacions: Castelló de la Plana, Spain, 2020; pp. 137–151.
10. Goñi, A.; Ibáñez, J.; Iturrioz, J.; Vadillo, J.Á. Aprendizaje Basado en Proyectos usando metodologías ágiles para una asignatura básica de Ingeniería del Software. In *Actas de las Jornadas de Enseñanza Universitaria de la Informática*; Universidad de Oviedo: Oviedo, Spain, 2014; pp. 20–35.
11. Knutas, A.; Hynninen, T.; Hujala, M. To get good student ratings should you only teach programming courses? Investigation and implications of student evaluations of teaching in a software engineering context. In Proceedings of the IEEE/ACM 43rd International Conference on Software Engineering: Software Engineering Education and Training (ICSE-SEET), Madrid, Spain, 22–30 May 2021; IEEE: Piscataway, NJ, USA; pp. 253–260.
12. Herranz, E.; Palacios, R.C.; de Amescua Seco, A.; Sánchez-Gordón, M.L. Towards a Gamification Framework for Software Process Improvement Initiatives: Construction and Validation. *J. Univ. Comput. Sci.* **2016**, *22*, 1509–1532.
13. Monteiro, R.H.B.; de Almeida Souza, M.R.; Oliveira, S.R.B.; dos Santos Portela, C.; de Cristo Lobato, C.E. The Diversity of Gamification Evaluation in the Software Engineering Education and Industry: Trends, Comparisons and Gaps. In Proceedings of the IEEE/ACM 43rd International Conference on Software Engineering: Software Engineering Education and Training (ICSE-SEET), Madrid, Spain, 22–30 May 2021; IEEE: Piscataway, NJ, USA; pp. 154–164.
14. Rodríguez, G.; González-Caino, P.C.; Resett, S. Serious games for teaching agile methods: A review of multivocal literature. In *Computer Applications in Engineering Education*; John Wiley & Sons: Hoboken, NJ, USA, 2021; pp. 207–225.
15. Alhammad, M.M.; Moreno, A.M. Gamification in software engineering education: A systematic mapping. *J. Syst. Softw.* **2018**, *141*, 131–150. [CrossRef]
16. Ivanova, G.; Kozov, V.; Zlatarov, P. Gamification in software engineering education. In Proceedings of the 2019 42nd International Convention on Information and Communication Technology, Electronics and Microelectronics (MIPRO), Opatija, Croatia, 20–24 May 2019; IEEE: Piscataway, NJ, USA; pp. 1445–1450.
17. García, F.; Pedreira, O.; Piattini, M.; Cerdeira-Pena, A.; Penabad, M. A framework for gamification in software engineering. *J. Syst. Softw.* **2017**, *132*, 21–40. [CrossRef]
18. Berkling, K.; Thomas, C. Gamification of a Software Engineering course and a detailed analysis of the factors that lead to it's failure. In Proceedings of the 2013 International Conference on Interactive Collaborative Learning (ICL), Kazan, Russia, 25–27 September 2013; IEEE: Piscataway, NJ, USA; pp. 525–530.
19. Vera, R.A.A.; Arceo, E.E.B.; Mendoza, J.C.D.; Pech, J.P.U. Gamificación para la mejora de procesos en ingeniería de software: Un estudio exploratorio. *ReCIBE Rev. Electrónica Comput. Inf. Biomédica Y Electrónica* **2019**, *8*, C1.
20. Morschheuser, B.; Hassan, L.; Werder, K.; Hamari, J. How to design gamification? A method for engineering gamified software. *Inf. Softw. Technol.* **2018**, *95*, 219–237. [CrossRef]
21. Sattarov, A.; Khaitova, N. Mobile learning as new forms and methods of increasing the effectiveness of education. *Eur. J. Res. Reflect. Educ. Sci.* **2020**, *7*, 1169–1175.
22. Tangirov, K. Didactical possibilities of mobile applications in individualization and informatization of education. *Ment. Enlight. Sci. Methodol. J.* **2020**, *2020*, 76–84.
23. Raelovich, S.A.; Mikhlievich, Y.R.; Norbutaevich, K.F.; Mamasolievich, J.D.; Karimberdievich, A.F.; Suyunbaevich, K.U. Some didactic opportunities of application of mobile technologies for improvement in the educational process. *J. Crit. Rev.* **2020**, *7*, 348–352.

24. Zhang, X.; Lo, P.; So, S.; Chiu, D.K.; Leung, T.N.; Ho, K.K.; Stark, A. Medical students' attitudes and perceptions towards the effectiveness of mobile learning: A comparative information-need perspective. *J. Librariansh. Inf. Sci.* **2021**, *53*, 116–129. [CrossRef]
25. Qureshi, M.I.; Khan, N.; Hassan Gillani, S.M.A.; Raza, H. A Systematic Review of Past Decade of Mobile Learning: What we Learned and Where to Go. *Int. J. Interact. Mob. Technol.* **2020**, *14*, 67–81. [CrossRef]
26. Qureshi, M.I.; Khan, N.; Raza, H.; Imran, A.; Ismail, F. Digital Technologies in Education 4.0. Does it Enhance the Effectiveness of Learning? A Systematic Literature Review. *Int. J. Interact. Mob. Technol.* **2021**, *15*, 31–47. [CrossRef]
27. Shaqour, A.; Salha, S.; Khlaif, Z. Students' Characteristics Influence Readiness to Use Mobile Technology in Higher Education. *Educ. Knowl. Soc. (EKS)* **2021**, *22*, e23915. [CrossRef]
28. Gupta, Y.; Khan, F.M.; Agarwal, S. Exploring Factors Influencing Mobile Learning in Higher Education–A Systematic Review. *iJIM* **2021**, *15*, 141.
29. Venkataraman, J.B.; Ramasamy, S. Factors influencing mobile learning: A literature review of selected journal papers. *Int. J. Mob. Learn. Organ.* **2018**, *12*, 99–112. [CrossRef]
30. Hu, S.; Laxman, K.; Lee, K. Exploring factors affecting academics' adoption of emerging mobile technologies-an extended UTAUT perspective. *Educ. Inf. Technol.* **2020**, *25*, 4615–4635. [CrossRef]

MDPI AG
Grosspeteranlage 5
4052 Basel
Switzerland
Tel.: +41 61 683 77 34

Computers Editorial Office
E-mail: computers@mdpi.com
www.mdpi.com/journal/computers

Disclaimer/Publisher's Note: The title and front matter of this reprint are at the discretion of the Guest Editors. The publisher is not responsible for their content or any associated concerns. The statements, opinions and data contained in all individual articles are solely those of the individual Editors and contributors and not of MDPI. MDPI disclaims responsibility for any injury to people or property resulting from any ideas, methods, instructions or products referred to in the content.